Special Drawing Rights (SDRs)

Special Drawing Rights (SDRs)

The First International Money

by
Christopher M. D. Wilkie

OXFORD
UNIVERSITY PRESS

OXFORD
UNIVERSITY PRESS

Great Clarendon Street, Oxford OX2 6DP

Oxford University Press is a department of the University of Oxford.
It furthers the University's objective of excellence in research, scholarship,
and education by publishing worldwide in

Oxford New York

Auckland Cape Town Dar es Salaam Hong Kong Karachi
Kuala Lumpur Madrid Melbourne Mexico City Nairobi
New Delhi Shanghai Taipei Toronto

With offices in

Argentina Austria Brazil Chile Czech Republic France Greece
Guatemala Hungary Italy Japan Poland Portugal Singapore
South Korea Switzerland Thailand Turkey Ukraine Vietnam

Oxford is a registered trade mark of Oxford University Press
in the UK and in certain other countries

Published in the United States
by Oxford University Press Inc., New York

First published 2012

British Library Cataloguing in Publication Data

Data available

Library of Congress Cataloging in Publication Data

Data available

Typeset by SPI Publisher Services, Pondicherry, India
Printed in Great Britain
on acid-free paper by
MPG Books Group, Bodmin and King's Lynn

ISBN 978–0–19–960646–7

1 3 5 7 9 10 8 6 4 2

To my mother and the memory of my father

When the people of any particular country have such confidence in the fortune, probity, and prudence of a particular banker, as to believe that he is always ready to pay upon demand such of his promissory notes as are likely to be an any time presented to him; those notes come to have the same currency as gold and silver money, from the confidence such money can at any time be had for them.

—Adam Smith, *The Wealth of Nations*

We set up a universal money; we make sure that its quantity shall be adequate; we share it out between the countries of the world in equitable amounts; we take what precaution we can against improvidence on the one hand and hoarding on the other. It is obvious that in this way we establish an immensely strong influence to expand the trade and wealth of the world, and to remove certain disastrous causes of inhibition and distress.

—John Maynard Keynes—House of Lords Debate—
International Clearing Union, 18 May, 1943

Before the end of this year, the Special Drawing Rights machinery of the International Monetary Fund should come into operation, ushering in a new era of multilaterally created international reserves. This is no small matter. The international community has not heretofore created anything so deadly serious as money.

—Edward R. Fried, *Foreign Affairs*, October, 1969

Preface

Following the Rio Agreement in 1967, the birth of the Special Drawing Right (SDR) was widely heralded as the first step towards a world international money. The SDR's intended purpose, though, was more modest: to help salvage the prevailing international monetary system that had evolved since Bretton Woods. Even this more limited objective was not realized, however, and this book begins with an examination of why this occurred. The approach is to emphasize the politics surrounding the SDR, for it quickly emerges that the reasons for the SDR's early marginalization did not lie solely in technical failures associated with it.

Despite their retreat from early acclaim, SDRs have recently re-emerged as a potential source of support and stability for the international monetary system underpinning the world economy. To understand why and how this has occurred, it is necessary to examine the changing roles of the United States (US) and the International Monetary Fund (IMF). This involves an investigation of the evolving role of the legislative and executive branches of the US government with a bearing on international monetary policy; office holders in the Administration and the evolution of US Congressional interest in the SDR are both important in this regard.

In addition, as international financial power diffused during the post-Bretton Woods era, the development of the IMF as an entity with an increasing willingness to express its own interests and an ability to influence the international monetary agenda is also an important part of this story. This manifests itself with respect to the Fund's influence on somewhat neglected provisions embodied in the Second Amendment to the IMF's Articles of Agreement, many of them relating to the SDR.

Two key themes thus characterize SDRs in the post-Bretton Woods era: first, following the breakdown of Bretton Woods, the US came to view the SDR as irrelevant—but not antithetical—to its national interest; second, the IMF, after viewing the SDR as a prime *casus belli* in the evolution of the Fund's role in the 1970s and early 1980s, also eventually came to a similar conclusion vis-à-vis the SDR as the post-Bretton Woods arrangements consolidated themselves. Despite these developments, however, quiet work continued, particularly at the Fund, on enhancing the potential of SDRs to contribute to international monetary stability. These accomplishments may yet prove fortuitous for the international monetary system as well as the world economy.

Finally, the SDR and the debate surrounding it is also an excellent prism through which to examine other important themes in contemporary international monetary political economy, such as international liquidity provision and international monetary reform. Ultimately, however, the policies of the US, the Fund, and the changing nature of the relationship between them emerge as fundamental themes for an understanding of the politics surrounding the marginalization of SDRs under post-Bretton Woods international monetary arrangements. Today, the promise and disappointment that has characterized the short history of SDRs is more important than ever as the world again examines these arrangements in the wake of the international financial crisis.

Acknowledgements

Above all, this book could not have been written without the support and indulgence of my family, all of whom deserve so much more than the gratitude expressed here. Financial assistance is gratefully acknowledged from Corpus Christi College, Oxford, as well as the University of Oxford, for sponsoring travel and research in the early days of my work. Throughout the publication process, the support and patience of Georgia Pinteau and Aimee Wright at Oxford University Press has been much appreciated. The views expressed in this book remain solely those of the author. They do not relate to current or former professional responsibilities and do not represent the views of the Government of Canada or any other entity.

The book benefitted greatly from helpful suggestions from two longstanding proponents of the Special Drawing Right (SDR) at the International Monetary Fund (IMF), the late Dr J. J. Polak and Sir Joseph Gold, both of whom met with me repeatedly to discuss this work in an earlier guise. Dr. Polak also agreed to examine large segments of this work while it was still evolving and I am indebted to him for his many helpful suggestions and the patience he took in explaining intricacies associated with the SDR and its evolution. And again, I would like to thank the other policy makers and academics listed in the bibliography who agreed to discuss issues related to this book in both England and the US early in its gestation.

I would also like to acknowledge the assistance of Gertrude Long, Leo van Houtven, and Jacob Frenkel—formerly archivist, secretary, and research director, respectively—at the IMF. These individuals kindly made available departmental and staff memoranda related to the SDR, as well as documentation associated with the negotiation of the Second Amendment to the IMF's Articles of Agreement, which helped me greatly in my research. I would also like to thank the International Monetary Fund for granting me permission to publish information used in the tables, illustrations, and figures as listed below. Similar thanks are due to Euromoney Institutional Investor PLC, London, for permission to reproduce photographs of an SDR certificate of deposit.

Finally, I would like to thank Loukas Tsoukalis and in particular Andrew Walter—both formerly at St. Antony's College, Oxford; Professor Walter now at LSE—at the London School of Economics, without whose help at crucially important stages this book would never have been completed.

Rabat, Morocco

Contents

List of Tables, Figures, and Illustrations

List of Abbreviations

BIS	Bank for International Settlements
BRIC countries (BRICs)	Brazil, Russia, India, and China
C-20	Committee of Twenty (IMF)
CRU	Composite Reserve Unit
DAA	Draft Article(s) of Agreement (IMF)
dfo(s)	development finance organization(s)
DM(s)	Deutschemark; Departmental Memoranda (IMF)
EBD	Executive Board Document (IMF)
EBM	Executive Board Minute (IMF)
ECE	Economic Commission for Europe (UN)
ECOSOC	Economic and Social Council (UN)
ECU	European Currency Unit
EEC; EC; EU	European Economic Community; European Community; European Union
EMS	European Monetary System
FDIP	Foreign Direct Investment Program (US)
FOMC	Federal Open Market Committee (US Federal Reserve)
FRB; Fed	Federal Reserve Board (US central bank)
G10	Group of Ten (major industrialized countries)
G20	Group of Twenty (major industrialized and emerging countries)
G24	Group of Twenty-Four (less developed countries) (successor to short-lived G31)
G30	Group of Thirty (distinguished experts in international economic and monetary issues)
GAB	General Arrangements to Borrow
IBRD	International Bank for Reconstruction and Development (World Bank)
ICU	International Clearing Union

IIE	Institute for International Economics
IIF	Institute for International Finance
IMF	International Monetary Fund
JEC	Joint Economic Committee (US Congress)
ldc	less developed country
MCA	Mutual Currency Account
NAC	National Advisory Council (on International Monetary and Financial Policies) (US)
OECD	Organization for Economic Cooperation and Development
OPEC	Organization of Petroleum Exporting Countries
SDR	Special Drawing Rights
SM(s)	Staff Memoranda (IMF)
UNCTAD	United Nations Conference on Trade and Development
UNDP	United Nations Development Programme
VFCRP	Voluntary Foreign Credit Restraint Program (US)
WP3	Working Party Three (of the Economic Policy Committee of the OECD)

Chronology

International Monetary Developments and the SDR since 1962	
Oct 1962	G10's General Arrangements to Borrow instituted
Feb 1963	Compensatory Financing Facility (for temporary shortfalls in export earnings) instituted
Sept 1963	President Kennedy tells IMF Annual Meeting that the US 'stands ready to support such measures as may be necessary to increase international liquidity'
June 1964	32 international economists (the Bellagio Group) issue the report 'International Monetary Arrangements: The Problem of Choice'
July 1964	G10 Study Group on Creation of Reserve Assets instituted
Sept 1964	Pierre-Paul Schweitzer becomes IMF's Fourth Managing Director
Feb 1965	President de Gaulle calls for return to gold standard
Feb 1965	President Johnson, in a series of measures that would continue for the next four years, announces restrictions on US capital outflows
Aug 1965	G10 publishes deputies report (the Ossola Report) on 'functioning of the international monetary system and of its probable future needs for liquidity'
Sept 1965	Managing Director Schweitzer tells IMF Annual Meeting in Washington that the Fund would intensify its studies into international liquidity
Nov 1966	Fund continues to maintain support for universal scheme for enhancing international liquidity. This culminates in the first joint meeting between IMF Executive Directors and G10 Deputies
Jan 1967	Second meeting of Joint Fund/G10 Committee
Jan 1967	At The Hague, EEC finance ministers agree to study for continuing improvement in international credit facilities, and recommend an increase in voting majority to 85% of Fund's Board for SDR allocation
Feb 1967	Fund circulates further liquidity plans
Mar 1967	US Treasury Secretary Fowler recommends early agreement for international reserve creation
Apr 1967	Munich Agreement; EEC finance ministers agree to joint position on SDR
Apr, June 1967	Third and Fourth meetings of Joint Fund/G10 committee produce broad agreement on SDR creation
July, Aug 1967	Meetings of G10 establish position on prospective SDR
Sept 1967	IMF Annual Meeting in Rio de Janeiro. IMF Board of Governors approves 'Outline of a Facility Based on Special Drawing Rights in the Fund', and requests Executive Directors to begin drafting amendments to the IMF Articles of Agreement
Nov 1967	UK devalues sterling 14.3% against the dollar
Mar 1968	G10 Stockholm meeting establishes final SDR provisions (France reserves its judgement). Two tier gold market instituted
Apr 1968	Executive Board submits proposed amendments to Board of Governors; Board approves amendments and submits them to members
May 1968	Fund Board of Governors approves proposed First Amendment; membership ratification process begins

July 1969	First Amendment of IMF Articles of Agreement establishing SDR reaches required support among the membership
Aug 1969	Special Drawing Account at IMF instituted
Sept–Oct 1969	Deutschmark revalued 9.3%
Oct 1969	IMF Board approves Managing Director's proposal for SDR 9.5 billion allocation over three years
Jan 1970	First annual instalment of first SDR allocation. SDR 3.5 billion allocated
Sept 1970	Fund publishes 'The Role of Exchange Rates in the Adjustment of International Payments', which recommends no major changes to exchange rate mechanisms. Bürgenstock Papers published, most of which advocate more flexible exchange rates
Jan 1971	Second annual instalment of first SDR allocation: SDR 2.9 billion
May 1971	Deutschmark and Dutch guilder float
Aug 1971	'Nixon shocks': US suspends general convertibility for the dollar and imposes a 10% import surcharge. Yen floated
Dec 1971	Pompidou–Nixon summit in the Azores; agree to currency realignments. G10 meeting at the Smithsonian Institution institutes new par values (with a narrow band for exchange rate fluctuation); dollar effectively devalued in terms of gold from $35 to $38 per oz.
Jan 1972	Third and final annual instalment of First SDR allocation: SDR 2.95 billion (total over three years: SDR 9.3 billion)
Mar 1972	IMF begins denominating accounts in SDRs
Apr 1972	EEC halves Smithsonian currency fluctuation margins to 2.25%: the 'snake' within the 'tunnel'; G24 inaugural meeting, Caracas
June 1972	UK and Denmark leave EEC snake
July 1972	Committee of Twenty (Committee on Reform of the International Monetary System) approved by IMF Board of Governors. (First meeting of C-20 in September)
Sept 1972	IMF publishes 'Reform of the International Monetary System'; US proposes system of 'reserve indicators' whereby changes in reserves serve as signal for exchange rate changes
Jan 1973	Second Basic Period for SDRs opens with no agreement to allocate any further SDRs. G24 reiterates support for 'link' between allocations for SDRs and provision for development finance
Feb 1973	Dollar devalued a second time: 10% in terms of gold to $42.22 per oz.
Mar 1973	Paris Agreement (G10 plus four remaining EEC countries). EEC allows joint float of EEC currencies against the dollar, signalling end of Smithsonian agreement. C-20 reiterates support for 'stable but adjustable' par values. DR redefined in terms of 16 currency basket, each with a world export share of greater than 1% from 1968 to 1972
Sept 1973	H. Johannes Witteveen succeeds controversial Pierre-Paul Schweitzer as fifth IMF Managing Director
Sept 1973	C-20 Deputies meeting in Paris results in deadlock over reformed system
Dec 1973	Second OPEC oil price rise in three months, effectively quadrupling oil prices
Jan 1974	BIS made first prescribed holder of SDRs outside the Fund
Jan 1974	C-20 meeting in Rome adopts 'evolutionary' path to international monetary reform. Support for fixed rates and primary role for SDR diminishes
Jan 1974	Franc leaves EEC snake; US abandons outward controls on capital while Germany eases restrictions on capital inflows
Mar 1974	Fund extends suspension of 'equal value provision', enabling European countries to use SDR holdings in payments among themselves
Apr 1974	Fund recommends work on legalizing prevailing international monetary arrangements, which would entail further amendment to the Articles. Fund begins work internally on proposed amendment
June 1974	Final meeting of C-20; establishment of Interim Committee and 'Outline of Reform' published

July 1974	Sixteen currency basket replaces gold/dollar denomination for SDR; five currency basket used for determination of SDR interest rate. Interest rate set at six monthly intervals, as a proportion of combined market rates (initially 5%)
Oct 1974	First meeting of Interim Committee
Jan 1975	Second Interim Committee meeting; agreement on the need for a Second Amendment, and that the role of gold should be reduced (i.e. no official gold price, and no obligatory gold transfers among Fund members)
Mar 1975	First Comprehensive Draft Amendment proposed by IMF staff to Executive Directors
June 1975	First SDR Eurobond issued by Alusuisse International NV (SDR 50 million)
July 1975	France re-enters EEC snake. SDR interest rate set at quarterly rather than half-yearly intervals; gradual move to full rather than a proportional interest rate
Nov 1975	First economic 'summit' at Rambouillet; France and US compromise paves the way for flexible exchange rate ratification under Second Amendment
Jan 1976	Jamaica Agreement; Legalization of prevailing international monetary arrangements including flexible exchange rates; decision to reduce role of Fund gold. Degree of flexibility embodied in agreement, including provisions accommodating alternative arrangements. Declaration that the SDR is to become the 'primary reserve asset' included twice in the new Articles of Agreement
Mar 1976	France leaves EEC snake again
Apr 1976	IMF Board of Governors submits Second Amendment to Fund members for ratification
Mar 1977	In addition to normal SDR transactions, and in addition to currencies made available from General Resources Account, Fund makes SDRs available from General Resources Account to members
Apr 1978	After two years, ratification of Second Amendment succeeds (three-fifths of Fund membership representing four-fifths of voting power). SDRs become freely usable in transactions by agreement among Fund membership (ie without Fund approval or balance-of-payments need); Fund begins to prescribe 'other holders' of SDRs (mostly other official institutions—BIS had been a prescribed institution since 1974)
June 1978	Jacques de Larosière succeeds Johannes Witteveen as IMF's sixth Managing Director
July 1978	Revised 16 currency basket (based on 1972–76 export shares) for SDR comes into effect
Nov 1978	US announces further measures to strengthen dollar, including sales of SDRs, issuing of 'Carter bonds' (securities denominated in foreign currencies), and an increase in swap lines with the major surplus countries
Jan 1979	Third Basic Period for SDR Allocations. SDR 12 billion allocation over three years; first annual instalment of second SDR allocation: 4 billion allocated. Reconstitution requirement for SDRs reduced from 30% to 15% of net cumulative allocations
Mar 1979	European Monetary System (EMS) instituted; ECU replaces EUA
June 1979	Third and last in a series of 1979 OPEC oil price increases (second oil price 'shock')
Oct 1979	Interim Committee meeting at Belgrade endorses substitution account; recommends continued Fund work on the mechanics of the plan
Jan 1980	Second annual instalment of Second SDR allocation: SDR 4 billion allocated
Apr 1980	Hamburg Interim Committee meeting; SDR substitution account fails
June 1980	First SDR-denominated Certificate of Deposit
Jan 1981	Third and final annual instalment of Second SDR allocation: SDR 4 billion allocated. Five currency basket replaces sixteen currency basket for SDR
Jan 1981	First SDR-denominated syndicated loan
Apr 1981	Reconstitution provision for SDR abrogated

May 1981	SDR interest rate reaches full combined rate of five major currencies
Aug 1982	Mexican debt moratorium and beginning of debt crisis. IMF, US Treasury, and private banks (Paris club) coordinate response
May 1983	Expansion of General Arrangements to Borrow (GAB) credit lines from SDR 6 billion to SDR 17 billion
July 1985	G10 Deputies issue Dini report 'The Functioning of the International Monetary System "promoting" convergence of economic performance'; acknowledges no consensus on the future of the SDR, but recommends that IMF continue research into its future role
Sept 1985	Plaza Agreement; cooperative agreement to lower the value of the dollar and reduce trade barriers
Oct 1985	Baker Plan, announced at IMF meeting in Seoul, solidifies US support for heavily indebted countries with support of multilateral institutions and private banks
Oct 1986	Baker–Miyazawa Accord; US acknowledges importance of currency stability
Jan 1987	Michel Camdessus succeeds Jacques de Larosière as IMF's seventh Managing Director
Feb 1987	Louvre Accord—aims to halt the dollar slide and promote currency stability
Mar 1987	Fund publishes 'The Role of the SDR in the International Monetary System', focusing on possible role for SDR in promoting international monetary stability
Apr 1987	Following four years of decline, IMF Executive Board decides to maintain Fund's SDR holdings at between SDR 0.75–1.25 billion
Oct 1987	IMF suspends SDR transactions at the Fund 'by designation'; henceforth all are 'by agreement' among the membership
Apr 1988	Institute of International Finance (IIF) in Washington, speaking on behalf of its international commercial bank membership, recommends a 'sizable allocation' (SDR 21.4 billion) of SDRs to maintain orderly exchange markets and to ease financing problems of both deficit and surplus countries
Nov 1989	Universal Postal Union commences denominating accounts in SDRs
Jan 1990	Germany authorizes private use of SDRs
June 1990	Minor Third Amendment proposals, involving the suspension of voting rights for members not fulfilling IMF financial obligations, accepted by IMF Board of Governors
Apr 1991	Japan recommends that Interim Committee discuss new SDR allocation
Sept 1992	In its annual supplement to the IMF *Survey*, the Fund continues to refer to the impasse over SDRs in maintaining that the future success of the SDR is linked to its role as principal reserve asset
Nov 1992	Third Amendment to IMF Articles of Agreement, approved in June 1990, formally ratified
Sept 1993	In an address to the Parliamentary Assembly of the Council of Europe, Jean-Claude Paye, OECD Secretary-General, calls for another SDR allocation
June 1994	G7 Summit at Naples discusses the possibility of an SDR allocation; US Treasury Secretary Bentsen believed to be amenable to limited discussion of SDR issues
Sept 1994	IMF fails to endorse compromise package of a limited SDR allocation for new Fund members at the IMF Annual Meeting in Madrid
June 1995	G7 Summit at Halifax, Canada, endorses an SDR allocation (as part of Fourth IMF Articles of Agreement amendments); New Arrangements to Borrow (NAB) proposed
Sept 1997	Fourth Amendment to IMF Articles of Agreement, and special one-time allocation of SDR 21.4 billion (Fourth Amendment to IMF Articles of Agreement) approved by Executive Board. Ratification by 85% of membership not attained until 2009
Nov 1998	New Arrangements to Borrow (NAB) instituted; SDR 34 billion (US$51 billion) in resources available for 26 participants

Jan 1999	Replacement of French franc and German deutschemark by the Euro in SDR valuation basket
Sept 1999	IMFC (International Monetary and Financial Committee) replaces Interim Committee
May 2000	Horst Köhler succeeds Michel Camdessus as IMF's eighth Managing Director
Nov 2000	European Central Bank (ECB) approved as 16th prescribed holder of SDRs
Feb 2002	At a Washington conference prior to the publication of *On Globalization*, George Soros calls for an immediate issuance of SDR 21.4 billion (ie Fourth Amendment amount), coupled with donations from rich to poor countries for pre-approved programs focusing on development, followed by annual allocations on a similar basis
Mar 2002	Monterrey Consensus (Report of the UN International Conference on Financing for Development) recognizes the value of '... innovative sources of finance, noting the proposal to use special drawing rights allocations for development purposes'
June 2004	Rodrigo de Rato succeeds Horst Köhler as ninth IMF Managing Director
Jan 2007	Crockett Report on funding IMF, highlights expanding Fund investment activities and an endowment fund through limited sale of Fund gold
Nov 2007	Dominique Strauss-Kahn succeeds Rodrigo de Rato as tenth IMF Managing Director
Fall 2008	Global financial crisis—seizure of international credit and liquidity markets
Mar 2009	Bank of China Governor Zhou Xiaochuan calls for the role of SDRs to 'play a greater role' in the international monetary system by acting 'as a super-sovereign reserve currency'
Apr 2009	London G20 Summit. G20 agrees to support a new SDR allocation of $250 billion, and the ratification of the Fourth Amendment to the Fund's Articles of Agreement
July 2009	IMF Executive Board approves a framework for the issuance of IMF notes, denominated in SDRs, that could be held by designated SDR holders (IMF members and central banks, and approved multilateral institutions)
Aug 2009	SDR allocation of $250 billion (SDR 161.2 billion)
Sept 2009	Following US approval in August, IMF reaches 85% of voting power necessary to ratify 1997 Fourth Amendment of the IMF Articles of Agreement; one-time allocation of SDR 21.4 billion—new members receive weighted disbursement to make up for previous allocations.
Sept 2009	UN Group of Experts on Reform of the International Monetary and Financial System, chaired by Joseph Stiglitz, recommends SDR allocations to be complemented by further reform of the monetary system to facilitate them.
Nov 2010	IMF Executive Board approves doubling of Fund quotas (to SDR 476.8 billion) with a corresponding rollback in the New Arrangements to Borrow (NAB), as well as changes to Executive Board
Jan 2011	France assumes chairmanship of G8 and G20; 'wider use of SDRs' to be discussed
July 2011	Following his resignation in May, Christine Lagarde succeeds Dominique Strauss-Kahn as eleventh IMF Managing Director

Introduction

At the International Monetary Fund (IMF)'s annual meeting in Rio de Janeiro in 1967, the IMF endorsed the first amendments to its Articles of Agreement since the Bretton Woods meetings in 1944. The most significant change in the amended Articles (which were ratified two years later) was the invention of Special Drawing Rights (SDRs). According to the first of 12 new articles, the primary purpose of SDRs was 'to meet the need, as and when it arises, for a supplement to existing reserve assets . . . '.[1]

Contemporary observers from both the policy making and academic communities felt that SDRs had much more potential than this, however. In the late 1960s and early 1970s SDRs were widely heralded as necessary not only to the functioning of the international monetary system, but also as a first step towards a world international money. Needless to say, this outlook was wildly optimistic, and this book asks why this initial and widespread enthusiasm was not sustained during the following decades.

The first and most obvious reason why SDRs did not live up to expectations is that they were designed for a different international monetary system than that which evolved after the breakdown of Bretton Woods only a few years later. After all, much of the initial analysis of SDRs was written with the needs of the international monetary system under Bretton Woods arrangements in mind.[2] Nonetheless what emerges in this book is that the central fact of the breakdown of Bretton Woods does not solely explain the SDR's demise from the 1980s until very recently. In addition, despite the retreat of prospects for the asset, its post-Bretton Woods evolution—particularly through the 1970s and the Second Amendment negotiations—nonetheless succeeded in confirming the role of the IMF in post-Bretton Woods monetary arrangements, including current prospects for the institution, and indeed SDRs, as the issue of international monetary stability again assumes a higher profile.

Although the economics of the SDR and international liquidity are important to this story, the main contribution of our investigation lies elsewhere. As a Fund historian perceptively noted:

> [M]uch of the discussion about the inadequacy of international liquidity, or projections of its future inadequacy, disguised in technical dress problems that were really political.[3]

Focusing on the politics of SDRs allows us to see that—whatever its technical merits or drawbacks—the failure of SDRs to live up to the optimism they engendered at inception also occurred because two of the principal actors in structuring post-Bretton Woods international monetary relations, namely the US and the IMF, gradually turned away from the asset. The SDR simply became increasingly irrelevant to the national interests of the US; importantly this also became true of the supranational institutional interests of the Fund.[4] Thus, their contribution to international monetary arrangements in the last two decades of the twentieth century was increasingly ill fated.

Although a subject of enquiry in the fields of contemporary economic history and political economy, the narrative approach in this book is that of a case study that lends itself to two investigative approaches in international relations literature. Politics and institutions are of course fundamentally important to international monetary relations, and this is no less true with respect to recent experience with the SDR. Indeed the evolution of the Fund as an international institution in our investigation is particularly illustrative of this. Acknowledging this places us within a neo-liberal institutional approach to international relations theory as articulated by Robert Keohane, who has argued forcefully that international institutions are of fundamental importance to an understanding of international relations.[5] This is not the sole approach to the investigation of the history of SDRs in this book, however, as the chapters on evolving US policy in the 1960s and 1970s demonstrate. The examination of the influence of US power on international monetary relations and the SDR also implicitly defers to a neo-realist perspective in maintaining that the importance of the state and state structures is the most useful means of capturing the strong US influence on the SDR and post-Bretton Woods international monetary arrangements.[6] Parenthetically, these two approaches have both been furthered by the contribution of a small group of influential individuals—many of whom were generous with their time in agreeing to be interviewed for this book—that also affected prospects for the SDR. Indeed the viewpoints and roles of important individuals such as successive IMF managing directors, and a number of influential economists, adds another dimension to our investigation, which lends additional insights into the development of post-Bretton Woods monetary arrangements.[7] Such an avowedly eclectic approach nonetheless facilitates an examination of the evolution of the Fund, the US, as well as their interrelationship, and simply contributes to a more comprehensive understanding of the significance of the

SDR and the evolution of international monetary relations as the post-Bretton Woods system emerged.[8]

The introductory chapter of this work examines the early history of SDRs. What emerges is that, contrary to the optimism for SDRs fostered in the wake of the Rio Agreement, a greater role for SDRs was circumscribed by the compromises necessary for the negotiation of the First Amendment. These limited prospects are thrown into sharper relief in historical perspective by examining the main precursors to the SDR, beginning with Keynes's Bancor proposal, but also including some of the later proposals of the 1960s.

In Chapter 2 we examine the basic mechanisms of SDR transactions during this period for an understanding of how SDRs worked. We also examine SDRs in the context of a monetary system in transition, noting the new system of liquidity provision and the role of reserves under the new exchange rate system. Triffin colourfully termed this development the 'abdication of responsibility [for liquidity provision] to the private market' in the 1970s;[9] it may be more neutrally said that under the new arrangements a move to market mechanisms was increasingly evident, which in turn contributed to an increasingly poor prognosis for the SDR. In this context the Committee of Twenty (C-20) and its proposals and disagreements regarding SDRs are also addressed here, not only for reasons surrounding their failure (which has been covered by John Williamson[10]), but to put the debates into a perspective that further experience with the new international monetary arrangements facilitates.

In Chapter 3 we focus primarily on the changing international monetary policy of the US administration, which in turn greatly affected prospects for the SDR after the First Amendment. First of all, though, we briefly examine the change in European approaches to the SDR in the 1970s. This is important because European indifference to the SDR during the 1970s contrasted with its much more unequivocal backing only a few years earlier. Importantly, part of the reason for the change in European attitudes lies simply in the continuing predominance of the US under post-Bretton Woods arrangements.[11] But in any case the shift away from support for the SDR was surprisingly abrupt in Europe. Thus we turn to the evolution of the US administration's policy towards the SDR for the remainder of this chapter in order to focus upon why the undeniable US enthusiasm for the SDR in the 1960s crumbled in the 1970s. For apart from a brief resurrection in the late 70s during the Carter administration, US support for the SDR waned markedly for the next 30 years.

Some of the reasons for this must be sought in an examination of the changing US policy process itself, which is the primary focus of Chapter 4. How did some of the broader structural influences on US policy change in the first years of the post-Bretton Woods era? As a relatively arcane subject for policy makers, the SDR was not a subject of intense media scrutiny or lobbying. It therefore lends itself well to an examination of international monetary policy determination within the US policy-making apparatus at all levels. This leads to an analysis of how the structure of the US international monetary bureaucracy changed in the 1970s, and how this influenced policy towards the SDR. As a consequence of this, we are led to other influences on US international monetary policy determination such as the Federal Reserve Board, and particularly the role of Congress, which, as we shall see, assumes increasing importance in the 1970s and 1980s. The US domestic policy environment is very important to the international monetary policy process, and in this context theoretical debates concerning US foreign policy determination are also of interest. Ultimately, changing US policy process in the 1970s strongly reinforced the moves away from the SDR in the US administration, and thereby contributed to the SDR's retreat on the international monetary stage.

A fuller understanding of the marginalization of the SDR entails returning in Chapter 5 to the changing role of the IMF vis-à-vis the SDR as post-Bretton Woods arrangements consolidated themselves. Central to any discussion of the Fund's role is the negotiation of the Jamaica Agreement (the Second Amendment to the Fund's Articles of Agreement), which included the provision that the SDR become the principal reserve asset in the international monetary system. Excellent source material is available for this examination, amongst which are seven volumes of documents and minutes of the Fund's Executive Board meetings entitled *Documents Relating to the Second Amendment of the Articles of Agreement of the International Monetary Fund.*[12] These comprehensive volumes, including the contributions and views of IMF executive directors and Fund staff, provide a fascinating window on international monetary policy determination in the early evolution of the post-Bretton Woods era.

Importantly, the Fund's Articles after the Second Amendment were more flexible than either of its two previous incarnations discussed in 1944 and 1967, and encompassed possibilities to enhance the role of SDRs. But the fact that this yielded few if any tangible results indicated that the Fund, too, would gradually divorce itself from SDRs, or at least from too closely identifying its own role with that of SDRs. Nonetheless to overlook the role of the Fund on the development of international monetary relations as a whole during this time is a mistake—indeed the influence of the Fund on the international monetary agenda (although not necessarily the results) in the late 1960s and 1970s is a fundamentally important development for international monetary relations during and indeed since that time.

In Chapter 6 the focus shifts to SDRs after the Jamaica Agreement. The debate over the SDR, when it occurred, reflected a growing impasse, the language of the G10's Dini report in 1985 typical of the stalemate that lasted for another 25 years.[13] Here we examine the second allocation of SDRs and review more recent issues for further illustrations of the impasse, including the uneasy grafting of the SDR on to post-Bretton Woods monetary arrangements. We noted in Chapter 2, for instance, that the mechanisms surrounding the SDR worked satisfactorily, and in this chapter it emerges that a tiny market in SDRs continued to develop. However, without the fundamentally important political support of the US and IMF, the SDR retired to the margins of international monetary arrangements where it languished until recently.[14]

Thus the politics surrounding the SDR—more specifically the key influences embodied in the US international monetary policy process, the institutional role of the IMF, and the inter-relationship between them—are fundamentally important for a more complete understanding of the SDR's marginalization under post-Bretton Woods monetary arrangements. In addition to the history of the SDR, this book also contributes to a fuller appreciation of the evolution of international monetary relations in the post-Bretton Woods monetary era.

In sum, the SDR's role as the new system emerged, and indeed what the experience with the SDR reveals about international monetary arrangements at the apogee of market-driven approaches to financial and monetary policy, has been a relatively neglected subject in contemporary international economic history, as well as in relevant political, economic, and international relations literature. Although the SDR was widely heralded at its birth, as new arrangements evolved the SDR was not germane to the interests of the US, and changes to the American international monetary policy process reinforced this. In addition, after halting attempts to improve its functioning and increase its profile, the SDR also became less integral to the interests and role of the IMF—and to systemic needs in general—in the international monetary arena under post-Bretton Woods arrangements.

However the fragility of these arrangements became evident extremely rapidly as the current international financial crisis unfolded in late 2008. Since the G20 meetings in London in April 2009, it is again evident that reform is near the top of the international monetary agenda.[15] The long overdue ratification of the Fourth Amendment to the Fund's Articles of Agreement endorsed first at the G20 meeting in London and subsequently by the IMF resulted in an SDR allocation of SDR 21.4 billion (with all new members receiving a weighted disbursement to make up for previous allocations that occurred prior to them joining the Fund). Most importantly, an SDR allocation of $250 billion (SDR 161.2 billion) as part of the $1.1 trillion G20 finance package (also agreed to at the London G20 summit) was issued in August, 2009.[16]

And within this rubric, once again latent but strong support for SDRs among much of the Fund membership heralds a prospectively greater role for the asset. Just prior to the G20 London Summit in 2009 Bank of China Governor

Zhou Xiaochuan called the SDR '... the light in the tunnel for the reform of the international monetary system'.[17] And President Sarkozy of France, on assuming the chairmanship of the G8 and G20, set the reform of the international monetary system as a G20 priority for 2011, having arranged with President Hu of China a 'working seminar' on the subject, including an examination of the role of SDRs.[18] Notably, it is not only liquidity needs, but, with the rise of the Euro and even renminbi as alternative reserve assets, interest in international monetary stability that has prompted reconsideration of a greater role for SDRs.

This may yet prove another in a long line of optimistic prognostications for the asset. But at the very least it now appears that that the SDR's very survival during a period when they seemed anachronistic is significant. It is partly thanks to previously unheralded work at the IMF and elsewhere—when SDRs appeared largely irrelevant to systemic needs—that this prospective contribution again appears possible.

Notes

1. Article XXI of *Articles of Agreement of the International Monetary Fund as Modified by the Proposed [First] Amendment* (includes typewritten palimpsests), IMF (Washington, DC: n.d. [1968]).
2. See Stephen Cohen, *International Monetary Reform 1964–69: The Political Dimension*, Praeger (New York: 1970); Dorothy Sobol, *Europe Confronts the Dollar—The Creation of the SDR, 1963–69*, Garland (New York: 1982); and Fritz Machlup *Remaking the International Monetary System: the Rio Agreement and Beyond*, Johns Hopkins Press (Baltimore: 1982).
3. Margaret Garritsen de Vries, *The International Monetary Fund 1966–71*, IMF (Washington, DC: 1976), *vol. 1, The System Under Stress*, p. 34.
4. As Robert Mundell succinctly observed: '... there is a tendency for the dominant country to reject the world currency'—see Mundell, Robert, 'The International Monetary System and the Case for a World Currency', Leon Koźmiński Academy of Entrepreneurship and Management (WSPiZ) and TIGER, Distinguished Lectures Series n. 12, Warsaw, available at: http://www.tiger.edu.pl/publikacje/dist/mundell2.pdf (accessed 8 June 2011), 23 October 2003, p. 4.
5. The importance of international institutions in international relations is largely the product of the proliferation of these organizations this century, particularly of the United Nations Organizations after World War II. See Robert Keohane, 'Neoliberal institutionalism: a perspective on world politics'—chapter 1 of R. Keohane, *International Institutions and State Power*, Westview Press (Boulder, Co: 1989). This essay builds on Robert Keohane and Joseph Nye's earlier classic work *Power and Interdependence: World Politics in Transition*, Little Brown and Company (New York: 1977).

6. An example of this approach is embodied in Robert Gilpin's *US Power and the Multinational Corporation*, Basic Books (New York: 1975). It is shared to a degree by the balance of power perspective in Kenneth Waltz's *Theory of International Politics*, Addison-Wesley (Reading, MA: 1979), and, as Keohane has noted, is also implied by the absence of a supranational authority in Hedley Bull's *The Anarchical Society*, Columbia University Press (New York: 1979).
7. Without addressing the relevance of constructivism to international monetary relations (i.e. that the international monetary system is a social construct), it is nonetheless possible to acknowledge the power of ideas and the influence of individuals on the emergence of post-Bretton Woods arrangements. See in particular John Odell's *US International Monetary Policy: Markets, Power, and Ideas as Sources of Change*, Princeton University Press (Princeton, NJ: 1982); also *Negotiating the World Economy*, Cornell University Press (Ithaca, NY: 2000).
8. This eclecticism is echoed and has important antecedents in contemporary international relations theory. As liberalism deferred to neo-liberalism and realism to neo-realism these schools implicitly deferred to respective explanations of international relations and international political economy. For instance, as indicated in the title to Robert Keohane's 1989 book, neo-liberal institutional theorists increasingly acknowledge the importance of the state in their analysis. See Robert Keohane, *International Institutions and State Power, op. cit*, pp. 162–6. The same dynamic is evident in neo-realist perspectives. Most importantly, eclecticism itself has recently been accorded formal legitimacy by one of the doyennes of international political economy theory, Peter Katzenstein—see Rudra Sil and Peter J. Katzenstein, 'Analytical eclectism in the study of world politics: reconfiguring problems and mechanisms across research traditions', American Political Science Association's *Perspectives on Politics*, vol. 8, no. 2, June 2010.
9. Robert Triffin, '"Europe and the Money Muddle" Revisited', *Banca Nazionale del Lavoro Quarterly Review*, March 1978, p. 55.
10. See John Williamson, *The Failure of World Monetary Reform*, Nelson (Sunbury on Thames: 1977).
11. Denis Healey, former Chancellor of the Exchequer and Chairman of the IMF's Interim Committee during an important time for the SDR (1977–9), reiterated that the US was fundamentally important to the success of international monetary initiatives, but that this was no less true of post-Bretton Woods monetary arrangements than it was in the 1960s. Correspondence with the author; see also Chapter 3, fn. 14, below.
12. This material consists of three volumes of documents, three volumes of Executive Board minutes, and an index, covering all intermediate phases of the negotiations, and comprises almost 5,500 pages. Though stamped 'not for public use', these volumes were made available to a limited number of researchers and libraries in 1986, and have since been declassified by the Fund. For detailed contents, see Appendix 1, below.
13. The report stated that '. . . the Deputies have discussed both normal SDR allocations and other ideas for developing the SDR, but found no consensus within the Group on any specific proposal', in IMF *Survey*, July 1985 (Supplement), p. 14. Similar

wording reflecting this and indeed other SDR-related impasses were a feature of successive communiqués through until the 2008 financial crisis.

14. Despite a failure to approve the Fourth Amendment to the Fund Articles until 2009, the US indicated sporadic rekindling of US interest in the SDR; for example a willingness to discuss it at the 1994 G7 summit in Naples, and a UK–US proposal for a limited SDR allocation. See 'US and Britain Propose Boost to Reserves of Poorer IMF Members', *Financial Times*, 19 September 1994, p. 18. And in the wake of the financial crisis the US quickly agreed to an SDR allocation of $250 billion as well as a ratification of the Fourth Amendments to the IMF Articles of Agreement (see: http://www.g20.org/Documents/g20_communique_020409.pdf (accessed 8 June 2011)).
15. Working Group 3 (G20 finance officials) was mandated by G20 leaders to advance actions in their 'Leaders Declaration' in November 2008 on 'reform of the IMF'. The WG3 report in March 2009 recommended ratification of the Fourth Amendment to the Fund articles which, as noted, was endorsed by G20 leaders in London. See: http://www.g20.org/Documents/g20_wg3_010409.pdf (accessed 8 June 2011).
16. See 'Leaders Statement—The Global Plan for Recovery and Reform, London, 2 April 2009', at: http://www.g20.org/Documents/final-communique.pdf (accessed 8 June 2011).
17. Governor Zhou's statement also noted that a 'super-sovereign reserve currency' could both 'create and control' global liquidity. See People's Bank of China, 'Reform the International Monetary System', 23 March 2009 as at: http://www.pbc.gov.cn/publish/english/956/2009/20091229104425550619706/20091229104425550619706_.html (accessed 8 June 2011).
18. 'G20 Summit Press Conference Given by Nicholas Sarkozy, President of the Republic', excerpts, Seoul, 12 November 2010, as at: http://ambafrance-us.org/spip.php?article1958 (accessed 15 June 2011). See also the French-inspired 'Palais-Royal Initiative' on the reform of the international monetary system in the run-up to the French chaired G20 meetings in 2011 as at: http://www.elysee.fr/president/root/bank_objects/2011-007.Palais-Royal_Initiative-Final_version_of_the_Report-Jan_18.pdf (accessed 8 June 2011).

1

The genesis of SDRs and the limitations of the Rio Agreement

1.1 Introduction

Although its prospects have often appeared moribund, the emergence of the Special Drawing Right (SDR) in the late 1960s was a highly significant development in the history of international monetary relations. The SDR was the first truly international money to be created by fiat. At the time, however, SDRs were seen simply as a means of bolstering the international monetary arrangements forged at Bretton Woods in 1944, and it was for this reason that International Monetary Fund (IMF) members ratified the creation of SDRs as part of the first amendment to the Fund's Articles of Agreement in 1969.

But even this more modest justification was not fully realized. Indeed, an inkling of the problems that lay ahead for the SDR may be discerned as early as 1967, the year of the SDR's first arrival on the international stage. For it was with flat institutional prose and some understatement that the IMF unveiled the SDR to the world at its annual meeting in Rio de Janeiro in September 1967. While this may have reflected the Fund's customary caution, or the years of negotiations that were still taking place, perhaps it was simply exhaustion which prompted the Fund to announce hesitatingly that:

> The facility described in this Outline is intended to meet the need, as and when it arises, for a supplement to existing reserve assets.[1]

Despite this muted language, the Rio Agreement was quickly seized upon by policy makers, the academic community, and bankers to be an important step in augmenting and regulating the provision of international liquidity—a step which would lead to an even greater role for the SDR.[2] This enthusiasm was strongly echoed at the Fund: in 1967 J. J. Polak forecast that by the year 2000 SDRs could account for over half the world's reserves.[3] In fact prevailing optimism among many financial observers at the time[4] even prompted the chairman of the US Federal Reserve Board to suggest that in regulating liquidity, SDRs were a first step towards an international money with a modified IMF as world central bank.[5] While the cool heads of the IMF and the battle weary negotiators cautioned that SDRs were simply a means of increasing liquidity, around the world many others warmly welcomed the SDR and speculated enthusiastically as to what this first step might herald.[6]

The SDR was more than an asset. At the time, some writers stated that they were money, or well on the way to becoming so.[7] More recently, John Williamson has pointed out:

> It is true that SDRs are only central bank money, because only central banks accept them in settlement of debts. But to the extent that they are so accepted, they are money.[8]

Most importantly, however, underlying the international agreement to create SDRs at Rio de Janeiro was the tacit understanding that the provision of international liquidity was to be supplemented at the international level—when it needed to be—by official agreement. In other words, international liquidity was to be managed not by a central bank, but collectively, with systemic interests paramount.

This chapter will examine SDRs in light of these conflicting and at times contradictory interpretations and aspirations. It should also be recalled at the outset that the optimism surrounding the first SDR allocation, and some of the more confident predictions for the role of the Fund itself, occurred at a time when increasing transnational interactions in economic, political, and social domains was increasingly seen as responsible for the evolution of a new international system. This was reflected in much international relations literature; in fact it underlay some of the rationale for the explosion in the discipline in the postwar period, including the rise of international political economy within it.[9] The early 1970s prompted an awareness of the importance of transnational corporations and also international organizations as both an impetus for and response to issues that affected people across international boundaries.[10] While this did capture some developments in international monetary relations at the time, such as the study of the various elements of the UNO, the changing and increasingly influential voice of the Fund in this context remains relatively ignored. Of course the Fund's was not the only voice in the international monetary reform debate: the very real changes which occurred in more traditional subjects for analysis, such as the US bureaucracy, or the nature of the international system as a whole, are also important. In any case, an account of the SDR and international monetary arrangements surrounding it without an examination of the institutional influence of the Fund is incomplete, and overlooks a vitally important determinant of what transpired under the new arrangements.

Part of the reason why the Fund's influence on international monetary relations has been relatively overlooked is that in the immediate postwar period the Fund's role was minimal. The SDR negotiations, however, revealed an IMF that was increasingly aware of its potential as an independent institution, willing to posit its own prospective solutions to international monetary problems. We can explore the early evidence of this through an examination of the SDR's progenitors.

1.2 The Postwar Legacy

The liquidity negotiations of the 1960s had important historical antecedents. In many respects these negotiations were a return to the discussions of John Maynard Keynes and Harry Dexter White in the 1940s over the merits of a supra-national reserve asset.

The postwar international monetary system as Keynes envisioned it did warrant a role for a truly international reserve asset to be called Bancor.[11] The now familiar story of how Keynes's plans were attenuated considerably in negotiations with the US meant that more comprehensive ideas about postwar international monetary relations were quickly shelved at the Bretton Woods conference in 1944. Indeed by then Keynes's attention to Bancor was distracted not by inherent difficulties with the plans per se but by other more domestically oriented considerations, among them encouraging support for the watered down agreement.[12] In the US, too, there was some difficulty in garnering support for an agreement which some perceived as unnecessarily generous to Britain and the Continent.[13] It quickly became apparent that the de facto role of the Fund was to be relatively circumspect.

Initially, however, Keynes had formulated his plans for Bancor before negotiations were entered into with the Americans. They were outlined extemporaneously in a number of speeches and articles and, as he readily admitted, they were not solely his ideas.[14] During the war, Keynes strongly advocated Bancor since he did not expect the American war boom to continue, and he felt that the proposed Fund liquidity would be more than adequate for the 'purposes for which [it is] intended'.[15] Of course, the US 'boom' did continue, and the corollary of this development was that the Bretton Woods system, including currency convertibility and the IMF's capacity to provide liquidity, was effectively stillborn.[16]

Keynes had hoped that an International Clearing Union (ICU), initially to be set up by Britain and the US with joint head offices in London and New York, would issue Bancor to all member countries proportional to their prewar importance in world trade. Bancor would be linked to gold, and no special role was contemplated for the dollar or sterling (although it was anticipated that the US Federal Reserve Board would have to lend its gold surplus to the ICU in the immediate postwar period). Importantly, countries in either deficit *or surplus* would, in conjunction with a Governing Board, decide what measures would be necessary to restore balance of payments equilibrium. And contrary to a common misconception, Keynes suggested slightly greater leeway for surplus countries:

> a member state whose debit balance has exceeded a *quarter* of its quota on the average of at least a year shall be designated a Deficiency Country; and a member state whose credit balance has succeeded *half* of its quota on the average of at least a year shall be designated a Surplus Country.[17]

Balance of payments deficits were thus discouraged as were, to a lesser degree, surpluses. In addition penalties were imposed on both surplus and deficit countries: a 1 per cent per annum charge whether in credit or debit up to half a country's quota, and a 2 per cent charge for countries in excess of half their quota. In effect the ICU would have had greater power to restore balance in the international monetary system by providing liquidity through the automaticity embodied in its provisions. This contrasted with the process that emerged by virtue of the powers of the IMF's Governing Body—an important distinction that Keynes tried to emphasize.[18] While the Bretton Woods agreement included a 'scarce currency' clause (article VII), which existed as a potential threat to surplus currency countries, a lack of automaticity in bringing it into force gave primacy to political considerations and it was never invoked. Notably, the official institution of SDRs in 1970 did not embody the automaticity of the ICU either. Again, it is important to note that through the automatic penalties of the ICU, the ICU would have enjoyed greater inherent support for its institutional arrangements—including Bancor—than the Bretton Woods arrangements that evolved even after the invention of SDRs.[19]

Keynes also proposed that the International Clearing Union would issue Bancor credits, which would *not* be convertible into other reserve assets. Again, in a foreshadowing of many later substitution account proposals for the SDR, they were also to be distributed to all members in proportion to their importance in world trade. The amount initially envisioned was $40 billion, which was similarly expected to increase with the growth in world trade flows.[20] Bancor would be backed by gold, or by quotas in the ICU that would be contributed by members in their initial subscription. The price of Bancor units would be fixed but adjustable. Sales of gold, overdraft privileges, and ICU charges (through penalties on countries with persistent deficits or surpluses) could also augment the level of Bancor available in the international monetary system.

At the time, these proposals were perceived as too radical by most in the US; much to the frustration of Keynes even the prospective location of the IMF itself was moved by the Americans from New York to Washington, which he believed made it more susceptible to political influence from its most important member.[21] Nonetheless, as the Bretton Woods system came into being, the overwhelming importance of the dollar and the health of the US economy to the functioning of the international monetary system strongly overshadowed the role of the IMF. The failure of sterling convertibility in 1946 threw this dynamic into sharp relief.

To illustrate this further: when it became apparent as early as 1947 that liquidity available through the IMF was inadequate, the US insisted on making funds available through the Marshall Plan rather than utilizing the Fund.[22] In April 1948 the IMF went on to state that any recipient of Marshall Plan aid should refrain from asking for Fund resources.[23] The subordinate status of the Fund vis-à-vis the US has thus been evident, but it was in the 1940s and 1950s that it was at its most obvious. After the Marshall Plan, the IMF remained on the margins of international monetary relations until the late 1950s.

In fact a par value system with full convertibility was postponed until 1958—let alone consideration of alternative assets. At first, the liquidity problem following the war was not accompanied by concern over gold supplies, and such concern as there was over sterling at the time only served to contrast it with the strength of the dollar (and the weakness of sterling also contributed to the postponement of currency convertibility—see Table 1.1). The prime concern addressed by the Marshall Plan was not achieved by directly increasing the amount, or type, of liquidity in the system but rather in redistributing it from capital-rich America to capital-starved Europe. And with US political, military, and economic power at its apex, it was not surprising that the US wanted to redistribute liquidity under its own auspices rather than through the IMF.

Throughout the 1950s then, the Fund remained on the periphery of international monetary relations—so much so that outside observers prodded it to increase its activities. For instance, in 1950 the Economic and Social Council (ECOSOC) of the UN commissioned a report entitled *Measures for International Economic Stability*, published in July 1952, which included the observation that 'our examination of existing reserves has convinced us that they are not in general adequate'.[24] The ECOSOC report went on to recommend an enlargement of Fund resources, and urged the Fund to address its report.[25]

The Fund greeted this challenge in October 1953 in a report ultimately published in the IMF's *Staff Papers*, revealingly titled 'The Adequacy of

Table 1.1. Development of the Gold Exchange Standard Gold, Foreign Exchange, and IMF Quota Contributions to international liquidity, 1937–60

US$ million

		1937				1948				1951			
		Gold	Foreign Exchange	IMF Gold Tranche Position	Total	Gold	Foreign Exchange	IMF Gold Tranche Position	Total	Gold	Foreign Exchange	IMF Gold Tranche Position	Total
	US	**12,790**	—	—	**12,790**	**24,399**	—	**1,359**	**25,758**	**22,873**	—	**1426**	**24299**
	UK	**4,141**	....	—	....	**1,605**	**404**	—	**2,009**	**2,172**	**202**	—	**2374**
	Sterling Area	**490**	....	—	....	**580**	**8,440**	**24**	**9,044**	**625**	**6,815**	**29**	**7469**
	Continental Europe	....	....	—	....	**3,710**	**2,015**	**44**	**5,769**	**4,345**	**3,080**	**93**	**7518**
	France	*2,749*	*5*	—	*2754*	*548*	*5*	—	*553*	*597*	*19*	—	*616*
of which	*Germany*	....	....	—	....	—	*295*	....	....	*28*	*427*	....	*455*
	Italy	*210*	....	—	....	*96*	....	—	....	*333*	*441*	—	*774*
	Canada	**180**	**20**	—	**200**	**401**	**610**	**75**	**1,086**	**842**	**984**	**75**	**1901**
	Rest of World	....	....	—	....	**2,365**	**4,005**	**59**	**6,429**	**2,065**	**4,050**	**90**	**6205**
	Japan	*279*	*17*	—	*296*	*3*	....	....	....	*10*	....	....	....
of which	*Latin America*	*765*	....	—	....	*1,490*	*1,395*	*37*	*2,922*	*1,955*	*1,025*	*65*	*3045*
	Total	....	....	—	....	**33,060**	**15,470**	**1,560**	**50,090**	**33,925**	**15,150**	**1713**	**50788**

		1954				1957				1960			
		Gold	Foreign Exchange	IMF Gold Tranche Position	Total	Gold	Foreign Exchange	IMF Gold Tranche Position	Total	Gold	Foreign Exchange	IMF Gold Tranche Position	Total
	US	**21,793**	—	**1,185**	**22,978**	**22,857**	—	**1,975**	**24,832**	**17,804**	—	**1,555**	**19,359**
	UK	**25,30**	**268**	**236**	**3,034**	**1,555**	**819**	—	**2,374**	**2,801**	**438**	**488**	**3,727**
	Sterling Area	**675**	**7,235**	**30**	**7,940**	**690**	**6,515**	**41**	**7,246**	**680**	**6,250**	**131**	**7061**
	Continental Europe	**6,055**	**5,555**	**261**	**11871**	**8,215**	**5,950**	**157**	**14,322**	**13,230**	**8,190**	**928**	**22,348**
	France	*708*	*553*	*3*	*1264*	*581*	*64*	—	*645*	*1,641*	*429*	*202*	*2,272*
of which	*Germany*	*626*	*1,870*	*83*	*2579*	*2,541*	*2,573*	*83*	*5,197*	*2,971*	*3766*	*309*	*7,046*
	Italy	*346*	*581*	—	*927*	*452*	*903*	—	*1,355*	*2,203*	*876*	*68*	*3,147*
	Canada	**1,073**	**882**	**75**	**2,100**	**1,100**	**736**	**90**	**1,926**	**885**	**951**	**153**	**1,989**
	Rest of World	**2,825**	**4,365**	**56**	**7,246**	**2,890**	**4,995**	**49**	**7,934**	**2,630**	**6,005**	**317**	**8,952**
	Japan	*21*	*717*	*.1*	*738.1*	*23*	*501*	—	*524*	*247*	*1,577*	*125*	*1,949*
of which	*Latin America*	*1,835*	*1,300*	*30*	*3165*	*1,890*	*1,930*	*40*	*3,860*	*1,360*	*1,580*	*127*	*3,067*
	Total	**34,950**	**18,305**	**1,845**	**55,100**	**37,305**	**19,015**	**2,313**	**58,633**	**38,030**	**21,830**	**3,570**	**63,430**

Source: *International Financial Statistics*, Supplement to 1963/64 issues, Washington 1964

Monetary Reserves'. The report concluded by pointing out that it was primarily individual countries themselves that were responsible for maintaining and increasing reserve levels. Even during economic depressions (in which case the ECOSOC report had concluded that international reserve levels were inadequate) the report argued that:

> ...primary reliance for the avoidance and cure of depressions must be placed upon appropriate measures at the national level, especially in industrial countries.[26]

For the first 15 years of its existence, the Fund's role was marginal with respect to international liquidity provision. This was also true concerning its self-professed role vis-à-vis aiding or disciplining its members. For a time Keynes's warnings about the Fund being perceived as a mere appanage of the US administration seemed prescient.

When the Fund next addressed this question comprehensively, however, its position on reserve adequacy had changed. The first of a series of increasingly active IMF managing directors, Per Jacobsson, sponsored a staff study called 'International Reserves and Liquidity' in 1958. The Fund then observed that between 1947 and 1957 world exports had increased by 90 per cent and that decreases in reserves had occurred because of 'decreases in primary product prices' or 'prolonged inflation' (Ceylon, India, and some Latin American states were particularly singled out as victims):[27]

> It is doubtful whether, in the circumstances of the world today, with world trade greatly expanded in volume and value, the Fund's resources are sufficient to enable it fully to perform its duties under the Articles of Agreement. (See Table 1.2 for changing reserve/import ratios)[28]

While alternative assets still seemed irrelevant to the needs of an international monetary system whose problems could be alleviated by the provision of more (or higher priced) gold or dollars, this Fund report, coincident with moves to general convertibility, signalled a shift in perception of the requirements of the international monetary system and the role of the Fund itself. Also, as Table 1.1 indicates and as Triffin and others were beginning to warn, it began to point to a disequilibrium between gold and dollar reserves, and thus a relative (but not yet absolute) decline in US liquidity.

The Fund then, was just beginning to develop a voice of its own. As well as the new Fund report, another manifestation of this was the willingness of the Fund's managing director to speak out on major issues. As we shall see, the post was beginning to assume increasing importance when articulating the nascent interests of the Fund on international monetary matters—a distinct voice increasingly less obviously beholden to the interests of its most important members.

1.3 The Liquidity Debate in the 1960s

Indeed by 1960, and reflecting this new concern of the Fund, international monetary circumstances were perceived as threatening prevailing Bretton Woods arrangements. A catalyst to this initial perception was the publication of Robert Triffin's *Gold and the Dollar Crisis* in 1960, although credit must be given to Keynes and his successors (such as Harrod and Kaldor) in Britain for their warnings regarding the limitations of Bretton Woods monetary arrangements throughout the 1940s and 1950s.[29]

Gold and the Dollar Crisis drew attention to the dependence of the world upon the US for the provision of reserve assets. As Triffin saw it, this was not a problem if the US could continue to provide the necessary liquidity without balance of payments deficits. However, if US balance of payments deficits were endemic, or perceived to be so, the rest of the world would increasingly exchange dollars for gold. *The Federal Reserve Bank of St Louis Review* succinctly summarized the delicate relationship between liquidity and confidence in the US's role as guarantor of the Bretton Woods system, which became known as the Triffin Dilemma:

> While other central banks were willing to accept dollars as reserve assets, foreign holdings of dollars could not expand sufficiently to satisfy foreign central banks' demand for reserves without a continuous U.S. balance of payments deficit. The United States could not continue running balance of payments deficits, however, without casting doubt upon the ability of the U.S. Government to maintain the fixed relative value of the dollar. This would ultimately reduce confidence in the dollar as an international reserve asset.[30]

One alternative solution, increasing the price of gold, was rejected early in the US, as we shall see. Rather, Triffin's point of view was increasingly accepted. The Bretton Woods system did not effectively provide for a dynamic international economy in that as the international economy grew (or if inflation took place), there would be an increasing shortage of dollars (rather than gold shortage relative to dollars).[31] This view took hold at the Fund as well as among many US policy makers and observers.

Attention was thus drawn to the corresponding difficulties of an international monetary system that thereupon depended upon continued US deficits to provide liquidity. Crisis first manifested itself in sterling—the dollar's first line of defense—and signalled involvement by the Fund and especially the US in international monetary management. These moves then led to a number of initiatives to shore up the dollar in the early 1960s, amongst them currency 'swaps' (short-term credit arrangements between central banks and the Federal Reserve in the US), the gold pool (which sought to stabilize the gold price at \$35/oz), and the enlargement of credit facilities to the G10 nations through

Table 1.2. Reserve/import ratios—major country groupings as a measure of reserve adequacy to 1957

		Value Figures in US$ millions								
		1928			1937			1948		
		Reserves	Imports	Ratio(%)	Reserves	Imports	Ratio(%)	Reserves	Imports	Ratio(%)
	US	**3,746**	**4,427**	**85**	**12,790**	**3,573**	**358**	**24,399**	**8,058**	**303**
	UK	**748**	**5,795**	**13**	**4,141**	**5,082**	**81**	**2,009**	**8,370**	**24**
	Sterling Area	**754**	**2,670**	**28**	**1,425**	**2,870**	**46**	**7,275**	**7,627**	**95**
	Continental Europe	**5,140**	**11,103**	**46**	**6,600**	**8,680**	**78**	**5,875**	**14,519**	**40**
	France	*2,541*	*2,097*	*121*	*2,784*	*1,689*	*165*	....	*3,443*	....
of which	*Germany*	*776*	*3,335*	*23*	....	*2,196*	....	*295*	....	....
	Italy	*583*	*1,173*	*50*	*212*	*734*	*29*	*539*	*1,539*	*35*
	Canada	**93**	**1,364**	**7**	**200**	**939**	**21**	**1,011**	**3,024**	**33**
	Rest of World	**2,560**	**5,266**	**49**	**2,400**	**3,990**	**60**	**5,925**	**10,497**	**56**
	Japan	*598*	*990*	*60*	*297*	*1,138*	*26*	....	*684*	....
of which	*Latin America*	*1,160*	*2,453*	*47*	*875*	*1,717*	*51*	*2,750*	*6,224*	*44*
	Total	**13,041**	**30,625**	**43**	**27,556**	**25,134**	**110**	**46,494**	**52,095**	**89**
		1951			1954			1957		
		Reserves	Imports	Ratio(%)	Reserves	Imports	Ratio(%)	Reserves	Imports	Ratio(%)
	US	**22,873**	**11,882**	**193**	**21,793**	**11,047**	**197**	**22,857**	**14,174**	**161**
	UK	**2,374**	**10,934**	**22**	**2,798**	**9,447**	**30**	**2,374**	**11,412**	**21**
	Sterling Area	**5,225**	**9,652**	**54**	**5,000**	**7,924**	**63**	**4,050**	**9,969**	**41**
	Continental Europe	**7,500**	**22,033**	**34**	**11,425**	**23,701**	**48**	**14,575**	**34,384**	**42**
	France	*912*	*4,457*	*20*	*1,369*	*4,221*	*32*	*775*	*6,170*	*13*
of which	*Germany*	*518*	*3,491*	*15*	*2,636*	*4,571*	*58*	*5,644*	*7,478*	*75*
	Italy	*1,003*	*2,167*	*46*	*1,041*	*2,439*	*43*	*1,532*	*3,626*	*42*
	Canada	**1,826**	**4,194**	**44**	**1,954**	**4,551**	**43**	**1,836**	**6,346**	**29**
	Rest of World	**6,725**	**14,685**	**46**	**6,550**	**14,755**	**44**	**7,175**	**20,475**	**35**
	Japan	*924*	*1,995*	*46*	*1,022*	*2,399*	*43*	*1,019*	*4,284*	*24*
of which	*Latin America*	*2,925*	*7,831*	*37*	*3,025*	*7,411*	*41*	*3,775*	*9,100*	*41*
	Total	**46,523**	**73,380**	**63**	**49,520**	**71,425**	**69**	**52,867**	**96,760**	**55**

Source: pp. 412–15 of statistical appendix to 'International Reserves and Liquidity: A Study by the Staff of the International Monetary Fund', in J. Horsefield (ed.), *The International Monetary Fund 1945–65—Twenty Years of International Monetary Cooperation* (vol III, Documents) the IMF (General Arrangements to Borrow). In this context, the SDR may simply be seen as another (but nonetheless ill-fated) step in a long line of attempts to shore up the dollar-based arrangements.

The US also began to make it more difficult to export capital outside its borders—through a Voluntary Foreign Credit Restraint Program (VFCRP) which restricted bank lending for reinvestment abroad, an Interest Equalization Tax (IET) that instituted a 1 per cent tax on domestic purchases of foreign securities, and finally the Foreign Direct Investment Program (FDIP), which in 1968 imposed compulsory restrictions on foreign direct investment abroad.[32] Notwithstanding the fact that these various measures also inadvertently contributed to the growth of Euromarkets (i.e. offshore markets in currencies, particularly dollars, outside the immediate reach of domestic monetary authorities), these various programmes came to be associated with 'ad hoccery', a pragmatic but loose response to international monetary management whose most well-known proponent was Robert Roosa, the Under-Secretary of the Treasury in the early 1960s.[33] Roosa recognized that the increasing US deficits were affecting confidence in the international monetary system. What was less unanimously acknowledged was how long term this deficit was likely to be, and whether it reflected fundamental disequilibrium within the US economy or the system as a whole. Whatever the case, it became apparent to many during the 1960s that reform of the international monetary system should aim to reduce the instability threatening liquidity arrangements under the Bretton Woods monetary system. The US Administration itself came to this conclusion by 1965; what guise this reform would take became a matter of increasing debate that eventually led to the plan to create SDRs.

Following Triffin, momentum gathered quickly for reform of liquidity arrangements. Many of these plans were ambitious, and some of these embodied features of Keynes' ICU and Bancor. Numerous surveys of the plans for reform in the 1960s already exist; indeed the US Congress published a taxonomy of various proposals as early as 1961.[34]

As the perceived liquidity crisis intensified during the 1960s, and despite very real differences among policy makers on both sides of the Atlantic, options were quickly narrowed. We may briefly group these myriad early plans roughly in order of relevance to the prevailing Fund arrangements:

1) The Triffin Plan.[35] Drawing upon Keynes, Triffin advocated an extended IMF (christened by Oscar Altman an 'XIMF'[36]) that would provide a limited amount of international liquidity in exchange for gold and foreign reserves.[37] International liquidity would be increased in proportion to the growth in world trade, or, to avoid deflationary tendencies during periods of trade decreases, 3 per cent to 5 per cent p.a. Williamson, using Aliber's distinction between supply- and demand-oriented theories of the supply of international reserves, shared Triffin's characterization of

the problem as supply-determined, which would be remedied by an increase in the supply of liquidity.[38] Triffin also advocated an end to the reserve currency system, with the IMF then acting as sole issuer of deposits and also acting in the open market by issuing interest bearing deposits in exchange for sales of gold and reserve currencies to the IMF—that is as a world central bank.

2) The Stamp Plan.[39] Stamp is usually credited with the first 'link' proposal, which linked the provision of liquidity to development finance. Stamp envisioned IMF-issued certificates distributed through central banks, backed only by agreement in settling debts.[40]
3) A composite commodity reserve currency. Hart, Kaldor, and Tinbergen, reviving a nineteenth-century idea, advocated an IMF sponsored stockpile of key commodities which would be exchanged for IOUs; their paper was presented at an UNCTAD conference in 1964.[41]
4) Bernstein and CRUs.[42] Edward Bernstein advocated that Composite Reserve Units (CRUs) linked to gold be created by key-currency countries, and that states receive reserve units to supplement gold in settling deficits within the limited group. This was a cause also championed by the French. In return states would agree to hold units to a specified percentage of gold holdings.
5) Robert Roosa, US Treasury Under-Secretary during the early 1960s, advocated an increased role for currency swap arrangements. In return, the US would agree to explore a multiple currency reserve system when the US official payments deficit returned to rough balance.[43] As mentioned previously, Roosa became the chief proponent for the extension of ad hoc arrangements such as the General Arrangements to Borrow (GAB), swap arrangements, and the gold pool, as well as the possibility of long-term loans between surplus and deficit countries. By 1963, however, Roosa began to acknowledge the possible necessity of addressing liquidity questions more comprehensively.[44]
6) Gold revaluation. Michael Heilperin, Roy Harrod, Milton Gilbert, and Peter Oppenheimer all advocated various proposals involving an increase in the price of gold, either by the US doubling the dollar price of gold (thereby revaluing existing gold reserves) or by raising the price for new gold purchases only.[45] Alternatively, Jacques Rueff, Valéry Giscard d'Estaing, and President Charles de Gaulle in the early 1960s promoted a return to the gold standard, in de Gaulle's case including his impromptu rhapsody to gold (as opposed to the dollar) at a press conference in February 1965.[46] The US, however, stood steadfastly against a greater role for gold, or even for increasing the gold price, a proposal that had been earlier rejected by President Kennedy. Even

earlier than this, during the 1961 Congressional investigation into the international monetary system, similar gold-related proposals were firmly rejected.[47] Whatever the merits of these ideas, the perceived antagonism of the French towards the US dollar, coupled with early US opposition to altering the dollar–gold price link, suggested that these proposals stood little chance of success.

7) The dollar-standard school received its main impetus from an article in *The Economist* in 1966 by Charles Kindleberger, Walter Salant, and Emile Despres,[48] and was supported later by other US theorists such as Ronald MacKinnon.[49] Basically, dollar-standard theorists argue that the US deficit was essentially demand-determined. Thus US efforts to curtail the deficit would harm the rest of the world's need for liquidity. Crudely, the US deficit was not a major cause for concern, as it simply helped to satisfy the world's demand for liquidity.[50]

8) Finally, flexible exchange rates, which essentially amounted to an abandonment of the Bretton Woods system, were advocated by a growing minority of academic economists. Machlup mentions over 20 of them quietly working on what were highly unfashionable ideas in the 1950s and early 1960s, among them Milton Friedman, Gottfried Haberler, and Fritz Meyer.[51] And Canada was an early outlier to Bretton Woods arrangements in this regard, having at first advocated (during Bretton Woods negotiations), and then embraced (during the 1950s), a limited flexible rate regime.[52] Needless to say, this was the solution to international monetary arrangements that ultimately prevailed—though more by default than by design.

In the mid-1960s, however, the solution to international monetary problems tended to be seen as resolvable through negotiation and international agreement. By 1964, academic discussion of reform proposals was usurped by an increasing number of official proposals, which nonetheless did not deter continued advice from respected observers. The Bellagio Group, consisting of 32 of the most influential macro-economists (among them Roy Harrod, Fred Hirsch, Harry Johnson, Peter Kenen, Charles Kindleberger, Jacques Rueff, and Robert Triffin) was the most illustrious example. This Group had arisen despite that fact that the G10, flush with the success of the GAB, no longer felt it necessary to consult academic experts on reform.[53]

Thus, it was rather developments within the Fund, hitherto underemphasized by most observers, and other official developments, that bear closer examination for an understanding of the path which led to SDRs. Among these, the Ossola Report, published under G10 auspices, quickly came to terms with the liquidity debate, in both recognizing the problems of US failure or unwillingness to adjust, and the confidence in the gold–dollar system that was thereby called into question over future sources of liquidity through the US dollar.[54]

Surveys abound on the liquidity problem, as noted.[55] Developments within the IMF that influenced international liquidity negotiations have been somewhat overlooked in this regard, however. While it is undoubtedly true that international monetary developments were primarily influenced by the major members of the Fund, particularly the US, the work at the IMF itself bears closer examination. It has already been shown that the change in appreciation of the liquidity problem by the Fund heralded a growing realization of the liquidity problem in the late 1950s with the publication of its report 'International Reserves and Liquidity'. This was an important step. Similarly, the sponsorship of a subsequent study by the Fund's managing director in the early 1960s, a process which was to intensify throughout the next 20 years, signalled an increasingly high profile for Fund initiatives. For instance, in a revealing statement made just 18 days after his appointment, the new Fund managing director Pierre-Paul Schweitzer noted problems with 'procedural aspects of the international liquidity problem'.[56] The US at the time disagreed. At a G10 meeting shortly afterwards, Douglas Dillon, US Treasury Secretary, argued that the 'present national reserves . . . seemed fully adequate in present circumstances'.[57] This was a very early signal of a rift between the new managing director and the US that was to assume increasing importance in the years ahead. And it presaged the growing role of a Fund willing to express what it perceived to be either systemic or indeed its own interests, beyond those of its most important members.

The negotiations leading to the Rio Agreement were of course marked by compromise, not only among key protagonists, but within the US administration, within the EEC and within the G10.[58] And international monetary reform was now firmly on the international agenda, and the Fund was also involved in the talks as it furthered a role for itself in a reformed system. The Fund's report 'International Reserves and Liquidity' signalled a higher profile and approach to reform at the IMF—a dynamic increasingly in evidence during the 1960s and particularly the 1970s. Whereas Machlup and others were able to write of a diverse number of reform proposals, many of which, as has been mentioned, did not even include the Fund, by 1964 options on the official plane had narrowed. The Fund also realized that it had to take more of an initiative if it was not to be overtaken by events.

As noted, not all proposals for reform involved the IMF. But as the 1960s progressed, more did. For example, the G10, essentially a vehicle for the GAB, quickly added to momentum in the liquidity debate by commissioning a report in 1964 under the chairmanship of Rinaldo Ossola of the Bank of Italy. The Ossola Report, while acknowledging disagreements among G10 members, grouped alternative proposals according to whether they recommended (a) creation of reserve assets by a group of countries (including CRUs); (b) creation of reserve assets through the Fund; or (c) schemes to provide holders of currency with an alternative asset.[59] The Fund was implicitly to be involved in most of these schemes for reform, unlike many of the proposals of the early 1960s.

And the Fund itself devoted increasing attention to international liquidity problems. After a sleepy 1950s, Machlup notes that at the IMF's annual meeting in 1961 officials first admitted that the international monetary system was 'not all well and sound'.[60] Two important staff papers were published in 1964,[61] both of which focused on the possibility of increases in unconditional liquidity provided through the Fund. While G10 and EEC members continued to attempt to resolve their internal differences,[62] revealed most clearly by the respective positions of the French and the Americans, the IMF quietly pursued its work. As we noted at the outset, IMF staff studies:

> ...noted that much of the discussion about the inadequacy of international liquidity, or projections of its future inadequacy, disguised in technical dress problems that were really political.[63]

So it was only natural that it was G10 and intra-European negotiations that embodied attempts to resolve these political questions, and it is to these latter developments that we now turn. It is worth noting, however, that the process of compromise that characterized the proceedings leading to SDRs did tend to evolve towards an understanding of the liquidity problem as the Fund conceived it to be. This is not to say that the US voice in the Fund or the G10, or indeed other country positions, were not paramount when SDRs were being discussed. However at a time when the US position was experiencing policy shifts, many of which were as a consequence of international monetary developments, the Fund was beginning to contribute to the debate in a way that had appeared unlikely only five years previously.

1.4 Forging a European Response

While the acceptance of the Triffin thesis by members of the US administration, and particularly the Treasury, influenced the steps taken that eventually led to the Rio Agreement,[64] the attitudes and policies of the major European states were also an increasingly important impetus behind negotiations in the 1960s. Dorothy Sobol, in *Europe Confronts the Dollar—The Creation of the SDR 1963–69*, examines the emergence of an eventual European policy on liquidity provision despite the very different attitudes towards liquidity and reserves by the French and Germans. This is not to say that policy differences among the major European partners were completely overcome, but during the 1960s they were subsumed temporarily within a united front.[65] In addition, the perception of a confidence crisis in the US's continued ability to remain responsible for the bulk of liquidity provision also influenced the Europeans in the negotiations leading to Rio.

The key European participants, representing the two strongest economies were France and West Germany, and it was these two countries that represented the most divergent views concerning the analysis of international monetary problems and recommendations. The UK's influence had declined commensurately with her worsening reserve position (see Table 1.3). The fact that both an intra-European and US–EEC debate took place so soon after the impetus of proposals from the Fund, and at so senior a level, indicates how quickly the liquidity question had come to dominate the international monetary agenda.

Germany was able to bargain from what was at first appearances the stronger position, that is a stronger economy with a successful and aggressive export-oriented trade policy that translated itself into a strong balance of payments surplus and reserve position. Even in 1960, Germany's reserves amounted to over US$7 billion, which was much greater than both the UK's $3.7 billion and France's $2.3 billion combined (see Table 1.3).

On the political plane, though, Germany had much less room to manoeuvre. Germany was beholden to the US for a large defence presence, and was much less willing to criticize the US publicly. As Sobol writes:

> The desire to ensure the presence of US troops on German soil for security purposes made the Federal Republic in matters of international economic policy probably the US' best ally on the continent in defence of the dollar: the wish to play an integral but not too dominant part in the evolving European Community made it perhaps more willing than most to try to compromise its differences with other Community partners.[66]

Robert Triffin also wrote of the US defense presence in Europe, emphasizing that this continued expenditure was perhaps the main reason for the US balance of payments deficit:

> ...last but not least, the current [1960] relaxation of world tensions may possibly enable us to reduce the terrifying and disproportionate defence burdens – internal as well as external – which probably account, more than any other single factor, for the revolutionary shift which has taken place in the international dollar balance from prewar to postwar days.[67]

Indeed, as Susan Strange pointed out, the UN's ECE (Economic Commission for Europe) noted that US troop expenditures in Germany 'were almost wholly responsible for the present imbalance in West Germany's balance of payments'.[68] These factors cannot be underestimated. Germany proceeded warily, not only because of a political sensitivity to US–European relations in general, but more concretely because of a Cold War military dependence on the US, the existence of which facilitated non-military expenditures that dovetailed well with domestic social and economic priorities.

In addition, Germany was a key holder of dollars as a component of its reserves. Whereas France was traditionally a gold holder and therefore held a smaller amount of dollar reserves, Germany's foreign exchange component was much higher, the vast majority of which were dollars. It was in Germany's interest to press quietly for an alternative reserve asset that supplemented dollar holdings. Reinforcing this, it also became apparent that Germany would *not* encourage the nascent moves into Deutschmarks as a reserve currency (a move continually discouraged by an export-oriented Germany that feared the potential of an overvalued currency).[69] Not for the first time, and certainly not for the last, successful export-led growth policies led naturally to upward pressure on exchange rates, which in turn tends to be resisted by economic policy makers as threatening growth. It is usually only after a time lag—sometimes a considerable one—that ostensible advantages of revaluing currencies and even reserve currency status appears advantageous and/or inevitable, and that higher exchange rates are welcomed. Parallels to 1980s Japan and current debates over Chinese exchange rate policies are striking.

Germany pursued negotiations, then, because it perceived that a potential reserve asset would strengthen its position under prevailing international monetary arrangements. Otmar Emminger, then a director of the Bundesbank, advocated increased and managed reserve growth for ostensible internationalist reasons since it:

> . . . signified a transition to a new reserve system in which future additions to world reserves would henceforth be related to the overall needs of the international system.[70]

While other German monetary officials (Dr Karl Blessing, president of the Bundesbank, for example) would have preferred the US to address its balance of payments problems, the diplomatic Dr Emminger pointed out that prospective SDRs could also be a supplement to gold—a point that was not lost on the French.

It also bears repeating that underlying the evolution of a German response was an approach that would enable Germany to continue to pursue her own trade policies of export-led growth. The apparent shift from reticence to enthusiasm at Munich in April 1967, where EEC finance ministers agreed to support the SDR later at Rio was, like the similar volte face in American pronouncements in 1965, inspired less by a shift in policy than by a changed perception of how to uphold existing policy.

In any event, momentum was with an international agreement to enhance liquidity. This momentum was both unofficial, vis-à-vis the earlier reform plans, and now also increasingly official in nature. Initially the Bundesbank, in common with most of Germany's EEC central bank partners, believed that the US deficit should first of all be cut in order to commence negotiations. But by 1965–6 it was believed that US deficits were, if not chronic, antithetical to international monetary health. A form of supplementary reserves would perhaps both relieve pressure on continued German accumulation of dollar holdings internally, and relieve pressure to diversify into the DM externally. By 1967 the key to Munich for the Germans lay in accommodating French postures very different in origin from their own.

French opinion on international monetary reform in the 1960s was influenced by several non-monetary factors. The attachment to gold was not merely a romantic idea based on the traditional French peasant's minor holding at the back of the garden. The French Treasury was not overly enamoured with reserves in the form of currency (see Tables 1.1 and 1.3) for understandable reasons. These not only reinforced private preferences, but also were rooted in historical preference for a liquid asset which tended to maintain its value in a continent whose varying fortunes often called into question paper reserves, even if they were interest bearing. Sterling reserves, for instance, had lost 30 per cent of their value in 1931 and again between 1949 and 1950. While the French devotion to gold often appeared intransigent to the Anglo-Saxons, to themselves it was simply part of a prudent portfolio strategy. The fact that it became an external constraint on US policy was only of later and secondary importance.

The other chief characteristic of French monetary posture was the relatively high public profile of the debate over international liquidity, and gold and the dollar in particular. As Sobol noted, this was not only because of the more obvious interest of de Gaulle, but also because of the institutional structure of French economic and monetary policy. Under the Fifth Republic—and indeed under the Fourth as well—the Banque de France has tended to exercise less influence than the Finance ministry. The Banque de France was more largely influenced by domestic and even agricultural considerations in the management of short-term credit, whereas the Finance Ministry, staffed by such influential men as André de Lattre as Director of External Finance from 1962–5, Valéry Giscard d'Estaing, and former Prime Minister Michel Debré (Finance Ministers from 1962–6 and 1966–8, respectively), tipped the balance of influence in favour of the Finance Ministry. President de Gaulle was also very much influenced by his pro-gold advisor, Jacques Rueff.[71] Under these circumstances, then, the reasons for the apparently intransigent attitudes of France concerning the dollar and gold are more easily discernible.

Table 1.3. G10 reserve holdings with foreign exchange component, 1960s

	US$ million							
	1960		1963		1966		1969	
	Reserves	Foreign Exchange Component	Reserves	Foreign Exchange Component	Reserves	Foreign Exchange Component	Reserves	Foreign Exchange Component
US	19,359	—	16,843	212	14,882	1,321	16,964	2,781
UK	3,719	431	3,148	174	3,099	1,158	2,527	1,055
Switzerland	2,324	139	3,122	302	3,545	704	4,425	1,783
France	2,272	429	4,908	1,282	6,733	507	3,833	286
Netherlands	1,861	289	2,099	295	2,449	305	2,530	370
Belgium	1,507	252	1970	461	2,350	458	2,386	712
Germany	7,033	3,753	7,651	3,255	8,029	2,480	7,129	2,748
Italy	3,251	980	3,619	1,050	4,911	1,612	5,045	1,226
Sweden	528	320	758	524	1,027	659	696	369
Canada	1,998	960	2,613	1,796	2,702	1,208	3,106	1,756
Japan	1,949	1,577	2,058	1,589	2,119	1,469	3,654	2,614
Total	45,801	9,130	48,789	10,940	51,846	11,881	52,295	15,700

Notes: 1. Residual is mostly gold (priced at US$35/oz), plus IMF tranches. 2. Minor differences between reserve totals in Tables 1.1, 1.2, 1.3 due to refining of Fund estimates

Source: *International Financial Statistics*—supplement series no. 6: 'Supplement on International Reserves', IMF, 1983

During the early 1960s France never wavered from her position that liquidity, especially the US dollar, did not really need to be supplemented. At the IMF's annual meeting in 1964, Giscard d'Estaing said:

> We have never concealed the fact that we do not consider the increase in international liquidity to be the main target of the studies which have been undertaken.[72]

Nonetheless, France took an active interest in the CRU proposals that would have supplemented liquidity in proportion to gold holdings. France's interest in the CRU, however, was not because it would add to world liquidity, but because it would enhance gold's profile as an international reserve. France felt adversely affected by the US apparent 'exorbitant privilege' to run indefinite deficits in the name of international liquidity provision; in effect they protested at what the dollar-standard theorists argued was beneficial.

Throughout the 1960s, France's participation in negotiations was often reluctant. Her decision at the Hague in 1966 at a G10 meeting to go ahead with joint discussions with the IMF on reserve creation was effectively under protest, reflecting a realization that an isolationist tack would be counterproductive to French aims.[73] While France was willing to pursue an independent course because of a belief in a primary role for gold, and because of relative political and military independence,[74] France was also extremely wary of the Anglo-Saxon cooperation that had shut them out at Bretton Woods. Should France exclude herself from G10 initiatives, the danger remained that she would be without a voice in international monetary negotiations once again. And France became dismayed at the rapidity with which negotiations progressed after the G10 Hague meeting, and this included the Rio Agreement in 1967. Again, it was not so much a reflective volte face, but in this case rather the exigencies of the student-worker revolt in 1968, which resulted in a new French willingness to accept what others had long advocated. Major domestic upheaval in that year provoked the resignation of de Gaulle, a run on the franc, and severely shook French confidence.

Ultimately, France signed The Hague and Munich agreements with EEC partners, and the Rio Agreement in 1957. Rather than stick to uncompromising policy stances, the decision to participate in successive discussions and agree to results that were often at odds with their positions pointed to a constructive willingness to be a part of any new arrangements that would emerge. While France argued for a return to a system more concretely based on gold (and less on the dollar) it also realized that it was impossible to pursue this course independently, despite aggressive attempts in early 1968 to redeem dollars for gold. France's stance was understandable and not at all as intransigent as it appeared. Above all, although appearing at times grudging if not obstinate, France also was expressing fears and concerns which many of her European partners shared but were more hesitant to express: concerns over the US deficit and the ability of the US to conduct an independent monetary policy seemingly oblivious to international concerns. France, too, was sensitive to the wishes of her EEC partners and the Munich agreement represented a willingness to forge a European response as much as it did a realization that the US was eager to conclude an agreement. Indeed Sobol argues that among the reasons for the significance of the Rio Agreement was the Franco–German compromises that led to a European front on the SDR.

Britain, perhaps surprisingly, played a comparatively small role in reform negotiations. Her influence waned roughly in proportion to the fortunes of sterling on the international exchange markets. Reginald Maudling, Britain's Chancellor of the Exchequer in the early 1960s, initiated a relatively modest proposal in 1962–3. The Maudling Plan included a 'mutual currency account', which was essentially an account at the Fund in which reserve holders could deposit excess reserves. In turn this could be used as a support system for deficit countries. The proposal, however, was snubbed by the US, who, under Kennedy, Dillon, and Roosa, were not yet willing to negotiate reform further than the ad hoc GAB and swap agreements then in place.[75] From 1964, with the bail-out of sterling under GAB, further borrowing in 1965, and then the devaluation of 1967, Britain became increasingly preoccupied with domestic economic problems reflected in the weakness of sterling. Suffice it to say that Britain was content with her 'bridging' role between Europe and America, and hid under the US monetary umbrella.

And the UK also did not wish to destabilize intra-European relations. After initially rejecting the EEC option at the beginning of the decade, Britain spent much diplomatic energy over the next dozen years attempting to join it. With this is mind, it was certainly not in Britain's interest to risk antagonizing prospective EEC partners. Thus, the forging of a European international monetary policy became increasingly a Franco–German affair, which lasted into the 1970s and the creation of the European Monetary System (EMS).

A few sentences on Japan will suffice at this stage. Japan's influence on and interest in the SDR during the 1960s was relatively small. Not surprisingly, Japan's was a muted voice in the reform negotiations at the time; after all, it was still running current account deficits in the mid-1960s. Although Robert Roosa acknowledged the role of the Japanese in agreeing to the SDR, he also pointed out that Japan did not become a member of the OECD (and WP3) until 1964, apparently at the suggestion of Roosa.[76]

Japan shared much in common with Germany as a successful export-oriented economy that consciously pursued export-led growth strategies and complementary exchange rate policies. Unlike Germany, it did not have to take into account relations with several powerful European neighbours. As long as Japan's access to the vast American market continued, and, like Germany, it enjoyed low defence expenditures, it preferred to take a low profile in the debates over reform. Indeed, as Japan was content to accumulate increasing dollar balances rather than gold (even more so than Germany), the US was also more amenable to increased Japanese access to US markets. Japanese foreign policy remained relatively accommodating of US views on international monetary matters until the early 1970s.

So the resolution of a European stance was important in the evolution of SDRs, and pointed to two developments: first, how quickly international monetary instability prevailed upon the consciousness of G10 negotiators, and second, how the acceptance of the Triffin thesis, and solutions such as the SDR, came to be accepted.

1.5 The Intensification of Negotiations

Although the US appeared to exhibit a volte face in Fowler's famous pronouncement to the American Bar Association in 1965 on international monetary reform, the essence of US policy had not really changed.[77] A means of upholding the dollar's role as core reserve currency remained the nucleus of US international monetary policy. All that had really changed was that the US now believed that the possibility of an internationally accepted reserve currency created by fiat was not a threat to the dollar, but rather a support for it at a time when concern over sterling and the US deficit was increasing. Moreover, the SDR could even replace gold and remove the constraint of dollar-gold convertibility.

In addition, the US chose a propitious time to announce its willingness to participate in reform negotiations. Fowler's announcement came at precisely the time when President Johnson's efforts at stemming the flow of dollars abroad from domestic sources were beginning to take effect. After recognition that the US would have to do something to strengthen its balance of payments position, Johnson announced a series of measures aimed at reducing the export of US capital and improving the balance of payments—continuing Roosa's policies of 'ad hoccery'.[78] In addition, it may also be noted that isolating the French and replacing the role of gold were not incidental effects. Indeed it could be argued further that these were fundamental to promoting the international role of the dollar. Unlike Odell, we must be wary, however, of reading more into this volte face in policy; rather than a sudden reversal in policy, the emphasis was an understandable constancy of self-interest with respect to the dollar.

During the mid-1960s, then, the extremes of position were represented by France and the US. In France, De Gaulle and Giscard d'Estaing both publicly called for an enhanced role for gold in the international monetary system. In February of 1965 Giscard itemized France's antipathy to the current system that centred upon the advantage held by reserve centre countries by virtue of their ability to run indefinite payments deficits.[79]

After 1965, the US championed reform, as well as a forum in which it had considerable influence. This was the IMF. We have already seen how the Fund tended to push for universal schemes at a time when the G10 was paying credence to a more limited involvement in enhanced liquidity options. While IMF and US interests did coincide at this time, this was due to a confluence of factors, particularly that the US came to champion the merits of a reserve asset to be administered through the IMF. This is important, although it would be wrong to read too much into this—other than to observe that reform became more likely once the Fund released its 1958 report signalling a willingness to consider increased liquidity options *and* once Fowler had announced US readiness to consider a new international reserve asset in 1965. Although it was true that interests were concurrent, as we have seen a nascent independence of views under Pierre-Paul Schweitzer and increasing divergence in the late 1960s and early 1970s suggest that interests at the time were coincident only temporarily. While the G10 ironed out the considerable divergence of views among its membership, the Fund quietly pushed its functionalist solutions to the liquidity problem that could be accommodated by the Fund either with or without amendments to the Articles of Agreement.[80] As we shall see, however, a gradual divergence of views between the US and the Fund was increasingly evident as the SDR came on stream in 1970.

In any case, the process of both intra-European and international negotiations intensified in the mid-1960s. Needless to say, core debates remained an affair of developed countries in this immediate post-colonial period, as weighted voting procedures within the Fund reinforced this tendency. The role of the G10 intensified this. Furthermore, with even the Bellagio Group of academics avoiding 'link' proposals between liquidity provision and development finance (because of 'highly political considerations'[81]), it was not surprising that developing country views were accorded little attention—a phenomenon which was to continue.[82]

But among developed countries, negotiators in the various groups discussing international monetary reform were tightly knit and overlapped considerably. In addition to the Fund and the G10, in 1966 the Fund set up a joint committee of the G10 Deputies and the Fund Executive Directors. The OECD had in the meantime set up Working Party No. 3 (WP3) of international financial officials in 1961. This was a subcommittee of its Economic Policy Committee, whose brief was to oversee OECD monetary and fiscal policies with particular reference to balance of payments disequilibria. WP3 published its own report in 1966 focusing on adjustment problems; however it too gave its approval to a concept of a new reserve asset while paying credence to the continental European view that adjustment of balance of payments disequilibria also remained a priority.[83]

Rapid progress was stalled briefly by a plethora of official proposals at this time. It was in 1966 that the Emminger Report of the G10 dealt with the proposed limited membership of the proposed new asset scheme.[84] The Emminger Report was essentially a summing up of EEC views, although France at this point was still focusing on the adjustment problem and promoting its own scheme of CRUs. Early in 1966, the US, UK, and Canada each submitted papers to the G10, all of which included the idea of a limited membership scheme.[85] The US paper, however, also considered a universal scheme of 'special reserve drawing rights' (SRDRs), a precursor to the only slightly less unwieldy moniker of SDR.[86]

Other developments soon prompted an intensification of negotiations, however. Among these were very real economic pressures on sterling and the dollar that increased throughout this period and were reflected in continued US balance of payments imbalances and use of the GAB. In addition, IMF-facilitated developments prompted negotiations to conclude within eighteen months.

As has been mentioned, the first of these was the Joint Committee of Deputies of the G10 and the Executive Board of the Fund. The first and second of these meetings in November 1966 and January 1967 served to provide another forum for delineation of differences and areas of convergence. It was at the second meeting that it was agreed that the prospective new asset would be operated through the IMF.[87] The third and fourth meetings prompted further agreement. It was increasingly Fund proposals, or proposals that promoted the Fund as the central clearing agency for a new asset, which were now considered by the G10 through this Joint Committee.

One of the reasons for this was that it was the Fund itself that was responsible for much of the increased output of documents and drafts of outlines for the new asset schemes. In addition to the managing director's proposals of 1966 ('Creation of Additional Reserves Through the International Monetary Fund'), the Fund published several illustrative schemes between February and June of 1967 that showed how the Fund or a Fund affiliate could accommodate a facility based on drawing rights on the Fund.[88] These outlines honed the proposals of the 1966 documents, the former of which was the basis for the outline agreed to at Rio in September of 1967. As Strange concedes it was 'the Fund staff who would be the ultimate draftsmen', and it was indeed Fund documents of 1966 and early 1967 which provided the basis for the Rio Agreement.

Finally, IMF staff, including managing directors, took a keen and growing interest in promoting the ideas of a universal scheme. Pierre-Paul Schweitzer replaced Per Jacobsson in September 1964, and Schweitzer, after quickly declaring his support for a universal scheme, reiterated his support following the publication of the Emminger report. By the Rio meeting in 1967, the Fund had already proposed an outline that was acceptable to its Board of Governors. The agreement, consisting of six short pages, established the foundation of the amended Articles of Agreement. Simply an outline for amending the Articles, it was agreed to at the Fund's annual general meeting held at the Museum of Modern Art in Rio de Janeiro. The requisite proportion of Fund membership ratified the amended Articles by 1969. In less than five years, the debate over international liquidity had essentially become a Fund affair,[89] and the Board of Governors approved the managing director's allocation proposals prepared by Fund staff on 3 October 1969.[90]

Obstacles between Rio and the eventual amendments did exist; the most important of which was resolved at the Stockholm meeting of the G10 in 1968 whereby a formula was agreed to which meant that a united EEC, like the US, would have effective veto power over subsequent large-scale changes to the operations of the Fund. It was the Rio Agreement, however, which established the principles of universality, allocation, and use of SDRs, and which heralded the first major change to international monetary arrangements since Bretton Woods. Other international liquidity issues had an influence upon negotiations as well, however, among them how the SDR was *expected* to work, and it is to these that we now turn.

1.6 Accomplishments and Limitations of the First Amendment

Following the Rio Agreement, provisions governing the SDR and the SDR Department were contained in Articles XXI–XXXII of the Fund's amended Articles of Agreement, with articles governing allocation, use, cancellation, participation, administration, and obligations.[91] Their avowed character as a supplement to reserve assets has already been alluded to; Article XXIV stated that SDRs would aid in avoiding stagflation, excess demand, and help balance of payments adjustment:

> . . . the Fund shall seek . . . to supplement existing reserve assets in such a manner as will promote the attainment of purposes and will avoid economic stagnation and deflation as well as excess demand and inflation in the world. The first decision to allocate special drawing rights shall take into account, as special considerations, a collective judgment that there is a global need to supplement reserves, and the attainment of a better balance of payments equilibrium, as well as the likelihood of a better working of the adjustment process in the future.[92]

The Fund's amended Article XV was to state 'the Fund has authority to create unconditional liquidity by allocating SDRs to participants in the SDR

Department. The Fund cannot allocate SDRs to itself or other holders'.[93] It must be recalled that a primary purpose of this liquidity was to aid in the maintenance of currency par values. At a time when US balance of payments deficits were deemed chronic and the deficits could not continue to be relied upon for liquidity (if only because of decreasing confidence in the gold–dollar relationship), SDRs were construed as a supplement to the dollar. The protestations of the French, who argued that the SDR was a supplement to gold, seemed examples of both wishful thinking and a refusal to recognize that the 'exorbitant privilege' to run deficits, coupled with the development of largely US dollar denominated Euromarkets, had become necessary to the functioning of the international monetary system. By the late 1960s, French and other proposals focusing on gold and/or its revaluation were practically off the agenda as the liquidity negotiations focused on new liquidity in the form of the SDR as a supplement to the dollar.

Fred Hirsch, in an article in the Fund's *Staff Papers*, viewed SDRs as a stabilizing influence on the international monetary system in that this addition to liquidity would be subject to the control of the IMF and hence over the composition of global reserve growth.[94] This was a positive attribute if it is accepted that international liquidity needs to be managed—and to Hirsch and others at the time recent international monetary history embodied the search for a stable, non-inflationary source of reserve growth as a precondition for other economic priorities.

This diagnosis, however, assumed fixed exchange rates with fixed par currency values and a necessary reserve ratio for these to be maintained (which could nonetheless vary from country to country). It also assumed a static relationship between reserves and GDP growth. It became difficult to include other variables such as the changing dynamics of the role of reserve assets in the monetary system as a whole. A crucially important development that was not captured here was the growth of Euromarkets that effectively weakened the link between owned reserves (such as gold, the dollar, or SDRs) and liquidity, not to mention the potentially destabilizing role of short-term capital movements. Indeed as it transpired the availability of borrowed reserves may be argued to be a contributing factor to the willingness with which the international monetary system accommodated itself to market-oriented liquidity provision, notwithstanding official paralysis in actually wanting to preserve the par value system. SDRs in principle might allow greater collective management of international liquidity. They did not, however, address other issues in the international monetary arena, and even with respect to their primary role were in danger of being outmoded by events. These problems included not only the rise of Euromarkets and increasing endogeneity of international liquidity, but also increases in short-term capital movements, rising US inflation, and chronic surpluses in Germany. Nor could they be used to help in the management of liquidity provision if the Fund membership and the Fund's most important member were unwilling to use them in that fashion. This is indeed what transpired very quickly as SDRs were allocated in three instalments from 1970–2.

SDRs were therefore seen as a stabilizing influence on the dollar, as well as with respect to reserve growth, since they were allocated and administered by an IMF whose structure remained unaltered. Although the articles were amended to allow the institution of a separately administered SDR Department, this facilitated effective accounting as voting procedures, quota administration, and management practices remained unaltered. Most importantly, US policy attitudes to the SDR had warmed not because the asset was an instrument of reform, but rather because it was perceived as a means of upholding and even increasing the role of the dollar within the system. Thus, some of the enthusiasm about SDRs that we noted at the beginning of this chapter was misplaced. Paradoxically, as will be shown in our analysis of the Jamaica agreement, condemnation of the timidity of the Second Amendments changes to the international monetary system was similarly misplaced. However in the latter case it was because accomplishments embodied in these Amendments have not been credited sufficiently. Nonetheless the First Amendment was a success. SDRs were allocated, at the time amounting to over 8 per cent of global non-gold reserves. Further, the economic mechanism of SDRs under fixed rates was important if only for reasons of historical precedent (the first truly international money created by fiat) and the fact that an instrument now existed to supplement international liquidity. And mechanisms surrounding the SDR proved to work well, including in ways that had not been foreseen as the world moved quickly to a floating exchange rate system. Above all, SDRs were on the international monetary agenda. In this context, the SDR also quickly became an entity of interest to many interested in further reform, rather than an asset whose sole purpose was to uphold existing international monetary arrangements, a theme that is addressed in the following chapter.

1.7 Summary

In an effort to shore up the Bretton Woods system the idea of fiduciary money created by fiat, first mooted by Keynes, was revived. The negotiations themselves revealed a Fund newly aware of the issues and eager to foster a new international reserve unit that it would administer. And the appeal of supplemented and internationally managed liquidity to aid stability was, if only briefly, almost universally attractive, the musings of the chairman of the US

Federal Reserve about the SDR representing a step to a world central bank being by no means unique.[95]

Nonetheless the Rio Agreement and the SDR did not save the system of managed liquidity provision that was quickly breaking down. Despite a temptation to draw an analogy between the SDR and the IMF with Keynes's Bancor and the ICU, the world was moving away from a system willing to be anchored by a supra-national money, even at a subsidiary level. Nor, in truth, was this what the negotiations in the 1960s were about, despite many optimistic pronouncements by the Fed chairman and many others noted at the outset of our investigation. In order to address the mechanism of the SDR as it was envisioned to work under fixed rates, it is important to be cognizant of these limitations. The accomplishments of the Rio Agreement, embodied in the clumsily named Special Drawing Right, were not a comprehensive enough development to address the continued march away from a gold exchange to a dollar standard.[96]

In addition, it was the US that still had the most bearing upon the success or failure of international monetary initiatives. Europe, after forging a temporary united response in the reform negotiations during the 1960s was not as united in the 1970s; furthermore its concerns subsequently were primarily with European issues, particularly a European monetary system.[97] This is not to say that Europe became less important but rather, as has already been noted, the main debates surrounding the SDR manifested themselves in Washington, either at the IMF or within the US government. Although the creation of the SDR was essentially a product of compromise in the Atlantic Alliance, a European approach to reform did little to determine the ultimate outcome of the liquidity negotiations as time went on. European support was necessary for reform, but it was not sufficient in and of itself. Of much more importance was the US acceptance or rejection of the idea. In the 1970s this process intensified: it was increasingly the dynamics of the relationship between the Fund and the US, and the roles of these entities individually, which we address as the most salient and important for an understanding of evolving attitudes not only towards the SDR but international monetary arrangements as a whole.

In sum, what has been explored in this chapter has been threefold: first to show that the institution of SDRs, apart from the important precedent of putting a form of liquidity created by fiat on the international monetary agenda, and despite the important compromises achieved which led to its birth, did not represent the fundamental change that it initially appeared to be. Second, we have addressed the role of the Fund in international monetary negotiations during the 1960s, and note that its growth as an independent institution—with its own interests and priorities—has tended to be overlooked. After all, it was not even evident initially that it would be the IMF that would administer the new liquidity scheme. Finally, a case has been made for examining changing US policy attitudes and the role of the IMF in the structure and functioning of international monetary relations in the post-Bretton Woods system. It has been argued that this is crucially important for an understanding of the institution of the SDR, and is true as well for an understanding of its subsequent marginalization.

As this chapter has illustrated, the marginalization of the SDR was inherent in the compromises surrounding its birth. Apart from brief periods, the US took the view that the SDR was not an alternative, but rather a supplement, to the dollar. For a while the Fund was to latch on to the SDR as a key vehicle to disseminate its views on systemic monetary needs, but even this was a temporary development that has only very recently reemerged in the wake of the 2008 global financial crisis. Thus it is now necessary to turn to contemporary policy attitudes—first during the First SDR Allocation, later during the Jamaica Agreement, and then during and after the Second Allocation of SDRs—in order to deepen our understanding of the evolution of the SDR and international monetary arrangements as they evolved in the post-Bretton Woods era.

Notes

1. 'Outline of a Facility Based on Special Drawing Rights in the Fund', 29 September 1967 (Board of Governors Resolution 22–8, Rio de Janeiro) in M. Garritsen de Vries, *The International Monetary Fund 1966–71*, Volume II: Documents, IMF (Washington, DC: 1976), p. 47.
2. Fritz Machlup noted central bankers' and finance ministers' praise for the agreement, including that of US Treasury Secretary Fowler, UK Treasury Callaghan, France's Finance Minister Debré, Jelle Zijlstra of the Netherlands Bank, and Delfim Netto, Brazil's Finance Minister. Machlup was pleased to note that the latter two were also economists. See F. Machlup, *Remaking the International Monetary System: The Rio Agreement and Beyond*, Johns Hopkins Press (Baltimore: 1968).
3. See J. J. Polak, 'Special Drawing Rights: The Outline of a New Facility in the Fund', *Finance and Development*, IV (4), December 1967, p. 280.
4. See, for example, 'SDRs—A New Asset Supplementing Reserves for Growth in Free World Trade', in *Business Review*, Federal Reserve Bank of Dallas, December 1970, pp. 3–16; and 'SDR: Super-Duper Reserve?', in Federal Reserve Bank of Philadelphia *Business Review*.

   The Bank of Nova Scotia wrote 'If the spirit of cooperation that has prevailed in recent years should continue, there is no reason why SDRs should not come to play an increasing role in the international monetary system'. 'A New International Reserve Asset', *Bank of Nova Scotia Monthly Review*, Toronto, October 1967, p. 4.
5. William McChesney Martin, 'Toward a World Central Bank?', Per Jacobsson Foundation Lecture, 14 September 1970, pp. 7, 26–7.

Indeed, by the time of the Rio Agreement the US was one of the most enthusiastic proponents of SDRs. At the time the US Administration pointed out that it was the first industrial nation to endorse their use (in 1968), and urged others to ratify the Rio Agreement 'as quickly as possible'. (US Treasury Press Release, 'Announcing the completion of US action on the Special Drawing Rights facility', 15 July 1968.)

6. Also, although having virtually no role in the negotiations, developing country reaction was largely positive. In an article in an Iranian journal in 1971, for instance, the author postulates that: '. . . one can, indeed, foresee a day perhaps in just a couple of decades—in which SDR's, if properly managed, enjoy the present position of gold'. Parviz Pārsā (Director of Economic Studies at the Ministry of the Economy, Tehran), 'Special Drawing Rights: Background and Analysis', *Tahqiqat-e eqtesadi* (*Quarterly Journal of Economic Research*), Tehran, vol. 8, spring 1971, p. 109. See also S. Aqdas Ali Kazmi, 'Special Drawing Rights and International Liquidity', *Punjab University Economist* (Pakistan), vol. VIII, 1970.

   Non-western support for SDRs has continued uninterruptedly since then—see Chapter 5, below, also, e.g. D. Jovović, 'Evolution of Special Drawing Rights', *Review of International Affairs* (Yugoslavia), no. 837, 20 February 1985; S. P. Gupta and Niropam Bajpai, ICRIER (Indian Council for Research on International Economic Relations), comments following Warren Coats Jr., *Special Drawing Rights—Operations and Role in Development Finance*, Allied Publishers (New Delhi: 1990), pp. 71–3.

7. In October 1969, Edward R. Fried, who later went on to become a US Executive Director at the World Bank, wrote: 'Before the end of this year, the Special Drawing Rights machinery of the International Monetary Fund should come into operation, ushering in a new era of multilaterally created international reserves. This is no small matter. The international community has not heretofore created anything so deadly serious as money.' See 'International Liquidity and Foreign Aid', *Foreign Affairs*, October 1969.

8. John Williamson, 'Why SDRs Could Rival the Dollar', Peterson Institute for International Economics, Policy Brief no. PB09-20, September 2009. But Peter Kenen has recently argued that SDRs, like gold, are reserve assets, not reserve currencies—see 'An SDR Based Reserve System', *Journal of Globalization and Development*, vol. 1, issue 2, 2010, p. 1. For central banks, however, classic characteristics of money—as a unit of account, store of value, and even medium of exchange—were and remain present to some degree. And discussions about a greater role for SDRs role entail enhancing these characteristics.

9. See J. Martin Rochester, 'The rise and fall of international organization as a field of study', *International Organization*, vol. 40, no. 4, Autumn 1986. On the rise of international political economy, including important differences between the US and British approaches, see Benjamin J. Cohen, 'The Transatlantic Divide: Why are American and British IPE so Different?', in *Review of International Political Economy*, vol. 14, no. 2, May 2007.

10. On corporations, see Ray Vernon, *Sovereignty at Bay: The Multinational Spread of US Enterprise*, Basic Books (New York: 1971).

11. Alternative names such as Byzant and Unitas were also proposed. See J. M. Keynes, in Doddridge, *The Collected Writings of John Maynard Keynes. Volume XXV, Activities*

1940–44, Shaping the Post-war World: The Clearing Union, Macmillan (London: 1980), p. 271.

See A. Van Dormael's *Bretton Woods: Birth of A Monetary System*, Macmillan (London: 1978) for a detailed account of the Bretton Woods negotiations.

12. Even though his influence on the Bretton Woods compromise was less than he would have liked, Keynes spent much time and energy in the House of Lords, in the letters column of *The Times*, and elsewhere, persuading his countrymen of the necessity and merits of the Bretton Woods agreement. See especially Doddridge (ed.) *Collected Writings of Keynes—vol. XXVI Activities 1941–1946, Shaping the Post-war World—Bretton Woods and Reparations*, Macmillan (London: 1980), pp. 1–238.
13. Hostility to Bretton Woods and to the terms surrounding American loans to the UK in the mid-1940s was in evidence in the House of Commons and especially concentrated in the US Congress. See Richard N. Gardner, *Sterling-Dollar Diplomacy*, Clarendon Press (Oxford: 1956), pp. 99, 237–8. This was a harbinger of periodic Congressional involvement in international monetary issues which manifested itself from the late 1970s (see Chapters 4 and 6, below).
14. Doddridge (ed.) *Keynes—Collected Writings—vol. XXV, op. cit.*, and van Dormael, *op. cit.* Indeed Keynes' thinking in this area had been evolving since 1933. He was aided by a number of colleagues and associates in the academic community, as well as senior bureaucrats in London, especially at the Board of Trade. (See also P. M. Oppenheimer, 'The Endogeneity of International Liquidity', in R. Z. Aliber, *The Reconstruction of International Monetary Arrangements*, Macmillan (London: 1987), p. 309.)
15. That is, not including reconstruction costs. *Keynes—Collected Writings—vol. XXVI, op. cit.*, p. 14.
16. Alan S. Milward, *War, Economy and Society 1939–1945*, University of California Press (Berkeley and Los Angeles: 1977), pp. 364–5.
17. *Keynes—Collected Writings—vol XXV, op. cit.*, p. 67.
18. Ibid. pp. 67–9.
19. As we shall see in Chapter 5, this automaticity was, however, embodied in the Jamaica Agreement to a small degree—an achievement that has been relatively overlooked in the literature.
20. In 1943 Keynes prepared a comparison of the British proposal for a Clearing Union and the American proposal for a Stabilization Fund. Keynes noted that under the Stabilization Fund total quotas would amount to 'at least $5 billion', whereas '[U]nder C.U. they might be more like $40 billion', in Doddridge (ed.), *Keynes—Collected Writings—vol. XXV, op. cit.*, p. 216.
21. On his way to Savannah, Keynes wrote to the Treasury: 'the Americans will be proposing that both the Fund and the Bank should be situated not at New York as we had been assuming but at Washington. I reacted very vehemently, declaring that in that case these bodies could not be regarded as international institutions but were being treated as an appanage of the American Administration'. Doddridge (ed.) *Keynes—Collected Writings—vol. XXVI, op. cit.*, p. 211.
22. T. Balogh, 'Old Fallacies and New Remedies: The SDRs in Perspective', in *Bulletin of the Oxford University Institute of Economics and Statistics*, May 1970, p. 85.

23. Margaret Garritsen de Vries, *The IMF in a Changing World, 1945–85*, IMF (Washington: 1986), p. 67. Indeed the last surviving US negotiator at Bretton Woods, Edward Bernstein, said that the Fund: '. . . suffers from *never* having been able to discipline its principal member, the United States.' See 'Bretton ćWoods Remembered—by Its Last Remaining Star', *Financial Times*, 1 August 1992, p. XI (emphasis added).
24. Chapter IV, *Measures for International Economic Stability*, as cited in de Vries, *The International Monetary Fund 1945–1965, vol. III, op. cit.*, p. 311.
25. IMF *Annual Report*, 1952, p. 45.
26. 'The Adequacy of Monetary Reserves', IMF *Staff Papers*, October 1953.
27. 'International Reserves and Liquidity—A Study by the Staff of the IMF', reproduced in de Vries, *The International Monetary Fund 1945–65, vol III* (documents), pp. 406, 410.
28. Ibid. p. 410
29. Robert Triffin, *Gold and the Dollar Crisis*, Yale University Press (New Haven: 1960). Liquidity provision had continued to concern British theorists during the 1950s. (See also John Williamson, 'International Liquidity: A Survey', in *Economic Journal*, 1973.) It is not surprising that this should have been a British preoccupation at the time: with sterling the 'first line of defence' for the dollar, and with British reserves called into question, attention was drawn to liquidity provision problems in the UK first.
30. Douglas Mudd, 'International Reserves and the Role of Special Drawing Rights', in *FRB St Louis Review*, January 1978, p. 11
31. This is not to say that the problem could have been conceived as Gilbert and others saw it (i.e. that the most important monetary problem was a gold shortage relative to dollars), but rather that at the time it was Triffin's observations that were increasingly accepted. See Milton Gilbert, *Quest for World Monetary Order* (P. Oppenheimer and M. Dealtry, eds.), Wiley (New York: 1980), pp. 216–17.
32. See also Brian Tew, *The Evolution of the International Monetary System 1945–77*, Hutchinson (London: 1979), pp. 116–20. Also, see Maurice Levi, *International Finance—Financial Management and the International Economy*, McGraw-Hill (Tokyo: 1983), pp. 195–9, for an explanation of how these measures, in addition to the strengthening of Regulation Q which limited interest payments on deposit accounts, encouraged the long-term growth of the Eurocurrency markets.
33. For Roosa's optimistic defense of 'ad hoccery', see R.V. Roosa, 'Assuring the Free World's Liquidity', *FRB Philadelphia, Business Review Supplement*, September 1962.
34. 'International Payments Imbalances—And Need for Strengthening International Financial Arrangements', Report of the Subcommittee on International Exchange and Payments (Henry Reuss, chairman), Joint Economic Committee, US Congress, 87th Congress, 1st session, 1961. For later summaries, see Fritz Machlup, 'Plans for the Reform of the International Monetary System', *Princeton Special Paper in International Economics*, No. 3, August 1962; Herbert Grubel, *International Monetary Reform: Plans and Issues* (1963), 'The Demand for International Reserves: A Critical Review of the Literature', *Journal of Economic Literature*, December 1971; John Williamson, 'International Liquidity: A Survey', *op. cit.*; and Benjamin

J. Cohen, 'International Reserves and Liquidity' (including comments by Ronald McKinnon and Rudi Rhomberg), in P. B. Kenen (ed.) *International Trade and Finance - Frontiers for Research*, Cambridge University Press (Cambridge: 1975).

35. In addition to *Gold and the Dollar Crisis* (*op. cit.*) see his two articles in the *Banca Nazionale del Lavoro Quarterly Review*, 'The Return to Convertibility' (March 1959), and 'Tomorrow's Convertibility' (June 1959).
36. Oscar L. Altman, 'Professor Triffin on International Liquidity and the Role of the Fund', IMF *Staff Papers*, vol. VIII, May 1961, p. 156.
37. Robert E. Cumby, 'Special Drawing Rights and Plans for Reform of the International Monetary System: A Survey' in G. von Furstenberg, *op. cit.*, p. 443.
38. J. Williamson, 'International Liquidity: A Survey', *op. cit.*, p. 706.
39. Maxwell Stamp, 'The Fund and the Future', *Lloyds Bank Review*, October 1958.
40. John Williamson later argued in his survey of international liquidity that this was 'a principle whose unacceptability to dimwitted bankers was vociferously proclaimed by numerous economists until it was discovered that the SDR agreement embodied precisely that principle'. J. Williamson, 'International Liquidity: A Survey', *op. cit.*, p. 716.
41. Albert G. Hart, Nicolas Kaldor, and Jan Tinbergen, 'The Case for an International Commodity Reserve Currency', in *Proceedings of the UN Conference on Trade and Development*, United Nations, vol. III, 1964.

    The idea of a commodity based currency was revived in the mid-1970s, especially as world commodity prices rose, and also by US Treasury Secretary Baker's proposal in the late 1980s for commodity indicators.
42. E. M. Bernstein, 'A Practical Program for International Monetary Reserves', *Quarterly Review and Investment Survey*, Model, Roland, and Co., 1963(4).
43. R. V. Roosa, 'Assuring the Free World's Liquidity', *FRB Philadelphia, Business Review Supplement*, September 1962.
44. R. V. Roosa, 'Reforming the International Monetary System', *Foreign Affairs*, vol. 42, no. 1, September 1963.
45. M.A. Heilperin, 'The Case for Going Back to Gold', *Fortune*, September 1962. Sir Roy Harrod, 'Imbalances of International Payments', *IMF Staff Papers*, April 1953. M. Gilbert, 'The Gold-Dollar System: Conditions of Equilibrium and the Price of Gold', *Princeton Essays in International Finance*, No. 70, 1968. P. M. Oppenheimer, 'The Case for Raising the Price of Gold', *Journal of Money, Credit and Banking*, August 1969.
46. '...Nous estimons nécessaire que les échanges internationaux soient établis comme, c'était le cas avant les grands malheurs du monde, sur une base monétaire indiscutable et qui ne porte la marque d'aucun pays en particulier. Quelle base ? En vérité, on ne voit pas qu'il puisse y avoir réellement de critères, d'étalon autre que l'or....' Extract from Charles de Gaulle *Discours et Messages*, Plon (Paris: 1970).
47. 'International Payments Imbalances—And Need for Strengthening International Financial Arrangements', Joint Economic Committee, 1961, *op. cit.*, p. 18. The relevant subcommittee was chaired by Henry Reuss, a respected Wisconsin Democrat who was to have an even greater influence on Congressional attitudes towards the SDR in the 1970s. See Chapter 4, pp. 126–130, below.

48. E. Despres, C. P. Kindleberger, and W. S. Salant, 'The Dollar and World Liquidity—A Minority View', *The Economist*, 5 February 1966.
49. R. I. McKinnon, *Private and Official International Money: The Case for the Dollar*, Princeton Essays in International Finance, no. 74, Princeton, 1969.
50. One implication for this vis-à-vis international liquidity provision is that SDR creation would affect reserve composition rather than the quantity of demanded reserves themselves.
51. F. Machlup, 'Plans for Reform of the International Monetary System', *op. cit.*, p. 12.
52. 'Canada's Experience with a Flexible Exchange Rate in the 1950s: Valuable Lessons Learned', Lawrence Schembri, International Department, *Bank of Canada Review* (Ottawa: Spring 2008), pp. 3–15, as at: http://www.bankofcanada.ca/wp-content/uploads/2010/06/schembri.pdf (accessed 15 June 2011).
53. F. Machlup *et. al.* 'International Monetary Arrangements: the Problem of Choice—Report on the deliberations of an international study group of 32 economists' (Princeton: 1964). See also Susan Strange, *International Monetary Relations*, vol. 2 of A. Shonfield (ed.), *International Economic Relations of the Western World 1959–1971,* p. 216.
54. (For a review of the Bellagio Group, see Machlup and Malkiel (eds.), 'International Monetary Arrangements: The Problem of Choice', *op. cit.*). The Ossola Report ('Report of the Study Group on the Creation of Reserve Assets', Group of Ten, Washington, 1965) recommended an increase in liquidity provisions.
55. See also fn. 34, above.
56. J. Keith Horsefield, *The International Monetary Fund 1945–1965, vol 1*—Chronicle, IMF (Washington: 1969), p. 541.
57. Ibid.
58. Machlup, Odell, Stephen Cohen, Susan Strange, and Dorothy Sobol cover this fascinating period in international monetary history in great detail, all with different emphases. Strange's work is the most comprehensive as she places the debates in her history of international monetary relations during the 1960s. S. Strange, *International Monetary Relations*, volume 2 of A. Shonfield (ed.), *International Economic Relations of the Western World 1959–1971*, RIIA and Oxford University Press (London: 1976). Machlup examines the relationship between the various plans for reform in the context of the larger countries in the international monetary system to avoid a confidence crisis. Fritz Machlup, *Remaking the International Monetary System: the Rio Agreement and Beyond, op. cit.*, 1968. Stephen Cohen concentrates on the financial diplomacy surrounding the reform debates and concluded from his analysis of US–European relations that countries sought to secure and further national power (i.e. ability to avoid adjustment) rather than maximizing national income. S. D. Cohen, *International Monetary Reform, 1964–69: the Political Dimension, op. cit.*, 1970. Dorothy Sobol examines the interesting intra-European debates during the 1960s as Europe sought to present a united and hence equal voice with the US in the negotiations. Dorothy M. Sobol, *Europe Confronts the Dollar—The Creation of the SDR, 1963–69, op. cit.*, 1982, we have already mentioned. Odell, in *US International Monetary Policy, op. cit.*, explored the influences of 'markets', 'power', and 'growth' on US international monetary policy

during the 1960s. His conclusions concerning the relatively ad hoc approach to US international monetary policy were strongly echoed in Joanne Gowa's *Closing the Gold Window*, Cornell University Press (Ithaca, NY: 1983), an exploration of the US's decision to abolish convertibility in 1971.

59. Garritsen de Vries, *The International Monetary Fund, 1966–71—The System Under Stress, vol. 1*, p. 60.
60. Fritz Machlup, *Remaking the International Monetary System: The Rio Agreement and Beyond, op. cit.*, p. 3. In fact as early as 1958 (ironically the first year of general convertibility under Bretton Woods) the Fund published a study hesitantly questioning the adequacy of reserves and liquidity arrangements: See 'International Reserves and Liquidity: A Study by the Staff of the International Monetary Fund', IMF (Washington, DC: 16 September 1958).
61. J. Marcus Fleming, 'The Fund and International Liquidity', IMF *Staff Papers*, vol. 11 (1964), pp. 177–215; and Oscar L. Altman, 'The Management of International Liquidity', IMF *Staff Papers*, vol. 11 (1964), pp. 216–47.
62. By 1967 observers from Switzerland, the BIS, and the OECD were officially kept abreast of liquidity negotiations (M. Garritsen de Vries, *The International Monetary Fund 1966–71*, vol. 1, p. 76). Many of the Fund deputy directors were also members of the OECD's Working Party 3 (of the Economic Policy Committee). WP3 membership, the focus of which was balance of payments disequilibria, was virtually coincident with the G10—less Belgium, plus Switzerland.
63. Garritsen de Vries, *The International Monetary Fund 1966–71, vol. 1, op. cit.*, p. 34.
64. J. S. Odell, *US International Monetary Policy—Markets, Power, and Ideas as Sources of Change*, Princeton University Press (Princeton, NJ: 1982), pp. 163–4, 363.
65. Stephen Cohen in *International Monetary Reform, 1964–69: The Political Dimension* developed this argument by suggesting that Europe's dollar conversion attempts at reform were a means of encouraging the US to adjust and promote further symmetry in the adjustment process.
66. Sobol, *op. cit.*, p. 187.
67. Triffin (1960), *op. cit.*, p. 8.
68. Strange, *op. cit.*, p. 47.
69. See Michael Kreile, 'West Germany: The Dynamics of Expansion', in P. J. Katzenstein, *Between Power and Plenty*, University of Wisconsin Press (Madison, Wisconsin: 1978) (also the fall 1977 issue of *International Organization*), pp. 191–224.
70. Sobol, *op. cit.*, p. 212. Emminger was later the Bundesbank's Deputy Governor and Vice-Chairman, as well as chairman of the deputies of the Group of Ten (from 1964–7) and vice-chairman of the Monetary Committee of the EEC.
71. Sobol, *op. cit.*, pp. 301, 302.
72. Ibid. p. 315.
73. Ibid. p. 326.
74. In contrast to Germany's defense predicament, by the mid-1960s France withdrew from NATO command (until 2005), and its nuclear '*force de frappe*' had already become a reality in the late 1950s
75. Strange, *op. cit.*, p. 101. This MCA was actually an early precursor to the substitution account. See Chapter 3, pp. 95–9 and Chapter 6, pp. 196–205.

76. See Robert Roosa, 'The United States and Japan in the International Monetary System 1946–1985', Group of 30 Occasional Paper 21 (New York: 1986).
77. In his speech at Hot Springs, Virginia on 10 July 1965, Treasury Secretary Fowler signalled a switch in US international monetary policy by saying that the US was willing to participate in international monetary negotiations to reform arrangements for international liquidity provision. Odell wrote that 'Fowler's speech stunned the international financial world, since the United States had labored for several years on behalf of a balance-of-payments policy that would avoid fundamental changes, and it had specifically and repeatedly rejected rival liquidity schemes.' See John Odell, *US International Monetary Policy, op. cit.*, p. 79.
78. Levi, *op. cit.*, pp. 195–9.
79. Garritsen de Vries, *The International Monetary Fund 1966–71, vol. 1, op. cit.*, p. 62.
80. In a paper of 3 March 1966, the managing director of the Fund made available two alternatives to the Executive Board, one of which involved amendments to the Fund's Articles, one of which did not. By now Fund documents on additional reserves began to presage the Rio Agreement: they were structured in sections which mirrored those of the existing articles on, for example, membership, transferability, and repurchase. See 'Creation of Additional Reserves Through the International Monetary Fund' (including supplement), in Garritsen de Vries, *The International Monetary Fund 1966–71, vol 2* (Documents), pp. 3–14.
81. Susan Strange, *International Monetary Relations*, vol. 2 of A. Shonfield (ed.), *International Economic Relations of the Western World 1959–1971*, p. 233.
82. See Chapter 6, below. Developing countries did pursue some avenues to promote their views. The Group of Thirty-One, a precursor to the Group of Twenty-Four formed in 1971, was set up as an adjunct to UNCTAD's Expert Group on International Monetary Issues in 1965. It published a document in 1966 cautioning against the possibility of any reserve asset scheme which did not incorporate a principle of universality. See UN document TD/B/75 (New York), 31 May 1966.
83. WP3, OECD, 'The Balance of Payments Adjustment Process, a Report by Working Party No. 3 of the Economic Policy Committee', Paris, August 1966.
84. Strange, *International Monetary Relations*, p. 235.
85. The US paper was entitled 'Outline of a Possible Dual Approach to the Creation of Reserve Assets, the UK's 'International Monetary Reform—Summary of United Kingdom Views', and Canada's 'Future Creation of Reserve Assets—Some Views of the Canadian Delegation'. See Garritsen de Vries, *The International Monetary Fund 1966–1971, vol. 1, op. cit.*, p. 79.
86. Ibid. p. 80.
87. Ibid. p. 126.
88. Garritsen de Vries (ed.), *The International Monetary Fund 1966–71, vol II*, documents, pp. 15–44. Illustrative schemes: (A) 'Outline of an Illustrative Reserve Unit Scheme' (23 February 1967), (B) 'Outline of an Illustrative Scheme for a Special Reserve Facility Based on Drawing Rights in the Fund' (28 February 1967); Tentative outlines: (A) 'An Outline of a Reserve Facility Based on Drawing Rights in the Fund' (29 May 1967), (B) 'An Outline of a Reserve Facility Based on Reserve

Units and Administered by a Fund Affiliate' (8 June 1967), (C) 'An Outline of a Reserve Facility Based on Drawing Rights in the Fund—Revised' (8 June 1967).

89. Garritsen de Vries, *The International Monetary System 1966–71, vol. I,* The System Under Stress, pp. 209–19. Garritsen de Vries also notes that academic opinion largely concurred with the allocation estimates prepared by the Fund (p. 214). See also *International Reserves: Needs and Availability*, IMF (Washington, DC: 1970).
90. Resolution No. 24-12, Board of Governors of the Fund, 3 October 1969.
91. *Articles of Agreement of the International Monetary Fund as Modified by the Proposed [First] Amendment* (includes typewritten palimpsests), IMF (Washington, DC: n.d. [1968]).
92. Ibid. p. 123.
93. 'The International Monetary Fund—Its Evolution, Organization, and Activities', IMF Pamphlet Series No. 37, p. 56.
94. Fred Hirsch, 'SDRs and the Working of the Gold Exchange Standard' *IMF Staff Papers*, vol. XVIII, p. 221.
95. See fn. 5, above.
96. R. E. Cumby, 'Special Drawing Rights and Plans for Reform of the International Monetary System: A Survey', *op. cit.,* p. 460.
97. Not coincidentally, in the run-up to the launch of the Euro in 1999, European international monetary policy priorities concentrated on European monetary integration and European/US monetary relations. In an earlier guise, see e.g. Kenneth King, *US Monetary Policy and European Responses in the 1980s*, RIIA/Routledge & Kegan Paul (London: 1982); and Chapter 3, below.

2

SDRs in the transition from Bretton Woods monetary arrangements

2.1 Introduction

We have seen in the previous chapter how the negotiation of Special Drawing Rights (SDRs) was an important but limited achievement. While SDRs implicitly increased liquidity, other difficulties, particularly over stability and adjustment, remained.[1] Before the US suspended its dollar convertibility into gold, and before SDRs had been in existence for even five months, Thomas Balogh surmised that recent reform had been 'too little, [and] a little late'.[2] Despite these qualifications, however, amendments to the Fund's articles were agreed to, and the first international money to be created by fiat was instituted. In addition, the International Monetary Fund (IMF) had begun to emerge as an entity in itself, with systemic interests of its own which it increasingly promoted. In the late 1960s and early 1970s international monetary reform and the SDR were often the vehicles for this.

This chapter will examine the role of SDRs between the first allocation in 1970 and the discussions that preceded the Jamaica Agreement in 1976. This involves, in turn, an examination of the first SDR allocation, the changing role of international reserves and SDRs as the fixed exchange rate system was breaking down, the discussions surrounding a post-Bretton Woods system, and emerging tensions in international monetary relations.

This was a period of flux for the SDR. The divergence between optimistic pronouncements on the future of the SDR and the rapid evolution of an international monetary system where the role of SDRs was increasingly tenuous, provides the backdrop to our investigation in this chapter.

2.2 The First SDR Allocation

How in fact did the first SDR allocation between 1970–2 work in practice? At the outset, it may be acknowledged that SDRs did not succeed in salvaging and strengthening the Bretton Woods monetary arrangements. But they did supplement international liquidity, which is what they were supposed to do. And in a more specific and limited sense, SDR operations were also a success: the SDR Department at the IMF ran smoothly during a difficult period of transformation in international monetary relations. Many safeguards which the Fund had instituted concerning the use of SDRs proved if anything to be superfluous. These safeguards were relaxed or modified, even going so far as abandoning the reconstitution provision (which, in the longer term proved to be a controversial decision).[3] Finally, it was also during this time that SDRs became a key element in reform plans, over-reaching their initial mandate as a supplement to existing reserve assets in the eyes of many ultimately chastened proponents of publicly-oriented liquidity management.[4]

SDRs were allocated on 1 January 1970.[5] This was not a normal working day, but it was deemed a significant enough event to warrant a special trip into Fund headquarters by senior Fund staff:

> ... the Acting Managing Director and a few senior officials ... could have waited for the first business day of the year, with the book entries to be made as of January first; but the symbolic importance of the event seemed to justify 'action'—which meant the signing of a computer print-out—on the day itself, even though it was a holiday.[6]

3.414 billion SDRs were allocated on that day, which, because of the exchange link between them and the dollar that then prevailed, equalled the same amount in US dollars.[7] On 1 January of the following two years, 2.949 billion and 2.952 billion SDRs were allocated respectively.[8] Importantly, this was more than the initial proponents of the SDRs had envisaged in 1967–8; at that time it was felt that one to two billion SDRs (representing a global reserve increase of 1.25 per cent to 2.5 per cent p.a.) would suffice.[9] At the time of the allocation, however, when the US had a relatively restrictive monetary policy, an excess of liquidity provision was not at the forefront of concerns. Indeed it was estimated by the IMF that the 'required' global reserve growth would be \$4 billion to \$5 billion per annum, an approximate increase of 5–6 per cent;[10] world trade during the period 1970–2 was expected to grow by 15 per cent, 11.5 per cent, and 19 per cent, respectively.[11]

In fact, however, reserves grew at a greater rate than expected during this period, and most of this was comprised of foreign exchange (a shift in US monetary policy towards expansion was one reason for this). SDRs accounted for a very small percentage of this increase, as Tables 2.1 to 2.3 indicate. Had reserves increased by the anticipated levels of $4 billion to $5 billion per annum, the same level of SDR allocation would have represented approximately 60 per cent of this increase, a considerable proportion in retrospect.

Table 2.1. Composition of total reserves, 1969–72

	(Value figures in billions of SDRs)							
	1969		1970		1971		1972	
	amount	% of total	amount	% of total	amount	% of total	amount	% of total
Gold*	39.1	50	37.2	40	36.1	30	35.8	25
SDRs**	–	–	3.1	4	5.9	5	8.7	6
Fund reserve positions	6.7	9	7.7	8	6.4	4	6.3	4
Foreign exchange	32.3	41	44.5	48	71.4	60	93.6	65
Total	78.1	100	92.5	100	119.8	100	144.4	100

* gold valued at US$35/oz
** allocations less SDRs held by Fund's General Account
Source: 'Operatons and Transactions in SDRs—The First Basic Period', IMF Pamphlet no. 17; IMF International Financial Statistics (various issues)

Table 2.2. Allocations and holdings of SDRs at 31 December 1972

	(Value figures in millions of SDRs)			
			SDR Holdings	
	Allocations	Net Receipt or Net Use (-)	Amount	As % of Allocations
Industrial Countries	**6,177.7**	**397.0**	**6,574.7**	**106**
United States	2,294.0	–490.9	1,803.1	79
United Kingdom	1,006.3	–401.9	604.4	60
Industrial Europe*	2,141.4	1,136.0	3,277.4	153
Canada	358.6	106.7	465.3	130
Japan	377.4	47.1	424.5	112
Other Developed Areas	**789.1**	**–140.5**	**648.5**	**82**
Less Developed Areas	**2,348.0**	**–885.2**	**1,462.9**	**62**
Latin America	879.1	–313.0	566.0	64
Middle East	239.4	–114.9	124.5	52
Other Asia	765.0	–275.2	489.8	64
Other Africa	464.5	–182.0	282.5	61
Total	**9,314.8**	**–628.7****	**8,686.1**	**93**

* Austria, Belgium, Denmark, France, Germany, Italy, Luxembourg, Netherlands, Norway, Sweden
** held by the Fund's General Account
Source: 'Operations and Transactions in SDRs—The First Basic Period', IMF Pamphlet no. 17, 1973

Table 2.3. SDR allocations as additions to reserves, 1970–2*

(Value figures in US$ millions)

	SDR Allocation, 1970			SDR Allocation, 1971			SDR Allocation, 1972		
	Reserves, End of 1969	Amount	As % of 1969 Reserves	Reserves, End of 1970	Amount	As % of 1970 Reserves	Reserves, End of 1971	Amount	As % of 1971 Reserves
Industrial Countries	***54,539***	**2,276.2**	**4.2**	***65,790***	**1,954.8**	**3.0**	***86,438***	**1,946.7**	**2.3**
United States	*16,964*	866.9	5.1	*14,487*	716.9	4.9	*12,149*	710.2	5.8
United Kingdom	*2,527*	409.9	16.2	*2,827*	299.6	10.6	*6,063*	296.8	4.9
Industrial Europe**	*28,288*	753.3	2.7	*38,957*	692.2	1.8	*48,828*	695.9	1.4
Canada	*3,106*	124.3	4.0	*4,679*	117.7	2.5	*5,251*	116.6	2.2
Japan	*3,654*	121.8	3.3	*4,840*	128.4	2.7	*14,148*	127.2	0.9
Other Developed Areas	***6,196***	**284.8**	**4.6**	***7,016***	**247.0**	**3.5**	***10,299***	**257.3**	**2.5**
Less Developed Areas	***12,519***	**853.1**	**6.8**	***14,150***	**747.5**	**5.3**	***15,491***	**747.4**	**4.8**
Latin America	*4,495*	330.0	7.3	*5,620*	275.8	4.9	*6,040*	273.3	4.5
Middle East	*1,904*	77.4	4.1	*1,869*	81.0	4.3	*2,585*	81.0	3.1
Other Asia	*4,060*	277.7	6.8	*4,247*	242.4	5.7	*4,320*	244.9	5.7
Other Africa	*2,060*	168.0	8.2	*2,514*	148.3	5.9	*2,546*	148.2	5.8
Total	***73,254***	**3,414.1**	**4.7**	***87,081***	**2,949.3**	**3.4**	***112,228***	**2,951.4**	**2.6**

* Excluding China and nonparticipants (Ethiopia, Kuwait, Lebanon, the Libyan Arab Republic, Portugal, Qatar, Saudi Arabia, Singapore, and the United Arab Emirates)
** Austria, Belgium, Denmark, France, Germany, Italy, Luxembourg, Netherlands, Norway, Sweden

Source: 'Operations and Transactions in SDRs—The First Basic Period', IMF Pamphlet no. 17; IMF International Financial Statistics (various issues) for Reserves

Table 2.1 indicates the composition of global reserves between 1969 and 1972. The most obvious change was the unanticipated increase in the foreign exchange component of reserves. While it could be argued that this increase in foreign exchange reserves was simply supplementing decreasing gold reserves, this can only be said of the *relative* composition of reserves. In absolute terms, total reserves roughly doubled between 1969 and 1972, and the foreign exchange component was responsible for well over 80 per cent of this increase, the amount of gold holdings falling slightly. SDRs represented 6 per cent of world reserves in 1972, or approximately 12 per cent of the reserve increase since 1969.

Table 2.2 focuses upon the receipt or use of SDRs by country and Table 2.3 indicates the amount of SDRs as a proportion of total reserves. Revealingly, the largest net users of SDRs between 1970 and 1972 were the US and UK, using more SDRs than all developing countries combined. Correspondingly, it was 'Industrial Europe' that received the most SDRs by designation, especially Belgium, the Netherlands, and West Germany.[12] Habermeier writes that in general flows of SDRs mirrored 'the direction of equalizing participants' holdings of SDRs as proportions of their reserves', as provided for in the guideline for designation.[13] This meant that countries such as the US, the UK, and Latin America, for which SDRs represented a higher than average addition to reserves, tended to be net users of SDRs, whereas recipients of SDRs (Industrial Europe, Canada, and Japan) tended to be in countries where allocated SDRs represented a smaller addition to reserves.[14] This is perhaps not surprising since SDRs were allocated in the same proportion as countries' IMF quotas, which in turn roughly reflected relative importance to world trade. Thus, there was a tendency for SDRs to represent another component of existing reserve policies of individual members. In short, the allocation of SDRs did not alter the tendencies of holders to maintain prevailing reserve policies for non-SDR reserves. Interestingly, those countries which, it could be argued (and the US did), should have revalued their currencies because of higher relative reserve positions before SDRs, did not experience any additional pressures following the SDR allocation. Thus, the experience of SDR use during the First Basic Period (the period of the first allocation) tended to reinforce the prevailing reserve portfolio policies and preferences of finance departments and central banks.

Of total SDR transactions during the first basic period, 60 per cent of them (representing SDR 1.873 billion of SDR 3.109 million in total) were between participants and 40% involved transactions with the General Account.[15] Of the transactions between participants, 60% of these were classified as subject to the requirement of balance of payments need; 40% involved other transfers. Again it was the UK, but also the US, that were particularly affected by balance of payments need. Regarding transactions with the General Account (generally repurchases), incentives for participants included the low rate of SDR interest and the lack of necessity to prove balance of payments need—even though the UK transacted with the General Account for this purpose in 1972 in its drawing of SDR 292 million as part of a gold tranche drawing. During the previous two years the UK tended to transfer SDRs *to* the General Account.[16]

Another important feature of SDR use during this time was that they tended to be used because of a reluctance of some holders—particularly Industrial Europe—to accept further dollars as reserves. As Habermeier writes concerning the relatively heavy use of SDRs by the UK:

> . . . the two major uses of SDRs by the United Kingdom were influenced by the unwillingness of other EEC countries to accumulate larger balances of US dollars.[17]

Already we can see that from a very early date the SDR was perceived by some as a potential substitute for the dollar rather than as a supplement. This is certainly not what was originally intended. While the use of SDRs to pay Europe was intended to relieve pressure on the US gold stock, it was not envisioned that its potential role as a substitute for the dollar would necessarily follow. Joseph Gold made this point clear in his discussion of the legal status of SDRs as they were allocated:

> Special drawing rights are intended to supplement existing reserve assets. They are not intended to be a substitute for existing reserve assets . . . [18]

For if SDRs were viewed as an alternative to other reserve assets, they would begin to assume the characteristics that were discouraged during the initial negotiations. The US made this clear in the Treasury press release announcing the American ratification of the Rio Agreement, describing SDRs as a 'facility to provide *supplementary* reserves'.[19] Pierre-Paul Schweitzer strongly echoed these sentiments, arguing forcefully that SDRs were not usurpers of the role of existing reserve assets:

> The new [SDR] facility is intended, when the need arises, to supplement, not to supplant, gold and foreign exchange. *This is no more than common sense.*[20]

Given US policy, if SDRs had been perceived as a substitute for the dollar at the time, US support for the asset, which was then very strong, would have quickly palled. For the US to support an SDR administered under Fund auspices, it was important for the Fund to make this clear.

However the trend towards the perception of the SDR as a possible substitute for the dollar continued following the breakdown of Bretton Woods. In 1972, after the Smithsonian Agreement and the ersatz devaluation of the dollar to $38/oz of gold, and as the expansion of US monetary policy was reflected in increased reserve holdings by other countries, the use of SDRs continued to indicate 'a desire on the part of some major industrial countries to minimize the use of US dollars as a means of settlement'.[21] Again, even at this early stage the SDR was not perceived, or used, solely as a supplement to the dollar. Admittedly, there was some slight reluctance to use SDRs as well—international monetary instability reflected upon all reserve assets at the time—although the relatively low interest rate of 1.5 per cent which prevailed (compared to at least twice this for major national currencies) may also be said to have had an influence on this.[22] As we shall see, however, this 'substitution potential' was seized upon by both supporters and detractors of an increased role for the SDR.

The issues of the SDR's value also became problematic during the first basic period. Under the First Amendment to the Fund's Articles, the unit of value of SDRs was defined as .888671 gm of fine gold.[23] In practice this meant that the SDR was equal to the gold-dollar.[24] Once the dollar began to float (the Fund issued a press release on 20 August 1971 confirming that this was so, five days after the Nixon 'shocks'), the SDR/dollar value link was called into question. A further difficulty then arose in that the unit of value of the SDR could not be changed without amending the Articles of Agreement. The eventual solution, whereby the SDR was related to a basket of currencies (see Table 2.4), enabled the Fund to value SDRs in terms of floating currencies, but also allowed par values to exist simultaneously. The implication of this was that the SDR was allowed to assume its own value, in effect de-coupled from that of gold and ultimately the dollar. As Joseph Gold put it:

Table 2.4. Composition of SDR currency basket (1 July 1974)*

Currency	Weight (%)	Amounts (units)
US dollar	33.0	0.40
Deutschmark	12.5	0.38
Pound sterling	9.0	0.045
French franc	7.5	0.44
Japanese yen	7.5	26
Canadian dollar	6.0	0.071
Italian lira	6.0	47
Netherlands guilder	4.5	0.14
Belgian franc	3.5	1.60
Swedish krona	2.5	0.13
Australian dollar	1.5	0.012
Danish krone	1.5	0.11
Norwegian krone	1.5	0.099
Spanish peseta	1.5	1.10
Austrian schilling	1.0	0.22
South African rand	1.0	0.0082

* J. J. Polak noted that the date of announcement was '... 30 years to the day after the beginning of the Bretton Woods conference, a day that is singled out in the Articles of Agreement in the expression "... the United States dollar of the weight and fineness in effect on 1 July 1944."' (Article IV, Section 1(a)). See also Chapter 5, pp. 170–1, Table 5.1, below

Source: J. J. Polak, 'Valuation and Rate of Interest of the SDR', IMF Pamphlet no. 18, 1974. p. 2

> ... the effect was to determine the value of gold by reference to the SDR instead of determining the value of the SDR by reference to gold.[25]

Or, as another senior Fund staff member wrote:

> ... the provision of the Articles that links the SDR to gold is now applied in reverse to determine the Fund's transaction price for a currency in terms of gold, in that one ounce of gold equals 35 baskets.[26]

This change from gold and then dollar equivalence to a separate valuation was symbolically very important in the evolution of the SDR as a reserve asset with its own attributes and limitations.

Related to the valuation question was the question of the SDR interest rate. This became important following the increase in inflation in Western economies in the early 1970s which succeeded in pushing up prevailing interest rates to 10 per cent, levels that had only briefly been approached once since 1945, during the Korean War. The initial SDR rate of interest of 1.5 per cent was kept low for two reasons: firstly, an SDR linked to gold could be expected to increase in value relative to currencies (between 1946 and 1967 revaluations—of the Deutschmark and guilder—had occurred only once), and secondly, and more revealingly, as a result of US pressure in 'order to minimize competition with the US dollar as a reserve asset'.[27] As the US pursued relatively low-interest rate policies with respect to dollar-denominated assets, it did not wish to risk further competition from SDRs.[28]

It was the reduction of the SDR currency basket to five currencies in 1974 that also fostered the solution to the SDR interest rate problem. The interest rate compromise was in fact reached in the final days of the Committee of Twenty: the C-20's *Outline* suggested that the SDR interest rate would be set from time to time by the Executive Board 'in the light of changing market interest rates'.[29] Table 2.5, below, shows the SDR interest rate formula agreed to, which prevailed until the Second Amendment negotiations.

As interest rates rose in the West following the oil price rise, the SDR interest rate was increased to 5 per cent on 13 June 1974. It was subject to semi-annual adjustment by a formula based on a sliding scale of the weighted average of short-term interest rates of US, UK, German, French, and Japanese currencies.[30] This was a precursor to the eventual adoption of SDR interest rates that eventually more closely reflected market rates of these five currencies as well (see Chapter 6). This was both resisted by the US and advocated by the Fund.[31]

Concerning other practical aspects of SDR operations, Habermeier observed that the distribution of SDR holdings between 1970 and 1972 'raised no difficulties for the operation of the Special Drawing Account'.[32] Even the reconstitution provision presented no pressing difficulties, although indications by 1972 were that it was beginning to inhibit the use of SDRs where the

Table 2.5. SDR interest rate formula, 1974

Composite Market Rate	SDR Rate (%)	Difference
3	1.5	1.50
4	2	2.00
5	2.5	2.500
6	3.25	2.75
7	3.75	3.25
8	4.5	3.5
9	5	4
10	5	5
11	5	6
12	5.5	6.5

Source: J. J. Polak, 'Valuation and Rate of Interest of the SDR', IMF Pamphlet no. 18, 1974, p. 20

need to reconstitute became a factor.[33] In this vein, John Williamson pointed out that a country could alternatively purchase sufficient SDRs in order to comply with the reconstitution provision as the end of the averaging period approached.[34] Despite an apprehension of difficulties, however, the reconstitution provision provoked little debate until the Second Amendment discussions.

Designation, another Article XIX provision governing operations and transactions in SDRs, is a process by which the Fund could ensure that participants use their SDRs 'by designating participants to provide currency for specified amounts of SDRs'. It too worked well.[35] The Fund designated a participant in cases where its balance of payments or reserve position was strong. As Joseph Gold argued when the first SDRs were issued: 'The acceptance of SDRs by designated participants is the rock on which the assurance of use must rest'.[36] During the 'First Basic Period' (i.e. 1970–2), growing currency instability overcame some natural bankers' caution with respect to SDRs, and the over 100 transactions which took place under designation (though representing less than half of total SDRs) took place willingly.[37] Admittedly, this willingness to accept mandatory designation was partly a reflection of international monetary instability. However, safeguards of the Executive Board which included general prescriptions regarding reserve asset portfolios, and the harmonization of SDR holdings, were relaxed during the First Basic Period.[38]

2.3 Continued Systemic Instability

In a limited sense, then, SDRs functioned as well as could have been expected during the First Basic Period. Praise for the SDR must be tempered, however, when we recall that the SDR did not aid in the preservation of the Bretton

Woods system. As J. J. Polak, who remained one of the most enthusiastic proponents of SDRs admitted:

> The two ruptures of the system that the SDR was intended to prevent: cessation of official convertibility of the dollar against gold and an increase in the dollar price of gold, occurred within the first basic period of allocation.[39]

SDRs per se cannot be blamed for failing to avoid these developments. Other changes in the monetary environment had a much greater bearing on international arrangements. Virtually simultaneous with SDR allocation, the relaxation of US monetary policy in 1971 and 1972 had the effect of facilitating increases in international reserves. This greatly affected prospects for SDRs at this time, and indeed called into question the need for enhanced international reserves in the form of SDRs at all.[40] The notion of a need for a supplement at the time verged on irrelevant, but in a pattern that was to be repeated, this only rarely translated into calls for SDR abandonment. Instead SDRs as a substitute (rather than a supplement) for reserve currencies increasingly preoccupied analysts both inside and outside the Fund during the 1970s. A first formal step in the realization that the SDR had this potential was the symbolic decision to express the value of gold in terms of the SDR, which was one of the inevitable consequences of floating rates and ultimately the demonetization of gold.

Even so, it must be acknowledged that despite the smooth functioning of SDR operations, it was hardly a propitious time to begin SDR operations. Already the divergence between optimistic pronouncements and the nascent marginalization of the SDR was apparent. This was recognized even as SDRs were allocated. One observer suggested that policy makers were well aware of problems that could transpire, and that this underlay the decisions to front-end-load the allocation, and to approve a three-year rather than five-year basic period.[41]

The period of the first allocation of SDRs also served to draw attention to the prevailing weakness of the dollar. As we have seen, in general central banks were not reluctant to accept SDRs as an alternative to dollars. This was true even given the SDR's supposed illiquidity and low interest rate. Nonetheless, the fact remained that while the perception of a reserve shortage in the early 1960s eventually led to SDRs, continued instability vis-à-vis the dollar led to old questions about liquidity being asked in a different guise. All parties to the SDR's creation had earlier sought something different from the SDR. The Fund had succeeded in masking these differences to a degree, but policy disputes among its membership persisted which ultimately contributed to the end of the Bretton Woods system. Reflecting evident power asymmetries between the Fund and its members in international monetary policy formulation, it was the outlook for SDRs rather than dollars that dimmed.

Nonetheless, the SDR department at the Fund worked smoothly, and indeed had even begun to assume an identity not initially envisioned for it. Despite the temporary suspension of allocations in 1972, a new examination of the SDR in academic literature took place, together with a reassessment of the asset by the Fund and its membership in the Committee of Twenty. Before we address these new reform plans, we must first examine the SDR in context of the wider liquidity debate in the 1970s.

2.4 The SDR and International Liquidity Provision

The issues relating to international reserves and liquidity became increasingly complex in the 1970s. As we saw in Chapter 1, these were controversial enough issues during the 1960s; needless to say the debates were much further complicated after the breakdown of fixed exchange rates and the moves to private liquidity provision. While the literature on this subject is substantial, and much of it technical, it is important in addressing the role of SDRs in a post-Bretton Woods system to be aware of the debates surrounding SDRs and liquidity.

Excellent taxonomies exist on this subject. Benjamin Cohen provided one,[42] and in a wide-ranging study mentioned earlier, John Williamson provided an early bibliographical study of the debate until the 1970s.[43] Credit was given to Triffin for promoting a theory of the functioning of the international monetary system; the literature, Williamson argues, grew from there.[44]

In the period following SDR allocations, the Fund continued to generate and sponsor studies on issues surrounding the SDR, at times at an even greater pace than the papers which led to the Rio Agreement in the 1960s. In addition to relevant articles in the IMF's *Staff Papers*,[45] and two published texts in 1970 and 1983 on the liquidity-reserve question (with particular emphasis on the SDR),[46] the Fund kept internally well abreast of developments through staff papers, departmental memoranda, and other information.[47] For example, William Hood, then research director at the Fund, produced an annotated bibliography on the role of international reserves in the world economy in an internal memorandum.[48] In addition, the Fund's research department prepared a summary of papers prepared for the Fleming Memorial Conference in 1977, which illustrated the divergent views on liquidity among economists and policy makers at the time.[49] This process was to continue intermittently, including the sponsoring of an important conference and volume on SDRs in 1996, during a period when SDRs appeared at irrelevant to the international monetary system, international development needs apart.[50]

One of the most striking observations that much of this literature acknowledges is that the demand for reserves did not markedly change as the flexible-exchange rate system evolved. This is surprising, for, theoretically, flexible exchange rates obviate the need for reserves: if balance of payments are in deficit, the exchange rate should simply fall. As Heller and Khan put it:

> The standard textbook view... argues that in a system of floating exchange rates the need for a country to hold international reserves disappears, since payments imbalances will be corrected by movements in its exchange rate.[51]

Needless to say this did not occur. In general, countries stuck with their historical inclinations and reserve portfolio whatever the exchange rate regime, and markets continued to take into account reserves in determining credit ratings and interest rates, not to mention suitability for loans. We have already seen how SDRs did not change the reserve portfolio mix greatly during the period of the first allocation.

Broadly, reserve ratios and portfolios continued relatively unchanged under flexible rates. This may have reflected the ambiguous status of SDRs as reserve assets—in practice they were more like a line of credit than an asset per se. In its 1974 *Annual Report* the Fund set out four reasons for the lack of change in reserve portfolios: (a) exchange rates tended to be 'managed' rather than freely floating, (b) the motives for using reserves as a backing for foreign borrowing had not changed (indeed as Triffin noted the increased liquidity of Euromarkets had increased this motive),[52] (c) reserve levels were maintained in the hope of a return to fixed exchange rates, and (d) reserves were maintained by many countries in an effort to shadow the exchange rate of another floating currency.[53] Moreover, while these arguments addressed the period immediately before and after the move to 'generalized' floating, other studies have also shown that the tendency to maintain a relatively constant reserve-import ratio continued through the 1970s.[54]

While it may therefore be said that SDRs did not skew policies affecting reserve assets, a further question arose: how *inflationary* were SDRs to the international monetary system? This became an important issue as increasing global inflation rates took hold in the 1970s, variously attributed to Eurocurrency markets, the oil price hike, domestic social unrest (wage-inflation), US macro-economic expansionism—and SDRs. Tables 2.2 and 2.3 illustrated that SDRs had little impact on the amount of international reserves, accounting for approximately 2.6 per cent of the annual increase in 1972. On the other hand, even as late as 1969 the Fund had expected international reserves to increase by about 5 billion SDRs between 1970 and 1972.[55] It turned out that total reserves increased by almost 50 billion SDRs between 1970 and 1972 (see Table 2.3), and over 65 billion SDRs from 1969. So even if the addition of some SDR 9.5 billion to reserve growth was culpable in inflationary pressures (and there was less reason to believe this was true under flexible rates[56]), they were not a primary cause in the early 1970s.[57]

And in fact even the question of whether Eurocurrency markets contributed to inflation, or whether they directly contributed to an increase in world liquidity, is not completely clear. We have noted, however, that they did act as a catalyst to the large increases in foreign exchange reserves already witnessed in the early 1970s. Alexander Swoboda published an examination of this question for the G30, which examined five main treatments of the question of credit creation during the 1970s.[58] These range from an 'initial deposit approach', which argues that Euromarkets exist independently from national banking systems, to Swoboda's own 'world money stock approach', which acknowledged that the lack of reserve requirements meant that world money supply increased by a greater amount than it otherwise would have because of Euromarkets.

Similarly, in his examination of the impact of the first oil price crisis, W.M. Corden argued that the rise in Euromarket lending did not necessarily lead to an increase in world liquidity, although in a later work he conceded the earlier possible link between reserve increases and inflation:[59]

> In fact, liquidity as a whole in the world did not increase. The risks borne by the banks were, to some extent, spread to their customers and, more important, to the governments that stood behind them as lenders of last resort. In practice, of course, there was a substantial reshuffling of liquidity. ... Broadly we can say that for the world as a whole official liquidity has increased and private liquidity has decreased ....[60]

On the other hand, critics such as Robert Triffin and Geldolph Kessler have chosen to emphasize that an increase in private international liquidity did take place, and had a negative and destabilizing effect on the international monetary system. Furthermore the increase in reserves following the first oil price rise was also inflationary:

> ... the current account deficits of even the most inflationary ... [countries] ... could be financed—and indeed overfinanced—by international borrowing.
>
> The flooding of world reserves by dollar and Euro-dollar creation has added new dimensions to this financing. It has increased the cash reserves of commercial banks, enabling them to expand their own foreign lending at a pace which they could not have sustained otherwise.[61]

We will return to the phenomenon of Eurocurrency markets in so far as liquidity provision is concerned in Chapter 6. The core point at this stage, however, is that the increase in inflation as well as in reserves which did took place in the 1970s negatively affected the prospects for SDRs. It is not controversial to observe, in addition, that the link between reserves and central bank credit creation was complicated by the explosion in international bank lending. This reflected the fact that, for the developed countries and also for the newly industrializing countries (nics), reserves were increasingly demand rather than supply-determined.[62] International reserves could more easily be borrowed by the creditworthy from the private market, which was flush with deposits from oil producers. Even the concept of creditworthiness, which had been criticized as restricting Euromarket access to developed countries, became more nebulous as debtor countries began to borrow to increase their reserves, which could in turn 'entitle' borrowers to increased market access because of healthy reserves. Indeed the rather perverse effect of all this during the 1970s was that industrial countries, who had easy access to private liquidity, managed a decrease in their reserve-import ratio. Conversely, developing countries actually increased their reserves during this period.[63] Later, during periods when this practice became difficult to sustain, sovereign developing country debtors tended to turn to more expensive short-term instruments.[64] Even so, if the point that reserves were now increasingly demand-determined is accepted, could one then argue that Euromarket generated reserves were not inflationary whereas SDRs were? One would then have to argue that reserves from the private market were truly demanded and not solely a function of an increased Euromarket supply, in contrast to the demand and supply for liquidity in the form of SDRs.[65]

These developments and debates led some critics to argue that the move to both flexible exchange rates and private liquidity provision meant that the whole question of international liquidity was becoming less important. At the Fleming Memorial Conference in 1977, Gottfried Haberler argued that:

> Generalized floating and other developments have made obsolete any attempt to define an optimum level of international reserves; similarly, control of international reserves is no longer an important task for the Fund.[66]

This lies at the heart of the matter concerning a role for the SDR in the post-Bretton Woods era—for if the argument that flexible exchange rates obviate the need for reserves, or if reserves may be obtained from Eurocurrency markets (at least by those deemed creditworthy), questions of any optimum level of international reserves, whether or not including the SDR, become much less relevant. In any event, the evolution of this debate, and its corollary about the growing fungibility of international liquidity, could not help but adversely affect prospects for SDRs under the new arrangements based upon private liquidity provision.

Plainly, however, the moves to flexible exchange rates were neither comprehensive nor complete, especially vis-à-vis reserve policies. Although currencies representing 70 per cent of world trade were not pegged to any specified level by the mid-1970s, this left the vast majority of currencies, admittedly representing only 30 per cent of world trade, which adhered to some sort of formal target. In addition, those that did float were subject to official intervention, which suggested the existence of some target level for exchange rates. Moreover, exchange rates often over-shot and were subject to long periods of misalignment, which again often prompted official intervention. This in turn required reserves, if only to iron out day-to-day or month-to-month aberrations. As we have seen, a number of studies argued that floating rates did not decrease the demand for reserves.[67] Furthermore, reserve/import ratios were generally higher in the 1970s than in the 1960s.[68]

An unattributed BIS Economic Paper in June 1988 also confirmed trends identified in the previous decade, and indeed also identifiable in the Fund's *International Financial Statistics*, namely that between 1970 and 1980 total holdings of non-gold reserves increased approximately ninefold in current dollar terms, from $40 to $366 billion.[69] Of course, these broad statistical trends do not reveal other potentially destabilizing changes, such as moves towards a multi-currency reserve system in the late 1970s (and again towards the end of the first decade of the twenty-first century), the effect of a revaluation in the price of gold, and differences in reserve preferences. Some of these points will require further examination later; others are more tangential to our argument. The important points to remember here are: (a) following the moves to private liquidity provision, international reserves remain an important variable in the examination of international liquidity needs; and (b) the flexible exchange rate system (in practice managed or 'dirty' floating), ostensibly making adjustment easier, also required liquidity. It simply did not work as smoothly as some of its proponents suggested it would.

If international liquidity management is deemed unnecessary, then the private market may perform this function. However, if only for the reason of the management of instability, a role could have been envisioned for the SDR—whose prime raison d'être would be the liquidity needs of the system as a whole. The experience of SDR use during the early 1970s had shown that this was beginning to be possible—although the question as to whether SDRs could be used effectively to reduce world liquidity remained problematic.[70] But in any case, SDRs had proven themselves during the First Basic Period in terms of both basic functioning and the potential to supplement *or* supplant some liquidity needs. Quickly, however, events transpired and decisions were taken that rendered them seemingly superfluous, at least for a time.

The story of the marginalization of SDRs through the 1970s has tended to focus upon more practical matters, such as their illiquidity, or unwieldiness, or the idea that they were a cause of inflation. None of these factors, however, was completely true in the early 1970s. And, of course, the explosion of reserves through the 1970s took place through other reserve growth and increasingly demand-determined liquidity through the provision of Euromarket liquidity.[71] Although the SDR was now on the international monetary agenda, and many attempts were made to enhance its role—not the least of which occurred at the highest levels of Fund membership in the Committee of Twenty—the politics related to SDRs had a bearing on their apparent irrelevance to evolving international monetary arrangements.

2.5 The Committee of Twenty and Prospects for Reform

The quadrupling of oil prices by OPEC in late 1973 was another catalyst for movements towards the private provision of international liquidity. While it was not an inevitable development, it did help to show that the new more market-oriented system was adaptable. However, at this very time, reform and the SDR were being examined at the highest levels of international monetary affairs—in the Committee on Reform of the International Monetary System and Related Issues (the Committee of Twenty). The Committee of Twenty and the reform negotiations between 1972 and 1974 have been well documented by the Fund: in Margaret Garritsen de Vries' comprehensive history of international monetary developments between 1972 and 1978 as well as in the C-20 Report itself together with its accompanying annexes and reports. In addition, John Williamson and others have analysed why responses to the Committee were so muted.[72]

There are three points to be made concerning the discussion of the ever-widening gap between the arguments of reformers who favoured the SDR and international monetary developments during the period of the C-20. First, and most importantly, we must remain aware of the growing disagreements taking place as the C-20 was instituted. Conventional wisdom suggests that the breakdown of the Smithsonian Agreement and then the quadrupling of oil prices led to the collapse of the Committee. In fact the seeds of its destruction were already in place at its foundation. These difficulties only intensified as the Committee was in session. Second, it is important to draw attention to a Fund report concerning a reformed international monetary system which predated the C-20. Third and finally, we must be aware of the brief of the C-20, and the powers which it did *not* enjoy. The gap between the reform plans and the evolution of the international monetary system in practice was an ever-widening gulf. This was mirrored with respect to the SDR, and sometimes illustrated a lack of political realism with respect to international monetary relations, including between the Fund and the US, as well as a failure to appreciate changing attitudes towards the SDR by both these entities.

The C-20 was instituted more as a means of resolving important differences in position for international monetary management rather than to expedite a comprehensive agreement on required reforms. Even before the C-20 was considered the Board of Governors of the IMF had passed a resolution in 1971 that pointed to international instability and requested the Executive

Directors to report 'any amendments of the Articles of Agreement which they consider necessary'[73]—and this was less than two years after the initial amendment of the articles. The report also resolved that members 'as promptly as possible... establish a satisfactory structure of exchange rates, maintained with appropriate margins'.[74] In an increasingly familiar pattern, 'reform' was advocated in some quarters, while at the same time international monetary pressures were causing widening fissures at the international level.

In the same way that political compromise and the increasing difficulties of maintaining international consensus led to the birth of the Committee, these same strains not surprisingly led to its demise and replacement by a new Interim Committee. Throughout this period, however, the Fund pushed ahead with recommendations for discussion. Immediately prior to the C-20, the Fund's Research Department under J. J. Polak produced a 'sketch' of a reformed monetary system, submitted to the Board of Governors by the Executive Directors in August 1972 entitled 'Reform of the International Monetary System'.[75] (It was also annex II (26 July 1972) of this report that established the Committee of Twenty.[76]) In the report, a 'substitution facility' was advocated—the first time it had been fully advocated at the Fund[77]—along with other proposals such as the allocation of SDRs to development agencies and a skewed allocation favouring developing countries.[78] Importantly, many of these issues defined the debates over the role of SDRs for the next 40 years.

In addition, among several proposals to enhance the attractiveness of the SDR as a reserve asset was the provision that 'remuneration paid to net creditor countries (and perhaps also the charges payable on debtor positions) might have to rise...'[79]—a provision not unlike Keynes' proposals in 1944 whereby surplus countries were to be treated slightly differently than deficit countries.[80] As with the First Amendment negotiations, however, it was the desire to preserve international monetary arrangements rather than to dramatically alter them which the Fund initially set in motion when it created the C-20.

The C-20 thus had a wide-ranging document preceding it produced by the Fund itself. But progress within the Committee was halting. Although there was a consensus within the Fund and among its membership that some sort of change was necessary, the direction of this change was increasingly in dispute. In addition, the brief of the C-20 was broad and its structure was unwieldy. In setting out the Committee's terms of reference, the Board of Governors stipulated that the C-20 should advise and report:

> with respect to all aspects of reform of the international monetary system, including proposals for amendments of the Articles of Agreement of the Fund.[81]

In considering proposals for amendments, the Committee was directed to:

> give full attention to the inter-relationship between [matters relating to reform] ...and existing or prospective arrangements among countries, including those that involve international trade, the flow of capital, investment, or development assistance, that could affect attainment of the purposes of the Fund under the present or amended Articles.[82]

In setting up the Committee, the Fund's Board of Governors created a committee consisting of members that replicated the profile of executive directors in the Fund, coupled with up to two deputies each.[83] The Committee itself decided upon the number of advisors allowed by each member.[84] In practice the number of officials at each meeting varied, sometimes up to 200 at meetings of the Committee, though fewer at the meetings of the Deputies.[85] Despite these complex arrangements, the C-20's powers were only to recommend. Decisions would be with member countries of the Board of the IMF.

It soon became apparent, however, that this new forum was set up in an effort to resolve positions which were becoming increasingly irreconcilable. For instance, at the IMF's annual meeting in September 1971, the Chancellor of the Exchequer, Anthony Barber, set forth his plans for reform, which included three central points: first, that the SDR should become the *numéraire* for all parities, revaluations, and devaluations, second, 'the SDR could become the main asset in which countries hold their reserves', and third, that the SDR scheme be expanded to allow for increased liquidity without reliance on the deficit position of one or more countries.[86] What was equally revealed in Barber's speech was that influential policy makers were now proposing comprehensive reform plans. The US response, however, was more muted. Increasingly isolated, George Shultz's speech acknowledged interest in the 'Grand Design', but did not set forth its position clearly, at least in public.[87] This was an early indication that the US position was shifting away from support for existing arrangements, or at least support for a managed liquidity system, despite official pronouncements.

Notwithstanding its terms of reference, and the international monetary turbulence swirling outside its meeting rooms, the agreement that did transpire took place within the first year of the Committee of Twenty's existence. In his report to the Board of Governors in September 1973, the Chairman of the Committee wrote that the 'general shape' of the reformed system had been agreed upon, and symmetrical arrangements for both deficit and surplus countries (the absence of which was blamed for the breakdown of Bretton Woods) had been identified as the key problem to be resolved.[88] With respect to the SDR, and following Barber's cue, the phrase that 'the SDR is to become the principal reserve asset' of the reformed system, which was eventually incorporated twice into the new Articles (Article VIII, Section 7, and Article

XXII), also appeared in the report.[89] The nine months following this preliminary report, however, produced no further progress in the C-20. And relations between the Fund and the US were increasingly strained.

2.6 Increasing Strains in International Monetary Management

Well before the Committee was instituted, the US bared the frailty of the Fund during periods when it was found necessary to do so. Pierre-Paul Schweitzer, managing director of the Fund until August 1973, was only notified of Nixon's 'shocks' of 15 August 1971 barely half an hour before they were made public.[90] Reflecting greater popular interest in international monetary relations, Schweitzer's public image (greater than that of his well-respected predecessor, Per Jacobsson[91]), and his success in further raising the profile of the IMF, contributed to occasionally difficult relations between the US and the Fund. It was plain that Schweitzer was a popular managing director within and outside the Fund. Importantly, he succeeded in garnering developing country support for IMF membership.[92] The IMF's historian, Margaret Garritsen de Vries, referred to his popularity in her brief history *The IMF in a Changing World 1945–85* by pointing out that he received a number of honourary degrees and appeared on the cover of *Time* magazine in the US.[93]

Revealingly, in the longer Fund histories, de Vries abandoned her normally diplomatic prose to endorse the widely held suspicion that Schweitzer was essentially pushed out of the Fund by the US.[94] Indeed, as we noted in Chapter 1, Schweitzer had disagreed with the thrust of US policy towards international reserve assets as early as 1964, within three weeks of his appointment.[95] Later, de Vries pointed out that President Nixon as well as Treasury Secretaries Schultz and Connally informally 'expressed opposition to a reappointment for Mr Schweitzer'.[96] What most angered the US in the end was that Schweitzer had called for a formal devaluation of the dollar—at precisely the time the US was calling for a revaluation of other currencies.[97] This was to lead to the non-renewal of Schweitzer's appointment as soon as it could be expeditiously arranged. As Susan Strange bluntly put it: 'Helped by the British, Washington . . . got rid of Pierre-Paul Schweizer [*sic*]'.[98] Simply put, the Fund's continuing support for the SDR throughout this period, epitomized by Schweitzer's public pronouncements as well as the sponsoring of successive staff studies and conferences, created tension between the Fund and the US. But, as we shall see, subsequent managing directors were often just as vociferous, if not more diplomatic, in their support for the SDR in the 1970s until this support became no longer consistent with the entrenchment of the new arrangements.

While the US' blackballing of Mr Schweitzer tends to support the notion that the US had the determining voice in the functioning of the international monetary system, it also points to the continued growing importance of the Fund as an entity in itself. Despite the bureaucratic limitations on Fund staff with respect to public statements, and no natural constituency through which to appeal, the Fund was quietly developing its own persona and policy interests. The managing director not only made controversial statements on the role of the Fund in the management of the international monetary system and appeared on the cover of *Time* magazine; he—and SDRs—even became subjects for idle gossip; surely a sign that his persona on the international stage was more than that of just another important financial dignitary.[99] More significantly, the initiatives and attitudes of the Fund were also assuming increasing importance. As we shall see, despite clear setbacks on international monetary management, these were to bear some fruit in the influence of the Fund on its Executive in the negotiation of the Jamaica Agreement, and indeed had already had some effect in the setting of the C-20's agenda.

Nonetheless, in this atmosphere of international monetary upheaval, it was not surprising that the voice of the C-20 was inconclusive with respect to many points. Indeed the final Outline of Reform was only 20 pages long. Most of the far-reaching proposals concerning a prospective substitution account and capital flows could not be agreed upon and were contained in annexes known as Technical Reports. As the Committee admitted in the preface to its final report:

> ...in view of present uncertainties related to inflation, the energy situation, and other unsettled conditions, it is not appropriate to attempt to determine the full details of all aspects of the future international monetary system, many of which can better be decided in the light of future developments.[100]

In addition, in John Williamson's *The Failure of World Monetary Reform*, in which he laments the inability to agree to comprehensive reform, he observes that:

> In comparison with the initial objective of writing a new monetary constitution for the world... [the]... results were meagre. There was no agreement on a set of rules for assigning adjustment responsibilities, no design of a viable adjustment mechanism, no introduction of an SDR standard, no substitution and no curb on the asymmetries. These facts explain the use of the word 'failure' in the title of... [my]... book.[101]

It is true that the Committee was unable to agree on a comprehensively reformed system. However, recalling the difficulties that led to the institution of the Committee, it would have been surprising had such an agreement been concluded. The actual institution of the C-20 was a manifestation of differences on the prospective system that were proving increasingly irreconcilable. In addition, this was compounded by the international economic upheavals taking place as the Committee met (and which the Committee referred to in the above excerpt). Above all, at this time the US had less and less interest in an SDR standard of any workable variety and the Europeans themselves were fairly half-hearted in the negotiations—at least in contrast to the search for a united voice which they attempted to find in the First Amendment negotiations.

Within the rubric of these irreconcilable differences the C-20 did succeed in making some limited headway. Paragraph 31 of the 'Outline of Reform' recommended that the Committee be replaced by a

> ... permanent and representative Council ... [which would] ... have the necessary decision-making powers to supervise the management and adaptation of the monetary system, to oversee the continuing operation of the adjustment process, and to deal with sudden disturbances which might threaten the system.[102]

While the Council did not become operative, it did become an important issue in negotiations surrounding the second amendment, and was incorporated into them should 85 per cent of the Fund's membership wish to see it enacted.[103] In the meantime, the C-20 also established the Interim Committee 'with an advisory role in the areas in which the Council is to have decision-making powers'.[104]

With respect to the SDR specifically, the C-20 in much of its Outline recommended that the SDR become the principal reserve asset (para. 2(d)), and made further suggestions to improve both its utility (a link with development finance was noted, as was the possible abolition of the reconstitution provision), and its characteristics (increasing its 'effective yield', authorization by the Fund of additional types of transactions, authorization of SDR transactions by parties 'without designation' by the Fund) were improved.[105] These were to provide the basis for much of the debate with respect to SDRs over the next several years. And finally, the C-20 Report was used by the Fund during the Second Amendment negotiations. It was an important element in setting the agenda of the negotiations, as we shall see in Chapter 5.

It is necessary here, however, to recall that international monetary arrangements were quickly moving away from a system in which SDRs would play the role advocated by their proponents. This was particularly true of the US administration. The US Treasury, once a champion of fixed rates and the SDR, began to look more benignly at floating. Jack Bennett was one example, but there were others. George Shultz replaced John Connally as Treasury Secretary after the latter's resignation in May 1972. By June 1974 Shultz had been replaced by William Simon, and Jack Bennett had replaced Paul Volcker, who had been a proponent of reform within the Committee of Twenty.[106]

Both of these latter appointees were proponents of floating exchange rates—for that matter so was George Shultz. Arthur Burns, chairman of the Federal Reserve, was not, however, but in any case in the increasingly politicized international monetary environment of the late 1960s and early 1970s, particularly during the tenure of John Connally at the Treasury, his opinions carried little weight and indeed began to change.[107] Thus by the time the C-20 released its documents in June 1974, after dubiously successful international agreements in Washington in December 1971 and in Paris in March 1973—compounded by the oil embargo and quadrupling of oil prices in late 1973 and early 1974 with its catalytic effect on the importance of Eurocurrency markets—prospects for a return to fixed rates were looking increasingly slim. Prospective paths to reform continued at the Fund and elsewhere. Within the US administration, however, enthusiasm was waning rapidly. As Paul Volcker noted:

> ...there was talk about the need for monetary reform to go far beyond the agreement that created Special Drawing Rights. Before the Smithsonian and after, every official speech and every international communiqué about monetary affairs included obligatory paragraphs about the need to proceed on reforming the system. But the fact of the matter was that, for a time, the United States was not interested in pursuing the matter aggressively.[108]

2.7 The Early Role of the SDR Outside the IMF

US ideas concerning international monetary reform were to move away from those where the SDR was to play a significant role. At least until the Second Amendment negotiations, however, the Fund promoted a system in which the SDR was to play a central role. Had this interest in the SDR been a preoccupation only of the Fund, it would not have reflected much. And it is notable that the SDR was even enjoying limited early acceptance in the marketplace—and not only as *numéraire*.

This initial acceptance of the SDR in the market has been overlooked. There are several examples of this nascent private market in SDRs: On 24 May 1975 the Suez Canal Authority announced that tolls would be expressed in terms of SDRs.[109] The first Eurobonds denominated in SDRs were also issued in 1975.[110] US authorities were increasingly uneasy about these developments, and two further instances of the emerging market in SDRs illustrate this in particular. The first of these was the OPEC meeting in Libreville, Gabon on 11 June 1975, when it was announced that:

> With regard to the protection of purchasing power of oil revenues on account of the dollar fluctuation, the conference has decided to adopt the use of the SDR

(Special Drawing Rights) as a unit of account, and that it will define the practical modalities for the implementation of the SDR at its next extraordinary meeting.[111]

While an SDR-denominated oil price did not transpire, (and the dollar remains the vehicle currency for commodity trade despite fluctuations in its value) the US was increasingly uncomfortable at the prospect of the dollar losing even its status as *numéraire*. When IATA considered denominating air fares in SDRs, not only did public authorities (the US Civil Aeronautics Board) raise objections, but the private US carrier Delta Air Lines also expressed reservations concerning SDR use.[112]

There were further indications that the US was crucially aware of the SDR's potential not only to become *numéraire*, but to become a substitute for the dollar. This was evident in 1969, even before SDRs had been allocated, when the initial SDR interest rate was being set. J. J. Polak admitted that among other reasons 1.5 per cent was agreed upon was '. . . mainly the result of the strong desire on the part of the United States. . . . to minimize competition with the U. S. dollar as a reserve asset.'[113] Quite plainly, although the Fund managing director had stressed only two years earlier that the SDR was to supplement and *not* supplant gold and foreign exchange,[114] some had become worried that this was precisely what could happen.

US reticence was expressed in new roles for the SDR being actively promoted by financial intermediaries. When private banks such as Banque Keyser Ullman en Suisse SA, Bankhaus Deak & Co. Ltd (Vienna), and Chase Manhattan offered transactions in SDR equivalents, again US policy makers blanched. The Federal Reserve Bank of New York requested that Chase Manhattan Bank 'delay initiation of the services in New York involving the use of the SDR as a unit while the services were being studied'.[115] Thus it was not only the way in which some IMF members used or advocated SDRs that revealed its potential substitutability for the dollar. Outside the Fund, this unease was also evident with respect to nascent interest in the marketplace.

2.8 Summary

Despite the decision not to allocate SDRs in 1973, the SDR was not yet an anachronism. What this chapter has demonstrated is that given the international monetary instability of the early 1970s, with the increases in private liquidity and moves to floating, the mechanisms surrounding SDRs—despite their limitations—worked surprisingly well. Despite a relatively low interest rate, and illiquidity, central banks accepted them willingly, in some cases in preference to existing reserve assets. Furthermore, they did not alter existing portfolio management policies by the authorities—indeed they tended to reinforce central bank reserve policies. Modifications to its method of valuation and interest rate were enacted smoothly, and the SDR was beginning to assume characteristics not initially envisioned—to which the Committee of Twenty gave further credence through its attempted endorsement of the SDR as primary reserve asset and its examination of proposals for a substitution account. But the C-20 was circumscribed from the beginning, largely because of the limitations of its terms of reference, and increasingly irreconcilable positions among its members. Nonetheless, at the time the Fund found in the SDR a means of focusing its reform initiatives once the SDR had demonstrated a sufficient acceptability amongst the membership. The increasing importance of the managing director, a growing bureaucracy, and a burgeoning literature and conferences on the SDR all reflected this.

In addition, the nascent acceptance of SDRs in the marketplace is revealing vis-à-vis the arguments pointing to the SDR's relative illiquidity as one reason for halting further allocations, or against increasing the role of SDRs in the international monetary system. Inherent technical difficulties with the SDR were less of a problem than their growing potential to evolve into a different instrument altogether. Further, while the tendency of the SDR to be used as a substitute for the dollar may have reflected weakness in the latter at the time, it did not point to problems customarily associated with an illiquid or irrelevant asset.

However, it would be wrong to assert that SDRs had succeeded in any broad sense either. They had not succeeded in their avowed purpose, namely to assist in the salvation of Bretton Woods arrangements. The fact that the SDR department at the IMF worked well, and that the C-20 and other reformers were advocating an increasing role for the SDR, flies in the face of international monetary developments moving away from a system that could easily accommodate this role. This reinforces the importance of taking into account the political and other developments that mitigated against a greater role for the SDR.

Balogh has written that SDRs had come 'too little, and a little late'[116] to save Bretton Woods. They had, however, established themselves relatively efficiently under trying circumstances. Conflict was looming, however, for their role in the post-Bretton Woods monetary system. Negotiations began in 1974, as soon as the Committee of Twenty published its report. Before we address these fascinating negotiations, however, it is the changes in US policy that now claim further attention.

Notes

1. John Williamson, *The Failure of World Monetary Reform, op. cit.*, p. 51. Susan Strange, in her examination of liquidity negotiations in the late 1960s, argued that the agreement to create SDRs '. . . was a compromise which left the major problems of the role of the dollar and of gold, the functioning of the adjustment process and the balance to be achieved in international monetary management between stability and liquidity, expansion and security, still undecided. It made no easier or harder the decision to substitute international for national monetary management.' (A. Shonfield (ed.), *International Economic Relations of the Western World 1959–71*, RIIA (London: 1976); Susan Strange, vol. 2, *International Monetary Relations, op. cit.*, p. 258.)
2. T. Balogh 'Old Fallacies and New Remedies: The SDRs in Perspective' *op. cit.*, p. 81. See also John Williamson, 'A New SDR Allocation?', IIE (Washington, DC: 1984), p. 3.
3. The reconstitution provision (abolished in 1981) stipulated that SDR holders had to hold 30 per cent of their total allocation over a five-year period.
4. Indeed the question of whether SDRs should be considered reserve assets at all (rather than drawing a more appropriate analogy to a line of credit) has been raised by one critic. See letter to the editor by K. Alec Chrystal, *Financial Times*, 28 July 1994, p. 10.
5. The 1970–2 period of allocation was known officially as the First Basic Period. Initially, periods of allocation were to be of five years' duration; prevailing international monetary instability during the late 1960s, however, prompted the managing director to propose a three-year allocation in 1969. See 'A Report to the Board of Governors of the International Monetary Fund Containing the Managing Director's Proposal on the Allocation of Special Drawing Rights for the First Basic Period', part II, section 5; 12 September 1969; reproduced in Garritsen de Vries, *The International Monetary Fund 1966–1971*, vol. 2, documents, pp. 251–65,
6. J. J. Polak, 'The Impasse Concerning the Role of the SDR', in Eizenga, Limburg, and Polak (eds), *The Quest for National and Global Economic Stability*, Kluwer (Dordrecht: 1988), p. 175.
7. Walter Habermeier (IMF Treasurer), 'Operations and Transactions in SDRs—The First Basic Period', IMF Pamphlet Series, No. 17, 1973, p. 5. The initial allocation, as has been mentioned, was 9.5 billion SDRs over three years. Habermeier notes that the actual figure allocated did not quite add up to the designated amount due to China opting out during the first basic period. (Nonetheless, because China was a participant in the SDR scheme, China's quota was included when the initial rate of allocations was decided.)
8. Ibid. p. 5.
9. J. Williamson, 'A New SDR Allocation?', *op. cit.*, pp. 9–10.
10. These estimates were shared by both Fund and academic observers. See *International Reserves: Needs and Availability*, IMF (Washington, DC: 1970).
11. 'Operations and Transactions in SDRs—The First Basic Period', IMF Pamphlet Series, No. 17, 1973, p. 6.
12. Ibid. p. 9. Industrial Europe was defined as comprising Austria, Belgium, Denmark, France, West Germany, Italy, Luxembourg, the Netherlands, Norway, and Sweden.

13. Ibid. p. 10.
14. Ibid.
15. Walter Habermeier, 'Operations and Transactions in SDRs—The First Basic Period', IMF Pamphlet Series, no. 17, 1973, p. 28. For a glossary of SDR terminology, see IMF *Survey*, 26 January 1981.
16. For an overall summary of SDR transactions from their inception until the early 1990s, see Chapter 6, Table 6.1, below.
17. 'Operations and Transactions in SDRs—The First Basic Period', IMF Pamphlet Series, No. 17, p. 15.
18. Joseph Gold, 'Special Drawing Rights—Character and Use', IMF Pamphlet Series, No. 13, 1970, p. 26.
19. Remarks by Secretary Fowler as Governor for the US, 1 October 1968 at Joint Annual discussion of Boards of Governors of the IMF & World bank. Reproduced in *1969 Annual Report of the Treasury*, exhibit 34, p. 295 (emphasis added).
20. *IMF Summary Proceedings, Annual Meeting 1968* (Washington: 1968), p. 25 (emphasis added).
21. 'Operations and Transactions in SDRs—The First Basic Period', IMF Pamphlet Series, No. 17, pp. 14–15.
22. 1.5 per cent was paid to holders of SDRs above their allocations and 1.5 per cent was charged to holders of SDRs below their allocations.
23. IMF *Articles of Agreement*—First Amendment edition (with typewritten palimpsests), IMF (Washington, DC: 1968). Article XXI, Section 2, p. 41.
24. Appendix C, Rules and Regulations: Original Rule 0–3, in Joseph Gold, 'Floating Currencies, Gold, and SDRs: Some Recent Legal Developments', IMF (Washington, DC: 1976), p. 84.
25. Joseph Gold, 'Floating Currencies, Gold, and SDRs—Some Recent Legal Developments', IMF Pamphlet Series, No. 19, p. 11.
26. J. J. Polak, 'Valuation and Rate of Interest of the SDR', IMF Pamphlet Series, No. 18 (Washington, DC: 1974), pp. 11–12. The '35 baskets' refer to the official price of gold (SDR 35 = 1 ounce of gold) under the First Amendment.
27. Ibid. p. 8. Polak also points out that the rate of 1.5 per cent already existed, '...having been established in 1961 as the rate that the Fund would pay when it borrowed under the General Arrangements to Borrow'.
28. Garritsen de Vries, *The International Monetary Fund 1972–1978, vol. 1, op. cit.*, p. 283. De Vries also notes that developing countries, net users of SDRs, also preferred a low interest rate for SDRs (p. 286).
29. J. J. Polak, 'Valuation and Rate of Interest of the SDR', IMF Pamphlet Series, No. 18 (1974), p. 20.
30. From 1981 SDR interest rates were 'expressed as an equivalent bond yield' for the relevant currency amount in an SDR of 1) the market yield for three-month US Treasury bills; 2) the three-month interbank deposit rate in Germany; 3) the three-month interbank money rate against private paper in France; 4) the discount rate on two-month (private) bills in Japan; and 5) the market yield for three-month UK Treasury bills. See Rule T—Interest, Charges, and Assessments in Respect of SDRs, 'By-Laws, Rules and Regulations', IMF (Washington, DC: 1986), pp. 65–6.

Rates of remuneration from 1 January 1979 to 31 January 1987 on the SDR varied between 85 and 100 per cent of the rate of interest. (See IMF *Annual Report 1984*, pp. 72–3, 84; and IMF *Annual Report 1989*, p. 77.)

31. Garritsen de Vries, *The International Monetary Fund 1972–1978, vol. II, op. cit.*, pp. 892–5.
32. Walter Habermeier, 'Operations and Transactions in SDRs—The First Basic Period', *op. cit.*, p. 39.
33. The reconstitution provision, as outlined by Article XXV (Section 6) and Schedule G of the First Amendment to the Fund's articles, stated that five years after the First Basic Period the average daily holdings of SDRs must be greater than 30 per cent of its allocation. The Fund had the power to force participants in the SDR Department to comply with this provision by using convertible currencies to obtain them (*Articles of Agreement of the International Monetary Fund—as modified by the Proposed Amendment*, IMF, 1968). With minor amendments this provision was incorporated into the Articles under the Second Amendment (Article XIX, Section 6 and Schedule G), although it was abolished in 1981. Its abolition was more easily facilitated following the reduction of the necessary majority voting power from 85 to 70 per cent under the Second Amendment (see also Chapter 5, below).
34. John Williamson, 'A New SDR Allocation?', *op. cit.*, pp. 39–40.
35. Article XXV, Section 5(a), IMF Articles of Agreement (First Amendment), p. 47.
36. Joseph Gold, 'Special Drawing Rights—Character and Use', IMF Pamphlet Series, No. 13 (1970), p. 65. According to Gold, the designation provision was originally included in the event of reluctance by members to accept SDRs.
37. Walter Habermeier, 'Operations and Transactions in SDRs—The First Basic Period', IMF Pamphlet Series, No. 17, p. 17.
38. Ibid. pp. 16–17. After this period, designation first increased following a change in Fund policy in March of 1977, whereby SDRs (as well as currencies) were increasingly provided from the General Resources Account to members. The practice of designation became less necessary, and rarer, in the mid-1980s, and was suspended in 1987. SDR recipients could then hold these SDRs or obtain foreign exchange, subject to the reconstitution provision.
39. J. J. Polak, 'The Impasse Concerning the Role of the SDR', *op. cit.*, p. 2.
40. 'The Role of the SDR in the International Monetary System', IMF Occasional Paper 51, March 1987, p. 7.
41. John Williamson, 'A New SDR Allocation?' IIE, March (Washington, DC: 1984), p. 10.
42. See Benjamin J. Cohen, 'International Reserves and Liquidity', in Peter Kenen (ed.), *International Trade and Finance—Frontiers for Research*, Cambridge University Press (Cambridge: 1975).
43. J. Williamson, 'Surveys in Applied Economics: International Liquidity', *op. cit.*
44. Ibid. p. 686.
45. See, for example H. Robert Heller and Mohsin S. Khan 'The Demand for International Reserves Under Fixed and Floating Exchange Rates' (IMF *Staff Papers* vol. XXV, 1978); and Rudolf R. Rhomberg 'Balance of Payments Financing and Reserve Creation' (IMF *Staff Papers* vol. XXXII, 1985).

46. *International Reserves: Needs and Availability*, IMF (Washington, DC: 1970); and G.M. von Furstenberg (ed.) *International Money and Credit: The Policy Roles*, IMF (Washington, DC: 1983).
47. See biblio on IMF publications. Internal Fund 'Departmental Memoranda' (DMs), and 'Staff Memoranda' (SMs) are not generally published, although many eventually appear in the *Staff Papers* series. The Fund has kindly made many of the relevant DMs and SMs available to this author (see Appendix 1).
48. DM/84/11, 'Demand for International Reserves and Effects of Reserve Increases on the World Economy: An Annotated Bibliography', IMF Research Department, Financial Studies Division, 22 February 1984.
49. DM/77/18 'Control over International Liquidity—A Summary of the Views Expressed by the Participants in the Fleming Memorial Conference', Research Department, Financial Studies Division, 28 February 1977.
50. Michael Mussa, Michael, James M. Boughton, and Peter Isard (eds), *The Future of the SDR in Light of Changes in the International Financial System—Proceedings of a Seminar held in Washington, D.C. March 18–19, 1996*, IMF (Washington, DC: 1996). Just over five years later, George Soros published a book advocating a resumption of SDR allocations that would be used largely for development purposes—a book that was widely reviewed at the time as promoting a worthy cause, but not realistic. See George Soros, *George Soros on Globalization*, Public Affairs—Perseus Books (Cambridge, MA: 2002).
51. H. Robert Keller and Mohsin S. Khan, 'The Demand for International Reserves Under Fixed and Floating Exchange Rates', IMF *Staff Papers*, vol. XXV (1978), p. 623.
52. R. Triffin, '"Europe and the Money Muddle" Revisited', *BNL Quarterly Review* No. 124, March 1978, pp. 55–6.
53. As outlined in Heller and Khan, 'The Demand for International Reserves Under Fixed and Floating Exchange Rates', IMF *Staff Papers*, vol. XXV, 1978, pp. 625–6.
54. See John Williamson, 'Exchange Rate Flexibility and Reserve Use', *Scandinavian Journal of Economics*, vol. 78, no. 2, 1976, pp. 327–39. Also Jacob Frenkel (former head of the Fund's research department) 'International Liquidity and Monetary Control', in *International Money and Credit: The Policy Roles*, G. M. von Furstenberg, (ed), IMF, 1983, pp. 65–109. These papers confirmed that, generally, patterns of reserve use and holdings in general remained relatively unchanged following the move to floating. With respect to developing countries, K. Alec Chrystal pointed out that during the 1970s the reserve-import ratio tended to fall for industrialized countries, and increase for developing countries. See 'International Liquidity and the Position of Developing Countries in the 1980s', in S. Dell (ed.), *The International Monetary System and its Reform, vol. II*, North-Holland for the UN (Amsterdam: 1987), pp. 370–2.

    Following work by Triffin and Harrod in the 1940s and 1950s, the reserve-import ratio was generally accepted as a measurement of reserve adequacy (see J. Williamson 'Surveys in Applied Economics: International Liquidity', *op. cit.*, pp. 688–9), although caveats and other alternatives do exist. (The most important of the former is that any such ratios are less important under a system of free capital movements.) Williamson acknowledges these in his article, as well as in 'A New SDR Allocation?' *op. cit.*, pp. 18–20.

55. *International Reserves: Needs and Availability*, IMF, 1970, pp. 500–1, as quoted in Williamson, *The Failure of World Monetary Reform, op. cit.*, p. 158. Williamson goes on to write that this poor estimate '. . . surely demonstrates that, if reserve growth is ever to be determined collectively in the IMF, an essential precondition is that control be established over forms of reserves other than SDRs' (p. 158).
56. See also John Williamson, 'A New SDR Allocation?', *op. cit.*, p. 33.
57. It is interesting to note that following SDR allocations in 2009, and as inflation has once again become a concern to international economists in 2011, the IMF has sponsored a study by Richard Cooper asking the question whether SDR creation is inflationary. After reviewing a number of scenarios, Cooper responds that '. . . the possible global inflationary impact of some increased import demand by developing countries following an allocation of SDRs will be fully neutralized by the monetary policies of the Federal Reserve, the European Central Bank, and other inflation-targeting central banks.' See Richard Cooper, 'Is SDR Creation Inflationary', http://www.imf.org/external/np/pp/eng/2011/010711a.pdf (accessed 6 June 2011).
58. Alexander Swoboda, 'Credit Creation in the Euromarket: Alternative Theories and Implications for Control', Group of Thirty Occasional Paper 2 (New York: 1980).
59. As he argued in his discussion of SDRs at the IMF sponsored conference on SDR-related issues: 'It is, of course, with fixed exchange rates that reserve levels determine, or at least influence, world inflation'. W. M. Corden, 'Is there an Important Role for the SDR?', in von Furstenberg, *International Money and Credit: The Policy Roles, op. cit.*, pp. 234–5.
60. W. M. Corden, *Inflation, Exchange Rates, and the World Economy—Lectures on International Monetary Economics*, Oxford University Press (Oxford: 1981), pp. 127–8.
61. R. Triffin, 'The Future of the International Monetary System', *BNL Quarterly Review*, March 1980, p. 37.
62. John Williamson wrote that the recognition of this fact was one of the reasons why the second SDR allocation was agreed to in his IIE study 'A New SDR Allocation?', *op. cit.*, p. 12.
63. See fn. 53, above.
64. Darrell Delamaide provides an account of this juggling act in Mexico in the months prior to August 1982. See D. Delamaide, *Debt Shock—The Full Story of the World Credit Crisis*, Lester & Orpen Dennys (Toronto: 1984).
65. In his booklet for the IIE promoting an SDR allocation of SDR 43 billion in 1985–6, Williamson makes the case that SDRs can add to reserves under flexible rates without stimulating inflationary pressures, maintaining that the increase in reserve assets lacks '. . . any counter part increase in the income, wealth, or liquidity of the private sector, as happens with every other form of reserve creation.' John Williamson, 'A New SDR Allocation?', *op. cit.*, p. 33. See also Richard Cooper, 'Is SDR Creation Inflationary?', *op. cit.*
66. G. Haberler, in IMF Research Department's 'Control over International Liquidity—A Summary of the Views Expressed by the Participants in the Fleming Memorial Conference' (DM/77/18), 28 February 1977, p. 3.

67. See, e.g. H. Robert Heller and Mohsin S. Khan 'The Demand for International Reserves Under Fixed and Floating Exchange Rates', *op. cit.*, pp. 623–5; K. Alec Chrystal, 'International Liquidity and the Position of Developing Countries' (*op. cit.*).

    A BIS study also found that although considerable intervention in the market place took place '... official intervention was predominantly of the stabilising kind and thereby put the burden of proof on those who, under the slogan "the market always knows best", claim the opposite'. See Helmut Mayer and Hiro Taguchi, 'Official Intervention in the Exchange Markets: Stabilising or Destabilising?', *BIS Economic Paper no. 6*, March 1983, p. 36. Empirical evidence was obtained from the UK, W. Germany, and Japan from 1974 to 1982.
68. *International Financial Statistics, Supplement Series no. 6*, 'Supplement on International Reserves', IMF (Washington: 1983), pp. 106–7. Access to private liquidity would tend to suggest that this ratio should fall—however in the 1960s, average reserves covered 9.3 weeks of imports, in the 1970s this rose to 10.8 weeks of imports.
69. 'Reserves and International Liquidity', Bank for International Settlements, Monetary and Economic Department. *BIS Economic Paper no. 22*, June 1988.
70. Mirroring a dilemma of national monetary authorities, another problem which would remain for a global authority would be the provision of an economically stagnant region with liquidity while restricting it in other (overheated) regions.
71. G. Kessler, 'The Need to Control International Bank Lending', *BNL Quarterly Review*, no. 132, March 1980, pp. 57–81. See also M. Aglietta (commentary) in *Europe, America and the World Economy*, L. Tsoukalis (ed.), Basil Blackwell (Oxford: 1986), pp. 260–4.
72. John Williamson, *The Failure of World Monetary Reform* (*op. cit.*); also see C. J. Morse, 'The Evolving Monetary System', an address to the International Monetary Conference in Williamsburg, Virginia, 7 June 1974. Morse also suggests that a 'lack of political will' was one of the reasons for the failure of the C-20, in IMF *Survey*, 17 June 1974. pp. 186–9.
73. Board of Governors Resolution No. 26–9, 1 October 1971; reprinted in de Vries, *The International Monetary System 1966–71, vol. II*, IMF (Washington: 1976), pp. 331–2.
74. Ibid. p. 331.
75. J. J. Polak, 'Reform of the International Monetary System', in M. Garritsen de Vries, *The International Monetary System, 1972–1978, vol. III* (documents), IMF (Washington: 1985). See pp. 3–17, 19–56, 151–3.
76. Ibid. pp. 151–3.
77. Ibid. p. 46.
78. Ibid. pp. 54–5.
79. Ibid. p. 47.
80. See Chapter 1, above. p. 12.
81. Resolution no. 27–10 of the Board of Governors of the IMF, 26/7/72, 'Establishment of a Committee on Reform of the International Monetary System and Related Issues' (C-20, *op. cit.*) para. 2(a), p. 230.
82. Ibid. para 2(b), p. 230

83. IMF Board of Governors Resolution no. 27–10, 26/7/72, 'Establishment of a Committee on Reform of the International Monetary System and Related Issues', as reprinted in IMF, *International Monetary Reform—Documents of the Committee of Twenty*, para. 3(a), p. 230.
84. Ibid. para 1(c), p. 230.
85. *International Monetary Reform—Documents of the Committee of Twenty* (IMF: 1974). Introductory note. p. vii. Williamson, in *The Failure of World Monetary Reform* (*op. cit.*) notes that up to five advisors assisted each constituent member. Observers from the EEC, UNCTAD, the OECD, GATT, the IBRD, and BIS were also present, in addition to senior Fund staff and their associates (of which Williamson was one). Williamson also observed that in fact Deputies meetings were not much less well attended than Committee meetings: about 180 attended the former, 70 of whom were entitled to speak (p. 68).
86. Statement by Anthony Barber, Governor for the UK, Summary Proceedings, IMF Annual Meeting, September 1971. (As Williamson wrote, this is what Robert Triffin had been pointing out for eleven years. See John Williamson, *The Failure of World Monetary Reform, op. cit.*, p. 55.)
87. Shultz statement at IMF Annual Meeting, September 1971, IMF *Summary Proceedings*.
88. 'Report to the Board of Governors of the International Monetary Fund by the Chairman of the Committee on Reform of the International Monetary System and Related Issues', 24 September 1973, reprinted in *International Monetary Reform—Documents of the Committee of Twenty, op. cit.*, pp. 227–8.
89. Ibid. p. 228.
90. Susan Strange, *International Monetary Relations, op. cit.*, p. 338. Schweitzer was not alone in being uninformed—Alfred Hayes, President of the New York Federal Reserve was not consulted before the August 1971 decisions either. (See Chapter 4, below. p. 141, n. 44.)
91. Jacobsson came to the IMF from the BIS and stamped his authority upon the Fund with some difficulty after the relatively passive tenure of the first two managing directors. His daughter and biographer noted that this was especially evident at the beginning of his term: 'If displeased, PJ was apt to lose his temper, pound tables, run round the room. At least once, to show his displeasure, he threw a document written by a Head of Department to the far corner of the room, in its author's presence; the staples came apart and sheets of paper scattered far and wide'. Erin E. Jacobsson, *A Life for Sound Money—Per Jacobsson, His Biography*, Clarendon Press (Oxford: 1979), p. 297. Ms Jacobsson went on to say, however, that after this period of sometimes traumatic adjustment, Fund staff were proud of '. . . the old man's' achievement in putting the IMF firmly on the map.'

    Others authors have echoed this assessment; W. M. Scammell has gone so far as to say that during the late 1950s and early 1960s the Fund '. . . . was brought by an able Executive Director [*sic*] into the centre of affairs'. W. M. Scammell, *The Stability of the International Monetary System*, Macmillan (Basingstoke: 1987), p. 143.
92. Margaret Garritsen de Vries, *International Monetary Fund, 1972–78, vol II, op. cit.*, pp. 1003–4.
93. M. Garritsen de Vries, *The IMF in a Changing World, op. cit.*, p. 93.

94. Margaret Garritsen de Vries, *The IMF 1972–1978—vol II: Cooperation on Trial*, IMF (Washington, DC: 1985), p. 1003.
95. See Chapter 1, p. 32.
96. Margaret Garritsen de Vries, *The IMF 1972–1978, op. cit., vol II*, p. 1003.
97. Ibid. p. 1003. See also John Williamson, *The Failure of World Monetary Reform, op. cit.*, p. 58.
98. Susan Strange, *Casino Capitalism*, Basil Blackwell Ltd, (Oxford: 1986), p. 42.
99. For example, in his autobiography, Denis Healey wrote: 'It was said that the... Managing Director, a world-weary Frenchman called Schweitzer, had kept a parrot in the atrium which he trained to say 'SDRs—up your ass'. Its words are still echoing there.' Denis Healey, *The Time of My Life*, Michael Joseph (London: 1989), p. 416. This is almost certainly apocryphal: while parrots have been kept in the OAS building, there were never parrots at the IMF.
100. *Committee of Twenty—Outline of Reform, op. cit.*, Preface, p. 7.
101. J. Williamson, *The Failure of World Monetary Reform, op. cit.*, p. 73.
102. *Committee of Twenty—Outline of Reform, op. cit.*, para. 31, p. 18.
103. Schedule D, *IMF Articles of Agreement* (after second amendment) (Washington, DC: 1978), p. 87. And the C-20 was replaced by the Interim Committee upon the publication of its Outline of Reform in 1974, which was itself replaced by the International Monetary and Financial Committee (IMFC), with a similar mandate, in 1999.
104. *Committee of Twenty—Outline of Reform, op. cit.*, para. 33, p. 19.
105. Ibid. paras. 24–7, pp. 15–16.
106. John Williamson, *The Failure of World Monetary Reform, op. cit.* p. 175.
107. Burns' natural inclinations to avoid closing the gold window in August 1971, and to support intervention in the exchange markets in 1973, were over-ridden by John Connally in the first instance, and a growing realization that there was growing support among private intermediaries in the US for floating exchange rates in the second. See John Odell, *US International Monetary Policy, op. cit.*, pp. 259–60, 320–1.
108. Paul Volcker and Toyoo Gyohten, *Changing Fortunes, op. cit.*, p. 114.
109. *New York Times*, 25 May 1975, p. 18.
110. See Chronology, above, p. xx.
111. *Petroleum Intelligence Weekly*, 16 June 1975, p. 4. As quoted in Joseph Gold, 'Floating Currencies, Gold, and SDRs—Some Recent Legal Developments', IMF Pamphlet No. 19, 1976, pp. 48–9.
112. Joseph Gold, 'Floating Currencies, Gold, and SDRs—Some Recent Legal Developments', *op. cit.*, pp. 50–1.
113. J. J. Polak, 'Valuation and Rate of Interest of the SDR', IMF Pamphlet Series, No. 18 (1974), pp. 7–8.
114. See p. 50, above.
115. Joseph Gold, 'Floating Currencies, Gold, and SDRs—Some Recent Legal Developments', *op. cit.*, p. 71.
116. See fn. 2, p. 45, above.

3

The influence of US policy on the SDR under post-Bretton Woods arrangements

3.1 Introduction

During the 1970s it became impossible to speak meaningfully of changes in prospects for the Special Drawing Right (SDR) without speaking of US policy. Aside from the Fund, the US was increasingly the key determinant of what transpired with respect to the SDR. As we saw in the last chapter, the US was somewhat concerned about the SDR's attractiveness both in the marketplace and in the international policy dialogue. This disquiet boded ill for the SDR, and we now shift our emphasis slightly to focus more intently upon the US. Continuing our previous line of enquiry, which emphasized the importance of international and European initiatives, simply does not capture what happened once the Bretton Woods system broke down—at least with respect to the SDR. Of course it will be impossible not to relate our examination of the US back to international monetary arrangements in general. However, our investigation will be much more successful if we acknowledge the increasing importance of the US with respect to the SDR and also to approaches for international monetary management.

While the US had power over the ultimate success of initiatives, this did not always manifest itself in clear policy direction. The lack of concrete policy direction, understandable at a time of great change in international monetary relations, is the focus of our investigation in this chapter, particularly as it manifested itself through the policies of the US administration. As we noted in the introduction, this represents a slight shift in approach to one that focuses on the influence of the state and state structures in international relations.[1] Until now, we have been inclined to emphasize the importance of international institutions in the international system (particularly the role of the International Monetary Fund (IMF) in international monetary relations), and we will return to this approach in Chapters 5 and 6.[2] In looking at US international monetary policy, however, which had such an influence on post-Bretton Woods international monetary arrangements, we are inevitably led to examine the US administration and role of key individuals within it in more detail. Our emphasis on the US administration in this chapter (particularly the Treasury, but also the State Department where relevant) is incomplete, however, without Chapter 4, which integrates this approach with a broader examination of other structural influences on US international monetary policy formulation, such as the changing role of Congress, the Federal Reserve, as well as the influence of changing international monetary conditions on these actors.

We will begin with an examination of waning US enthusiasm for the SDR and other formalized arrangements in the early 1970s. Before we do this, however, we must at least briefly address how the EC addressed SDRs during the 1970s. While we have set out from the beginning to concentrate on the US and the Fund, we need to address why this became an increasingly valid approach in the 1970s. It could be argued that the EC warrants more attention; after all we examined each of the main EC protagonists during the 1960s in Chapter 1 when the precursors to the Rio Agreement were examined. Also, US international monetary diplomacy itself continued to be almost solely concerned with its G10 partners, all but two of which were European. It was this European predominance in the G10, however, that preoccupied the US, and in the early 1970s the US sought a less European dominated and more inclusive forum in which to express its views on international monetary matters.[3] By default, this became the Fund-inspired C-20, and later the Interim Committee and International Monetary and Financial Committee, as well as non-Fund institutions such as the G20. Within all these groups, European influence and interest with respect to international monetary issues, including the SDR, diminished.

3.2 Europe and SDRs in the post-Bretton Woods Era

As our investigation into the marginalization of SDRs progresses, we have chosen to narrow our focus to that of the US and the Fund. In some respects this is simply more practical, for evolving European foreign economic policy is a vast subject. But through the 1970s it was also increasingly evident that Europe had in fact turned away from the SDR. We have noted that, in the 1960s, the Rio Agreement was partly a result of US and European compromise. As the Bretton Woods Agreement broke down, it was possible to characterize the debate over SDRs as a largely 'anti-SDR' US versus a 'pro-SDR' Europe, as Williamson did. This was not true for long, however, and also confuses European policy concerning a fixed exchange rate system with their less discernable approach to the SDR. A less controversial observation is that as the 1970s progressed Europe became less able to speak with one voice with respect to SDRs, and hence to influence international monetary policy towards it.

The European position with respect to SDRs changed because of developments in Europe itself. In effect, the success of first the EEC, then EC, and today the EU in the international arena paradoxically resulted in a new preoccupation with intra-European relationships in this same arena.[4] The resultant changes were crucially important for the focus of international monetary initiatives emanating from the EC in the post-Bretton Woods era. On the international monetary plane in the 1970s Europe simply changed focus away from the SDR—continued academic interest notwithstanding.[5] The limited success of the grand neo-functionalist experiment in Europe naturally led to further attention to intra-European initiatives, both to consolidate these initiatives and to establish an institutional framework whereby these successes could blossom further.

Second, intra-European monetary differences seemed to be thrown into sharpest relief at the Fund: German policy, for example, became hostile to SDR initiatives, fearing inflationary pressures, whereas Italy and France were much more sanguine about international monetary prospects with a greater role for SDRs.

Third, the EC as a collection of still sovereign states was becoming frustrated to some degree with truly global monetary initiatives. After all the US still enjoyed an effective veto over fundamental change in the IMF, even though the EC as a collectivity now had a greater percentage of voting rights at the Fund. It also seemed that European concerns were lost among domestic US concerns in Washington, and that the diplomatic energy required to ensure that its views were considered (with respect to exchange rate policies, for example) was often not commensurate with the results attained. In any case the success of the EC did not lend itself to increased power, or, arguably, even increased influence on international monetary initiatives.

The EC and its member governments still cared passionately about the dollar and its relative strength, but this was only in so far as it affected the EC; it was not a systemic concern in itself. As Kenneth King wrote in a Chatham House study:

> Nor, of course, are the major European monetary authorities particularly internationalist in their thinking. What they object to most strongly is the impact of US policies on the management of their respective economies. . . . They would welcome the opportunity to influence US monetary policy so that in its repercussions abroad it took greater account of their problems.[6]

EC policy thus became more preoccupied with policies over which it had more immediate influence. While the EC lost interest in the grand design schemes for international monetary reform, however, it did not ignore other extra-

Community international relations over which it had more influence. One of the most important results of heightened EC activity in this sphere was the negotiation of the Lomé Convention, an early trade treaty between EC members and most of their former colonies.[7] In retrospect it is evident that a strong independent strain in the US international monetary policy, coupled with an increasing self-preoccupation within the EC in the 1970s, did not lend itself well to successful global monetary initiatives. Rather these phenomena contributed in part to what business theorists identified in the 1980s as a 'Triad' of global economic powers whose influence was increasingly regional: Europe, the US, and Japan.[8]

It is not as if interest in ideas surrounding public liquidity provision diminished, as continued intra-European initiatives demonstrated. Jacques Polak noted with some concern the implications of these new European monetary arrangements in an internal document for the IMF in 1979.[9] While his study acknowledged that EMS arrangements were not analogous to liquidity provision at the Fund, he cautioned that, with respect to the supply of liquidity to the international monetary system in general, the EC seemed to be providing considerable short- and medium-term financial assistance to its members at the inception of the EMS, which was 'generous in comparison with the agreement, laboriously arrived at just previously, to increase IMF quotas by 50 per cent'.[10] While Polak stressed that this did not suggest 'that EC members have a closed mind to the needs of other members',[11] it may be inferred that the EC had found it more compelling to institute financial mechanisms for a European system rather than to promote increased quotas or the allocation of SDRs for the system as a whole. In addition, this begs the question of whether the rest of the Community would have been successful in persuading Germany to support them on SDRs. In any event, the lack of success in influencing US attitudes and policies contributed to the EC turning away from global initiatives.

Signs of European disinterest appeared immediately after the demise of the Smithsonian Agreement. In 1973, at the first conference of the International Center for Monetary and Banking Studies in Geneva, some of the papers presented on Europe and the system did address SDRs—though in turn, these tended to be presented by Americans.[12] Even at this early stage, when the C-20 was only half way through its deliberations, the conference moved to a discussion of European monetary integration and then international capital flows. More notably, by 1977, at a conference on US–European monetary relations sponsored by the American Enterprise Institute and attended by senior officials from both sides of the Atlantic, there was no published discussion of SDRs at all.[13] A similar conference in 1986 echoed this silence on SDRs, although this did not apply at Fund-sponsored events.[14] The frustration that Europe felt with respect to international monetary initiatives was succinctly captured in 1990 by Denis Healey, chairman of the IMF Interim Committee meetings between 1977 and 1979, who observed with some frustration that '...no change could be made in the structure of world finance without the consent of the United States'.[15]

Changing US attitudes towards the SDR thus remained crucial to its further development. The influence of the US was paramount at the Fund and in the international monetary arena as a whole, as both policy makers and academics have noted. Importantly, this was as true for international monetary arrangements in the 1970s as it was in the 1960s, increased interdependence notwithstanding. Following his comments on European monetary interests in the international arena, Kenneth King also wrote of the continued influence and importance of US monetary policy and international initiatives:

> US monetary policy determines world monetary policy. The scale of the US and Eurodollar markets dwarfs all other financial markets.
>
> Even under a regime of floating exchange rates other countries have been unwilling or unable to insulate themselves against the rapid changes in US interest rates and the strength of the dollar.[16]

He goes on to say that this relationship is neither obvious to, nor deemed desirable in, the US. There has been a whole branch of international relations literature devoted to whether or not this US monetary power and influence is monolithic (much of it in the debate over the pervasiveness of US hegemony). It is not the intention to enter this debate, which has in any case polarized on transatlantic lines. However it should be pointed out that the failure of international monetary reform should not be seen as a manifestation of weak political will on the part of the US, as Williamson does. Much to the exasperation of the Europeans, the US increasingly promoted a more market-oriented system in which US interests were less constrained than under a more managed system.[17]

It was not only observers such as Jacques Polak at the Fund who had observed that Europe was turning away from interest in global initiatives—there was at least one candid admission from within Europe that concentration on the EMS and ECU and then Euro almost necessitated less emphasis on the SDR. While a successful ECU or Euro *and* a successful SDR are not mutually exclusive, the Dutch central bank argued in its annual report in 1984 that this could indeed be the case:

> Promotion of the ECU as a new reserve currency will inevitably be detrimental to the cause of the SDR...
>
> In summary, do we regard the ECU as the future common currency of Europe, as a substitute for the national currencies? Or do we see it as one of the world's reserve currencies, contrary to our earlier intention to replace these reserve currencies by the SDR? It seems desirable to discuss this choice frankly and openly:

> The 'Europeans' among the politicians should not evade this discussion with their more 'world-oriented' colleagues.[18]

While European experience with the ECU and Euro lies largely outside our field of enquiry, the Dutch central bank's observation is a revealing illustration of the existence of a shift between internationalist concerns and a European preoccupation in Europe. And despite flashes of interest, European attention towards the SDR most certainly did not lead to any important successful initiative.

Whatever the extent of European influence on the Fund and its SDR progeny, the fact is that official European interest in the question had declined dramatically following the C-20's demise in 1974. US interest declined as well but, perhaps surprisingly, neither as completely nor as quickly. Henceforth, the US–European discussion about SDRs that did take place largely occurred at the Fund. This remains important to our investigation, and we will examine it in future chapters on the Second Amendment and second SDR allocation. Nonetheless, it is evident that Europe turned away from the SDR in the 1970s, so much so that it occasionally provoked comment from outsiders.[19]

Thus our attention turns back to that of the Fund and the US, which we pointed out would be the focus of our investigation at the outset. In the 1970s, despite the lack of successful initiatives at the Fund, the SDR periodically enjoyed academic and policy interest in the US. In one respect this interest may be seen to be because of the Fund's continuing interest in its progeny and the IMF's physical presence in Washington—Keynes' cautions about the Fund being an appanage of the US government taking an ironic twist. In any case, the history of the SDR and its gradual demise during the 1970s is most intertwined with that of the US and the IMF.

Thus our focus for the remainder of this chapter will be on the US, and centres on the change in US policy, with minor exceptions, to becoming an opponent of SDRs. It is also important to examine how the politics of international monetary relations *within* the US administration affected prospects for the SDR.

3.3 Waning US Enthusiasm for the SDR and Other Formalized Post-Bretton Woods Arrangements

When President Nixon, in a now famous burst of hyperbole, announced that the new Smithsonian Agreement was the greatest monetary agreement in the history of the world, behind the scenes there was already a sense that it would not last long. As Paul Volcker wrote: 'what was lacking was the sense of commitment necessary to make it all work'.[20] In fact it was remarkable how quickly enthusiasm waned for a fixed rate system and the original role of SDRs in supporting it. This was particularly so with respect to US policy, for a period of waning support in the early 1970s followed a very high degree of enthusiasm with respect to the SDR within all branches of the US government. The key purpose of the remainder of this chapter will be to examine this change from proponent to opponent, and then, briefly, to proponent again.

Let us review this early enthusiasm. In a 1968 press release, the US Treasury proudly announced that it was the first major industrial nation to approve SDRs officially.[21] The US Treasury Secretary, Henry Fowler, went further at the annual Joint Fund–World Bank meeting to encourage other nations to ratify the Rio Agreement as quickly as possible, so that the following year (1969) the Fund could 'consider the activation of the facility to provide supplementary reserves in the years ahead'.[22] He went on to note that the new SDR facility enjoyed wide support amongst a broad cross-section of economists, academics, and monetary officials, and more importantly, wide and enthusiastic bipartisan support in the Congress.[23] Lisle Widman, in an insider's account of international monetary policy formulation within the US Treasury, recounts how smoothly the Special Drawing Rights Act moved through Congress in 1968, 'despite allowing an international institution to create money'.[24] His account also provides a simple explanation of how easily international monetary policy then proceeded from the executive to the administrative branch of the US government:

> [The Bill]...was presented as a technique for reducing the threat to the U.S. international payments position, and therefore of special benefit to the United States. It moved through the Congress with unusual rapidity and little opposition despite the fact that a presidential election was under way. President Johnson transmitted the request for legislation April 30, 1968. Fowler testified before the House Banking and Currency Committee on May 1 and the House approved the bill ten days later. After review by the Senate Foreign Relations Committee, it was approved by the full Senate on June 6, six weeks from the date of the request.[25]

The belief that the SDR would supplement the dollar and thereby relieve the pressure on the dollar was largely accepted at the time. As international monetary affairs increasingly entered the political domain in the late 1970s, however, this relatively acquiescent attitude of Congress did not continue. As we shall see, the waning of Congressional support for SDRs, and Congressional incursion into what the administrative branch considers its foreign policy domain in the 1970s, was an increasingly important stumbling block to further initiatives. This was as true for the monetary system as it was for the international trading environment.[26]

It is paradoxical that despite avowed US policy objectives, American banks succeeded in furthering the internationalization of capital markets that contributed to destabilizing Bretton Woods and contributed indirectly to reform initiatives. These phenomena also acted as a catalyst to the politicization of monetary issues by drawing attention to the spectacular growth of Euromarkets. Hindsight allows us to observe that, if only for this reason, attempts at upholding Bretton Woods through the addition of an official source of liquidity through SDRs were insufficient to halt the moves towards an explosion of liquidity provision by unofficial sources (see Table 3.1 below).

It is also important to recognize here too that this Euromarket liquidity was made available under different institutional auspices and under different conditions (the poorest credit risks, for instance, would be largely ignored by the private market as they always had been) but also that the very nature of these reserves (i.e. borrowed vs. owned) had changed (see Table 3.2). This served to make the nebulous concept of liquidity that much more fungible, which would also have negative implications for the SDR in the 1970s. While the change from proponent to opponent of SDRs was coincident with the move from fixed to flexible exchange rates, and, even more importantly, the move from public to private responsibility for liquidity provision, this is not the only explanation for the shifting US stance. It is also important in the context of the growing divergence between reform initiatives and international monetary changes which were having such an influence on US policy.

We have already mentioned US difficulties with the IMF's managing director Schweitzer and the direction of reform negotiations. Other dissention also began to manifest itself in this relationship. Following the Nixon shocks, the persistent US encouragement of other countries to revalue was not only based on an antipathy to devalue vis-à-vis gold. Some were becoming increasingly uneasy about the role of the SDR—and its possible gold-like qualities. We have already seen signs of this, and a not incidental effect could have also served to increase the role of the IMF in international monetary management. If the dollar was devalued, the price of the SDR in terms of the dollar would increase. Again, this could have given further credibility to the SDR as a potential substitute for the dollar (despite its prevailing low interest rate) rather than a support for it. We saw in Chapter 2 that there were nascent signs of this in the very early 1970s—as a few on both sides of the Atlantic had initially presaged. This was realized before fixed parities had been abandoned—but even after generalized floating the SDR assumed some of the attributes upon which many of the plans for international monetary reform were hinged.

Thus, the US was beginning to realize that it had less of a stake in reform plans. This was especially true if they restricted the US's ability to pursue a more independent monetary policy. At this stage Jack Bennett, first Deputy Assistant Secretary for International Affairs at the US Treasury (1969–70), and then Deputy Under Secretary for Monetary Affairs (1971–5), became

Year	SDRs			Reserve Position in the Fund			Foreign Echange			Gold		
	Amount	Period to Period % Change	Percent Share in Total Reserves	Amount	Period to Period % Change	Percent Share in Total Reserves	Amount	Period to Period % Change	Percent Share in Total Reserves	Amount	Period to Period % Change	Percent Share in Total Reserves
1951				1.71		3.51	13.47		27.62	33.58		68.87
1952				1.78	3.78	3.60	13.99	3.87	28.33	33.62	0.11	68.07
1953				1.89	6.41	3.68	15.35	9.71	29.91	34.09	1.39	66.41
1954				1.85	−2.47	3.48	16.45	7.18	31.03	34.72	1.87	65.49
1955				1.88	1.90	3.50	16.73	1.70	31.12	35.16	1.25	65.39
1956				2.28	21.18	4.07	17.77	6.21	31.79	35.86	1.99	64.14
1957				2.31	1.53	4.10	17.05	−4.05	30.21	37.08	3.41	65.69
1958				2.56	10.59	4.45	17.08	0.16	29.76	37.82	1.99	65.83
1959				3.25	27.08	5.69	16.11	−5.66	28.20	37.76	−0.50	66.11
1960				3.57	9.86	5.95	18.49	14.79	30.83	37.92	0.41	63.22
1961				4.16	16.48	6.70	19.13	3.46	30.84	38.75	2.20	62.46
1962				3.80	−8.74	6.04	19.90	3.99	31.66	39.16	1.05	62.30
1963				3.94	3.83	5.89	22.69	14.03	33.94	40.22	2.70	60.16
1964				4.16	5.46	6.01	24.22	6.74	35.05	40.72	1.24	58.93
1965				5.38	29.39	7.55	24.02	−0.83	33.75	41.78	2.60	58.70
1966				6.33	17.74	8.69	25.70	7.00	35.29	40.80	−2.34	56.02
1967				5.75	−9.20	7.71	29.41	14.44	39.43	39.42	−3.37	52.86
1968				6.49	12.88	8.34	32.59	10.80	41.87	38.76	−1.69	49.80
1969				6.73	3.66	8.54	33.07	1.48	41.99	38.95	0.50	49.47
1970	3.12		3.35	7.70	14.43	8.25	45.47	37.49	48.72	37.03	−4.94	39.68
1971	5.87	88.05	4.75	6.35	−17.48	5.13	75.55	66.16	61.04	36.00	−2.78	29.08
1972	8.69	47.86	5.89	6.33	−0.42	4.29	96.75	28.07	65.62	35.69	−0.85	24.20
1973	8.81	1.39	5.74	6.17	−2.47	4.02	102.79	6.25	66.95	35.78	0.25	23.30
1974	8.86	0.58	4.89	8.84	43.39	4.88	127.76	24.29	70.52	35.71	−0.20	19.71
1975	8.76	−1.06	4.47	12.62	42.73	6.44	138.88	8.70	70.86	35.66	−0.15	18.20
1976	8.66	−1.24	3.87	17.74	40.50	7.93	161.77	16.48	72.32	35.50	−0.44	15.87
1977	78.13	−6.04	3.06	18.09	1.99	6.80	203.77	25.96	76.59	36.02	1.48	13.54
1978	8.11	−0.28	2.86	14.84	−17.97	5.24	224.17	10.01	79.08	36.29	0.74	12.80
1979	12.48	53.87	4.06	11.76	−20.75	3.83	249.86	11.46	81.34	33.06	−8.91	10.76
1980	11.81	−5.37	3.33	16.84	43.16	4.74	293.12	17.32	82.55	33.33	0.84	9.39
1981	16.41	38.98	4.43	21.32	26.66	5.76	299.01	2.01	80.80	33.30	−0.09	9.00
1982	17.75	8.12	4.86	25.46	19.38	6.97	288.61	−3.48	79.08	33.15	−0.47	9.08

Notes: 1. Gold valued at SDR 35/oz., including as a component of total reserves. 2. Percent changes and percent shares based on amounts in SDRs

Source: IMF International Financial Statistics, Supplement Series no. 6: 'Supplement on International Reserves', Washington, 1983

Table 3.2. G10 reserve holdings with foreign exchange component, 1973–82

	SDR million							
	1973		1976		1979		1982	
	Reserves	Foreign Exchange Component	Reserves	Foreign Exchange Component	Reserves	Foreign Exchange Component	Reserves	Foreign Exchange Component
US	11,919	7	15,767	275	15,170	2,890	29,918	9,257
UK	5,368	3,916	3,641	2,302	15,626	14,022	11,904	8,769
Switzerland	7,063	4,151	11,183	8,018	15,391	12,269	16,930	13,544
France	7,070	3,088	8,373	3,767	16,212	12,222	17,850	13,230
Netherlands	5,427	2,740	6,358	3,025	7,301	4,911	10,723	7,852
Belgium	4,227	1,632	4,480	1,793	5,329	3,132	4,757	2,560
Germany	27,497	20,787	29,954	21,958	43,225	35,942	43,909	35,917
Italy	5,335	1,808	5,727	2,762	16,149	13,128	15,107	11,431
Sweden	2,097	1,699	2,144	1,603	2,880	2,314	3,397	2,802
Canada	4,782	3,266	4,995	2,945	2,944	1,426	3,428	2,324
Japan	10,151	8,458	14,292	11,949	15,667	12,417	22,001	17,380
Total	90,936	51,552	106,914	60,397	155,894	11,4673	17,9924	12,5066

Notes: 1. Residual is mostly gold (priced at SDR35/oz), plus IMF tranches. 2. See also Tables 1.3 and 1.4
Source: *International Financial Statistics*—supplement series no. 6: 'Supplement on International Reserves', IMF, 1983

increasingly convinced that floating rates would essentially allow the US to continue to pursue its policies of non-intervention in the exchange markets—to the benefit of the US and the international system.[27] With respect to the SDR, Bennett argued that while he was at the Treasury in the early to mid-1970s (a crucially important time for the SDR), it was never an important part of US international monetary policy; instead Bennett viewed it as mainly a means of providing limited finance to developing countries.[28] Growing US antipathy towards the asset in some quarters, however, suggests that US concerns were more deep-rooted.

The growing US disenchantment with a fixed rate system and the role that SDRs might play in defending it intensified after the failure of the Smithsonian Agreement to hold. Within 18 months the US again had to devalue the dollar by increasing the price of gold in February 1973 to $42.2 per ounce. Partly because of increasingly liquid Eurocurrency markets, this did not halt exchange rate pressures, so that within a month the so-called Volcker Agreement, made in February, had also broken down.[29] The next month, foreign exchange markets continued to haemorrhage, the market price of gold hit $90 per ounce, and on 1 March European foreign exchange markets were closed for two weeks.

Shortly thereafter, the Paris Agreement was negotiated among the G10 plus the remaining four EC countries, which ostensibly jointly ensured 'an orderly exchange rate system'.[30] In fact, however, by then Canada, Japan, Italy, Britain, and Switzerland had floating currencies, and the members of the

European 'snake' (Germany, France, Benelux, and Denmark, as well as Sweden and Norway) continued their joint float with varying degrees of success until the official abandonment of the Werner Plan for European Monetary Union in 1977.[31] It was becoming evident that, temporarily at least, the Paris Agreement had approved a de facto floating exchange rate system. Even before the conference had taken place on 16 March 1973, Helmut Schmidt acknowledged as much by admitting that the most recent currency floating meant the 'end of Bretton Woods'.[32] Although the actual number of currencies floating was small, by 1975 eighteen floating countries (including the seven European currencies floating jointly) accounted for 70 per cent of trade flows among the IMF's membership.[33]

Within the short 15 months or so of the Smithsonian Agreement's existence, it also became evident that the move to private responsibility for liquidity provision obviated the immediate need for the US administration to assume the same degree of responsibility for strong and overt international liquidity management following the breakdown of Bretton Woods. This was at least partially reflected in the increased US political emphasis on international adjustment. Adjustment—inevitably of other surplus countries—had never been far from US concerns. Indeed even as the first SDRs were being allocated in 1970, the Council of Economic Advisors (yet another part of the US bureaucracy supporting SDRs in its earliest incarnation) chose to emphasize that the creation of SDRs would aid in allowing nations 'more time to redress their balance-of-payments disequilibria in an orderly fashion'.[34] When it appeared that SDRs were not helping in this regard, and when the Smithsonian Agreement broke down, US policy makers were free to emphasize the importance of individual country (as opposed to systemically generated) adjustment as well as to downplay liquidity issues.[35]

It is perhaps not surprising that, in a flexible exchange rate world when Euromarkets flush with petrodollars provided liquidity, pressure on the US administration to take responsibility for liquidity provision also dissipated. Again, as Guido Carli, the Governor of the Bank of Italy, put it in the 1976 Per Jacobsson Lecture at the IMF:

> The private banking system took over the functions proper to an official institution possessed of the power to finance balance-of-payments disequilibria through credit-granting and to create international liquidity.... The function of creating international liquidity has been transferred from official institutions to private ones.[36]

Inevitably this also had a bearing on the marginalization of what was inherently an asset that was created to enhance public liquidity provision, and at a time when the US was not oblivious to the market opportunities for US banks under the new system. And, not incidentally, at the time it took just over a year for the domestic controls established at the time of the Nixon 'shocks' in August 1971 (including mandatory wage and price controls) to be dismantled.

As the new international monetary arrangements consolidated themselves, the accompanying move from public to private responsibility for liquidity provision removed the primary raison d'être for the SDR, at least as initially constituted. While SDRs did not disappear once Bretton Woods broke down, the original impetus behind them shifted so that SDRs became associated with reform initiatives rather than the preservation of existing arrangements. This shift also contributed to waning US support. We have already seen in the last chapter that the SDR mechanisms worked as well as could be expected, and yet US policy makers were quietly apprehensive about the prospect for a greater role for the SDR. In addition, under a flexible rate system an internationally managed reserve asset seemed clumsy and unwieldy; the flexibility of burgeoning Euromarkets and the availability of borrowed rather than owned reserves (see Table 3.2) made SDRs as initially constituted seem part of a monetary system that had failed. By the beginning of 1973, with both business and labour complaining, Nixon signalled a shift in policy towards the market by the rapid dismantling of controls that was echoed by the promotion and appointment of officials sympathetic to a floating dollar.[37] In addition, private liquidity provision also reduced the absolute *necessity* of public international agreement to provide liquidity, aside from for the 'non-creditworthy'.

Table 3.3. Deposit bank's total foreign assets, 1971–86

	US$ billion		
	Industrial Countries	Developing Countries	Total
1971	183.73	24.65	208.38
1972	226.46	37.05	263.52
1973	324.08	55.00	379.08
1974	389.26	86.19	475.45
1975	455.09	120.09	575.18
1976	543.77	177.11	720.88
1977	663.01	227.43	890.43
1978	883.92	296.07	1179.98
1979	1122.70	359.37	1482.06
1980	1358.72	465.09	1823.81
1981	1599.84	583.80	2183.64
1982	1732.19	631.30	2363.49
1983	1785.56	664.01	2449.57
1984	1830.23	692.24	2522.46
1985	2206.44	764.22	2970.66
1986	2820.46	910.88	3731.33

Note: Tables 3.3 and 3.4 for comparative purposes only

Source: *International Financial Statistics*, Supplement Series no. 14 on International Liquidity, 1987

Table 3.4. Total currency claims of BIS reporting banks and BIS estimates of total net international bank lending, 1973–90

	US$ billion			
	Foreign Currency Claims	Domestic Currency Claims	Total Currency Claims	Net International Bank Claims
1973	247.6	49.0	296.6	-
1974	282.5	78.4	360.8	220.0
1975	342.9	99.4	442.4	260.0
1976	418.4	129.6	549.5	330.0
1977 I	503.1	153.9	657.1	405.0
1977 II	514.3	175.5	689.8	435.0
1978	659.7	233.5	893.2	530.0
1979	828.9	282.1	1111.0	665.0
1980	980.0	341.9	1321.9	810.0
1981	1124.8	425.4	1550.2	945.0
1982	1135.9	558.6	1694.5	1020.0
1983 I	1186.7	570.4	1757.1	1085.0
1983 II	1527.3	570.6	2097.9	1240.0
1984 I	1565.1	586.4	2151.5	1280.0
1984 II	1573.9	586.5	2160.4	1280.0
1985	1881.4	692.9	2574.3	1420.0
1986	2374.4	903.1	3277.5	1735.0
1987	3039.9	1168.0	4207.9	2185.0
1988	3287.1	1233.3	4520.4	2545.0
1989 I	3770.4	1370.0	5140.4	2905.0
1989 II	3954.2	1401.1	5355.3	2920.0
1990 I	4703.0	1555.8	6258.8	3530.0
1990 II	4712.4	1559.4	6271.8	3535.0

Notes: 1. Above figures include banks in the European reporting area as well as in Canada, Japan, the US, and offshore branches of US banks in the Bahamas, Cayman Islands, Panama, Hong Kong, and Singapore. 2. Austria, Denmark, and Ireland are not included until 1977. 1977 II: Finland, Norway, and Spain are not included until 1977. 1983 II: Offshore branches of non-US banks until this time. Other differences between 'I' and 'II' due to minor changes in time series. 3. Net international bank lending column is total claims (column 3), less BIS estimates of interbank deposits. 4. Tables 3.3 and 3.4 for comparative purposes only

Source: BIS Annual Reports, BIS 'International Banking and Financial Market Developments' (Oct. 85 issue) (see also B. J. Cohen, *In Whose Interest? International Banking and American Foreign Policy*, 1986). Figures for 1985–90 from BIS 'International Banking and Financial Market Developments', statistical annex, tables 2(A) and 2(C), Feb. 1991 and May 1992

Thus, the simple existence of private intermediaries also succeeded in reducing the pressure on the US administration to address responsibility for liquidity provision. Indeed, whether or not one attributes the inflationary pressures of the mid-1970s to the explosion in Eurobank lending, it is perhaps surprising that the liquidity provision inherent in the SDR remained on the international monetary agenda *at all* during this period. (The by now familiar expansion in bank lending is the focus of Tables 3.3 and 3.4, representing IMF and BIS estimates, respectively. While absolute amounts are not directly comparable, the trend in both indicates an explosion in private lending.)

Prospects for international monetary reform that focused on fixed rates, the primacy of public liquidity provision, and the SDR thus quickly receded, the demise of the C-20 also reflecting this. This was furthered by policy changes within the US government. Despite this, however, the SDR was not abandoned in policy discussion in the US as quickly as it had been in European pronouncements, nor indeed from academic interest. Until 1974, for instance, the Fed was recommending further work on the SDR, and Congress recommended reforming the SDR to make it a more useful asset in 1976.[38] This seems surprising given policy shifts away from the SDR—but it does give some credence to a certain lack of coordination in US international monetary policy. This was to continue later after the election of President Carter in 1976, when the SDR enjoyed a brief renaissance in the US administration.

3.4 Continued 'Ad Hoccery' and US Accommodation of Floating Rates

Despite the quick accommodation of the new arrangements by the US administration, it could be argued that aside from a general interest in the dollar, the US recognition of even its *own* particular interests in international monetary policy decisions during the early 1970s was somewhat unclear. Its own balance of payments policy, for instance, was difficult to ascertain, as what was to be called 'benign neglect' continued.[39] Revealingly, in 1972, with the US just having invested much political capital in the salvaging of a fixed rate system in the form of the Smithsonian Agreement, the US did not even have clear international monetary goals with respect to consolidating reform, as Paul Volcker admitted:

> Not long after Shultz became secretary [of the Treasury], he asked me about our plans for monetary reform. I had to confess they did not exist.[40]

Even with respect to Euromarkets, which furthered the expansion of US banks abroad, the US Fed did not officially drop its bar on foreign currency deposit taking by its own banks until 1989.[41] Like everyone else, the US adminstration was adapting to, as much as some elements of it were promoting, a new post-Bretton Woods environment.

Another development which contributed to this, and also adversely affected the prospects for SDRs, was that the political desire for an alternative system of flexible exchange rates and market-oriented solutions to international monetary problems continued to rise in intellectual popularity in the US. This was roughly coincident with President Nixon's ill-fated second term and continued under President Ford, and reinforced the changes occurring as the Smithsonian Agreement broke down. Herbert Stein succeeded Paul

McCracken as Chairman of the Council of Economic Advisers, George Shultz was to be moved from his post as Director of the Office of Management and Budget to Treasury Secretary (and was also named Assistant to the President), and Peter Flanigan became Executive Director of the Council on International Economic Policy. As Stein admitted: 'Shultz, Flanigan, and I were ideological floaters'.[42] This could also be said of Jack Bennett, Deputy Under-Secretary and Under-Secretary for Monetary Affairs at the Treasury between 1971 and 1975. Furthermore, President Nixon's growing impatience with international monetary questions, and the frustration he felt at any international circumscription of US domestic and foreign policy, also contributed to the waning of support for formalized arrangements.[43]

However it was still true that reform in the guise of public international liquidity management was still on the international monetary agenda at the Fund at least. The problem for the US was in determining a response.[44] It was at the IMF that the US had to respond to the most consistent reform pressure, first at the C-20, then during Second Amendment negotiations. Partly in response to the earlier pressure, the US did float a 'reserve indicator' proposal at the IMF annual meeting in 1972.[45] The proposal, compatible with an evolving dollar standard, did not go anywhere. The US Treasury, increasingly characterized by its enthusiastic market-oriented staff such as Shultz and Jack Bennett, were clearly not as disappointed when reform negotiations broke down as the US Treasury would have been only a few years earlier.

While much debate was forthcoming on the willingness of the US to discuss international monetary reform within the Fund and even the UN (where initiatives were under the jurisdiction of the State Department, which remained more sensitive to international criticism), the US was content with a new monetary system as long as policy latitude for the dollar remained. It was apparent that structural relationships could favour this latitude in both the Bretton Woods and post-Bretton Woods systems. More by default than by design, a 'dollar standard' came to be advocated by the Treasury. Diplomacy suggested that this had to be promoted quietly, for the US:

> could not take a position which might permit foreign countries to charge that we were attempting to *impose* a dollar standard. This would smack too much of imperialism.[46]

In 1972–4, the US position was relatively isolated internationally. Reform was on the minds of most of the C-20, and the US representative on this Committee, Paul Volcker (then Under-Secretary of the Treasury), realized that the character of the debate on international reform had changed in that most were still willing to accommodate a greater role for SDRs.[47] The Europeans—even the Germans at this stage—were in a reformist mood, and were willing to concede the link between SDR allocations and development finance for developing countries, for example. At the time, however, the US was beginning to perceive reform completely differently in the guise of a flexible rate, market-oriented system. And in truth, aside from the C-20, formal proposals from elsewhere were not prevalent.[48] Furthermore, with most G10 countries deciding to float their currencies against the dollar in the light of severe speculative pressures and macro-economic divergence among them, the US was able to abandon any real commitment to heavily structured reform more easily.

It was plain that by the mid-7190s, with private liquidity markets growing exponentially, sufficient desire to embark upon a new Bretton Woods, or a regulated system to replace it, had dissipated in Washington as much as elsewhere. The growth of Euromarkets acted as a catalyst to the arguments supporting floating exchange rates and private liquidity provision. While Euromarkets had been growing exponentially from the late 1960s, it was from a virtually non-existent base. A swelling of the market by petrodollars following the first oil price rise in late 1973 also contributed to a hiatus in reformist tendencies. The international monetary system had changed, the intellectual climate had changed, and so had US preparedness to entertain plans that would include a greater role for the SDR. Although the US was briefly willing to entertain ideas associated with the SDR during the Carter administration, as the new international monetary arrangements consolidated themselves it became increasingly evident to the administration that the SDR was far from essential to meet any specific national interest of the US. Furthermore, the brief flirtation with the SDR in the late 1970s was increasingly ill fated because of the changing face of monetary policy determination in the US, particularly given the growing role of the US Congress.

By the mid-1970s the post-Bretton Woods monetary arrangements had come in through the back door. Although flexible arrangements had had their respected advocates throughout the Bretton Woods era, they were still on the margins of the debate as late as the early 1970s. While it could be argued that the time was ripe for a new system, or even that serendipity played its part, it gradually became evident that waning enthusiasm for the preservation of Bretton Woods arrangements by US policy makers, particularly in the second Nixon administration, also had an effect. It is evident that the power of ideas—in this case support for flexible exchange rates and a more market-oriented international monetary system—played a role in the demise of prospects for Bretton Woods arrangements, including a role for the SDR.[49]

The fact that apparent US policy drift during the early post-Bretton Woods years may have also served US interests has been mentioned by some analysts as a contributing factor to the consolidation of the new arrangements.[50] Others, including Williamson, lamented intellectual failings (or technical inadequacy, as Williamson also characterized it in another guise) and weak political will in accounting for the failure of international monetary reform. This lack of political will was also identified by the IMF when it published a critique by Jeremy Morse in an issue of its *Survey*.[51] In any case, by the mid-1970s US opposition applied to most of the C-20's recommendations on enhancing the role of the SDR, from the substitution account to the link. In this context it may be recalled that the failure of the Smithsonian Agreement had left a bitter legacy. As late as 1972 the US, even President Nixon, despite his impatient remarks on international monetary issues (culminating in his infamous 'I don't give a [expletive deleted] about the lira'), was on the record as favouring an agreement on a new monetary system.[52] This was a genuine desire—after all, the Smithsonian Agreement had been a child of the US, particularly Nixon's Treasury Secretary John Connally. Nixon's second term, however, was different. Domestic political difficulties intensified. The Treasury was much more willing to entertain the prospect of floating exchange rates, especially when the Smithsonian Agreement seemed increasingly unlikely to hold.

In addition, difficulties in economic policy coordination within the US bureaucracy tend to give credence to the notion that US policy in this sphere was often made on an ad hoc basis, and subject to a large degree of inter-bureaucratic jealousy and rivalry. For instance, Charles Coombs writes that it was not until 1973–4 that American policies of 'benign neglect' in the foreign exchange market were abandoned, implying that the New York Fed's (or at least Coombs') preferences were disregarded.[53] As we shall see, the difficulties of Watergate also had a profound effect on international monetary policy determination in the US. At this stage it is enough to note that, although George Shultz's Treasury in the second Nixon administration started with a relatively clear willingness to embrace a new system, as the term progressed domestic political difficulties severely hampered effective policy management.

Compounding and contributing to this vacillation in US policy was continued upheaval in international monetary relations. 1971–6 witnessed the Smithsonian Agreement and its collapse, the C-20 negotiations, and the oil price hike; in addition, domestic difficulties intensified the flux in US policies until an accommodation of, and then support for, flexible rates occurred coupled with a commensurate decline in support for SDRs.

Further instances of policy vacillation and indecisiveness are revealed in another senior mandarin's writings, those of C. Fred Bergsten, Assistant Secretary of the Treasury in the Carter administration. (Bergsten had earlier advised Henry Kissinger as International Economic Affairs Assistant at the National Security Council.) During the C-20 negotiations, and at a time when many were turning away from the SDR, Bergsten (though not then a member of the administration) advocated that '[reserve] growth should be achieved wholly through creation of SDRs'.[54] Later, in discussing international monetary reform in 1975, Bergsten repeated this strong support:

> Most importantly... the liquidity focus of the new system should clearly be Special Drawing Rights... they could leap immediately to first place among existing reserve assets. At the margin, Special Drawing Rights would provide the bulk of the growth of world reserves, and perhaps all of it. The main objection to an increase in the official price of gold was always that it would imply a return of gold to the center of the international monetary system, a costly reversal of the historical evolution of money. This objection does not hold in a context which clearly elevates Special Drawing Rights to the center of the system.[55]

While Bergsten's support for the SDR was later to be tempered, his sense of prevailing policy drift in the mid-1970s was clearly evident. In a speech to the Chicago Council on Foreign Relations, Bergsten referred to the policy legacy as Carter took office:

> ...international economic policy had been hampered by major institutional problems: rancor, and often open hostility among the key departments of government with responsibilities in this area (notably, State and Treasury); mistrust and noncooperation between the administration and Congress; and a general failure to integrate domestic and international economic policy effectively.[56]

Bergsten went on to say, no doubt somewhat facetiously, that after his appointment 'total détente between the State and Treasury Departments' was accomplished within the first two days of office, and also claimed that relations between Congress and administration had improved.[57] While this was clearly an exaggeration, the Carter government of 1977–81 being subject to its own divisiveness, the administration during Bergsten's time once again entertained notions of a coordinated response to international monetary problems, which briefly encompassed serious discussion of a greater role for the SDR.

And it is interesting to note that work in the US on the SDR continued after the breakdown of the Smithsonian Agreement. This particularly reflected academic interest in the idea, echoing earlier interest in the liquidity question a decade earlier. The list of international monetary specialists—many of whom lived and worked in America—who advocated an increased role for the SDR was long. Admittedly, many at the time, such as Richard Cooper and Marina v. N. Whitman, hedged their support with the disclaimer that SDRs were unlikely to assume much greater importance in the foreseeable future.[58] Others, such as John Williamson (at the IMF and later at the Institute for International Economics) and Peter Kenen argued more forcefully for an expansion of the SDR's role under existing or modified international monetary arrangements.[59] Still others who had advocated different schemes in the 1960s, such as Edward Bernstein, maintained that an enhanced role for the SDR through a substitution account could strengthen the existing flexible exchange rate system.[60] This support for the SDR occasionally manifested itself in support for its role as primary reserve asset, but this was never reflected in US international monetary policy, and rarely by those who made the crossover from academia into public service.

But in any case, it is worth recalling that until 1973 the US actively promoted the SDR as a new, international reserve asset that could buttress the role of the dollar under fixed rates, including by providing policy space for the US to deal with its balance of payments problems, which at the time were a matter of growing concern domestically and internationally. The failure of the Smithsonian Agreement, however, was the catalyst to shifts in US policy already taking place. The administration quickly accommodated a flexible exchange rate order under Nixon and Ford, but this did not translate into complete or universal rejection of SDRs, which was particularly evident during the Carter era. 'Ad hoccery' in its newer guise prevailed, and it cannot be denied that this was more easily accommodated within the new arrangements. Thus the US came to reject the SDR as a means of anchoring a system of fixed rates, particularly if it threatened to substitute for the role of the dollar. Nonetheless there was a brief period when precisely this latter concept was entertained: during the serious US discussions of an SDR substitution account in the late 1970s.

3.5 The US Discussion of an SDR Substitution Account

As early as 1969, the Volcker Group recommended exploration of 'reserve settlement accounts' for balance of payments purposes.[61] While the idea suffered a setback following the breakdown of Bretton Woods monetary arrangements, it remained in the shadows for years. It was true that the US strongly opposed the idea of 'asset settlement' during the C-20 discussions, much to the frustration of observers at the time such as Jeremy Morse and Fred Hirsch (which John Williamson elaborates upon in exasperation):[62]

> [The US] ... held out against asset settlement through thick and thin, defending her position with arguments ... that were invalid if the comparison were with a system of on-demand convertibility, as it ostensibly was since this was the position that she was espousing.[63]

Nonetheless, the idea refused to go away in the US, even as the post-Bretton Woods arrangements took hold.

For instance, in a written submission before the Subcommittee on International Finance and Resources of the Senate Finance Committee in 1973, Jack Bennett, Deputy Under-Secretary at the Treasury, testified that under a prospective reformed system, 'possibilities for funding or exchanging part of existing dollar holdings into SDR obligations [a substitution account] warrant careful consideration'.[64] During the Nixon–Ford term, however, Bennett and the US administration did not pursue moves in this direction. In fact in an article in *Foreign Policy* in 1975, Bennett wrote 'A Free Dollar Makes Sense' and maintained that 'the world's economies have benefited from the absence of governmental attempts at 'firmer management'.[65] Also of great importance, by the time Bennett made his second statement, Congress had increased its profile with respect to international monetary matters; this latter development merits further attention in the next chapter.

Initially, the bare bones of a substitution account, whereby currencies could be exchanged for SDRs at the Fund, appealed to many US policy observers. After all, in times of dollar weakness, the dollar was often weak because of balance of payments or inflationary concerns, and anything that served to reduce attention to, or ameliorate, this problem might have been welcomed in the US. A key problem that emerged in this regard, however, was that of exchange risk. Why should the US shoulder future responsibility for exchange rate changes that did not favour the dollar?

We have seen that Volcker considered a substitution account as a possibility early on, although later his support weakened. Even Jack Bennett had reported to Congress that the US should carefully consider the possibility of funding or exchanging dollar holdings into SDR obligations.[66] Bergsten, too, favoured a 'Reserve Substitution Account', one reason being concerns about the possibilities of gold revaluation; his enthusiasm was longer lasting. Henry Fowler, by 1976 with Goldman Sachs, the Treasury Secretary in the 1960s who had changed the US policy to one which embraced reform, argued that some sort of 'substitute account process' was desirable *because* SDRs were subject to governmental control. This he deemed preferable to the provision of unrestrained liquidity through national currencies and gold.[67]

Despite these sentiments it must be recalled that the US had come to support the freedom of a post-Bretton Woods system with all the enthusiasm of a recent convert to a cause. This was still true of the Carter administration from 1977–80, which included many of the academics, such as Cooper and Whitman, who nonetheless acknowledged an interdependent world with a consequent imperative of multilateral cooperation. Thus the residual support for SDR schemes and a substitution account would still have to be accommodated within the context of the new arrangements. The logic for this greater role for SDRs was clearly less compelling under flexible rates.

But the US had more than flirted with a substitution account, even if F. Lisle Widman admitted that some of US interest was feigned in order to appeal to developing countries. Widman admitted that Treasury debate on the account was serious during the early 1970s, when '. . . thousands of man hours were spent in attempting to develop a proposal which would be acceptable both to the United States and to the major dollar holders'.[68] While much of the early discussion in the US dissipated after the break-up of the C-20, during the Carter administration momentum gathered behind the idea again. In addition to Bergsten and Anthony Solomon, other officials such as Richard Cooper and Peter Kenen spurred a minor but ill-fated renaissance for SDR proposals. With Bergsten at the Treasury, Anthony Solomon at the New York Fed, and Richard Cooper at the State Department, SDRs had senior supporters at all major international monetary policy units in the administration. (See Appendix 2 for a summary of senior Treasury staff from 1965–90.) In a bureaucratized policy environment it was committed individuals who were most effective in their advocacy of these new ideas; we witnessed much the same thing with personnel changes during the second Nixon administration, and the notion also bears closer examination when we address the influences of changes to the policy structure in the determination of US foreign economic policy.

Despite challenges, it is important to realize how close to fruition the substitution account appeared during the Carter administration. Speculation became particularly intense in the second half of 1979. In the weeks preceding the Hamburg meeting of the Interim Committee in 1980, some in the press confidently forecast its official endorsement.[69] As we shall see in Chapter 6, the Fund was so confident of its institution that it even leaked the proposed size of the account. This reflected the fact that the Treasury was giving the idea very serious consideration.

In fact the battle for the substitution account was lost just before the Hamburg meeting of the Interim Committee in 1979, although the *New York Times* reported from Hamburg that the plan had been 'unexpectedly' shelved. The paper reported that while many officials had expected some compromise, the Treasury Secretary, G. William Miller had met privately with his G5 counterparts the previous week to say that the Americans could not support the plan.[70] Miller had effectively torpedoed the plan semi-publicly when he spoke against the substitution account before an audience of bankers.[71]

Why did this change occur, particularly given the work in Washington and the support at senior levels of the bureaucracy throughout the administration? This time it appeared to be because of practical concerns associated with the complicated mechanisms involved in the operations of a substitution account. The main problem that emerged in this context, particularly (but not exclusively) from the perspective of the US, was that of exchange risk, that is how settlement would occur in the event of withdrawals when the dollar (or other reserve currency deposit with the account) exchange rate relative to SDRs fluctuated from the rate that existed at the time of the initial substitution. A G30 paper at the time partially avoided this latter scenario by advocating that the substitution account be permanent.

Peter Kenen, an early supporter of the substitution account both at the Treasury and in academia, addressed these problems in a series of simulations that hypothesized the existence of a substitution account between 1964 and 1978.[72] The article is valuable for an indication as to how the proposed substitution account could work, and how exchange risk could be apportioned. With respect to interest payments, they are assumed to be paid in either SDR claims, or by the US in US dollars at a variety of alternative rates (e.g. US Treasury Bill rate, government bond rate, or various combinations of these). In turn it is initially assumed that SDR interest payments would be added to SDR claims, and US dollar payments would not be converted to claims on the substitution account.

Importantly, in all Kenen's simulations, the net benefit is positive (though not necessarily optimal) for the depositors—but also costly to varying degrees to the US. Kenen attempts to minimize these costs to the US by extrapolating the effects of the US paying half the interest payments, supplemented by a 'deficiency payment' from Fund gold sales. If liquidation of the account is also considered, then it is this latter simulation that results in the least net cost to the US. (However, Kenen also points out that gold sales to support a substitution account was an unlikely scenario for a number of reasons, not least of which was the possibility of quickly exhausting Fund gold holdings.[73])

As Kenen concedes in the conclusion to his paper there were 'large costs to the United States under all of the interest rate arrangements examined'. Somewhat surprisingly, however, Kenen goes on to say that even though the initiative had failed in 1980, this was all the more reason:

> ...to start talking soon again about a substitution account. To wait until cyclical forces weaken the dollar may be worse than trying to reach agreement at a time when holders of dollars have no wish to part with them.[74]

Finally, at the same time, Kenen suggests that new talk of a substitution account, outside the crisis atmosphere of 1979–80, should take place 'inspired by the need for a better reserve system rather than the fear of a worse one'.[75] Whether the US administration, which had been shown that virtually all simulations involved a net cost, would agree with this was another matter. In addition, this cost problem was compounded when the possibility of access to private markets by public authorities was taken into consideration—theoretically the US could be found liable for substitution ad infinitum.

While exchange risk was the main problem in the US, there were other factors as well. In addition to a lack of Congressional interest in the issue at the time, the importance of the changing character of the SDR, as well as political considerations, cannot be discounted.[76] In fact, Richard Cooper claimed that it was his opposition at the State Department that sounded the death-knell for US consideration of the substitution account.[77]

As the Hamburg meeting floundered, US Treasury officials also argued that in an election year, and when Congressional interest in US international monetary policy was increasing, President Carter would have enough problems in pleading for increases in quotas to the Fund and increasing aid budgets.[78] This was an additional and crucially important complicating factor. The Carter administration's consideration of the SDR ultimately led to failure and the abandonment of attempts at a Substitution Account. It is nonetheless illustrative of strains in US policy determination that we have begun to identify, including a pragmatic, ad hoc approach to international monetary policy, and the influence of individuals in a complex, bureaucratized policy environment. The debate over the substitution account reveals different things at the IMF; we will return to examine this in Chapter 6.

3.6 State Department Involvement in the Evolution of US Policy Towards the SDR

While the Treasury's approach to the SDR following the breakdown of Bretton Woods fluctuated, this was generally less true of the State Department. This was particularly evident during the Carter administration, when appointments were made in an effort to bolster the economic branches of the Department, which had witnessed a comparative decline in economic expertise since the heyday of the 1940s. During Bretton Woods negotiations, the US Treasury and State Department cooperated well; conflict was most clearly evident in the administration's relations with Congress. Indeed, at the time it could be argued that the State Department enjoyed as much influence on international monetary matters as the Treasury.[79] As Bretton Woods arrangements consolidated themselves, however, the rivalry and interaction between the two departments became similar to the dynamic in other Western states, although the technical expertise increasingly required to engage in relevant debates tended to favour finance departments and treasuries over time.

In the US, the State Department's responsibilities are broadly those of foreign policy, including the UN, but not necessarily its specialized agencies. While international monetary policy is within the jurisdiction of the Treasury, the potential for overlap and conflict between these two departments exists, and manifested itself in the wake of the breakdown of Bretton Woods and the repoliticization of international monetary questions. Treasury staff tend to downplay the importance, and question the competence, of State Department officials to grasp the subtleties of international monetary policy.[80] Indeed, when questioned, Treasury and ex-Treasury staff are at pains to emphasize that it is the Treasury that has virtually sole responsibility for international monetary policy. No doubt some of this sensitivity was due to the encroaching upon what was thought of Treasury Department territory, particularly in the 1970s. State Department staff, however, emphasize their own contributions: as we have seen, Richard Cooper went so far as to claim responsibility for pointing out irresolvable difficulties with the substitution account.

And it may also be said that the Treasury gradually increased its influence on international monetary policy during the transformation to post-Bretton Woods arrangements. Importantly, during the 1970s the Treasury fought successfully for increased representation in several US missions abroad. While some finance ministries—particularly in smaller countries—rely on foreign affairs staff taking responsibility for economic intelligence and representing domestic economic interests abroad, the US Treasury convinced the State Department and the President's staff of the necessity of the Treasury expanding its legations in its most important trading partners, particularly the G10.[81] In common with other Western states, this points to a certain wariness—and potentially conflicting objectives—of finance ministries in their dealings with foreign ministries in representing financial interests and garnering an appreciation of these interests abroad.[82]

But the influence of the State Department in international monetary policy arguably had an effect upon US policy towards the SDR, particularly during the Carter administration. Certainly Richard Cooper and later Edward Morse (both Carter appointments) succeeded in raising the profile of the State Department in matters of international monetary policy. Indeed a recognition of State and Treasury Department rivalry during the Carter administration also aids in accounting for the resurgence of US discussion of the Substitution Account. Contributing to the resurgent role of the State Department at this time was the fact that many senior officials in other departments had State Department or other political experience. Fred Bergsten, for example, became Assistant Secretary (International Affairs) at the Treasury, and Anthony Solomon became Under-Secretary for Monetary Affairs, having had experience of the State Department as Assistant Secretary of State for Economic Affairs during the Johnson administration.[83]

As we have seen, the State Department is especially sensitive to international considerations in the political sphere; Cooper's appointment signalled that this also applied to the international monetary arena. Also, Carter's Treasury Secretaries tended to be weaker. (See Appendix 3 on senior US Treasury appointments.) W. Michael Blumenthal was generally not as strong as his predecessors, although it is interesting to note that he too had State Department experience (he served as Deputy Assistant Secretary of State during the Johnson years). Widman observed that Blumenthal's appointment led to difficulties, among them 'some resentment and morale problems with the senior members of his own organization', and inefficient duplication of tasks among branches of the Treasury.[84] (On the other hand Robert Roosa observed that by late 1978 Blumenthal, unlike his predecessors Shultz and Simon, was more convinced that neglect, benign or otherwise, 'would not do'.[85] Needless to say, inflation was proving stubborn in the US and the dollar was falling—Blumenthal's public comments occasionally exacerbating the latter.) To compound matters these changes in the Treasury occurred at a time of mounting monetary dislocation and rising inflation among America's G10 partners. This culminated in ill-fated efforts at policy coordination, prompted by President Carter at the Bonn Summit of 1978, among the US, Germany, and Japan, which was quickly abandoned as the second oil shock occurred and inflation fears mounted.[86] The EC, continuing its emphasis on the refinement of its own monetary mechanisms, inaugurated the EMS on 13 March 1979. Robert Roosa confirmed the EC frustration with the US (which was one of the characteristics we noted in the first part of this chapter) by noting that the EMS was organized largely because the EC was:

> ...increasingly discouraged by what was then an apparent indifference toward the dollar on the part of the US Treasury. [They] carried on extensive negotiations concerning a possible new approach toward currency stability in Europe.[87]

As a result of these dislocations, both within the US administration and in the international system, there was again a discernable drift in international monetary policy. At the time Euromarkets were expanding rapidly, seemingly efficiently recycling petrodollar imbalances in the wake of the first oil crisis. Neither the Fund, the State Department, the Federal Reserve, nor even the US Treasury were to become involved in any significant way in tackling this phenomenon until the consequences of this policy became apparent with the Mexican debt moratorium in 1982.

A less consistent (but arguably more realistic) Treasury, and Treasury–State rivalry, particularly during the late 1970s, exacerbated problems associated with the lack of coordinated policy mechanisms to deal with international monetary questions. Stephen Cohen noted that this policy vacillation has a long history, with new ad hoc economic committees created in successive US administrations (the Economic Policy Board, the Economic Policy Group, and the Senior Interagency Group on International Economic Policy—later Economic Policy Council, respectively), each proving relatively unsuccessful in mediating policy interests.[88] Destler and Henning have also observed that this lack of continuity has hurt US policy in his investigation of exchange rate policy making in the 1980s.[89] Also in the 1980s, other institutions with a long association with international monetary questions concerning the IMF, such as the permanent National Advisory Council on International Monetary and Financial Policies (chaired by the Secretary of the Treasury and known as the NAC), had

> ...withered to the point where today [1988] its major continuing function is to routinely extend staff-level interagency approval of the Treasury Department's proposals for the US government's votes in the IMF... it has long been outside of the policy mainstream.[90]

Cohen believed that international economic policy coordination worked 'unusually well and harmoniously' during the Carter administration. Whether this was the case is arguable; what is less contentious is that with the second oil shock in 1979, the failure of the substitution account in 1980, and a change in administration in 1981, the outlook for the SDR worsened even further. In addition the malaise which characterized the US approach to SDRs had another source which would overwhelm any interdepartmental rivalry within the administration—that of the growing role of Congress.

Thus, the SDR nor the substitution account never again enjoyed the consideration it enjoyed in 1978–80. Even though it was a mechanism that failed before being tested, it was not a utopian dream as the 'thousands of man-hours' at the Treasury indicated. There were other mitigating factors as well: the Congressional reticence concerning the account as early as 1975, the strengthening of the dollar after the oil shock, drift in the administration as a whole, and exchange risk all led the idea to be buried at Hamburg. Finally, as Peter Kenen has observed:

> There is never a good time to negotiate major changes in the international monetary system. One U.S. official put it well. When the dollar is weak, he suggested, the United States cannot obtain acceptable terms. When the dollar is strong, no one else is interested.[91]

In sum, the demise of the SDR in the eyes of the US administration, including the disparate strains of thought over the substitution account, was a complicated but nonetheless undeniable process as post-Bretton Woods arrangements consolidated themselves. But, more broadly, this latter process was itself another manifestation of a policy of muddling through, identified by one theorist as explaining US policy earlier influencing foreign policies during the immediate post-Bretton Woods debates.[92] The varying influence of the State Department in the equation, at least as far as the SDR was concerned, complicated matters still further. Ultimately these strains all complemented each other, for as the post-Bretton Woods era unfolded, the belief in the US administration intensified that almost all proposals to do with the SDR were not in its national interest.

3.7 Summary

Much can be learned about the difficulties that immediately arose for the SDR as it came into being through changes in US international monetary policy. Initially, the US agreed to SDRs as a means of upholding the role of the dollar within Bretton Woods and thereby viewed it as a substitute for gold rather than the dollar. This is precisely what the French feared throughout the 1960s. As the Smithsonian Agreement quickly broke down, and in a process that was to intensify through until the Carter administration, international monetary instability increased. Ideas associated with the SDR enjoyed a brief resurgence to address this, and the US did consider various SDR proposals seriously, especially the substitution account. Thus, the outlook for the SDR fluctuated during the 1970s more than might have been expected, although it would be misleading to suggest that this amounted to any meaningful reverse in a march away from ideas associated with the SDR in the post-Bretton Woods era, particularly in the US.

As this chapter has explored, conflict and some drift within the administration, all in the context of a new exchange rate system that included an increased role for private providers of international liquidity, proved to be to the detriment of SDR proposals. In addition the US, like everyone else, was reeling from oil shocks and the new important role of international capital markets. For the US, taking into account the domestic ramifications of international events was a relatively new phenomenon in the postwar world. This all contributed to a rejection of an enhanced role for the SDR in the international economy.

Kenen's observation that there is only support for major change when the dollar is weak (and then the US cannot obtain acceptable terms) is true. With respect to US consideration of an SDR substitution account, however, we may extend this notion to say that in periods of dollar weakness, the US tends to consider the SDR as a support for the dollar, or to make a multi-currency reserve system seem less appealing.

In any case, the US administration's reluctance to consider fundamental reform along the lines of the C-20, extending to the defeat of proposals enhancing the role of the SDR, were pronounced by the mid-1970s as international monetary arrangements acclimatized themselves to a floating rate system. Unsurprisingly, US interests remained closely identified with the dollar, whatever the international monetary arrangements. At the conclusion to the last chapter we noted US disquiet at the nascent acceptance of the SDR in the private market; this, too, would continue. Although the US administration continued to consider the role of SDR occasionally, this was only in the context of its supporting role vis-à-vis the dollar.

In addition, it was not only the continuation of 'ad hoccery' and drift in US international monetary policy which adversely affected the SDR. We have begun to point to other influences on policy determination in the US administration, including the role of Congress, which complemented moves away from the SDR in the US. Thus it is useful to examine further these structural as well as political influences on US policy, and to do this we need to delve deeper into the American international monetary policy process.

Notes

1. This implicitly defers to a neo-realist approach to the study of international relations. See, For example Destler and Henning, *Dollar Politics* (*op. cit.*); also Robert Gilpin, *US Power and the Multinational Corporation* (*op. cit.*).
2. This does not negate the importance of the structure of the international system but does require that we emphasize the influence of international institutions on this structure. See Robert Keohane, *International Relations and State Power* (*op. cit.*), esp. ch. 1, also ch. 7: 'International Institutions: Two Approaches', p. 174.
3. Paul Volcker and Toyoo Gyohten, *Changing Fortunes, op. cit.*, pp. 115–16; John Williamson, *The Failure of World Monetary Reform, op. cit.*, p. 61.
4. Formally, the EEC (European Economic Community; less formally, the 'Common Market') existed from the ratification of the Treaty of Rome in 1957 until the Maastricht Treaty came into effect in 1993. Its successor entity, the EC (European Community) was replaced by the EU (European Union) with the ratification of the Treaty of Lisbon in 2009.

   On the monetary plane, functions associated with the European Monetary System (EMS), instituted by EEC member states in 1979 to enhance intra-European monetary management and exchange rate stablity, were intensified through the EMI (European Monetary Institute) founded in 1994, and then the ECB (European Central Bank) in 1998. Notwithstanding continuing strains in intra-European exchange rate stability under the European Exchange Rate Mechanism (ERM)—which reasserted itself after a honeymoon period for the Euro from its introduction through until 2010—the EMS led to the establishment of Economic and Monetary Union (EMU) as a goal in 1990. EMU also contributed to the establishment of the ECB in 1998, which introduced the Euro for most EU member states in 1999 (in turn replacing a unit of account known as the European Currency Unit (ECU)). See also nn. 31 and 44, below.
5. In France, see for example Michel Lelart, 'L'Utilisation du DTS et de l'ECU par le secteur privé', *Banque* (Paris), nos. 433 and 434, November and December 1983. Academic interest in Germany was more prevalent—see M. Bargelame, *Die Sonderziehungsrechte im internationalen Währungssystem*, Duncker & Humblot (Berlin: 1981); H. Ith, *Die Sonderziehungsrechte und die internationale Währungsreform*, Verlag Rüegger (Diessenhofen, Switz: 1975); K. Theile, *Die Koppelung der Sonderziehungsrechte mit der Entwicklungsfinanzierung—Reihe Weltwirtschaft Band 3*, Verlag Rüegger

(Diessenhofen: 1981), especially the latter's bibliography. Interest in the UK was more pronounced, and the Anglo-Saxon cross-fertilization of ideas meant that much SDR scholarship was better known—and published—in both the UK and US. In the early 1970s, for example, see P. Bauer, 'Inflation, SDRs, and Aid', *Lloyds Bank Review*, no. 109, 1973, K. A. Chrystal, 'International Money and the Future of the SDR', Princeton Essay in International Finance no. 128, 1978; Fred Hirsch, 'An SDR Standard: Impetus, Elements, and Impediments' Princeton Essay in International Finance no. 99, 1973.

6. Kenneth King, *US Monetary Policy and European Responses in the 1980s*, Chatham House Paper 16, Royal Institute of International Affairs/Routledge & Kegan Paul (London: 1982), pp. 2–3.
7. The Lomé Convention conferred preferential access to EC markets by its developing country signatories. In some cases the EC agreed to purchase goods by quota or to establish stabilization funds for developing country export earnings. See 'The Lomé Dossier', reprinted from *The Courier—Africa-Caribbean-Pacific-European Community* (European Commission) no. 31, special issue, March 1975, p. 3.
8. As we noted in Chapter 1, the Japanese role was relatively muted with respect to the SDR in the 1960s, and this remained largely true of the 1970s and 1980s. In his sympathetic account of US–Japanese international monetary relations, Robert Roosa notes that Japan often proved a useful intermediary between Europe and the US. See Robert Roosa, 'The United States and Japan in the International Monetary System 1946–1985', Group of Thirty Occasional Paper no. 21 (New York: 1986), pp. 17–18. Otherwise, Japan's key international monetary policy interest remained the dollar/yen exchange rate. See Yoichi Funabashi, *Managing the Dollar: From the Plaza to the Louvre*, Institute for International Economics (Washington: 1988); also Toyoo Gyohten's excerpts in Volcker and Gyohten, *Changing Fortunes (op. cit.)*

   Preoccupied with a successful adjustment process following successive oil shocks, Japan was an advocate of SDR allocation, then an opponent in the 1980s, then an advocate again in the early 1990s. During the IMF Second Amendment negotiations, Japan's profile remained relatively discreet, a phenomenon that has remained true of Japan in most international fora until very recently. By 1991, however, Japan had changed its policy from opposition to the promotion of an SDR allocation for 'short-term financing difficulties'. See 'Japan Suggests SDR Issue to Meet Finance Demands', *Financial Times*, 26 April 1991, p. 8.
9. DM/79/91, *The European Monetary Fund: External Relationships* (based on a paper presented at a conference in Geneva 7–8 December 1979 on 'The European Monetary Fund: Internal and External Relationships), J. J. Polak, 10 December 1979.
10. Ibid. pp. 5–6.
11. Ibid.
12. Fritz Machlup, 'The Expanded Role of SDRs and the Possibilities of an SDR Standard'; C. Fred Bergsten, 'International Monetary Reform: A Viewpoint from the United States'; Richard N. Cooper, 'Eurodollars, Reserve Dollars, and Asymmetries in the International Monetary System', in Alexander K. Swoboda, *Europe and the Evolution of the International Monetary System*, proceedings of the first conference of

the International Center for Monetary and Banking Studies, Institut Universitaire de Hautes Etudes Internationale, A.W. Sijthoff (Leiden: 1973).

13. Samuel I. Katz (ed.) *US–European Monetary Relations*—papers from a 1977 conference sponsored by the American Enterprise Inst. for Public Policy Research and Georgetown University (Washington, DC: 1979). Participants included Edward Bernstein, Sir Alec Cairncross, Tom de Vries, J. J. Polak, Andrew Shonfield, and other economists and policy advisors such as Haberler, Lamfalussy, Thygesen, van Ypersele, Wallich, and Williamson. The conference themes included global versus regional monetary integration; the problems of regional (European) integration, especially the controversial notion of urging German reflation, were also discussed.
14. See L. Tsoukalis (ed.), *Europe, America and the World Economy*, Basil Blackwell/College of Europe (Oxford: 1986). On Fund sponsored work, in addition to staff papers, memoranda, etc., see two volumes in particular: George M. von Furstenberg, *International Money and Credit: The Policy Roles* (Washington, DC: 1983), most of which dealt with aspects of the SDR; and Michael Mussa, Michael, James M. Broughton, and Peter Isard (eds), *The Future of the SDR in Light of Changes in the International Financial System—Proceedings of a Seminar held in Washington, D. C. 18–19 March 1996*, IMF (Washington, DC: 1996).
15. D. Healey, *The Time of My Life*, Michael Joseph (London: 1989, p. 416). Healey's frustration with the US was also expressed to this author: 'The work of the IMF in my time, and even more today, is that its efficacy depends entirely on active support from the US [...This]...is even lower today than it was at my time' (correspondence with the author).
16. Kenneth King, *op. cit.*, p. 3.
17. See A. Walter, *World Power and World Money*, St Martin's Press (New York: 1993), chapter 6.
18. De Nederlandsche Bank *Annual Report* (General Survey) 1984, p. 18. I am indebted to René Smits, former chief of the Banking Supervision Department at De Nederlandsche Bank for drawing this passage to my attention.
19. Both American and IMF commentators noted this new emphasis on intro-European rather than internationalist initiatives—see Jack Polak's and Robert Roosa's comments, pp. 80 and 101, respectively.
20. Paul Volcker and Toyoo Gyohten, *Changing Fortunes*, *op. cit.*, p. 90.
21. US Treasury Press Release, 'Announcing the completion of US action on the Special Drawing Rights facility', 15 July 1968. Also reproduced in *1969 Report of the Secretary of the Treasury*, Exhibit 51, p. 368.
22. Remarks by Secretary Fowler as Governor for the United States, 1 October 1968, at the Joint Annual Discussion of the Boards of Governors of the International Monetary Fund and the International Bank for Reconstruction and Development and its affiliates. Reproduced in *1969 Annual Report of the Treasury*, Exhibit 34, p. 295.
23. Ibid. p. 297.
24. F. Lisle Widman, *Making International Monetary Policy* (Washington, DC: 1982), p. 189.
25. Ibid. p. 189.

26. On trade issues, see I. M. Destler, *American Trade Politics*, Institute for International Economics and the Twentieth Century Fund (Washington and New York: 1992).
27. J. Bennett, 'A Free Dollar Makes Sense', *Foreign Affairs*, no. 21, Winter 1975–6, pp. 64, 75.
28. Interview remarks with the author, New York.
29. Paul Volcker, then Under Secretary of the Treasure for Monetary Affairs, spent most of February on secret missions to Japan and Europe negotiating what was essentially the second devaluation of the dollar by raising the official price of gold to $42.2 per ounce. See John S. Odell, *U.S. International Monetary Policy, op. cit.*, pp. 313–18; also Paul A. Volcker and Toyoo Gyohten, *Changing Fortunes—The World's Money and the Threat to American Leadership*, Times Books (New York: 1992), pp. 108–12.
30. US Dept of State *Bulletin*, 16 April 1973, p. 454.
31. Herbert G. Grubel, *The International Monetary System*, 4th edn, Penguin Books (Harmondsworth: 1984), p. 188. The idea was revived in the guise of the EMS agreed to by Helmut Schmidt and Valéry Giscard d'Estaing at Bremen in 1978, whereby varying exchange rate bands would be established according to an individual country's ability to intervene successfully in exchange rate markets, and the institution of the European Currency Unit (ECU), aspects of which were similar to the SDR.
32. *New York Times*, 12 March 1973, p. 1.
33. Brian Tew, *The Evolution of the International Monetary System 1945–77*, Hutchinson & Co. (London: 1979), p. 184.
34. *1970 Annual Report of the Council of Economic Advisers* (Washington: 1970), p. 133.
35. R. Triffin, 'The Future of the International Monetary System', in *Banca Nazionale del Lavoro Quarterly Review*, March 1980, p. 48. The lack of an official link between gold and the dollar no doubt also contributed to this as well.
36. As quoted in Benjamin Cohen, *In Whose Interest? International Banking and American Foreign Policy* (New Haven, 1986), p. 70.
37. Paul Volcker and Toyoo Gyohten, *Changing Fortunes*, *op. cit.*, pp. 105–6.
38. The Fed in its 1974 *Annual Report*, while acknowledging the 'changing [international] economic environment', went on to express hope that monetary reform discussions would aid in promoting a stable international system, including the 'possible consolidation of outstanding reserve currency balances'. Federal Reserve Board of Governors, 1974 *Annual Report*, 30/5/74, p. 70.

    In its confirmation of the Jamaica agreement, Congress accepted that the character of the SDR had changed: it authorized the US Governor of the IMF (the Secretary of the Treasury) to accept the amendments to the Articles of Agreement concerning 'changes in the characteristics and uses of SDRs, and simplification and modernization of the IMF's financial operations and transactions' (Congress Public Law 94-569, 19/10/1976). Henry Reuss, chairman of the House Committee on Banking, Currency and Housing, again strongly influenced Congressional interest in these questions. As we have seen, this influence on international monetary matters was apparent 15 years earlier in Congress's rejection of an increased role for gold in 1962. See above, Chapter 1, pp. 19–20, 40.

39. This phrase had initially been used by Daniel Patrick Moynihan in the context of civil rights in the 1960s. Only later did the financial press use it in the context of apparent US international economic policy drift. (See Volcker and Gyohten, *Changing Fortunes, op. cit.*, pp. 61–2.)
40. Paul Volcker and Toyoo Gyohten, *Changing Fortunes, op. cit.*, p. 118.
41. The argument against changing the policy was simply that to do so would 'make it more difficult to conduct monetary policy'. Letter from Peter Bakstansky (vice-president, Federal Reserve Bank of New York) to the author.
42. Odell, *U.S. International Monetary Policy, op. cit.*, p. 309.
43. Paul Volcker and Toyoo Gyohten, *Changing Fortunes, op. cit.*, p. 104. See also A. Walter, *The Role of Hegemony and International Monetary Order, op. cit.*, Chapter 6.
44. Although Europe had not yet turned away in frustration from internationalist initiatives, already a change of emphasis away from the global in favour of the regional level was taking place with the formation of an EEC 'snake' in 1972, limiting exchange rate movements to a 2.25 per cent band.
45. Paul Volcker and Toyoo Gyohten, *Changing Fortunes, op. cit.*, pp. 119–21.
46. F. Lisle Widman *Making International Monetary Policy, op. cit.*, p. 158 (emphasis added).
47. Williamson, *The Failure of World Monetary Reform, op. cit.*, p. 175.
48. Paul Volcker and Toyoo Gyohten, *Changing Fortunes, op. cit.*, p. 121.
49. John Odell's classic *U.S. International Monetary Policy: Markets, Power and Ideas as Sources of Change*, Princeton University Press (New Haven: 1982) argued that ideas were among the key influences motivating policy makers and are thus a key variable in policy determination in the field.
50. See Susan Strange in 'Cave hic dragones. A Critique of Regime Analysis', in *International Organization*, Winter 1985; A. Walter, *World Power and World Money, op. cit.*, chs. 6, 7.
51. As quoted in John Williamson, *The Failure of World Monetary Reform, 1972–74, op. cit.*, p. 173.
52. *New York Times*, excerpt from Watergate tapes, 7/8/74, p. 47.
53. Charles Coombs, *The Arena of International Finance, op. cit.*, pp. xiv–xv.
54. C. Fred Bergsten, *Toward a New International Economic Order; Selected Papers of C. Fred Bergsten 1972–1974*, Lexington Books (Lexington, MA: 1977), p. 71.
55. C. Fred Bergsten, *The Dilemmas of the Dollar*, Council on Foreign Relations and New York University Press (New York: 1975), p. 530.
56. C. Fred Bergsten, 'The International Economic Policy of the Carter Administration', in *The International Economic Policy of the United States: Selected Papers of C. Fred Bergsten, 1977–1979*, p. 7.
57. Ibid. p. 7.
58. Cooper was also Under-Secretary of State for Economic Affairs at the State Department under President Carter and served on the staff of the Council of Economic Advisers and the National Security Council. During his sojourn at the State Department he sought to increase the Department's profile in questions of international monetary policy during his time there in the late 1970s. In the 1980s, after he had left office, although warning of the possibility of the SDR 'atrophying into irrelevance', he also deemed it 'prudent to improve and to allocate the SDR' (von

Furstenberg (ed.), *International Money and Credit: The Policy Roles* (Washington, DC: 1983), pp. 361, 367.

Marina v. N. Whitman also made the crossover from academia to the US administration, first as an economist and then as a member of the Council of Economic Advisers between 1970–1 and 1972–3. In a 1977 article for the Departments of State, Treasury and Labor she wrote somewhat ambiguously: 'Until some new conceptual framework evolves it will be difficult even to arrive at the consensus required to permit further allocations of SDRs, which may well become important in the not-so-distant future' (Princeton Essays in International Finance, no. 121, June 1977): 'Sustaining the International Economic System: Issues for U.S. Policy', p. 175.

59. Williamson in a pamphlet for the Institute for International Economics: 'A New SDR Allocation?' (Washington, 1984). Kenen supported a substitution account in 'The Analytics of a Substitution Account' in the *BNL Quarterly Review*, December 1981 and in 'Use of the SDR to Supplement or Substitute for Other Means of Finance' in von Furstenberg, *op. cit.*
60. E. M. Bernstein, 'The Future of the Dollar and Other Reserve Assets', in Dreyer, Haberler, and Willett (eds), *The International Monetary System—A Time of Turbulence* (Washington, DC: 1982), pp. 410–29.
61. Joanne Gowa, *Closing the Gold Window—Domestic Politics and the End of Bretton Woods*, p. 130.
62. John Williamson, *The Failure of World Monetary Reform, 1971–74, op. cit.*, pp. v, 173–4. See also Fred Hirsch, *An SDR Standard: Impetus, Elements and Impediments*, Princeton Essays in International Finance No 99, Princeton, 1973; and C. J. Morse, 'The Evolving Monetary System', as quoted in the IMF *Survey*, 17/6/74; and in Williamson.
63. Williamson, *The Failure of World Monetary Reform, 1971–74,* pp. 173–4.
64. Hearings before the Subcommittee on International Finance and Resources of the Senate Committee on Finance. 93rd Congress, 1st Session. 30 May, 1–5 June 1973. Communication by Jack Bennett, Deputy Under Secretary of the Treasury, pp. 149–50.
65. Jack Bennett, 'A Free Dollar Makes Sense', *Foreign Policy*, No. 21, Winter 1975: p. 72.
66. See footnote 65 above. Bennett made these comments in June of 1973, after the Smithsonian parities had been effectively abandoned, but before his arguments for the benefits of a 'free dollar' outlined in his article in *Foreign Policy*, No. 21, Winter 1975. He later became a strong opponent of the substitution account.
67. Henry Fowler, statement to the Subcommittee on International Finance and Resources of the Senate Finance Committee. 94th Congress, 2nd Session. 26 January and 17 February 1976, pp. 72–3.
68. F. Lisle Widman, ch. 9.8 'Shifting Policy on the Substitution Account', in *Making International Monetary Policy, op. cit.*, p. 157.
69. 'Monetary Swap Plan Outlined', *New York Times*, Monday, 4/2/80, p. D1; *The Economist*, 9/2/80, p. 84.
70. See 'Dollar Plan for IMF is Shelved', *New York Times*, Friday, 25/4/80, p. D 1.
71. Ibid.

72. Peter Kenen, 'The Analytics of a Substitution Account', *BNL Quarterly Review*, no. 139, December 1981.
73. Ibid. p. 424. The other two reasons were because developing countries would have preferred gold sales for their own benefit, and because gold sales would have implicitly favoured countries in balance of payments difficulties.
74. Ibid. p. 425.
75. Ibid.
76. Congress showed virtually no interest in the substitution account during Carter's tenure (interview with Peter Kenen, Chatham House, London, June 1988). (It had expressed hostility to the notion in 1975, however. See below, p. 128.)
77. Interview with Richard Cooper, Center for International Affairs, Harvard University, Cambridge, Mass. Treasury officials disputed this State department influence.
78. 'Dollar Plan for IMF is Shelved', *New York Times*, Friday, 25/4/80, p. D 1.
79. Gardner in *Sterling-Dollar Diplomacy*, Clarendon Press (Oxford: 1956). The economic expertise and governmental experience of Cordell Hull as Secretary of State, coupled with the State Department's strong influence on negotiations (equal to that of the Treasury of Henry Morgenthau and Harry Dexter White, and the Board of Economic Warfare under Vice-President Henry Wallace), meant that the State Department enjoyed great influence over international monetary policy questions, although this was gradually usurped by the Treasury.

    Widman also refers to the difficulties inherent in the State/Treasury department relationship that was also true of the Carter era despite—perhaps because of—close liaising between the two agencies. See Widman, *Making International Monetary Policy, op. cit.*, ch. 7.9, 'State-Treasury Detente' and 7.10 'Endorsement of the European Monetary System [despite the State Department's reluctance]', pp. 132–5.
80. Interviews with Helen Walsh, Assistant Treasury Representative, US Embassy, London; Jack Bennett, former Deputy Assistant Secretary for International Affairs at the Treasury (1969–70) and then Deputy Under-Secretary for Monetary Affairs (1971–75), New York.
81. Widman, *Making International Monetary Policy, op. cit.*, pp. 26–7.
82. Ibid. pp. 132–5.
83. Despite the influence of the National Security Council under Kissinger, Bergsten's influence as his (Kissinger's) deputy was not commensurate in the Volcker Group, no doubt because relations between Bergsten and Kissinger were cool. (Bergsten compared working as an economist for Kissinger as 'being in charge of the military for the Pope'.) See Gowa, *Closing the Gold Window, op. cit.*, pp. 124–5, and 95.
84. Widman, *Making International Monetary Policy, op. cit.*, pp. 44 and 38–9. According to Widman, overlap in responsibilities, particularly between the Office of the Assistant Secretary for International Affairs (OASIA) and the staff of the Assistant Secretary for Economic Policy, 'created problems throughout the Blumenthal regime' (p. 39).
85. Robert V. Roosa, *The United States and Japan in the International Monetary System 1946–1985*, Group of Thirty occasional paper 21 (New York: 1986), pp. 36–7.

86. The high-profile nature of economic summitry also dictated State Department involvement in their organization and adminstration.
87. Roosa, *The United States and Japan in the International Monetary System 1946–1985, op. cit.*, p. 37.
88. Stephen Cohen, *The Making of United States International Economic Policy*, Praeger (New York: 1988), pp. 86–8.
89. Although he does not mention the State Department as an important factor in 1980s policymaking, the role of Congress, private institutions and especially the Treasury-Fed relationship are all addressed in Destler and Henning's recommendations for exchange rate determination for the IIE. See I. M. Destler and C. Randall Henning, *Dollar Politics: Exchange Rate Policymaking in the United States*, IIE (Washington, DC: 1989).
90. Stephen Cohen, *The Making of United States International Economic Policy, op. cit.*, p. 96.
91. P. B. Kenen, 'The Analytics of a Substitution Account', *op. cit.*, Dec. 1981, p. 425.
92. J. Gowa, *Closing the Gold Window—Domestic Politics and the End of Bretton Woods, op. cit.*, pp. 141–9.

4

The SDR and the US international monetary policy process

4.1 Introduction

In the last chapter we looked at changing US administration policy towards the Special Drawing Right (SDR), focusing mostly upon Treasury attitudes to international monetary reform in the post-Bretton Woods period. What emerged is that US policy gradually turned away from initiatives with respect to the SDR, particularly when the SDR appeared to threaten the role of the dollar. These tendencies were reinforced by the political resurgence of market-oriented policies in the US as the post-Bretton Woods monetary arrangements consolidated themselves. There were brief times when the US reconsidered the SDR, particularly during the Carter administration, but these were also times when the dollar appeared weak and it seemed as if the SDR could bolster the role of the dollar internationally. This chapter delves further into the nature of US international monetary policy determination in the post-Bretton Woods era. It emerges here that the changing structure of the US international monetary policy apparatus also affected policy outcomes vis-à-vis the SDR in the post-Bretton Woods era. In effect this more structural approach to an analysis of the US state during the transition to post-Bretton Woods arrangements reveals that the political moves away from the SDR were further reinforced.

As an entity that did not attract much media or lobbying interest, the SDR is an excellent means of addressing changing policy processes in the bureaucratic environment. This inevitably widens our discussion to include other elements of the US state, such as the Federal Reserve and Congress. We will also have to take into account the political influences on the structure of the US state at the time, not the least of which was the changing balance between the administration and Congress in the wake of the Watergate scandal. While international monetary policy was rarely the cause or effect of changes in the US policy process, the combination of international monetary upheaval with domestic changes in the policy process in the 1970s meant that additional constraints were established on a wider role for the SDR. Hitherto this has been relatively neglected in the literature, but given the upheavals in US politics at the time, it remains important. The debate over the influence of domestic policy on US policy determination allows us to enter this discussion.

4.2 Domestic Policy Considerations in the Determination of US International Monetary Policy

The primacy of domestic considerations in the forging of US international monetary policy is understandable for the familiar reason that the US economy is relatively well insulated from the rest of the world. This has been an important theme in international relations literature.[1] It was less true in the 1970s and 1980s, however, than it was during the 1950s and 1960s. Nonetheless, whether measured by comparative import penetration, or imports as a percentage of GDP (see Table 4.1 below), the US economy is less dependent upon foreign transactions for its economic well being than its industrialized trading partners.[2] Conversely, the relative size of the US economy, and the influence it has had upon the international monetary system since World War II, mean that the international ramifications of US monetary policy remain fundamental, irrespective of the continuing debate over whether the US is a *declining* hegemon.[3]

Because American international monetary policy still exerted primary influence over the post-Bretton Woods system, relatively few US policy makers found it incumbent to give systemic goals priority. Foreign policy was important in so far as it could aid US domestic policy goals, but as with any other state US responsibility for the system was rarely emphasized.[4] In the immediate post-Bretton Woods era as much as during it the US administration remained cognizant of the importance of the dollar to the international monetary system, notwithstanding any gains that accrued to the US.[5] This status for the dollar was as important to the US after Bretton Woods as it had been during the Kennedy administration, although the demands this put upon US policy makers was increasing. Paul Volcker referred to a testy Arthur Burns replying to a question from the press in early 1973 in Paris that 'American monetary policy is not made in Paris; it is made in Washington'.[6] Although Volcker was uneasy with the outburst and the sentiment behind it, it did point to increasing tension between US domestic and international responsibilities, and a growing realization in Washington that international ramifications on domestic policy were increasingly evident.[7] The unease with which the US viewed the SDR as a substitute for the dollar, witnessed in previous chapters, also reflected this.

Table 4.1. G10 countries—ratio of imports to GDP (%), 1966–86

	1966	1968	1970	1972	1974	1976	1978	1980	1982	1984	1986
US	3.6	4.0	4.2	4.9	7.6	7.5	8.4	9.6	8.2	9.2	9.2
UK	15.6	18.0	17.7	17.3	27.6	24.5	23.5	21.6	20.6	24.5	22.8
Switzerland	26.0	25.9	30.7	27.7	30.5	26.0	28.1	35.8	29.7	32.4	30.3
France	11.2	11.2	13.4	13.8	19.5	18.1	16.9	20.3	21.0	20.9	17.8
Netherlands	39.3	37.6	39.7	35.6	45.2	42.1	39.2	46.1	46.2	49.9	43.1
Belgium	—	—	—	—	—	—	—	—	—	—	—
Germany	14.9	15.2	16.2	15.6	18.3	19.8	19.0	23.1	23.6	24.8	21.4
Italy	12.7	12.7	14.9	15.0	24.1	23.3	21.6	22.1	21.7	20.6	16.4
Sweden	19.5	18.9	21.0	19.0	28.9	25.1	22.6	26.9	27.6	27.7	24.9
Canada	16.8	17.5	16.8	18.3	22.0	20.0	21.8	23.6	19.1	22.7	23.4
Japan	9.0	8.8	9.3	7.8	13.5	11.6	8.2	13.3	12.1	10.9	6.5
Average	*16.9*	*17.0*	*18.4*	*17.5*	*23.7*	*21.8*	*20.9*	*24.2*	*23.0*	*24.4*	*21.6*

Note: Average is unweighted, not including Belgium

Source: *International Financial Statistics*—supplement series no. 15: 'Supplement on Trade Statistics', IMF, 1988

In addition, US officials in Washington are under no illusions that foreign economic policy is at best a minority taste. President Nixon once observed that there were only two to three thousand individuals in the entire country who specialized in any aspect of foreign policy, let alone foreign economic policy.[8] More revealingly still, Barry Newman, Director of the Office for International Monetary Policy at the US Treasury in the late 1980s, went even further in estimating that there were 'fewer than a dozen' people in Washington whose prime responsibilities were international monetary policy issues in so far as they affected the Fund and the SDR.[9] This has led some theorists to reflect that it is not only domestic priorities, but rather isolationist and neomercantilist strains among them, which lend to a more complete understanding of US policy choices and goals.[10] Indeed international monetary policy is relatively unimportant to policy makers in Washington because the international orientation of the US economy has never approached that of the country with which it is most often compared concerning its international monetary role, namely Britain at the height of the gold standard.

Although an appreciation of domestic policy considerations is vitally important for an understanding of US international policy change, it is not, of course, solely responsible for explaining it. There are other international and domestic considerations, not only concerned with policy, which are important. Some studies point to the importance of domestic electoral cycles in US policy making.[11] One critic has observed that this is perhaps not surprising, 'since foreigners do not vote in American elections', and citizens do not consider other countries' economic welfare when voting.[12] However this observation is immediately countered by the suggestion that if domestic economic 'welfare' could be enhanced by policy makers taking seriously the potential gains from international policy coordination, then they would be rewarded at the next election.[13] In general, of course, this does not happen—but this does point to additional strains inherent in the changing nature of foreign economic influences on the US. And it also helps to remind us that questions about the SDR and international systemic questions in general seemed remote to the average American 'outside the beltway'.

As we have noted, the SDR, as a relatively arcane subject for media and other private interests, is relatively immune from purely domestic political pressures, including lobbying, and is thus an excellent vehicle for examining the international monetary policy process. What is perhaps surprising given these almost laboratory-like conditions for examining the forging of US policy is how haphazard the process, and the structure of the bureaucracy itself, seems.[14] There are elements of constancy in this; it had been christened in the early 1960s as 'ad hoccery' associated with the policies of Robert Roosa, and somewhat later as 'muddling through' by Joanne Gowa.[15] We also noted aspects of it with respect to policy towards the SDR in the last chapter, and an examination of the structure of the US state, at least with respect to international monetary policy determination, tends to reinforce it. Changing ideas and policy processes, the individuals involved in these changes, and indeed the structure of the state itself, like the ultimate subject of international monetary policy itself, are increasingly fungible. This is certainly not to argue that international monetary policy is not taken extremely seriously by its practitioners, nor that it is not open to outside influences. However, it does seem that contributing to a sense of malaise in US policy determination was a lack of coordination within the policy process and in the growing complexities of the structure of the state itself. As Bergsten argued in his attack on the Ford international economic policy process in 1975:

> The absence of any effective machinery to formulate, coordinate, and implement the foreign economic policy of the United States has now become exceedingly costly to the nation and is, indeed, scandalous.[16]

We have noted these themes before, the point here, however, is that this lack of coordination also tends to confirm the importance of domestic policy considerations—including a relatively fluid delineation of responsibility—in the determination of US policy. Although the US came to support floating rates, there was no evident grand design in this, and the US experience with the SDR suggested that the flexibility and pragmatism that had characterized policy during previous periods continued to prevail, not least because it was a longstanding and successful approach.

A reinforcing phenomenon in the absence of coordination is a strong, but still nebulous, conception of national interest, and this includes equally vague but just as important attitudes towards the dollar. Thus the remainder of our investigation must keep these phenomena in mind: the prevalent but increasingly strained primacy of domestic politics, the lack of coordination of US international monetary policy, and a relatively strong conception of 'national interest', due in part to its geo-political influence.

4.3 US International Monetary Policy Responsibilities in the Legislative and Executive Branches

In examining the international monetary policy process within the US, let us now focus more closely upon the institutional structure of the bureaucracy itself. The principal 'actors' involved in US international monetary policy in their institutional context (both legislative and executive) are illustrated on pp. 117 and 118, below. It may be seen at a glance that the dispersion of power and influence within both the US Congress and administration is very diffuse, although in each case policy primacy lies with a smaller group. (And also recall that the number of people working *solely* on international monetary questions is tiny.)

We began to address the administration in the last chapter. However, Congressional influence has increased so much in recent years that the structure of the legislative branch on foreign economic questions is also important. This point has been made to a degree with respect to US exchange rate policy-making in the 1980s.[17] Our investigation of policy towards the SDR shows that Congressional interest in the SDR was surprisingly long standing, and also had an increasing bearing on US policy towards the asset through the 1970s. Although Congress's legislative role is by definition not analogous to the executive role of the administration, those branches of Congress whose influence extends to international monetary policy are increasingly evident, and indicated on Illustration 4.2.

While the power to 'regulate Commerce with foreign Nations' rests with the legislature under Section 8, Article I of the US constitution, in common with most Western states, foreign policy increasingly became vested in the executive. This tendency was reinforced historically for two reasons, the first of which was the increasing importance of a quick response at times of military tension. Somewhat paradoxically reinforcing this, the growing relative power of the US internationally meant that international considerations did not have to be taken into account as much as in other countries in the forging of domestic policy. In addition, the constitutional prohibition against restricting interstate commerce also had the effect of distancing the day-to-day business of the legislature from involvement in the international economic sphere.

The balance between Congressional and Executive influence has shifted back and forth over the years—however the recent difficulties experienced by successive administrations, particularly since Watergate, have meant that Congress has been increasingly active in foreign policy issues during the past 35–40 years. As one critic has argued:

> Congress now tries to micromanage those affairs—foreign policy—for which its members are held least responsible.... [E]ver since sensing the opportunities for expanding congressional power during the Nixon administration, legislators have made unprecedented incursions into the ability of the executive branch to set and to administer foreign policy.[18]

This is a particularly notable development given the tendency of power to be increasingly concentrated in the executive in other democratic jurisdictions, particularly those under Anglo-Saxon parliamentary systems.

It should also be noted that the structure of neither the legislative nor the executive branch of the US government lends itself to policy continuity. Two-year terms of office in the House of Representatives and a relatively politicized

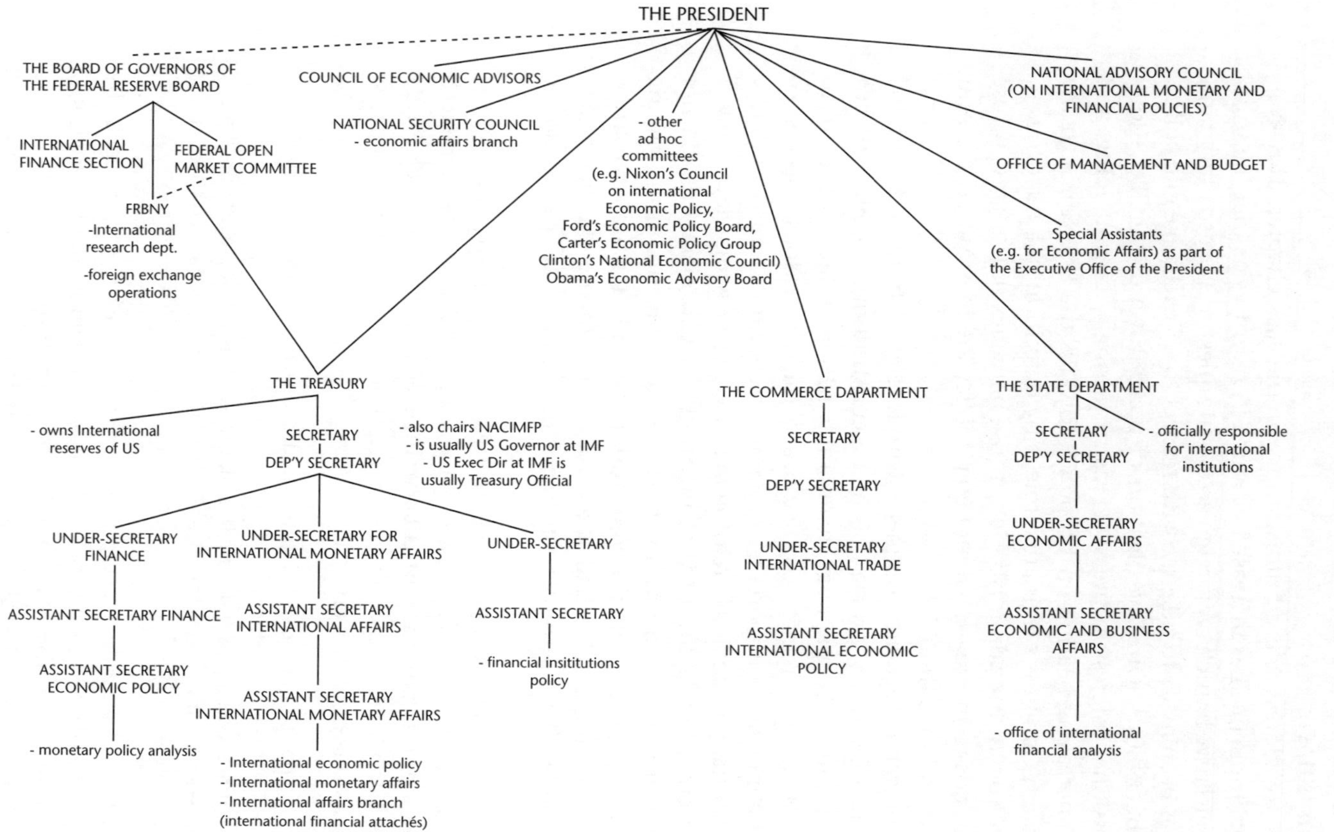

Note: 1. The structure of each department is subject to change, and often does, with a change in administration
2. For the vast majority of individuals within departments (in both the executive and legislative branches) international monetary policy is not their sole responsibility

Illustration 4.1. US government—international monetary policy bureaucracy representational organization chart—executive branch

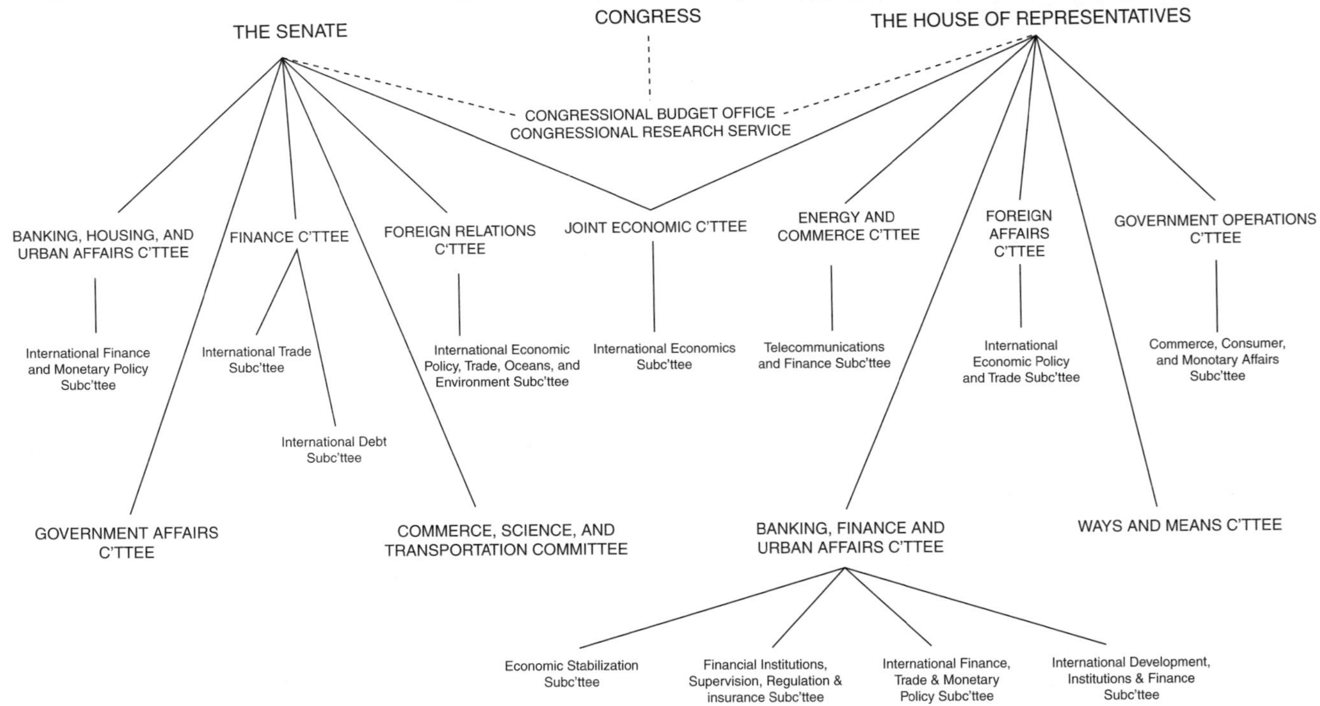

Notes: 1. Except for the Joint Economic Committe, Committees listed above are all Standing Committees. Other Special Committees and subcommittes may be instituted
2. Hearings of Congressional committees provide important Insight into the policies of the adminstration, since testimony is usually published

Illustration 4.2. US government—international monetary policy bureaucracy representational organization chart—legislative branch

bureaucracy in the administration does not easily lend itself to policy stability, particularly when complicated by frequent personnel changes as a matter of course. John Zysman links these phenomena:

> The large number of political appointments available with each shift in administration opens the bureaucracy to direct infiltration by groups concerned with specific agency decisions. The top officials of these agencies are often drawn from the groups affected by the agency. The legislature itself is fragmented, with power devolving to particular committees and in recent years to shifting and unstable congressional coalitions.[19]

It is interesting that few American observers argue that the bureaucracy is invigorated by the regular infusion of fresh blood. On the contrary it is argued that this hinders the bureaucracy from long-range decision making and contributes to a 'weak state' in terms of policy determination processes in the US. Notwithstanding this debate, the economic and political power of the US means that apparent lack of vision, structure, and continuity in policy processes is no less influential for that.

We have already witnessed rapid policy shifts and differences in approach with respect to the balance-of-payments crisis in the past: President Kennedy's cabinet committee on the subject was followed by President Johnson's Advisory Committee on International Monetary Affairs. President Nixon also created new committees, such as the Council on International Economic Policy and the Volcker Group, in an effort to come to terms with international monetary issues that were demanding increasing attention. Later, the experience of the Council on International Economic Policy, at least through the eyes of Fred Bergsten in testimony to a Senate Committee, is illustrative not only of the problems which can occur during the same administration, but also of those who analyse them:

> The Council on International Economic Policy (CIEP) was created in early 1971.... But it never even began to fulfil its function. CIEP has been without an executive director for six months. Its role has virtually disappeared, as indicated by the (ineffective) transfer of even its nominal responsibilities to the Economic Policy Board. Indeed I recommended its abolition before this subcommittee in May 1973, when Secretary of the Treasury George Shultz—whose role as economic czar was made clear by his designation as Assistant to the President for Economic Affairs—was effectively managing most international economic issues. Now, however, I see no alternative but to create a strong CIEP.[20]

Later still, there was a change of tack during the Reagan administration, when promotion of market solutions extended itself to delaying appointments within the Treasury or by approving a reduction within the departments (see Appendix 3).[21] President Clinton instituted the National Economic Council in order to help direct economic policy, and in the wake of the international financial crisis in 2008, President Obama instituted the Economic Recovery Advisory Board, calling upon Paul Volcker to be its first head before reorienting it to become a Council on Jobs and Competitiveness in early 2011. Therefore, while Illustrations 4.1 and 4.2 begin to illustrate how complex policy making has become in the US, they also oversimplify the overlapping of jurisdiction, of influence, and of potential dispute. This, too, also lends some credence to the importance of individual policy makers themselves in influencing policy direction in the US, a theme that emerged in the previous chapter, for instance when we witnessed the temporary increase in influence of the State Department in international monetary policy during the Carter administration. In order to address these bureaucratic questions more fully, let us review the role of yet another entity influencing US international monetary relations, the Federal Reserve Board.

4.4 The Federal Reserve Board

The Federal Reserve is responsible for US monetary policy, and derives its ultimate constitutional power from Congress. Questions of *international* monetary policy are the prerogative of the Treasury. Nonetheless, it is the New York Federal Reserve Bank, one of 12 constituent members of the Fed, which is responsible for managing foreign exchange transactions for the US government. Inevitably, the Fed is involved in questions of international importance, and these have included the SDR. Like other central banks, the Fed shuns publicity—but this has become increasingly difficult under a succession of influential heads (Paul Volcker and Alan Greenspan in particular), so that its role has come under increasing scrutiny.[22]

There are different roles for its constituent elements. Few of the 12 member reserve banks have much to do with international policy, except for the New York Federal Reserve, which is responsible for conducting monetary policy operations including foreign exchange. It is the Federal Open Market Committee, however, which issues directives to the New York Fed for these operations, and the FOMC and US Treasury (the latter having legal authority over exchange rate policy) that direct operations in foreign exchange markets, although again it is the New York Fed which performs the transactions. In turn, the New York Fed, as *primus inter pares* on the 12-member FOMC, traditionally provides the FOMC's vice chairman, with the chairman of the Board of Governors in Washington acting as the FOMC's chair.[23]

The attitudes of the Fed towards the SDR are interesting. At the conclusion to Chapter 2 we saw how the New York Fed in the early 1970s recommended that private sponsorship of SDR denominated assets be halted—and this very shortly after they had appeared. This was apparently due to the Fed's policy against the acceptance of foreign deposits by member banks[24] (which also served to support the role of the dollar)—but is interesting nonetheless given the strong early US support for the SDR by the Treasury. What it also pointed to was that privately US officials were more wary than their official pronouncements indicated.

Later, the Fed then hinted at support for the SDR in 1974 by saying that it had reconsidered the 'possible consolidation of outstanding reserve currency balances'.[25] Also at this time, the Administration's National Advisory Council on International Monetary and Financial Policy (NAC) had shifted its stance. The NAC's 1973 Annual Report hinted at some support for the SDR, noting that the US favoured a 'comprehensive approach to reform' and that:

> ... there is general agreement that the role of special drawing rights (SDRs) should be greatly enhanced, and that instrument would take on the role of unit of account, or *numeraire*, and central reserve asset in the new system. The United States has proposed a number of modifications to the present rules relating to the SDR to make it a more usable and attractive asset.[26]

As noted, however, the breakdown of the Smithsonian Agreement in the spring of 1973 was the watershed for changing commitments to reform. The Federal Reserve, which in its 1973 Annual Report noted the necessity of continued work on the Committee of Twenty's First Outline of Reform as presented at the Fund's annual meeting in Nairobi in September of that year, equivocated strongly the following year.[27] It noted that in periods of severe economic change, progress would be difficult on the basic issues of the international monetary system.[28] Instead it advocated the adoption of floating exchange rates and a decision on the role of gold. Evidently, the Fed was pleased with post-Bretton Woods arrangements, and this was a further indication that US national interest was not served by the 'grand designs' of the C-20 and publicly-oriented international monetary reform proposals that advocated a stronger role for the SDR.

Somewhat echoing the changes during the Carter administration, Federal Reserve attitudes towards the SDR shifted briefly again later in the decade, although strained relations between Washington and New York muted them somewhat. Alfred Hayes and then Anthony Solomon in New York, for instance, were more sympathetic to the SDR. Indeed in Solomon's case, his views—at least while at the Treasury in the late 1970s—were very supportive of SDR initiatives. This included the period when the substitution account was under discussion, when he said in a 1979 address to the Royal Institute of International Affairs:

> Certainly we would expect the SDR to take on a growing role in the system ... We in the United States have great hope for the progress of the SDR.[29]

However the Fed became more hostile towards the late 1970s when discussion of the substitution account at the Treasury reemerged. In a question and answer session following the 1980 Per Jacobsson Lecture, Charles Coombs, the former vice president in charge of the Foreign Department and special manager of Federal Open Market Account, was asked if he thought that there was any hope of the SDR becoming an international currency, and if so, how soon. He replied:

> I would say that it has not the chance of the proverbial snowball in hell. I think that the SDR may have certain importance as a limited reserve asset.[30]

While other former US officials (William McChesney Martin and Frank Southard) were quick to interject that they were more optimistic, the comments of the respected Coombs are interesting. Coombs' reticence about the viability of the SDR was longstanding; he wrote that despite it being apparent to him and colleagues at the New York Fed that the Bretton Woods system 'was heading into serious trouble' as early as 1960, he never advocated anything like an SDR-based system:

> The initial bright hope of 'paper gold' in the form of the SDR has also faded, and as someone who was skeptical of its technical feasibility from the outset I am neither surprised nor saddened. But in any case, the SDR was never really needed.[31]

This candid admission, admittedly from an official after his retirement from active service, revealed that even when the US was publicly supporting the SDR, there were strong reservations about its role. (We have already witnessed more concrete manifestations of this during the first SDR allocation.) But in any case, by the late 1970s the Fed was increasingly preoccupied with both the level of inflation and the falling dollar exchange rate, which made SDR initiatives, especially in the guise of a substitution account, seem irrelevant at best. Admittedly, the US used SDRs as part of a package to rescue the dollar by the end of 1978,[32] but the importance of this gesture was that it reflected using SDRs in their traditional guise—as a support and *not* a substitute for the dollar.

It was also at this time that President Carter appointed Paul Volcker as Chairman of the Federal Reserve. (Anthony Solomon had moved from the New York Fed to the Treasury shortly beforehand.) With its relatively high public profile under Volcker's chairmanship and its role during the fight against inflation during the early 1980s, the Fed exercised further caution in its approach to international reform and the SDR (as Coombs's words presaged). Paul Volcker had a long experience with the SDR from his work at both the Treasury and the New York Fed in the 1960s and 1970s. Initially, he thought the first SDR allocation of 9.5 billion was 'a little below my highest hopes'.[33] After some experience of floating rates, however, he wrote of their 'relative disuse', and mused about the political impracticalities involved in more power for a supra-national world central bank (i.e. the IMF) that would presumably be necessary for an enhanced role for them.[34] Much more recently, however, as one of a number of former central bankers and finance ministers, he has called for reexamination of the SDR's potential role:

> ... in serving the public common good of monetary and financial stability in the new context of today's globalized and increasingly multi-polar world.[35]

Concerning increasing scepticism towards the SDR by the Fed, there were other reasons for its change in policy, which lie in the wider context of international monetary policy determination in the US. Federal Reserve Annual Reports reveal an organization that often felt it necessary to pay heed to prevailing political trends, as well as to its responsibilities for the international monetary system. Although the Federal Reserve is relatively separate from other government institutions (the Fed characterizes itself as 'independent within government'[36]), even it gradually became more beholden to Congress. As early as 1946, with the passage of the Employment Act, the Federal Reserve was required to pursue 'maximum employment, production and purchasing power'.[37] Thirty-two years later, with the passage of the Full Employment and Balanced Growth Act (the Humphrey–Hawkins Act) the Fed Chairman was required to report twice a year to the House Committee on Banking, Finance and Urban Affairs, and the Senate Committee on Banking, Housing, and Urban Affairs on the economy, and on 'the relationships of monetary objectives to the economic goals and policies of the administration and the Congress'.[38]

Congress's growing interest in foreign policy and foreign economic policy also manifested itself in an increasing number of legislative initiatives that had changes to Fed policy as an objective. Much of a New York Fed paper analyses these attempts between 1979 and 1990; it identifies 200 bills in the period (over three-quarters of which were in the first few years when the Fed's policies produced such historically high interest rates).[39] Most of these attempts were unsuccessful; perhaps the strongest prohibition against successful Congressional interference lying in the fact that, technically, the Fed is not part of the administration. (It is also organized regionally, which diffuses power.) Above all, since the Fed finances itself from its own earnings, Congress or the administration per se cannot use the appropriations or funding processes to control Fed policies.[40]

Nonetheless the Fed does stand in a delicate position. As we have seen, it is responsible for 'monetary policy', although it is the Treasury that is responsible for 'international monetary policy'. It has to report directly to Congress, which delegated power to the Fed through its constitutional responsibilities outlined in Article I, section 8 to 'coin money, regulate the Value thereof, and of foreign Coin'. Congressional attacks have sometimes been indirect as well, and have included recommending coincident terms for the Chairman of the Federal Reserve and the President, and trying to add the Secretary of the Treasury or even the Chairman of the Council of Economic Advisers to the FOMC. Occasionally the Fed has even had to withstand challenges to its legal standing and authority.[41]

In addition to Congressional suspicion, the Fed is subject to periods of strained relations with the administration as well. Much of the Chairman of the Federal Reserve's formal and informal contacts remain with or on behalf of the administration—with the various executive offices themselves (the Council of Economic Advisers and as a member of the National Advisory Council on International Monetary and Financial Policies, for example), at weekly meetings between senior members of the Board of Governors and the Treasury (at the Deputy or Under-Secretary level), and as the US alternate governor of the IMF. Despite these links, these relationships have at times been fraught with mistrust. In his candid work on international finance already mentioned, Charles Coombs noted that relations between the Fed, the US Treasury, and other administrative offices could deteriorate markedly, as they did during Nixon's presidency. He noted that as the Nixon administration took office in January 1969, the Federal Reserve Bank of New York, of which Coombs was vice president, was abruptly cut off from Washington discussions of foreign financial policy.[42]

> ...The cordial and candid working relationships Treasury officials I had enjoyed under Secretaries Dillon and Fowler soon withered away. Despite frequent visits to the Treasury during those early years of the Nixon administration, I was cut off like [FRBNY President] Hayes from Washington meetings. Nor could I even discern who was in charge of foreign financial policy. The new Treasury team seemed indecisive and lacking in initiative, and frequently gave the impression of simply executing policy instructions originating elsewhere—presumably in the complex of White House advisers.[43]

Parenthetically, we noted in Chapter 1 that Nixon's August 1971 shocks were a surprise to the Fund's managing director and to US allies abroad. While this may seem surprising, it seems that not even senior Federal Reserve officials were involved in the decision.[44] And this is despite the Special Manager for Foreign Operations at the New York Fed being responsible for carrying out the directives of the FOMC and the Treasury. That the president of the New York Fed was not informed of the 71 decisions to impose a 10 per cent import surcharge and suspend prevailing international monetary arrangements is surprising, and certainly gives further credence to the notion that US monetary policy, at least as far as the international aspects are concerned, is often made on an ad hoc basis.

Finally, and paying heed to its international context, it may be observed that despite the constitutional system of checks and balances within the US system, and despite the fluctuating fortunes of the legislature and administration vis-à-vis the Fed, it is again the importance of individuals at the Fed that has had a great bearing on the success of this institution to pursue its goals. In a study of the US and European central banks, the economic historian Richard Sylla observed:

> The Fed's independence depends more on the character and strength of its leaders, the outstanding examples being Benjamin Strong in the 1920's, Marriner Eccles in the 1930s, William McChesney Martin, Jr. in the 1950s and 1960s, and Paul Volcker in the 1980s.... If the independence of the Federal Reserve System is to remain a viable concept, it will be because central bankers through their actions earn the right to it, not because it is conferred upon them by mutable laws.[45]

Thus it may be said that the Federal Reserve as a whole lost interest in the SDR following the Smithsonian Agreement; whether during this time of upheaval it had pursued a policy with this goal in mind is less apparent. It is worth noting that in a wide-ranging Hirsch memorial lecture in 1978,[46] Paul Volcker, then at the New York Fed, did not even mention the SDR, and despite a more recent change of heart, he mused about the SDR's growing irrelevance to post-Bretton Woods in the 1990s.[47]

It could thus be stated simply that once Bretton Woods had broken down, the Fed effectively abandoned the SDR, even during the late 1970s when other branches of the US government were reconsidering it. And the growing influence of Congress on all entities of the US state, including the Fed, must also be taken into account. Perhaps, then, the best way of encapsulating the role of the Federal Reserve vis-à-vis the SDR is that it can exercise a 'negative capability', that is reflecting the caution with which it as a banker's bank is naturally charged, its power lies more in deflating or opposing policies rather than in proposing them. It could also be argued that the Federal Reserve disenchantment with the SDR sometimes anticipated the policies of the administration towards it. It is interesting to note that in a 1990s summary of US exchange rate policy since the war in the *Federal Reserve Bulletin*, the birth of SDRs is dealt with in some detail. Since then only a brief mention of them appears in the context of the IMF's Second Amendment and the SDR as principal reserve asset.[48] In any case, Fed policy was more hostile to the SDR as time went on. It was the Treasury, occasionally the State Department (especially during the Carter administration), and also the Congress that made the SDR its business after the breakdown of Bretton Woods.

4.5 The Growing Role and Influence of the US Congress on International Monetary Questions

Another key development that again reinforced US moves away from the SDR was the growing profile of Congress in matters of international monetary policy. This paralleled increasing Congressional involvement in other international economic questions in the 1970s and 1980s, including trade policy. We have already witnessed this with respect to its role in general in Chapter3, and above concerning the Federal Reserve; it also became increasingly true of Congress's relationships with the Executive.

Congressional influence on foreign policy, particularly that of the House of Representatives, is relatively new. Admittedly, Congressional influence on the Executive and foreign policy has always been cyclical. Woodrow Wilson observed in 1885 that US government was dominated by a Congress—'the central and predominant power of the system'—which in turn 'lay foundering in a confusion of warring committees'.[49] Almost one hundred years later, in the 1970s, Congress's influence on many economic issues was pursued aggressively again in the wake of the Vietnam War and Watergate. We have seen how Congressional initiatives increasingly affected the role of the Federal Reserve. While the role of Congressional 'oversight' of international monetary questions has been acknowledged, its growing legislative influence on these questions merits further attention.[50]

But first of all it is worth noting the absolute growth in manpower that increased Congress's ability to address foreign issues. To begin with, the number of Congressional staff increased from approximately 5,600 in 1955 to 6,800 in 1960, to 17,700 in 1974.[51] Many of these staff members were recruited for their foreign policy expertise—this was particularly true of the post-Watergate era:

> It... became the norm for each senator to have a foreign policy specialist on his personal staff, something highly unusual in 1965, and a growing number had more than one.[52]

In addition to this simple increase in staff, (something Congress shared with legislative branches throughout the industrialized world after the war) institutional changes within Congress meant that it took an increasing role in the formulation of policy. Whereas policy making in the past has been characterized by Robert Dahl as the Executive being 'the car-driver [while] Congress applies the brakes',[53] by the mid-1970s it would have been more appropriate to stretch the metaphor to argue that Congress was attempting to reach for the steering wheel as well. It has already been observed that Congress's influence escalated remarkably, particularly through the authorization and appropriations process that the growth in Committees has fostered (see the organization charts Illustrations 4.1 and 4.2). While some of this was cyclical, as has been noted, previous Congressional influence tended to be exercised through the Senate. In the 1960s, however, the House of Representatives, which had virtually no foreign policy role before World War II, also started to play a 'vital role . . . in the formulation of U.S. foreign policy'.[54]

The increasing size of government and complexity of issues also contributed to the growth in importance of Congressional subcommittees and their influence on policy.[55] While similar committee systems have evolved in other Western states, the growth in power vis-à-vis the executive in the US has not been as evident in the governments of its allies. With this growth in importance of subcommittees it is now vital for any researcher of US international monetary policy to take into account the role of Congress. This is not an easy task; the overlapping jurisdiction of committees and subcommittees as outlined in Illustration 4.2, coupled with the sheer volume of Congressional documents published, as well as the more common investigation of policy attitudes in the US administration, makes for increasingly complex foreign policy determination. However, the undeniable growth in importance of Congress, extending to the 'micromanaging' of foreign policy,[56] makes this an increasing necessity from an International Relations perspective.

Let us examine Congress's increasing involvement in issues affecting the SDR, including the SDR itself. Recall that in Chapter 1, we learned that as early as 1961 a Congressional committee under Henry Reuss had rejected an increasing role for gold in international monetary arrangements.[57] Recall also that in 1968 Treasury Henry Fowler made much of the fact that Congressional support for SDRs was wide and bipartisan.[58]

This enthusiasm, however, was even more short-lived than that of the administration. In fact, as early as 1970 Congress voted to limit the American IMF governor's latitude to create SDRs up to the amount equal to the US quota. Henceforth, any amount in excess of this would have to be authorized by Congress.[59] This was only the first of a gradual encroaching upon the influence of the US administration on international monetary policy.

As noted, under Article I, section 8, of the US Constitution, Congress has responsibility 'to coin money, regulate the Value thereof, and of foreign coin'. Thus, under section 5 of the Bretton Woods Agreement Act, the gold value of the dollar was established by statute. Nonetheless the practical exigencies of exchange rate management and the fact that the same section of the Constitution said that all 'duties, Imposts and Excises shall be uniform throughout the United States' meant that Congress assigned most of this responsibility to the Treasury and Fed.[60] As Congress attempted to reassert its role under flexible rates, however, it began to further impede what successive administrations felt was under their jurisdiction under Article II of the constitution, namely that of making treaties, etc. Given the grey area that therefore existed with respect to international initiatives, this also affected relations between the two branches of government concerning the SDR, when Congress effectively raised its profile.

In what was perhaps the clearest example of this, Henry Reuss, the House Democrat from Wisconsin and the most respected international monetary specialist in Congress throughout the 1960s and 1970s, supplied an unequivocal 'no' to what amounted to the substitution account in 1975:

> In sum, most dollar balances retained by foreigners are held willingly, and to the extent that they are not, the holders have no claim based in equity that the United States should guarantee the value of their holdings. An exchange of dollars for special drawing rights or other obligations bearing a foreign exchange value or purchasing power guarantee is neither necessary nor desirable.[61]

Reuss's report went further to recommend that for the 'foreseeable future, no dollar balances should be exchanged for [SDRs]', or for 'other long term obligations bearing exchange rate or purchasing power guarantees'.[62] Although the concern at the time was specifically the dollar overhang, the implications for a substitution account were far-reaching, as they were for increasing Congressional influence on questions of international monetary policy. Whether successive administrations in the US would have been able to overcome these concerns, particularly in the wake of Watergate, is debatable: as we noted in our discussion of the substitution account during the Carter administration, Congress did even feel it necessarily to take the proposals seriously.[63] But in any case, having opposed the idea so early (in 1975), and by a Committee chaired by a strong Democrat, this suggests that even if the administration had supported such an account at Hamburg in 1980, Congressional support would not have been easily won.

Other instances also exist of Congressional involvement in issues closely related to the SDR. In 1976, the Senate Foreign Relations Committee was again looking at international monetary questions. In its consideration of the Amendment of the Bretton Woods Agreements Act, the Committee was recommending further Congressional 'oversight... with regard to United States participation in the international monetary system'.[64] It was argued that more oversight of foreign economic policy was necessary under a system of flexible exchange rates. Although it was difficult to see how Congress could deepen its involvement in practice, Congress was indicating to the administration that international monetary matters should be subject to greater Congressional oversight.

Congress continued to pass laws throughout the 1970s and 1980s that subjected US international monetary policy to increasing Congressional involvement. Increases in the US quota at the IMF, for instance, became subject to Congressional approval. In 1976 Congress agreed to an increase in the US quota in the Fund to SDR 1.705 billion, while also suggesting that the administration seek 'changes in the characteristics and uses of SDRs'.[65] By 1983, Congress passed a bill that made it illegal for SDRs to be allocated at all without Congressional approval.[66]

This was one of Congress's most overt interventions into international monetary policy as it affected the SDR. Importantly, it remains a further stumbling block in the event the IMF agrees to additional SDR allocations. The most overt illustration of this is the 12-year delay between the successful IMF Fourth Amendment negotiations in 1997 and the US ratification in 2009. US congressional opposition to the Fourth Amendment was a constant factor during that time, notwithstanding early support during the Clinton administration.[67] Indeed, during continued Congress–administration battles over SDR quota authorization, the Treasury and Congressional Budget Office (CBO) agreed that increases to SDR quotas were a 'budgetary item', which indeed became law in 1998.[68] In turn, this now meant further Congressional committee involvement (particularly the powerful House Ways and Means Committee) with respect to the Fund and international monetary policy that had hitherto not existed, with additional reporting requirements of the Treasury.

Thus additional hurdles were created in the already complicated forging of US international monetary policy post-Bretton Woods. Growing Congressional strength in the wake of Watergate assumed increasing importance with respect to questions of international monetary policy and could not help but complicate prospects for the SDR. This was particularly in evidence in the wake of the Fourth Amendment to the IMF Articles of Agreement—despite the fact that it was championed by the US Treasury upon approval in 1997, once the Omnibus Consolidated and Emergency Supplemental Appropriations Act became law in 1998 the Administration was reluctant to submit it to a Congress that could have demanded additional changes to the Articles.[69] In addition, the Congressional committee system and also subcommittee system[70] (see Illustration 4.2) succeeded in further entrenching Congress's role with respect to international monetary matters. Future US administrations would have to think long and hard before presenting an SDR with complex and esoteric attributes to a Congress increasingly determined to play a role in almost all aspects of foreign policy. Richard Gardner had noted that international monetary policy considerations had been a hard sell in Congress even at the ratification of Bretton Woods. Although there was a rapprochement in the 1960s, which allowed the Fund's First Amendment, in the 1970s battles had once again become much more difficult.

Congressional strength has varied considerably in relation to the Executive, and during the 1970s Congress's influence increased at a time of considerable flux for international monetary relations. After Watergate, with a growing Congressional unwillingness to defer to the administration, and with growing expertise through an expanded Committee system and bureaucracy of its own, questions of international monetary policy, hitherto relatively ignored, were now sometimes aggressively addressed. The contrast between the acquiescence as SDRs were first allocated, with later opinions on the substitution account and even IMF quotas, was striking. It could be argued that Congress was attempting to re-assert its constitutionally mandated authority over the 'value' of the dollar, or with respect to foreign commerce. What was undeniable was a greater Congressional interest and influence over US international monetary policy—an influence that arguably extends to IMF policy itself.[71] Prospects for the SDR, already extremely limited under evolving Treasury attitudes, were undoubtedly adversely affected by a Congress that had only briefly entertained the SDR sympathetically. The growing role of Congress cannot be underrated in any account of US policy turning away from the SDR as the post-Bretton Woods era unfolded.

4.6 Post-Bretton Woods US International Monetary Policy and Theories of US Foreign Policy Determination

A theme underlying much of the past two chapters has been what our discoveries may contribute to theories of US foreign policy determination. One of the discoveries that emerged in the last chapter was that in general, as post-Bretton Woods arrangements evolved, the US was willing to entertain SDR-related initiatives only when they could be viewed as supporting the international role of the dollar. As the new arrangements consolidated themselves, this became less and less likely, discussion of the substitution account notwithstanding. In this chapter we have observed that Congressional and Fed reticence concerning the SDR was if anything even more pronounced, and that this, combined with a structural analysis of the US state (including the growth in importance of Congressional committees and subcommittees) has complicated both the determination and analysis of US international monetary policy.

We have seen that during the negotiations that preceded the Rio Agreement the US was an enthusiastic proponent of the SDR. With respect to theoretical aspects of US foreign policy determination, Stephen Cohen and John Odell have explored this initial enthusiasm to some degree. However, both these works concentrate on how US policy changed in favour of an international reserve asset during the 1960s. Later literature has not addressed in as much depth why this enthusiasm was not sustained, and indeed why it was reversed. The increasing complexities of international monetary policy determination in the US undoubtedly played their part.

Much international relations literature has sought to provide a theoretical basis for explaining international monetary policy change. This has sometimes proved useful in our examination of policy change towards the SDR in its early days. Later experience with the SDR has not been addressed in as much detail, although some explanatory variables can easily be transposed to our investigation. The question of the primacy of domestic considerations over international ones, for instance, is one such example. Also, in a work with which we are already familiar, John Odell emphasizes how these conditions affected bureaucratic decision-making in the administration while also paying credence to the economic conditions which spawned the decision to support discussions which led to the SDR.[72] The central argument of his influential work in international monetary relations is to note the explanatory power of markets, power, and ideas as key explanatory factors—and later experience with the SDR lends support to this thesis. To give credence to ideas in particular—and the people who hold them—could further be said to nod to economic constructivist strains of international relations theory, in that the social construct governing international monetary relations clearly changed as Bretton Woods arrangements broke down.[73] At the very least the debate over SDRs under post-Bretton Woods arrangements—and commensurate decline in prospects for the asset—was certainly coincident with the ascendance of new ideas associated with monetarism and private liquidity provision, versus traditional Keynesian notions of public liquidity provision that had characterized the prevailing international consensus up until the birth of SDRs in the dying days of the Bretton Woods system.

But these observations do not supply a complete picture. Our examination of the changing role and influence of the IMF suggests that institutions are indeed important in their own right. Furthermore, changing international monetary interests at the Fund had an influence on domestic policy determination, even among its most important members. This gives credence to Peter Gourevitch's classic work on longstanding international sources of domestic politics. This influential idea is important to our discussion of the role of the Fund in the story of the SDR and even to the evolution of the international monetary policies of its most important members. But more importantly, in the context of our discussion of US foreign policy, it may also be recalled that Gourevitch not only noted the importance of international relations to domestic politics, but how intertwined these influences are on each other:

> The international system is not only a consequence of domestic politics and structures but a cause of them . . . International relations and domestic politics are therefore so interrelated that they should be analysed simultaneously, as wholes.[74]

Ultimately then, how far can we say the decision to support the creation, allocation, and further discussion of a new international money lends itself to a theory of foreign economic policy making in the US during the 1970s? Odell argued that one of the main influences behind the decision to support the SDR initially was the acceptance of the Triffin thesis. Those who argue from a different perspective than Odell, such as Henry Nau, Fred Bergsten, and Joanne Gowa, also give credence to the influence Triffin's ideas had on the US administration.[75] Hence ideas, as well as markets or a change in international power relationships, is one of the main impetuses for US policy change in this instance. This is echoed later in the Bürgenstock papers, a collection of papers in which, as editor George Halm noted, policy makers tended to favour prevailing Bretton Woods monetary arrangements, whereas academics tended to favour freely floating rates.[76] Ideas presage policy change, promulgated by individuals who hold office, negotiate, or have influence over those who do. Odell acknowledged this in his examination of those involved in international monetary policy in the early 1960s:

> President Johnson named Henry H. Fowler, an adherent of the Triffin school, to replace Douglas Dillon as Treasury Secretary, in early 1965. Johnson's relatively new White House economist, Francis M. Bator, like his predecessors, also followed Triffin. Meanwhile, Dillon and Roosa also abandoned key earlier beliefs about international liquidity after leaving office.[77]

Just as important as the evidence for the influence of Triffin's ideas, there are also more subtle indications that some policy makers anticipated the Triffin paradox. Charls [*sic*] Walker, US Deputy and then Under Secretary of the Treasury during Nixon's administration, observed that the Triffin thesis was foreseen in American policy circles during the Eisenhower administration. At the Fund meeting in New Delhi in 1959, for instance, US officials warned of the 'dollar problem', and that the international community would have to start thinking about necessary changes to resolve it (there had been a marked deterioration of the US gold stock in the late 1950s—see Table 1.1). Walker emphasized, however, that the importance of this was impressed upon incoming Treasury officials during the Kennedy administration by the then Eisenhower staff, thereby anticipating Triffin's later influence as described by Odell.[78]

Until the US balance of payments problem became worse in the late 1960s, much energy was spent in the US avoiding the ramifications of the Triffin thesis through 'ad hoccery'. But rather than a change in ideas it could be argued that the apparent conversions in attitudes amongst senior Treasury officials was due to worsening balance of payments figures, rather than an appreciation of the finer points in Triffin's arguments or a new-found confidence in international reserve asset proposals. An early example of this possibility is revealed in declassified Treasury Department documents: although the US balance of payments position and international backing for the dollar in the early 1960s is noted, no explicit mention of what this means—including with respect to alternative assets—occurs in Dillon's arguments, either internally nor with his G10 counterparts. Most of the time was spent organizing what was to become the General Arrangements to Borrow among the G10 in 1962.[79] Also, Stephen Weatherford has observed that whereas the Basle Agreement and the Gold Pool of 1961 succeeded in relatively painlessly establishing short-term swap agreements, the medium term support inherent in the General Arrangements to Borrow was only achieved by Treasury Secretary Dillon after compromises with the G10 that constrained debtor access to the funds.[80]

US policy makers tended to be concerned with the grander elements of prestige attached to the geo-political role of the US. In the early 1970s, when the SDR added to world liquidity, the US was absolved from having to agree to an increase in the price of gold, which had been seen as a prime responsibility.[81] Although the US then seemed prepared to discuss further enhancement of the role of the SDR, domestic considerations and apparent sovereignty gains continued to take precedence with the breakdown of the Smithsonian agreement in 1973.[82]

Thus, although the acceptance of the Triffin thesis, and ideas in general, are certainly important to US international monetary policy determination, it is perhaps more important to note that the decision to support the SDR represented a continued side-stepping of some issues inherent in the Triffin thesis. It also tends to confirm the importance of domestic policy considerations in the forging of US international monetary policy. Other considerations, among them the appeal of apparently avoiding the domestic ramifications necessary to alter existing institutional arrangements necessary for the consideration of international issues, were also important, as were the changes in the prevailing intellectual climate as exhibited by policy makers themselves.

Odell refers to a secret group of individuals who were to promote a new international system to include exchange rate flexibility. These were brought together by Connally's successor at the Treasury, George Shultz, who had been named Assistant to the President in late 1972. The committee included Henry Kissinger or a deputy, neither of whom attended regularly, Arthur Burns, Herbert Stein (chairman of the Council of Economic Advisers), Peter Flanigan (the Executive Director of the Council on International Economic Policy), and Paul Volcker, then Under-Secretary at the Treasury.[83]

Using later examples, we may witness a change in office holders—for instance Jack F. Bennett, a supporter of flexible rates—as denoting a change in Treasury policy. Conversely, individuals who were prepared to listen sympathetically to ideas concerning the SDR during the Carter administration, such as Bergsten and Anthony Solomon, also had an influence on the brief US rekindling of interest in the substitution account. Later still, it was difficult to imagine a Federal Reserve supporting SDR initiatives while headed by Alan Greenspan from 1987–2002 (and who had also been Chairman of the Council of Economic Advisers in the mid-1970s under President Ford). We have already noted that the identity of individual Presidents of the Fed was important to the way in which this institution addressed international monetary policy, and to the 'negative capability' it exercised.

It is thus useful to acknowledge an important human element in policy formulation, US international monetary policy being no exception. This, too, has been recognized as an important consideration in the development of theories of foreign economic policy—at least in so far as the administration is concerned, one branch also noting psychological attributes of leaders and groups.[84] Paul Egon Rohrlich has also attempted to add 'cognitive analysis' (on the personal or social level) to what he terms more traditional '*realpolitik*' and 'behavioural' theories, which is consistent with growing 'scientism' in international relations theory.[85] Again, this is not to suggest that *personalities* may explain US foreign economic policy, but merely to point to a line of enquiry which has drawn attention to the importance of individuals and ideas, which has also enjoyed a great deal of credibility within the discipline and which should be integrated into any structural analysis of US international monetary policy determination. And it may go some way to contributing an explanation of the vagaries of US policy, which, as we have seen, has been termed successively 'ad hoccery', 'muddling through', and 'benign neglect', and may also be said to have continued in the post-Bretton Woods system. This is not to say that there were not important policy changes during this time, but simply to suggest that a comprehensive theory that explains US foreign economic policy may be premature, especially in dealing with the myriad influences on US policy makers. Yes, the primacy of domestic political priorities and a strong conception of national interest vis-à-vis the role of the dollar are constants. To argue further than this, however, does not necessarily make understanding the process of policy change any clearer. Indeed it may be observed that theorists (and often policy practitioners) with a more prosaic interpretation of policy determination and more narrative approaches to explaining change—including Fred Bergsten, F. Lisle Widman, or Henry Nau—come closer to explaining change than their more theoretical counterparts. Furthermore, without an integration of the growing role of Congress, either theoretically (as a reinforcement of the importance of domestic policy considerations), or practically (as contributing to an explanation of policy change), the present debates do not sufficiently capture the international policy changes in the US in so far as the SDR was concerned.

This is also not to say, however, that although US international monetary goals may at times seem obscure or even contradictory that cohesive theoretical elements may not be ascertained if some basic concepts are kept in mind. Domestic considerations in particular are a constant theme that aids in explaining how attitudes to international monetary policy change. Related to this is the notion that economic and financial policy is often seen as subsidiary to US geopolitical questions as a whole. This is an observation made by theorists[86] as well as practitioners of international policy in the US. Third, the identity and motivations of the policy maker is also a factor. In comparing the US to other countries' international monetary policy formulation processes, Widman makes some basic but nonetheless illustrative points referring to the importance of both individuals and larger geo-political questions as important variables in explaining US policy change:

> In Europe . . . it is often the individual with the greatest knowledge and experience in economic issues who rises to the top. Callaghan, Schmidt and Giscard d'Estaing all served as ministers of finance before they became heads of state. So did Fukuda and Ohiha in Japan. The minister of finance is often a more influential figure than the Prime Minister. The United States political system doesn't work that way. . . . Presidents have not been noted for their . . . understanding of the effects of macroeconomic policy. . . . [In the US] . . . more aspects of international economic policy [may be] in the hands of the Secretary of State than other countries place in their Foreign Offices. Occasionally this mismatch of responsibilities has unfortunate consequences for US economic policy.[87]

Thus, although larger geo-political questions and narrower issues involving individuals and ideas may not *both* be given credence in explaining international policy change in the US, it should be acknowledged that these factors make their influence felt through the structure of the state itself. We can thus integrate these findings into a neo-realist approach to international relations that we mentioned would characterize our approach to US international monetary policy formulation. Individuals, domestic political considerations, fluctuating institutional considerations, and the primacy of the US in geopolitics are constants in the fluctuating influences on policy determination in the US—and all had a bearing on the disillusionment with the SDR that occurred in the US. But, together, these do not take into account other factors to do with the IMF and other international institutions, nor the importance of ideational aspects of change as the world increasingly turned away from public responsibility for international liquidity provision as Bretton Woods arrangements broke down.

Parenthetically, and on a more practical note, it is interesting to note that several of the most respected observers of US international economic policy use their investigations to plead for the necessity of a better coordination of

US foreign economic policy in the future.[88] It may be noted that the disparate strains noted in this chapter give some credence to these suggestions. Equally, however, the contribution of each of these strains suggest that it is perhaps premature to posit a single theory of US foreign economic policy making in so far as the evolution of post-Bretton Woods arrangements and the SDR is concerned.

4.7 Summary

In addition to the shifting role of the Federal Reserve Board, a glance at the organization charts Illustrations 4.1 and 4.2 also indicates the diffusion of power within other layers of the US bureaucracy over international monetary policy (see also Appendix 3 on US Treasury officials during the all important period for SDRs in the 1970s). While in practice it is the Treasury that deals with questions of international monetary policy, other branches of the US government, such as the Federal Reserve and the Congress, may lay legitimate and varying claims to a role in the determination of policy.[89]

A relative diffusion of power has also served to slightly downgrade the importance of ideology in US policy. In our investigation it has been more productive to examine individuals *and* their beliefs within the bureaucratic structure of the US government, and in turn the determination of national policy in the national interest. Henry Nau has argued a related concept, in that ideas are formed within the bureaucracy surrounding policy makers, and it is these ideas, from many different layers of the 'cocoon of consensus building', which then determine changes in US policy.[90] This also lends credence to a notion of many influences on policy makers, and therefore tendencies towards fluctuating, or at least ad hoc, policies. In turn, it is not too obvious to observe that a concept of national interest is important to policy makers and academics,[91] and it is not a contradiction to observe that fluctuations in policy may be entirely consistent with a strong sense of national interest. National interest, however conceived, may be expressed in a variety of ways. It may have been Charles de Gaulle who coined the famous maxim that: 'Nations have not friends . . . Nations have only interests', but it was the American banker and chief of the quasi-governmental Municipal Acceptance Corporation, and later US Ambassador to France, Felix Rohatyn, who added that 'De Gaulle was right'.[92] Following from this, the US conception of national interest only briefly formally endorsed the SDR. Our exploration of interest in the SDR in the previous chapter, coupled with the ad hoc nature of policy determination and deepening complexities of a diffuse policy environment in the US, suggest that a revival of interest in the idea will be that much more difficult to sustain.

We have also witnessed the primacy of domestic policy priorities, and our investigation into the growing role of Congress, with its built-in electoral bias towards short-term and sometimes domestic considerations, substantiates this. Somewhat mitigating this was the decline in the relative insularity of the US economy noted by many theorists.[93] The importance of these developments should not overshadow the prevalence and importance of the structure of domestic institutions within the US bureaucracy. In the domestic context the structural framework of the US bureaucracy has shown itself to be a key influence on US policy, and this was no less true of its policy attitudes towards the SDR.

In particular, the growing role of Congress, including its Committees and subcommittees, and epitomized by the early 'no' to the substitution account in 1975 and interference with the work of the Federal Reserve Board, suggests that no investigation of contemporary international monetary policy in the US is complete without an examination of Congress. While the increasing importance of the committee system is a phenomenon witnessed throughout Anglo-Saxon legislatures during the past 30 years, in the US, with its defined constitutional focus upon the legislature, it has had a marked effect on international monetary policy formulation including towards the SDR.

And finally, apart from Congress, this chapter has also illustrated that the changing and increasingly complex structure of the US state reinforced the moves away from the SDR in the administration as the post-Bretton Woods arrangements consolidated themselves. That the administration soon determined that SDRs were not germane to the national interests of the US was a critical factor in their marginalization; that other elements of the state in the form of the Fed, the Congress, and indeed the changing structure of the state in the 1970s all intensified this severely muted prospects for the SDR in the post-Bretton Woods era until the international financial crisis in the 1990s. And even then a small part of the response, involving the Fourth Amendment to the IMF Articles of Agreement and an SDR allocation to new members, would not be ratified by the US until another, more severe crisis in 2008–9.

With this in mind, it is now important to return to examine more closely the IMF and the SDR in its international context. US policy remained fundamentally important to SDR initiatives, and the simple geographical location of the IMF made it subject to influence from the US, as Keynes had warned when the IMF was founded.[94] The structure and policies of the Fund, however, remained crucially important to international monetary arrangements and the SDR. This became more true as the Fund developed into an institution with its own ideas on these very arrangements—and the role of the SDR. Indeed much remains to investigate in the recent history of post-Bretton Woods monetary arrangements around the role of the institution that is ultimately responsible for Special Drawing Rights. In particular, the framework under which future prospects for the SDR exist, namely the Second Amendment to the Fund's Articles of Agreement, was negotiated during the mid-1970s and remains fundamentally important to the SDR—and it is these discussions that now demand our attention.

Notes

1. See M. Stephen Weatherford, 'The International Economy as a Constraint on US Macroeconomic Policymaking', *International Organization*, Autumn 1988.
2. In Table 4.1 also note, however, the fact that from 1966–86 the US had the greatest increase in import penetration among the G10.
3. On the continuing debate over whether the US is a declining hegemon, see the special issue of *International Organization*, Winter 85; also Charles Kindleberger, *The World in Depression: 1929–1939* (University of California Press: 1986) and Joseph S. Nye, *Bound To Lead—The Changing Nature of American Power*, Basic Books (New York: 1991). Following Vietnam and the first oil price shock the view that US influence on the international economy was declining became widely held in the US, and received its greatest initial spur from the impact of Nye and Keohane's interdependence thesis. (Joseph Nye and Robert Keohane, *Power and Interdependence*, Little, Brown & Co. (Boston: 1977.) However, this view was not so common among American trading partners, who remained vulnerable to US policy changes. See Chapter 3, 'The EC and SDRs' (above); also Andrew Walter, *World Power and World Money*, St Martin's Press (New York: 1993), chs. 6–7.
4. Some observers, however, lamented the other side of the coin: that in fact that policy latitude was not as great for the US as it was for others precisely because these changes had greater systemic ramifications. See Paul Volcker and Toyoo Gyohten, *Changing Fortunes, op. cit.*, p. 63; also B. J. Cohen, *In Whose Interest? International Banking and American Foreign Policy*, Yale University Press (New Haven: 1986), pp. 7–8.
5. The real gains of seignorage are a subject of some debate. Suffice it to say that the apparent gains of seignorage, intertwined as they are with the international prestige perceived by vehicle currency countries, *once obtained*, are jealously guarded. (See S. Gill and D. Law, *The Global Political Economy*, Johns Hopkins University Press (Baltimore: 1988), pp. 161–3; also H. Grubel, *The International Monetary System*, Penguin Books, 3rd edn, (Harmondsworth, Middx: 1977), pp. 143–5.) A prime example of this is the US concern expressed in the mid-1970s by the US administration when OPEC threatened to price oil exports in SDRs (see pp. 66–7, above). Most recently, DeAnne Julius cites a Mckinsey Global Institute Study in stating that the gains from US seignorage are now 'very small—equivalent to less than one half of one percent of its GDP' (DeAnn Julius, 'A Roadmap for SDR Evolution', in Subacchi and Driffill (eds), *Beyond the Dollar: Rethinking the International Monetary System*, A Chatham House Report (London: 2010), p. 41. As at: www.chathamhouse.org.uk/files/16146_r0310_ims.pdf (accessed 6 June 2011).)

6. Paul Volcker and Toyoo Gyohten, *Changing Fortunes, op. cit.*, pp. 113–14.
7. See also P. Gourevitch on 'The Second Image Reversed: The International Sources of Domestic Politics' *International Organization*, vol. 32, Autumn 1978, pp. 881–912.
8. Nixon, as quoted in *International Herald Tribune* leader, 25/2/88, p. 5.
9. Interview with Barry Newman, Director, Office for International Monetary Policy, US Treasury, Washington, DC.
10. In the wake of Keohane and Nye's extremely influential *Power and Interdependence*, foreign policy determination in the US was characterized by a classic debate about domestic influences upon foreign policy. See Peter Katzenstein, 'International Relations and Domestic Structures: Foreign Economic Policies and Advanced Industrial States', *International Organization*, vol. 30, no. 1, 1976, pp. 1–44.

    A more statist approach to US foreign policy was Stephen Krasner's *Defending the National Interest*, Princeton University Press (Princeton: 1978) which succeeded in re-conferring academic respectability upon neo-mercantilist theories of foreign policy, and Peter Gourevitch reminded observers about the international influences on domestic politics—certainly evident to non-US audiences, but less obvious in the US ('The Second Image Reversed: The International Sources of Domestic Politics', *International Organization*, vol. 32, Autumn 1978.)
11. Nathaniel Beck, 'Parties, Administrations and American Macroeconomic Outcomes', *American Political Science Review*, 76 (March 1982); James E. Alt, 'Political Parties, World Demand, and Unemployment: Domestic and International Sources of Economic Activity', *American Political Science Review*, 79 (December 1985).
12. M. Stephen Weatherford, 'The International Economy as a Constraint on US Macroeconomic Policymaking', *International Organization*, vol. 42, no. 4, Autumn 1988, p. 608.
13. Ibid.
14. Keohane and Nye, and Joanne Gowa, pointed out that the lack of interest groups in the international monetary policy process may itself have an influence on monetary policy. See Joanne Gowa, 'Public Goods and Political Institutions: Trade and Monetary Policy Processes in the United States', *International Organization*, vol. 42, no. 1, Winter 1988, p. 19.
15. Joanne Gowa, *The Closing of the Gold Window, op. cit.*
16. C. Fred Bergsten, 'Organizing the International Economic Policy of the United States', *Managing International Economic Interdependence: Selected Papers of C. Fred Bergsten, 1975–1976*, Lexington Books, D.C. Heath and Co. (Lexington, MA: 1977), p. 295. A similar point has also been made Stephen Cohen and also I. M. Destler, the latter with C. Randall Henning in *Dollar Politics, op. cit.*, as well as, with respect to trade politics, in *American Trade Politics,* 2nd edn, Institute for International Economics (Washington, DC: 1992).
17. I. M. Destler and C. Randall Henning, *Dollar Politics, op. cit.*, pp. 99–116. Destler and Henning point out that Congress lost influence on exchange rate policy once the formal link between gold and the dollar was abolished, but by the 1980s had become 'very effective' in influencing exchange rate policy, pp. 99–100.
18. L. Gordon Crovitz, 'Micromanaging Foreign Policy', in *The Public Interest*, Special Issue on The American Congress, no. 100, summer 1990, p. 102.

19. John Zysman, *Governments, Markets, and Growth—Financial Systems and the Politics of Industrial Change*, Cornell University Press (Ithaca: 1983), p. 267.
20. C. Fred Bergsten, 'Organizing the International Economic Policy of the United States'; testimony before the International Finance Subcommittee of the Senate Committee on Banking, Housing and Urban Affairs, 16 June 1975, as published in *Managing International Economic Interdependence: Selected Papers of C. Fred Bergsten, 1975–1976*, Lexington Books, D.C. Heath and Co (Lexington, MA: 1977), p. 298. Destler and Henning in *Dollar Politics* also make suggestions for improving policy-making with respect to exchange rate policy, among them a reconstitution of President Ford's Economic Policy Board, the forming of a private-sector Advisory Group on Exchange Rates (AGXR), and another Congressional committee on the subject.
21. According to President Reagan's first appointee to the Treasury, Donald Regan, while serving as Secretary to the Department, never saw the President alone 'and never discussed . . . fiscal and monetary policy with him one-on-one'. (As quoted in Destler and Henning, *Dollar Politics, op. cit.*, p. 20).
22. William Greider, in his sensationally titled but interesting examination of the Federal Reserve from a populist perspective, captured the Fed's dilemma in international affairs neatly: 'Reforming the instabilities of international money. . . . contained an ironic possibility: The Federal Reserve would become less powerful'. See *Secrets of the Temple—How the Federal Reserve Runs the Country*, Simon and Schuster (New York: 1987), p. 690. See also Bernard Shull, *The Fourth Branch: The Federal Reserve's Unlikely Rise to Power and Influence*, Praeger (Westport, CN: 2005).
23. M. A. Akhtar and Howard Howe, 'The Political and Institutional Independence of US Monetary Policy', Federal Reserve Bank of New York Research Paper no. 9110, May 1991, pp. 5–6. The FOMC membership is comprised of the Board of Governors of the Federal Reserve plus five Reserve Bank presidents. The latter rotate among the member banks, with the exception of the president of the New York Fed, who is a permanent member. The primary role of the FOMC is to direct the Fed's open market operations, that is the buying and selling of US government securities, which is the main monetary policy instrument.
24. Peter Bakstansky, then vice president of the Federal Reserve Bank of New York, wrote: 'Our best institutional memory is that the relatively informal request to Chase was made to be consistent with a broader bar on foreign currency deposit taking. That policy, which was not formalized by regulation but which was spelled out in a letter of a chairman of the Federal Reserve Board, simply stated the Federal Reserve's preference for banks not to accept foreign deposits, fearing that such a practice would make it more difficult to conduct monetary policy. Acceptance of this informal policy by banks was widespread. The restriction was lifted by the Board of Governors as of the end of 1989.' (P. Bakstansky, correspondence with the author.)
25. *1974 Annual Report*, Federal Reserve Board of Governors, 30/5/74, p. 70.

26. National Advisory Council on International Monetary and Financial Policies, *Annual Report*, 1 July 1972 – 30 June 1973, US Government Printing Office, 1973, p. 13.
27. Federal Reserve Board, *Annual Report*, 1973 (Washington: 30/5/1974), pp. 69–70.
28. Federal Reserve Board, *Annual Report*, 1974 (Washington: 16/6/1975), p. 68.
29. Anthony M. Solomon, 'The Evolving International Monetary System', in *The International Economic Policy of the United States: Selected Papers of C. Fred Bergsten, 1977–1979*, Lexington Books, D.C. Heath and Co. (Lexington, Mass: 1980), p. 41.
30. Charles A. Coombs and Guillaume Guindey, *Reflections on the International Monetary System*, The 1980 Per Jacobsson Lecture (Basle: 1980), p. 25.
31. Charles A. Coombs, *The Arena of International Finance*, John Wiley and Sons (New York: 1976), p. x.
32. Support for the dollar at this stage included increasing swap lines by $7.6 billion with the German, Japanese, and Swiss central banks (to total $15 billion), borrowing $10 billion in foreign currency denominated bonds (christened 'Carter bonds'), drawing $3 billion from the IMF, as well as $2 billion in SDRs.
33. Paul Volcker and Toyoo Gyohten, *Changing Fortunes, op. cit.*, p. 70.
34. Ibid. p. 295.
35. Palais-Royal Initiative (Michel Camdessus, Alexandre Lamfalussy, Tommaso Padoa-Schioppa *et. al.*), 'Reform of the International Monetary System: A Cooperative Approach for the Twenty First Century', 18 January 2011, as at: http://www.elysee.fr/president/root/bank_objects/2011-007.Palais-Royal_Initiative-Final_version_of_the_Report-Jan_18.pdf (accessed 6 June 2011). Para. 15, p. 7. This call was made consistent with cautioning against the potential of excessive global liquidity. Notably, the authors also quoted Article VIII, sect. 7, of the IMF Articles of Agreement, in the context of the role the SDR could play in addressing potential demands '... consistent with the objectives of promoting better international surveillance of international liquidity and making the special drawing right the principal reserve asset in the international monetary system.' See also fn. 47, below.
36. *The Federal Reserve System—Purposes and Functions*, Board of Governors of the Federal Reserve System (Washington, DC: 1984), p. 2.
37. M. A. Akhtar and Howard Howe, 'The Political and Institutional Independence of US Monetary Policy', Federal Reserve Bank of New York Research Paper no. 9110, p. 9.
38. Ibid. p. 3.
39. Ibid. pp. 14, 16.
40. Ibid. p. 6.
41. Ibid. pp. 20, 24–5.
42. Charles Coombs, *The Arena of International Finance, op. cit.*, p. 204.
43. Ibid. p. 205.
44. Ibid. p. 217. Coombs wrote that Alfred Hayes, President of the Federal Reserve Bank of New York 'was not consulted, nor even informed of the decision'. (As noted in chapter two Pierre-Paul Schweitzer was not informed of the US decisions either—until half an hour before they were made public.)

45. Robert Sylla, 'The Autonomy of Monetary Authorities: The Case of the US Federal Reserve System', in Gianni Toniolo (ed.), *Central Banks' Independence in Historical Perspective*, Walter de Gruyter (New York: 1988), pp. 37–8. Sylla notes that another critic makes the same observation: Donald Kettl, in *Leadership at the Fed*, Yale University Press (New Haven: 1986).
46. Paul A. Volcker, 'The Political Economy of the Dollar'—The Fred Hirsch Memorial Lecture, Warwick University, Coventry, England, 9 November 1978, as reproduced in FRBNY *Quarterly Review*, vol. 3, no. 4, Winter 1978–9.
47. Interview with the author, Princeton, New Jersey. In 1992, Volcker wrote that to replace the present multicurrency system with, say, a new issue of SDRs 'would be as politically unacceptable as it would be economically impractical'. See Volcker and Gyohten, *Changing Fortunes—The World's Money and the Threat to American Leadership, op. cit.*, p. 305. At the end of the decade, however, he was more equivocal, arguing that although he was unlikely to live to see it, '... if we are to have a truly globalized economy, a single world currency makes sense', and concluded that '... the underlying tendencies are in that direction'. Paul Volcker, 'Toward a Single World Currency to Level the Playing Field', *International Herald Tribune*, 31 January 2000, as at: http://www.iht.com/articles/2000/01/31/edpaul.2.t_0.php (accessed 6 June 2011). See also n. 35, above.
48. B. Dianne Pauls, 'US Exchange Rate Policy: Bretton Woods to Present', in *Federal Reserve Bulletin*, vol. 76, no. 11, November 1990, pp. 895–6, 899.

    Parenthetically, it may be noted that the New York Fed, particularly its heads such as Alfred Hayes and Anthony Solomon, were more sympathetic to the SDR than the Board of Governors in Washington (and Solomon was more vocal in his support for the SDR once he had moved to the Treasury during the Carter administration). This is not surprising given that it is New York which is responsible for international dealings and whose international contacts are more common.
49. Woodrow Wilson, *Congressional Government: A Study in American Politics* (1885), p. 23, as quoted in Robert A. Pastor, *Congress and the Politics of US Foreign Policy 1929–1976*, University of California Press (Berkeley: 1980), p. 15.
50. In US Congressional parlance, 'oversight' always refers to the process of Congress 'overseeing' other work, particularly of the administration, rather than an omission or mistake.
51. Robert Pastor, *Congress and the Politics of US Foreign Economic Policy 1929–1976, op. cit.*, p. 18.
52. I. M. Destler, 'Trade Consensus, SALT Stalemate: Congress and Foreign Policy in the 1970s', in Thomas Mann and Norman Ornstein (eds), *The New Congress*, American Enterprise Institute for public Policy Research (Washington, DC: 1981), p. 332.
53. Robert Dahl, *Pluralist Democracy in the US: Conflict and Consent* (1967), p. 136, as quoted in Robert A. Pastor, *op. cit.*, p. 348.
54. Robert Pastor, *op. cit.*, p. 252.
55. Roger Davidson, 'Subcommittee Government: New Channels for Policy Making', in Thomas E. Mann and Norman J. Ornstein, *The New Congress, op. cit.*, pp. 99–133. Davidson also goes on to write about the ramifications of this diffusion of

congressional subcommittee policy making, as mirroring the atomization of political life in the US as a whole.

56. L. Gordon Cravitz, 'Micromanaging Foreign Policy', *op. cit.*, p. 102.
57. See Chapter 1, pp. 19–20, above.
58. See Chapter 3, p. 83, above.
59. SDR Limitation Proposal. House Committee on Banking and Currency (Hearings). 91st Congress, 2nd session, 16 and 17 April 1970, p. 156.
60. I. M. Destler and C. Randall Henning, *Dollar Politics, op. cit.*, p. 99. Destler and Henning also examine the Treasury-Fed relationship with respect to exchange rate management. They acknowledge 'clear primacy' to the Treasury, but in practice close cooperation between the two is the norm. Note that the Treasury is relatively weaker than many of its OECD counterparts in that its budgetary powers and responsibilities are few. (The OMB and especially Congress are the most important institutions in this regard.)
61. 'Exchange Rate Policy and International Monetary Reform', Report of the Subcommittee on International Trade, Investment and Monetary Policy (House Committee on Banking, Currency and Housing), and the Subcommittee on International Economics (Joint Economic Committee), 94th Congress, 1st Session, August 1975, p. 10. (Reuss was chairman of both the House Committee and the Subcommittee of the Joint Economic Committee. It is worth recalling that he was a member of the House of Representatives—an institution that had effectively no influence on foreign policy before WWII. Reuss had had a long career in Congress; as chairman of a Joint Economic Committee subcommittee Reuss had contributed to the debate over international monetary arrangements as early as 1961 when Congress rejected liquidity plans which would increase the role of gold in international monetary arrangements (see Chapter 1, pp. 19–20).)
62. Ibid. p. 9.
63. See also Peter Kenen on this point on p. 98, above.
64. Amendment of the Bretton Woods Agreements Act, Senate Foreign Relations Committee Report, 10 August 1976, 94th Congress, 2nd Session, p. 6.
65. US Congress, Public Law 94–569, 19/10/76.
66. US Congress, Public Law 98–181, 30 November 1983. This law also instructed the US Executive Director of the Fund (invariably a Treasury official) to work for stable exchange rates and opposed using Fund money for any 'Communist dictatorship or any country that practices apartheid'. It also opposed using Fund resources 'drawn principally to repay loans imprudently made by banking institutions', and it favoured 'bringing the rate of charges on Fund drawings in line with market rates', and also sought to insure that debt rescheduling was 'consistent with safe and sound banking practices and with the country's ability to pay'.
67. Ernest Aryeetey, 'A Development-Focused Allocation of Special Drawing Rights' United Nations University, World Institute for Development Economics Research (WIDER), Helsinki. Discussion Paper No. 2003/3, January 2004, p. 7.
68. Peter Kenen interview with the author. This became law during the second Clinton Administration with the passage of the 'Omnibus Consolidated and Emergency Supplemental Appropriations Act' in 1998.

69. See 'What is the US Position?', para. 6 of in Note by HM Treasury on Special Drawing Rights, as at: http://www.parliament.the-stationery-office.co.uk/pa/cm200102/cmselect/cmintdev/785/2051410.htm (accessed 6 June 2011).
70. Roger Davidson, 'Subcommittee Government: New Channels for Policy Making', *op. cit.*
71. See J. Lawrence Broz and Michael Brewster Hawes, 'US Domestic and International Monetary Fund Policy' (later version published as 'Congressional Politics of Financing the International Monetary Fund' in *International Organization*, vol. 60, no. 2, Spring 2006), as at: http://dss.ucsd.edu/~jlbroz/broz_hawes_isnie.pdf (accessed 6 June 2011).
72. Odell, *US International Monetary Policy, op. cit.*
73. See Jacqueline Best, *The Limits of Transparency: Ambiguity and the History of International Finance*, Ithaca, NY (Cornell University Press: 2005).
74. Peter Gourevitch, 'The Second Image Reversed: The International Sources of Domestic Politics', *International Organization*, vol. 32, no. 4, Autumn 1978, p. 911.
75. Joanne Gowa, *Closing the Gold Window, op. cit.*, p. 43; Henry Nau, *The Myth of America's Decline—Leading the World Economy into the 1990s*, Oxford University Press (New York: 1990), p. 138; Fred Bergsten, *The Dilemmas of the Dollar—The Economics and Politics of United States International Monetary Policy*, Council on Foreign Relations and New York University Press (New York: 1975), p. 201.
76. George N. Halm (ed.), *Approaches to Greater Flexibility of Exchange Rates—The Bürgenstock Papers*, Princeton University Press (Princeton: 1970), pp. vi–vii.
77. Odell, *US International Monetary Policy, op. cit.*, p. 130.
78. Interview, Mr Charls Walker. Washington.
79. Papers of Dean Acheson, Harry Truman Library. Douglas Dillon, memorandums to the president, 8/8/62 and 12/9/62—US proposals to support the dollar and negotiations with European states. US Declassified Government Documents, nos. 86–1918 and 86–1919.
80. M. Stephen Weatherford, 'The International Economy as a Constraint on US Macroeconomic Policymaking', *International Organization*, vol. 42, no. 4, Autumn 1988, p. 613. The main compromise was that although the pool was administered by the through the Fund, it was governed under G10 rules 'which prevented the United States and Britain (with Canada and Japan) from determining outcomes without the assistance of at least one other major participant'.
81. Remarks by Secretary Fowler, 24 September 1968, before the 6th International Conference of the Forging Industry Association. Reproduced in *1969 Report of the Secretary of the Treasury*, Exhibit 32, p. 287. Indeed throughout the 1960s Presidents Kennedy and Johnson spoke of the 35 dollar per ounce gold price as sacrosanct.
82. In fact the Volcker Group (a committee under the chairmanship of Paul Volcker, then Under-Secretary for monetary affairs at the Treasury, which also consisted of officials from the Treasury Department, Federal Reserve, Council of Economic Advisers, State Department, and National Security Council) was highly sensitive to its international systemic responsibilities. The Group recommended in 'Basic Options in International Affairs' (23 June 1969) that the US follow a multi-lateralist approach to change. This included 'early and sizeable activation of the Special

Drawing Rights scheme . . . expansion of I.M.F. quotas . . . [and the examination of] . . . the feasibility and desirability of reserve settlement accounts.' Despite the credentials of this group, their recommendations were ignored at the Camp David meeting in 1971—signalling the end of Bretton Woods with the suspension of dollar convertibility. See Joanne Gowa, *Closing the Gold Window, op. cit.*, pp. 62 and 129–30.

83. John Odell, *op. cit.*, p. 307.
84. See, for example, Robert Axelrod (ed.), *Structure of Decision*, Princeton University Press (Princeton: 1976), and Ole R. Holsti, 'Cognitive Dynamics and Images of the Enemy: Dulles and Russia', in D. Finaly, O. Holsti, and R. Fagen (eds), *Enemies in Politics*, Rand McNally (Chicago: 1964); also Paul Egon Rohrlich, 'Economic Culture and Foreign Policy: The Cognitive Analysis of Economic Policy Making', in *International Organization*, vol. 41, no. 1, Winter 1987; and Janice Gross Stein, 'Psychological Explanations of International Conflict', in Walter Carlsnaes, Thomas Risse, and Beth A. Simmons (eds), *Handbook of International Relations*, Sage Publications (London: 2005).
85. Paul Egon Rohrlich, *op. cit.*; see also Benjamin J. Cohen on this trend more broadly in the field of international political economy, including with respect to what John Kenneth Galbraith termed as 'imitative scientism': 'The Multiple Traditions of American IPE', in Mark Blyth (ed.), *Routledge Handbook of International Political Economy (IPE)—IPE as a Global Conversation*, Routledge (Abingdon: 2009).
86. Paul Rohrlich refers to these theorists as sensitive to the realpolitik of economic goals as subsidiary to political power. See, For example Hans J. Morgenthau, *Politics Among Nations*, Knopf (New York: 1972); Stephen Krasner, *Defending the National Interest*, Princeton University Press (Princeton: 1978); and Robert Gilpin, *US Power and the Multinational Corporation*, Basic Books (New York: 1975).
87. F. Lisle Widman, *Making International Monetary Policy*, The International Law Institute and Georgetown University Law Center (Washington, DC: 1982), p. 267. See also Richard Sylla's and Donald Kettl's similar points with respect to the influence of the individuals holding the office of President of the Federal Reserve, p. 125, above.
88. See I. M. Destler, *Making Foreign Economic Policy*, the Brookings Institution (Washington, DC: 1980), pp. 211–28; I. M. Destler and C. Randall Henning, *Dollar Politics, op. cit.*, pp. 145–65; Stephen D. Cohen, *The Making of United States International Economic Policy—Principles, Problems, and Proposals for Reform*, 3rd edn, Praeger (New York: 1988), pp. 256–60.

    Bergsten, as noted in *The Dilemmas of the Dollar*, also periodically criticized the institutional structure of US international economic policy making. These criticisms do have an effect: virtually every president has attempted to address policy coordination, the most recent example being President Obama's 2009 Economic Recovery Advisory Board (on the retirement of Paul Volcker as chair in early 2011, renamed the Council on Jobs and Competitiveness).
89. As we saw in Chapter 3, during the Carter administration, economic expertise in the State Department may also be called upon in international monetary policy questions. (The Department of Commerce is only tangentially involved in these issues although, because of its links to industry, it is often a part of the international

economic policy making process in the US. Parenthetically, in trade matters protectionist strains in the administration have been viewed with the most sympathy at the Commerce Department.)

90. Henry Nau, *The Myth of America's Decline, op. cit.*, p. 47.
91. See Stephen Krasner *Defending the National Interest, op. cit.*
92. See Felix Rohatyn, 'America's Lost Independence', *The New York Review of Books*, vol. XXXV, no. 2, 18 February 1988, p. 10. In Chapter 1 we noted similar fluctuation in French international monetary policy within the context of a strong conception of national interest.
93. P. Gourevitch on 'The Second Image Reversed: The International Sources of Domestic Politics', *International Organization, op. cit.*; Joseph Nye, *Bound to Lead, op. cit.*, pp. 238–42; also Table 4.1, above.
94. Keynes, *Collected Writings, vol XXVI—Activities 1941–46, Shaping the Post-war World—Bretton Woods and Reparations*, ed. D. Moggridge (London, 1980), p. 211. See also Chapter 1, p. 13, above.

5

SDRs and the negotiation of the Second Amendment to the Fund's Articles of Agreement

5.1 Introduction

In this chapter we return to examine the evolution of the International Monetary Fund (IMF) and the influence this institution has had on international monetary relations. The focus now is on the negotiation of the Second Amendment to the IMF's Articles of Agreement, with special emphasis on the Special Drawing Right (SDR). In particular, we draw attention to some of the hitherto ignored attributes of the Second Amendment, in order to redress the tendency to downplay the real achievements that took place at the Jamaica meeting. Our investigation leads to the conclusion that the accomplishments of Jamaica were more than simply the de jure recognition of floating exchange rates. Changes were embodied in the agreement, such as diminishing the role of gold, and enhancing access to Fund resources by developing countries. Other features—including accomplishments—were less explicit, but nonetheless bear closer examination with respect to SDRs and the functioning of the international monetary system. The most important of these include the important 'enabling' provisions of the agreement, and the continued development of the Fund as an institution under the new arrangements, both of which emerge as key themes as this chapter develops. The latter aspect is vital since, at the time, the relevance of an organization established to uphold the exchange arrangements devised at Bretton Woods, and then essentially abandoned, was being called into question.

It is also just as important to investigate other aspects of the amended Articles which in fact occupied the negotiators to a greater degree. Many of these dealt at least partially with the SDR. It is revealing to note the many provisions which affected prospects for the SDR, especially since the SDR as initially constituted was ostensibly becoming less relevant to the liquidity needs of post-Bretton Woods arrangements focusing on private liquidity provision. Our efforts in this task have been considerably aided by examination of documents of the Fund and minutes of the Executive Board pertaining to the Second Amendment.[1] In addition, many internal Fund documents relating to SDRs since the Second Amendment, as well as other Fund information and relevant press reports have been examined.[2]

5.2 Precursors to the Jamaica Agreement and the Legacy of the C-20

In retrospect, many observers have viewed the Jamaica Agreement as a failure. Immediately after the meeting, though, reviews were positive. Press comment, for instance, tended to be laudatory—the *International Herald Tribune* headlined one story 'A Monetary Order is Born in Jamaica'.[3] US Administration comment, as we have seen, was also favourable, Treasury Secretary Simon observing that Jamaica was comparable to Bretton Woods,[4] while his French counterpart remarked that it was 'the beginning of a new monetary and political era'.[5]

This time, however, dissenting comment was also forthcoming and quite quickly. That which came from the president of the Bundesbank, Otmar Emminger, was typical:

> The new system which was adopted at the Jamaica Conference was not the outcome of the long drawn-out reform discussions of earlier years. The IMF Ministerial Committee simply acknowledged the existing realities concerning exchange rates and gold, as they have evolved since the breakdown of the Bretton Woods System in 1973, and legalized them.[6]

The divergent reactions echoed reactions to the Smithsonian Agreement (and even the First Amendment), although in this case hardened observers were even more inclined to criticize.[7] Partly as a result of this, however, and given that the Second Amendment was introduced in an atmosphere of disappointment—especially concerning supporters of a fixed exchange rate system—the accomplishments which were enacted have been overlooked. Above all, the Second Amendment succeeded in introducing elements of flexibility into the functioning of the Fund and its constitutional abilities to adapt to changing international monetary conditions.

Many critics have spoken of the latter as a negative development; the familiar jibes at the Jamaica Agreement being a compromise of the lowest common denominator that simply legalized the floating exchange rate system post facto epitomize this. This exasperation became public early; Williamson's *The Failure of World Monetary Reform* was a harbinger, expressing frustration at the lack of success of the C-20.[8] However, the groundwork laid by the C-20 had great influence upon the negotiations for the Second Amendment and on subsequent initiatives.

Although many economists expressed disappointment at the lack of progress towards international monetary reform at Jamaica, to some this was no longer surprising. One of the best known accounts of the Agreement was entitled 'Jamaica, or the Non-Reform of the International Monetary System'.[9] In a collection of essays on the Agreement, Fritz Machlup also characterized Jamaica as an opportunity missed:

> Unfortunately, only empty phrases from the *Outline* [of Reform of the C-20] were preserved in the final accord; the important phrases were lost in the shuffle, or deliberately dropped.[10]

Subsequent assessment of the Second Amendment, when it has appeared at all, simply mention it as the de jure recognition of a floating exchange rate system which already existed.[11] Indeed the collection of essays in which the above remark appeared—which included contributions from John Williamson, Robert Triffin, and Fritz Machlup—all tended to express disappointment at the final outcome of the Second Amendment.

However, a closer examination of SDRs during the Second Amendment negotiations further demonstrates the continued evolution of the Fund's ability to influence the negotiations, in much the same way that we witnessed in the 1960s and early 1970s. This time, however, the Fund's influence—on the agenda if not the results of the negotiations—was even more pronounced. The role of the Fund had changed as a result of the very real changes in the international monetary system in the early 1970s. Its prospective role was increasingly difficult to discern. Paradoxically, however, unlike the 1950s and even 1960s, when the Fund at times seemed an adjunct to reform negotiations—albeit an increasingly important one—by the 1970s the Second Amendment was negotiated to a large extent within the institution of the Fund itself. Although international monetary relations had become more politicized by the 1970s, with the important exception of the new Economic Summits (the first official summit took place at Rambouillet in 1975), the vast majority of the Second Amendment discussions took place at the Executive Board level at the IMF,[12] backed up by the important contributions of Fund staff. There are more than 6,000 pages of IMF material relating to the Second Amendment, half of which are documents of relevant Fund departments. As we shall see the latter reflect the stamp of an institution that was increasingly aware of its own interests and influence, despite its essentially subordinate status vis-à-vis the executive directors and Board of Governors. The documents point not only to a staff carrying out necessary studies for the directors, but also setting out options that influenced negotiators in their deliberations.

While the legacy of the Second Amendment was such that SDRs failed to secure the status which the C-20 advocated, the negotiations surrounding the Second Amendment and the role of the Fund as an institution had evolved considerably, which had important implications for the SDR.

Although the direct negotiations concerning SDRs in the post-Bretton Woods monetary system were not the only phenomena discussed during the Second Amendment, they were important to the intended roles of both the Fund and the SDR under the new international monetary arrangements. Following the disarray of the C-20's efforts at international monetary reform, the Fund quickly embarked upon attempts at reconciling itself to the prevailing international monetary arrangements embodied in freely floating exchange rates. It had not yet, however, abandoned the cause of international monetary reform, or of the SDR.

The C-20's hastily assembled documents were released in June 1974. Two months previously, in April, the executive directors had already begun to consider possible changes to the General Account that would 'provide a broader role for SDRs'.[13] Ultimately the negotiation of the Second Amendment that ratified these arrangements took four years from the initial discussions and the final ratification of the Second Amendment on 1 April 1978, a process that the Committee of Twenty initially expected to take eight months.[14] Part of the reason for the length of these discussions was growing international monetary instability, but within the discussions at the Fund, some of the time was spent on agreeing upon a role, or at least a prospective role, for SDRs under the new arrangements.

In part, the two years spent agreeing on the text of the Second Amendment, and the two following years it took to obtain ratification,[15] were a direct result of the C-20's efforts.[16] Although an influential staff member's review of the second amendment for the Fund does not go as far as to say this,[17] an examination of the documents and Executive Board minutes reveals that the Fund gave serious and lengthy consideration to many of the C-20's recommendations. An example of this was the discussion of a Council, as the C-20 simply described it, which would succeed the C-20 and which would have decision-making powers:

> ...to supervise the management and adaptation of the monetary system, to oversee the continuing operation of the adjustment process, and to deal with sudden disturbances which might threaten the system.[18]

The possible establishment of this Council—the title of the Interim Committee belied its status as successor to the C-20 until a Council could be agreed upon—was one of the first topics for discussion by the Executive Board and the relevant departments in mid-1974. Although the Council was not agreed upon, mechanisms for its functioning were established in Schedule D of the

Articles of Agreement resulting from the Second Amendment, and a provision for its institution was included in Article XII, section 1.[19] While this may be viewed as a very limited achievement, especially in view of the fact that the Interim Committee showed little signs of gaining the powers envisioned for it as a Council, it nonetheless was a core issue in the draft amendments, and we must not overlook the fact that provision for it was included in the new Articles. And time and again Fund documents refer to the Committee of Twenty as the basis for further study and debate among the executive directors.

Even before the C-20's failure to agree on reform, which was apparent by 1973, Fund staff continued to devote time to SDRS. As we have seen, months before the C-20 broke down, Fund staff prepared a memo for the executive directors to consider facilitating a 'broader role for SDRs'.[20] It was acknowledged that 'these changes, which are of different degrees of importance, would require amendment of the Articles.'[21]

On 13 June 1974, the day before the release of the C-20's report and supporting documents, the Fund's Board of Governors issued a press release confirming that the C-20 was about to publish its recommendations.[22] The Board signalled its willingness to further many of the recommendations of the C-20, and through the executive directors and relevant Fund departments (particularly the Treasurer's, Legal, and Research Departments, as well as the Secretary) work began publicly on what was to become the Second Amendment.

Most importantly, the structure of the discussions was shaped by the C-20's *Outline* for Reform. In addition, Fund staff relied heavily on the *Outline* in their preparation of documents for the executive directors. This was perhaps not surprising: most of the debates and unresolved issues still characterizing the debate over international monetary reform—such as a Council, SDRs, and development assistance—were all specifically addressed in the C-20 Report. This is not to say that the frustrations ultimately expressed by Williamson, and many of the Fund's members themselves, over the Second Amendment's equivocal approach to reform were not partly justified—after all, the Second Amendment effectively abandoned the cause of public responsibility for the functioning of a fixed-exchange rate international monetary system-envisioned at Bretton Woods. Nonetheless, given the policy attitudes of the US and, with variable consistency, G7 partners, the inherent approach to compromise embodied in the Second Amendment ensured that mechanisms for future reform were included in the Fund's Articles for the first time. The fact that reformist notions and flexibility were encompassed within the Second Amendment at all in the face of prevailing attitudes towards private liquidity provision and the Fund in general has been little credited. This is not a hollow accomplishment either: the Second

Amendment has fostered a role for the Fund under existing monetary arrangements, but also in establishing conditions for its role in a future of still different international monetary arrangements.[23]

Many of the recommendations of the C-20 were compromised in the Second Amendment. Others were not included at all. Despite the fact that some provisions were not included (such as the link), or were watered down (the Council), the negotiations over these issues proved important if only for the successful preservation of a role for the Fund in the new system, as well as providing a strong role for it should monetary arrangements change. Again, these considerations also lead to the conclusion that the accomplishments of the Second Amendment were more than simply the de jure recognition of floating exchange rates. The smooth way in which the Fourth Amendment and special SDR allocations took place in 2009 as part of the response to the international financial crisis is indeed a testament to this. Admittedly, it was the G20 that provided a forum and important political legitimacy, but it was the IMF that could respond. It was a seamless process, largely facilitated by the Second Amendment.

5.3 The Structure of the Second Amendment Negotiations

A brief examination of the process of the negotiation of the Second Amendment is illustrative of some of the themes just discussed. The evidence of the executive directors' minutes and documents of the Fund point to the initial impetus provided by the Committee of Twenty. While the Executive Directors did consider alterations to the General Account which would have meant enhancing the role of the SDR,[24] it was the C-20 that first suggested, and had the power to recommend to the executive directors, that possible amendments to the Articles of Agreement be drafted, in particular:

(a) the establishment of a Council;
(b) to enable the Fund to legalize the position of countries with floating rates during the interim period;
(c) to give permanent force to the voluntary pledge avoiding trade restrictions for balance of payments purposes;
(d) to authorize the Fund to establish, as and when agreed, a Substitution Account;
(e) to amend the present provisions concerning gold;
(f) to introduce improvements in the General Account and in the characteristics of, and rules governing the use of SDRs, as well as any other consequential amendments.[25]

All of these recommended topics were discussed during the Second Amendment negotiations. But the Second Amendment negotiations did not take place at the C-20 and it is important to understand the structure of the Second Amendment meetings. Present at the executive directors meetings were the managing director, the 20 executive directors (or their alternates), as well as a Fund secretary and an assistant, and other staff as necessary. Executive directors at the IMF are appointed by a country (in the case of the five or six individual members most important to world trade) or country group, and are responsible for 'devoting all the time and attention to the business of the Fund that its interests require'.[26] This extends to preparing, in conjunction with the Fund's managing director, an agenda for each meeting of the Board of Governors.[27] While it is usually apparent for which national constituency executive directors speak, in practice this is rarely blatant at meetings. And minutes identify each executive director by name only, not by geographic constituency. Divided loyalties could not help but exist between systemic (or Fund) and country responsibility, and in this vein it is interesting to note that sometimes staff members became executive directors, or vice versa. During the period of the negotiations culminating in the Second Amendment, Lamberto Dini, first senior advisor and then deputy director of the African Department, became an executive director for Italy, Malta, Portugal, and Spain in 1976.[28] Conversely, J. B. Zulu, the alternate executive director for most sub-Saharan nations between 1974 and 1976, then became a Fund staff member in heading the African Department.[29] In addition, one of the Fund's most respected staff members, J. J. Polak, became an executive director for the constituency comprising the Netherlands, Cyprus, Israel, Yugoslavia, and Romania in 1981.

Length of service varied greatly amongst the directors; Peter Lieftinck (Netherlands) had been an executive director since the mid-1950s, although this was exceptional. Among the five appointed directors during the negotiation of the Second Amendment, by mid-1974 Sam Cross had replaced William Dale as the US director, although William Dale continued to chair many Executive Board meetings in his new capacity as deputy managing director (traditionally a US post).[30] Of the other appointed directors between 1974 and 1976 the French and Japanese directors remained Jacques Henri Wahl and Kaichi Kawaguchi, respectively; William Ryrie replaced Anthony Rawlinson for the UK in 1975 and Eckard Pieske replaced Günther Schleiminger for West Germany in 1974.[31] (Appendix 2 summarizes senior Fund staff and IMF executive directors during the negotiation of the Second Amendment.) Unlike the formulation of US policy, where the identity and ideas of individual policy makers is a very important factor in looking at policy change, at the Fund this is less apparent. This is simply because some executive directors, despite country groupings of roughly equal strength, are more important than others in the institutional structure of the Fund, and are able to articulate national policies more cohesively. This is particularly true of executive directors who speak only for their own individual countries (the US, UK, Japan, Germany, France, and also Saudi Arabia).

All executive director meetings were chaired by the managing director (or his deputy); also present were senior Fund staff, including those responsible for the preparation of the papers under discussion. Negotiations for the Second Amendment continued throughout 1975; indeed there were 208 formal meetings of the Executive Board, lasting 495.5 hours.[32] Of these nearly 500 hours, approximately 175 hours were devoted solely to the draft documents for the Second Amendment.[33] It was Fund staff who introduced the papers, clarified points, and/or informally mediated during the discussion, and staff regularly outnumbered the executive directors.[34] General Counsel was called upon to speak most of all, and to mediate unofficially between apparently irreconcilable positions.

During Executive Board meetings it is a rule of the Fund that 'the Chairman shall ordinarily ascertain the sense of the meeting in lieu of a formal vote',[35] although formal votes may be requested. Throughout these negotiations no votes were requested. Actually, 'by the 1970s it had become almost impolite for an Executive Director to call for a formal vote.'[36]Although disagreements obviously took place, Fund staff and the managing director successfully intervened to ensure that meetings continued relatively smoothly.

5.4 The Process of Negotiation—The Council

The first item on the list initially suggested by the C-20 was an IMF Council. And the first Draft Second Amendments for discussion were entitled 'On the Establishment of a Council', which were prepared by the Legal Department of the Fund.[37] These were in turn discussed by the Executive Board on 24 July 1974.[38] After this directors meeting, supplementary versions of the Council proposals were prepared, taking into account executive directors recommendations. In this case four further drafts were prepared, with explanatory notes.[39] In addition to the 24 July 1974 meeting, the executive directors discussed these drafts at six further meetings—on 25 October 1974, 1 November 1974, 8 November 1974, 3 March 1975, 3 May 1975, and 5 August 1975.[40] The latter were meetings at which the Council was discussed almost exclusively. In addition, the executive directors commented upon the Council in preparing for meetings of the Interim Committee, as well as when Comprehensive Draft Amendments of the Articles of Agreement as a whole were published.[41]

Fund documents as part of these negotiations were wide ranging. Furthermore, while usually prompted by the directors, many of them tended to propose amendments promoting the SDR, in turn also reflecting the

Committee of Twenty's legacy. While it was the directors who were ultimately responsible for amending the Articles, it is interesting to note how Fund staff continuously promoted the SDR and other amendments that would have enhanced prospects for the SDR by referring to the Committee. The Council was one of these proposals, and in the first draft articles[42] the Council was proposed as an integral part of the Articles of Agreement—as a new Article XII. In this case, although a consensus of executive directors was established, by the time of the first Comprehensive Draft Amendments in March of 1975 the Council had been relegated to a schedule (Schedule J; ultimately Schedule D under the Second Amendment).

Interestingly, the US supported a Council. Opposition formed behind developing countries, particularly the Brazilian executive director, Alexandre Kafka.[43] One of the reasons why developing countries were reluctant to support the creation of a Council was apprehension over its apparent irreversible nature once constituted. This was a legitimate concern; Alexandre Kafka pointed out that the notion of a Council derived from an idea of the Group of Ten when agreeing to the proposed SDR amendment in 1968.[44] It was argued that if the G10 dominated a prospective Council then developing countries could potentially be denied a larger voice in the functioning of the international monetary system. Unlike most Fund committees, 'split voting' was to have been allowed, whereby the director of each constituency would be entitled to cast individual member's votes separately.[45] In a later article, Kafka again asserts that by a Council *not* coming to pass, developing country interests were better served. As a longstanding participant on the Executive Board, his reasons are worth noting in detail:

> The Council foreseen in Schedule D, but never established, would exercise de jure the Interim Committee's de facto powers. It is preferable (not only speaking as an Executive Director from a developing country) that the Council should not have come into existence. Jurisdictional disagreements could occur; strictly speaking, such disagreements between the former and the Interim Committee are impossible. Open disagreements could be very disruptive; and could, moreover, be reflected in a disruption of the relationship between Management and Executive Board. Nor would it be practical to attribute to the Council a different jurisdiction than to the Executive Board. Since the Council would make decisions by voting, rather [than] by consensus, as [in] the Committee, the influence on the forum of the developing members would be smaller.[46]

Thus it was viewed as preferable to continue to observe the progress of the Interim Committee before developing countries committed themselves to a Council.[47] The US, however, in supporting a Council, reflected continued US interest in moving away from a forum such as a G10 dominated by European members; we witnessed US support for the C-20 for this same reason in Chapter 3. Sam Cross asserted that there was room for a 'political' committee in the Fund, which would be fulfilled by a Council. He argued that:

> The creation of the Council would represent an important structural change that would provide the Fund with the opportunity to play a far more significant role in the management of international monetary matters ... [T]he Council's creation ... would strengthen the Fund. Mr. Cross said he had been struck by the timidness of the approach in the draft amendment [DAA/74/1, including supplements] rather than by its boldness.[48]

Our examination of the Council should also serve as a warning against the temptation to ascribe the scuttling of international monetary reform initiatives as solely US inspired. In this case, the US was in favour of a Council; developing countries were wary. Admittedly, Kafka felt that the cause of international monetary reform would have been hurt by a Council. Subsequent experience with the Interim Committee, however, which until its replacement by the very similar IMFC in 1999 had evolved into semi-permanent status in the absence of a Council, would suggest that international monetary reform issues might have had a higher profile if a Council had been instituted. To a degree this is hypothetical, but there are indications—strong Interim Committee support for a substitution account at Belgrade and Hamburg in the 1979 and 1980, for example—that provide some basis for this conjecture.

In any case the Council was relegated to the status of a Schedule (though also provided for under Article XII, a provision that could be enacted should there be 85 per cent support within the Board of Governors to activate Schedule D[49]). While this may be viewed as a very limited achievement, especially in view of the fact that the 'Interim' Committee became less interim as years passed, it nonetheless was a core issue in the negotiation of the draft amendments. It should also be pointed out that as the difficulties in negotiating a Second Amendment mounted, and as it became apparent that an 85 per cent majority would be necessary for further amendments,[50] the importance of the Second Amendment as a more permanent legacy increased. This point was increasingly realized by the negotiators, and, as we shall see, had a bearing on the results of the negotiations.

Thus it may also be said that the provision which was made for a Council in the new Articles was a limited achievement, especially since many contentious issues, such as the substitution account for SDRs, and the link proposal,[51] were not included in the final version of the Second Amendment, despite widespread discussion during the negotiations. The demise of the SDR/Aid link proposal was perhaps the most dramatic development in this regard, since the link was not incorporated into the Second Amendment at all. It is to this demise that we now turn in greater detail for a further insight into the process of the negotiation of the Second Amendment, and in order to understand other institutional developments that took place in the late 1970s and 1980s that adversely affected the prospects for SDRs. In concentrating on these institutional developments, leaving aside for the moment the broader question of the changing international monetary environment in which SDRs would have to function, it is worth noting that these developments were in marked contrast to those which heralded the SDR prior to the Rio Agreement only six or seven years previously.

5.5 The Failure of the SDR/Aid 'Link' Proposals

It must first of all be pointed out that the Committee of Twenty did not wholeheartedly endorse the idea of a link between SDR allocation and the provision of development finance. Whereas, for instance, the Committee explicitly proposed a Council to succeed it, and also that the SDR become the 'principal reserve asset of the international monetary system',[52] the link was not approved of in as forthright a manner; indeed in 1972–3 there was only one executive director among the developed member countries (Mr Palamenghi-Crispi of Italy) who supported it.[53] While paragraph 29 of the *Outline* proposed that 'an increasing net flow of real resources'[54] should accrue to developing countries, it went on to incorporate a caveat: '*IF* these arrangements were to include a link between development assistance and SDR allocation this could take one of . . . [two] . . . forms.'[55]

Thus, although the Committee acknowledged that a link could be implemented by the Executive Board, it was not specifically endorsed by the Committee, and in its technical group's report 'On the SDR/Aid Link and Related Proposals', arguments in favour and arguments against a link were both incorporated into the report.[56] In turn, it was not surprising that the conflict over the link then manifested itself in the Executive Board discussions surrounding the Second Amendment. While these discussions continued to reflect the Fund's practice of establishing consensus at executive directors meetings, rather than putting issues to a vote, one can discern in the minutes of the meetings that at times the discussions of a link verged on acrimony. This reflected frustration at the evident developed/less developed country split in opinion concerning the link.

Notwithstanding the Committee of Twenty's equivocal stand concerning the link, Fund staff, as they had done with the Council, again drafted a proposal integrating a reform initiative—a link in this case—as an integral part of the proposed amended articles. This time it submitted a provisional Article XXIV on 31 July 1974 and again on 8 January 1975.[57] The first of these again used the *Outline* as a basis for its proposal by proposing two alternatives (either a disproportionate allocation of SDRs directly to developing country members, or alternatively to development finance organizations) for an SDR/aid link. The 8 January draft further honed these alternatives by simplifying the wording and improving the structure of the amendment.

Between these two drafts, the executive directors discussed these proposals on 18 October 1974.[58] Most of the meeting was spent discussing the relative merits of Plan A (allocations direct to developing countries) or Plan B (allocations to development finance organizations). The US quickly made its reservations known: the American executive director, Sam Cross, expressed alarm at the Fund 'mixing aid with monetary issues such as liquidity creation'.[59] (This was one of the reservations which had originally appeared in the C-20's Technical Report.) Indeed disapproval of both plans was expressed:

> As to the drafts before the Executive Directors for discussion, both Draft A and Draft B would be adequate for those that liked them; he [Mr Cross] happened to like neither.[60]

The Acting Chairman of the meeting (in the absence of the Fund's managing director it was the deputy managing director, William Dale) suggested that further proposals be drafted. However when the managing director convened a meeting in November of 1974 to discuss a Program of Work in general (prior to a progress report by the executive directors to the Interim Committee), it was time constraints rather than the specific link proposals which were blamed for the lack of further consideration of the link.[61] Whatever the reason, it was plain that an impasse had been reached. At this meeting some frustration was expressed at these developments: Alexandre Kafka (Brazil) felt that the executive directors 'should pursue discussion on the amendments affecting gold, the "link", and the legalization of floating'.[62] P. S. N. Prasad (India) also expressed enthusiasm for the link, arguing that to ignore it

> ... would be to neglect the often expressed opinion of more than 80 per cent of the countries of the Fund. The achievement of broad reform would seem unbalanced if that topic were neglected.[63]

These sentiments were echoed by many developing country directors, particularly by Mr Yameogo[64] (Upper Volta), Mr Deif[65] (Egypt), and Mr Suarez[66] (Mexico). However the Chairman urged that the Interim Committee be advised as soon as possible of those proposals which had been agreed to and it was plain that the link did not have sufficient support to merit this. Thus while the Fund's legal department, in conjunction with other relevant departments (including the research, exchange and trade relations, and treasurer's department), continued to publish papers on the link, the stalemate on the proposal meant that the link never appeared on any comprehensive draft of the amended articles, let alone received further consideration by the Interim Committee.

The link discussions were in fact marked by strong disagreement, although well-couched in diplomatic language. Much to the frustration of most of the Fund's directors, some of whom had come to support the link only since 1973, at the time it was apparent that there were only two countries openly opposing it, one of which (the US) had an effective veto over proposals. Unlike in the discussion of the Council, at this time the US (and West German) views prevailed. At a meeting to discuss their report to the Interim Committee, some delegates expressed frustration at the diplomatic language of their report, arguing that countries that opposed the link should be officially exposed. Mr Zulu (Zambia) argued that after all the Interim Committee

> . . . would be aware of which two countries opposed the link', even if they were not specifically mentioned in the report. A third version of the draft amendment had been proposed but not extensively discussed, he added.[67]

There was a flurry of activity at this time by both the executive directors and Fund staff. Fund staff continued to draft amendments that included link proposals; in addition to the DAA/74/9, which had caused so much debate among the directors, staff documents continued to hark back to the C-20's direction to the Fund to implement a link.[68]

However, the second meeting of the Interim Committee, in Washington on 15–16 January 1974, had already indicated that progress on the link had halted. Seven months previously the Committee of Twenty had recommended to the Executive Board that draft amendments be prepared that *could* lead to the implementation of a link between development finance and SDR allocation; the press communiqué of the Interim Committee on 16 January 1975 reflected an impasse that had still not been breached. In language that hid the real rifts among executive directors, but was to be repeated over the next few years, the Committee acknowledged discussion of:

> . . . a possible amendment that would establish a link between allocations of SDRs and development finance, but there continues to be a diversity of views on this matter. It was agreed to keep the matter under active study, but at the same time to consider other ways for increasing the transfer of real resources to developing countries.[69]

Thus the link proposal died. Discussion of the link during the negotiations did indicate strong developing country support for the idea. It could be argued that because there was lukewarm support for the link during the C-20 negotiations, developing countries were flogging a dead horse by insisting that it continue to be discussed during the Second Amendment negotiations. Yet this more accurately reflects the attachment of developing countries to the idea.

The fact that it was one of the most acrimonious debates during the Second Amendment, however, also revealed the relative lack of power of developing countries at the IMF. This is doubly so given that during the mid-1970s developing country influence in international relations was at its peak (witnessed by the real attention of the G77 and other entities to notions of a New International Economic Order, a New Information Order, etc.).

More importantly, without US support the link could not have begun to succeed. It is also interesting to reflect that, although US support for an issue such as the Council did not automatically lead to the Council coming into fruition, US veto power over resolutions to which it was opposed, such as the link, prevailed. US power in the Fund is not absolute. In much the same way as the Federal Reserve manifests international monetary policy influence in the domestic economy in the US, the US at the Fund has a stronger capacity to block initiatives that it opposes rather than guarantee support for initiatives that it supports. Again, it is more of a 'negative capability'; US approval of a proposal will not necessarily lead to its acceptance, but firm US opposition to a proposal will prevail. Furthermore, it is interesting to note here that the link was further away from fruition than other proposals that were considered as reforming initiatives, in that it was essentially rejected in principle, unlike the later initiative of the substitution account, which *was* agreed to in principle. Also, given the conflict between the two proposals for the link (Plans A and B, above), even if the link had been agreed to on principle, it would not necessarily have followed that it would then have been enacted. After all, an initiative such as the substitution account would fail even after being agreed to in principle.

US influence did succeed in obtaining support for some of its objectives during the Second Amendment, including the legalization of de facto floating exchange rates (also supported by other important members such as West Germany). It did not succeed as fully as it had during the First Amendment, however, and certainly not as it did when Bretton Woods was conceived. The negotiations over the Second Amendment therefore go some way to confirming the observation that although US power was still paramount in the international system, it was not quite as pervasive as it had been even a decade earlier. This is not to suggest inexorable 'hegemonic' decline—the break-up of the Soviet Union and spread of US-inspired economic doctrine that came to be known as the 'Washington consensus' witnessed a resurgent US ascendancy from the 1980s for the next 30 years. But in the mid-1970s the future direction of international economy was not as clear cut.

Also, it has been noted that developing countries may have even hurt the cause of the SDR by their advocacy of the link. Peter Kenen, for instance, argues that because of opposition to using the SDR as a form of development aid, some Fund members may have become wary of any SDR initiative, including that of an allocation because of general liquidity or balance of payments need:

> The developing countries have already hurt themselves by their tenacious defense of the case for linking SDR creation with development assistance, because they have led other governments to be suspicious of *any* argument for an SDR allocation . . . allocations have [thus] been small and intermittent.[70]

Given their lack of real power, this perhaps ascribes too much blame to developing countries, but in any case, noting the lukewarm support of the link as early as the C-20 proposals, it is perhaps not surprising that the idea did not come to fruition. Ultimately, however, as an idea supported by Fund staff, it also hints at the influence of the Fund on the negotiations. That the link failed, though, was perhaps the first indication that the Fund would have to decouple its role in international monetary relations from that of the SDR—a notion that was to become increasingly evident in the years to come.

5.6 The Gold Substitution Account

Another reformist notion affecting SDRs that received attention at the Fund during the 1970s was the substitution account. Much of the impetus behind an SDR substitution account initially lay in proposals for substituting Fund members' *gold* holdings for SDRs.

A substitution account per se was first formally mooted at the Fund by the C-20 in its *Outline of Reform* in Annex 7.[71] Again this was a controversial proposal, reflected in two reports of technical groups on Intervention and Settlement, and on Global Liquidity and Consolidation. The reference to an idea behind a gold substitution account, however, was simple:

> Arrangements have also been proposed whereby the Fund would be authorized to purchase gold from monetary authorities in exchange for SDRs at a price between the market and the official price, and to sell gold gradually over time in the market.[72]

Following the C-20 report the Interim Committee called for further study of the proposal by the Executive Board at its second 1975 meeting.[73]

During the Second Amendment negotiations Fund staff also submitted technical papers dealing with the gold substitution account. The first of these, presented to the Executive Board on 24 April 1975, suggested that a 'once-for-all' opportunity to convert gold holdings into SDRs be made.[74] The second of them, on 28 July 1975, followed the by now familiar path of incorporating executive director suggestions for improvement, among them that the proceeds from the gold sales would be held in a gold substitution account, and that this account would have the authority to buy, hold, and sell gold and invest and reinvest the proceeds of gold sales.[75] These documents provoked much discussion among the directors, prompting two of them, Jacques de Groote (Belgium) and Alexandre Kafka each to submit a paper of his own.[76] Among other things, Mr de Groote pointed out that the staff schemes, while addressing the problem of member's gold holdings, left unresolved the question of Fund gold holdings.[77] Instead, he proposed a Gold Consolidation Account, among whose objectives would be to

> ...ensure a phasing down of the role of gold in the international monetary system while enhancing the role of the SDR, thereby increasing the volume of international liquidity that would be brought under international management.[78]

De Groote's plan was arguably the more ambitious of those proposed; he reasoned that if central banks were urged to reduce their gold holdings, the 'opportunity for the Fund as well as its members to convert gold holdings into stable and more usable assets' should be institutionalized.[79]

Mr Kafka's paper emphasized the importance of enhancing the role of the SDR; he also expressed fears that:

> ...even the possibility of an immense increase in liquidity for the major gold holders will at the very least impair the likelihood of further allocations of SDRs.[80]

However, the discussions of a gold substitution account concentrated on the effective demonetization of gold, notwithstanding the comments of Mr Kafka and Mr de Groote concerning the opportunity to enhance the role of the SDR. Once the difficulties of a gold substitution account with SDRs were realized, its prospects began to diminish. Second, in much the same way that discussions of the link reached an impasse, discussions of a gold substitution account began to be greeted with indifference by some executive directors. Reducing the role of gold was difficult enough to negotiate, and while Fund staff and some executive directors felt that a gold substitution account would present an opportunity to enhance the role of SDRs, to others it meant a weak resolution of the gold 'problem'. For instance, the Japanese director felt that while a gold substitution account was an attractive proposition, he did worry about 'the extent to which the gold holders were willing to participate in the scheme'.[81] Mr Pieske (Germany) referred to a time constraint,[82] which, as in the case of the link, indicated an impasse among the directors and suggested that the plan would remain dormant. Again it was an upcoming Interim Committee meeting—this time the Jamaica meeting—which loomed. He also wondered aloud whether a gold substitution account was worth discussing:

> ...he shared Mr. Wahl's [France] view that there were more deserving subjects, including the control of international liquidity in general, to which the Executive Directors could devote their energies. Indeed, he would not wish to discuss, even *in abstracto*, a scheme which was likely to create major problems for the international monetary system...[83]

Thus the gold substitution account was condemned to the same fate as the link. J. J. Polak pointed out that, technically, it had also proved a very complicated issue as well.[84] Despite the suggestions of Fund staff, and some support among the directors, support for the gold substitution account was not widespread enough for it to be agreed upon. And, finally, the US also admitted that one reason for this was that the issue was again linked to the allocation of SDRs. Sam Cross, the US executive director, explicitly rejected the idea, by pointing out that one motive for a gold substitution account:

> ...was to redistribute international liquidity as between countries holding large amounts of gold and those that did not. Both Mr. Kafka and the staff appeared to hope to bring about a redistribution through the allocation of special drawing rights. Again, he did not consider that an appropriate basis for the establishment of a gold substitution account in the Fund.[85]

By late 1975 US antipathy to SDRs during the Ford administration was becoming more evident. The gold substitution account, in so far as it addressed gold, was acceptable to the US. However, in so far as it promoted the SDR, it was not of interest.

The time spent on the gold substitution account reflected the Fund's interest in the gold question. After the impasse over the account, however, the gold issues that eventually took precedence were the further steps in the demonetization of gold. This was facilitated and sweetened by an acceptance of a market price of gold and by an agreement to set up a Trust Fund to distribute profits of one-sixth of the Fund's gold sales for the benefit of developing country members, which is indeed what happened.[86] Tangentially, however, the gold substitution account proposals kept alive the interest in a substitution account per se. This consideration was reflected in the serious discussions surrounding a currency substitution account for SDRs only three years later. Nonetheless the failure of the gold version of the account, like the failure of the Council before it, was another indication that SDR-related proposals were failing to take hold despite the sympathy and support of the IMF.

5.7 Reconstitution

The reconstitution provision, whereby IMF member countries could be obliged to 'reconstitute' SDRs used over the long term, was part of the first amendment to the Articles of Agreement agreed to at Rio. Its avowed purpose was to avoid financing chronic balance of payments deficits through the use of SDRs. This could be said to have effectively militated against their use, particularly by developing countries and, as we have seen in Chapter 2, by the end of the First Basic Period of SDR allocations, pressure for abolition of the reconstitution provision was mounting. While it was not abolished until 1981, this abolition was facilitated by the Second Amendment.[87]

Section 6(b) of the Articles after the *First* Amendment stipulated that:

> ... an eighty-five percent majority of the total voting power shall be required for decisions to adopt, modify, or abrogate the rules for reconstitution.[88]

In its draft paper on reconstitution in July of 1975, Fund staff acknowledged that there was some support for the 'deletion of reconstitution from the Articles'.[89] The paper went on to promote the idea of eliminating the provisions (for the reasons given in Chapter 2) and argued that 'the balance of advantage is in favor of amending the Articles to eliminate reconstitution'.[90] Once again Fund staff made its position clear, though the draft articles went on to say that should this proposition not find sufficient support the Board of Governors should consider abrogating the rules for reconstitution under the existing Articles.[91]

Again an impasse was evident amongst the directors. They considered this paper in July 1975,[92] and while most directors said that they favoured abolition of reconstitution, several, including Mr Schneider (Austria), Mr Laske (Germany), and Sam Cross favoured its retention. Mr Laske argued that reconstitution was a 'safeguard for the SDR',[93] and Mr Cross made the point that the staff argument maintaining that the 'balance of advantage' in favour of eliminating reconstitution was 'somewhat surprising' since:

> ... the staff seemed to argue in favor of reconstitution when it held that reconstitution enabled the Fund to sell SDRs to members that needed them to pay charges.[94]

Similar stalemate was in evidence when the directors considered the provision in October,[95] but when they met in December it was an impromptu remark by Mr Palamenghi-Crispi (Italy) that prompted the compromise incorporated into the Second Amendment. Mr Palamenghi-Crispi repeated his conviction that reconstitution should be abolished, and then proceeded to wonder aloud whether a reduction of the voting majority required for altering the reconstitution provision might be acceptable:

> Speaking personally, Mr. Palamenghi-Crispi wondered whether those Executive Directors who favored retaining reconstitution might be able to accept lowering

> the majority required for adopting, modifying or abrogating the rules for reconstitution from 85 per cent to 70 per cent of the total voting power.[96]

At this point many of those executive directors who had opposed tampering with the proposition, such as Mr Lieftinck (the Netherlands), said that they could perhaps accept such a reduction. The US Alternate Executive Director, Mr Leddy, said that 'he would inform his authorities of Mr Palamenghi-Crispi's proposal; presently, he could not comment on it'.[97] After some further discussion the Chairman of the meeting, Johannes Witteveen, observed that the directors were 'progressing toward a compromise on the basis of Mr Palamenghi-Crispi's proposal',[98] and suggested that the idea be reconsidered in the near future. Fund staff then incorporated the notion in their paper on the draft report of the executive directors to the Interim Committee on 12 December.[99] The new 70 per cent majority was one of the topics discussed at the Executive Board meetings in preparation for the Interim Committee meeting. The first of these was on the 15 December,[100] and although agreement could not be reached, subsequent redrafts of the report by the staff were quickly compiled (on 19 December, 23 December, and 24 December[101]) in an effort to complete them before Christmas and submit them before the Interim Committee meeting in early January. Hurried discussion of the proposal by the executive directors also took place on 22 December[102] and on 23 December. [103] The final staff document (SM/75/292, Revision 3) was submitted to the Interim Committee in time for their meeting in Kingston Jamaica on 7 and 8 January 1976, and it was agreed there:

> ...that the amended Articles should authorize the Fund to review the rules for reconstitution at any time and to adopt, modify, or abrogate these rules by a 70 per cent majority of the total voting power.[104]

This was incorporated into a comprehensive draft of the amendments for the first time on 14 January 1976.[105] After the final comprehensive draft was approved in March 1976,[106] the directors reviewed the reconstitution provision in 1976 and 1977. Although no changes were then recommended, in October of 1978 the Executive Board allowed members to maintain a 15 (rather than 30) per cent average of SDR allocations over five years,[107] and in 1981 the reconstitution provision was abolished entirely. This was supported by the G24.[108] It is interesting to note that the two major countries most reticent to accepting further SDR allocations (the US and West Germany), also opposed changes to the SDR's characteristics such as the abolition of the reconstitution provision.

In a further ironic twist, only three years later, one prominent proponent of SDRs asked whether the reconstitution provision should itself be 'reconstituted' in some form, arguing that with the predominance of private liquidity provision a new allocation of SDRs in this case would promote 'reserves to hold' rather than 'reserves to spend'.[109] Williamson also argued that a new reconstitution provision could reduce the reticence of industrial countries in agreeing to a new allocation by promoting an improvement in developing country reserve positions without real transfers from industrial countries. Augmenting the attractiveness of SDRs as reserves to hold would in turn in turn enhance the role of the SDR per se. Interestingly, two of the executive directors who had argued against the abolition of the reconstitution provision in 1975 had implied much the same thing: Tom de Vries (the Netherlands) argued that 'reconstitution helped prevent members spending their SDRs imprudently'[110] and Sam Cross pointed out that proponents as well as opponents of reconstitution 'maintained their different positions out of a common desire to strengthen the asset quality of the SDR'.[111] While proponents of SDRs during the negotiation of the Second Amendment favoured the abolition of the reconstitution provision on the grounds that they should be treated like any other reserves, by the mid-1980s the abolition of reconstitution was viewed as having been premature and reconsideration of the idea was advocated to bolster its declining attributes.

In the mid-1970s, despite the moves to private liquidity provision, SDRs had not yet been marginalized completely; indeed the seriousness with which the directors discussed them during the Second Amendment negotiations strongly belies this notion. In addition, the Second Amendment also incorporated the phrase that SDRs should become the principal reserve asset of a reformed international monetary system, and it is to the discussions on this proposition that we now turn.

5.8 The SDR as Principal Reserve Asset

In late 1974 Fund staff submitted a document to the executive directors outlining the objectives of the draft amendments already issued.[112] The negotiations had been running officially for only three months; at this early stage the document still included provisions for a link and a Council as part of the prospective articles. Also in this document was the strong statement referring not only to the SDR as principal reserve asset, but to improvements to the mechanisms surrounding it as well:

> [I]n view of the agreed objective that the SDR should become the principal reserve asset, [the Fund should seek] to improve the characteristics and relax the restraints on the use of the SDR.[113]

Again, the C-20's influence is apparent: SDRs were to become the 'principal reserve asset' of the international monetary system, a phrase which initially appeared in the Introduction of the C-20's *Outline of Reform*.[114] It is worth recalling that under the First Amendment of the Articles, the express purpose of allocating SDRs was to 'meet the need, as and when it arises, for a supplement to existing reserve assets'.[115] This statement was also incorporated in the Second Amendment under Article XV.[116] In Article XXIV of the First Amendment, it was also stated that SDRs would be allocated to promote the goals of the Fund and to 'avoid economic stagnation and deflation as well as excess demand and inflation in the world'.[117] Also in considering the first allocation, 'special considerations' may be taken into account, which were 'the attainment of a better balance of payments equilibrium, as well as the likelihood of a better working of the adjustment process in the future'.[118] Articles XXI to XXXII, which dealt with the new SDRs, went on to stipulate rights and obligations of members concerning the use of the new asset.

SDRs under the Second Amendment were treated slightly differently. To begin with, the primary raison d'être for SDRs under the First Amendment, namely reserve inadequacy, had largely disappeared with the explosion of Eurocurrency markets and loosening of US monetary policy, as we saw in Chapters 1 and 2.[119] Indeed in light of the difficulties over the link and the gold substitution account, and the acceptance of flexible exchange rates under Article IV, the incorporation of this 'principal reserve asset' phrase was perhaps surprising. SDRs had not yet lost their relevance to the Fund (or to many of its members) however; indeed the phrase was incorporated into the Fund's Articles of Agreement twice, in Article VIII and Article XXII.[120] This may be interpreted as mere crumbs of comfort to those, including those within the Fund, who still believed passionately in the future of the SDR. On the other hand, a much less comprehensive statement could have been offered, and the phrase remains a fascinating legacy to this day for those who view the SDR as a potential buttress to stable international monetary arrangements, let alone a (or the) principal reserve asset.

Curiously, the inclusion of the phrase at the time prompted little discussion, as an examination of Fund documents and minutes of the Executive Board reveals. Under the first comprehensive draft amendment, under Article VIII, it was stipulated that:

> ...each participant undertakes to collaborate with the Fund and with other participants in order to facilitate the effective functioning of the Special Drawing Account and the proper use of special drawing rights in accordance with this Agreement.[121]

In a supplementary revision to this draft, however, which appeared on 12 May 1975, the above phrase appeared with the addendum '... and with the objective of making the special drawing right the main reserve asset'.[122] A proposition appeared ten days later, in a staff memorandum, that the SDR should be the 'main' reserve asset.[123] Consideration of either proposition provoked little comment by the directors. There are two possible explanations for this. The first is that by ignoring the proposition and allowing its acceptance, all parties would be satisfied. By 1975 there was a realization that avoiding controversial debate was the only hope for the Second Amendment. The difficulties in negotiating the Second Amendment had made it clear to everyone that it should be drafted to incorporate enough flexibility to accommodate international monetary reform without further amendment.[124] This was an important change in emphasis. Evidence that this realization existed also came from the US Executive director in February 1975 during a discussion of the use of the Fund's resources, when Sam Cross:

> ... remarked that as no one knew what the international monetary system would be in the period ahead, he hoped that Section 3(b) [dealing with the purchase of Fund member's currencies] could be redrafted with sufficient flexibility so that if there was ever a return to a par value system, countries like the United States or the United Kingdom would be eligible to use the Fund's resources ...[125]

Indeed the rubric of flexibility in the Second Amendment was also reflected in the language that treated SDRs per se, as we shall see. As far as the SDR as principal reserve asset in the international monetary was concerned, the key to the incorporation of this provision in the amended articles was the word 'objective'. After little executive director comment on the idea (in Witteveen's statement and subsequent discussion of the comprehensive draft amendment DAA/75/2 there was no comment at all),[126] it was included in the second supplement to this draft article. It was rarely addressed directly again and, when it was, it was usually in conjunction with the role of gold in the international monetary system. The compromise embodied in the amended articles was such that it was agreed that the *objective* was to make the SDR the principal reserve asset. At one meeting Mr Lieftinck suggested that the words 'over time' be inserted in Article VIII, Section 7;[127] the General Counsel maintained that this would be superfluous since there were other provisions in the Articles which used the same language.[128] At this same meeting, a compromise solution of deleting Article VIII, Section 7, altogether was again suggested, although the compromise that was eventually agreed to was the submission of the proposal to the Interim Committee for further consideration—and acceptance.

The other point to be made here is that once gold had been abandoned as the lynchpin of the international monetary system, the SDR's potential importance as symbol in a fragile new system that had not yet proved itself became further evident. With the inclusion of the phrase that one of the objectives of the Fund was to make the SDR the principal reserve asset, the SDR could symbolically fill the vacuum that the effective demonetization of gold had left, as well as providing SDR supporters with what seemed an important statement.

Another reason why these provisions on SDRs were included in the Articles was in the eventuality that the new system legalized by the international community after the Second Amendment experienced further difficulties. As we have seen, the same was true of the Council. These were important steps to the success of the Amendments itself—after all, had not Sam Cross admitted that no one really knew what the international monetary system would be like in the future?[129] To accommodate this uncertainty, the nature of the Articles changed—from inherent rigid disciplines to flexibility. As Alexander Mountford of the IMF's Independent Evaluation Office has written:

> Broadly, one can say that the original Articles put a clear emphasis on firm rules, especially as regards exchange rates and the financial rights and obligations of members, and provided less room for discretion. The balance then shifted markedly in the late 1970s, with the Second Amendment of the Articles, towards a system in which there are fewer rules and greater reliance on Principles . . . [130]

Discussions of Article VIII began on 6 October 1975,[131] and resumed in earnest after agreement had been reached on a gradual reduction on the role of gold in the international monetary system at a meeting the previous week.[132] The 6 October meeting was one of many to discuss the first draft agreement of the Second Amendments, presented on 27 May 1975.[133] Three short alternative versions of Article VIII were offered, all of which obliged members to cooperate with the Fund in the reduction of the role of gold in the international monetary system.[134] It is interesting to note too, that despite the effective legalization of the new arrangements, many executive directors from a variety of countries insisted on the inclusion of a primary role for the SDR in this amendment.

In addition, the Interim Committee continued to promote the SDR, picking up where its predecessor, the C-20, had left off. In its meeting in Washington in January 1975, which effectively quashed the link, it continued to maintain that the SDR should become the principal reserve asset, as it had pushed for the adoption of a decision-making Council to replace it. (This also alluded to its supposed status as a truly *interim* committee.) In this vein, it must also be acknowledged that the C-20's last meeting in June of 1974 (the same one that proposed an Interim Committee, the establishment an oil facility, and recommended the establishment of new guidelines for floating rates), also secured approval for a reduction in the number of currencies in the SDR basket from an unwieldy 16 to 5 (see Table 5.1). This made the SDR a more manageable entity, as well as lending some early plausibility to a role for it under post-Bretton Woods arrangements.

Table 5.1. SDR valuation basket, July 1974 – December 2015

Currency	1 July '74 – 30 June '78		1 July '78 – 31 Dec '80		1 Jan '81 – 31 Dec '85		1 Jan '86 – 31 Dec '90		1 Jan '91 – 31 Dec '95		1 Jan '96 – 31 Dec '98		1 Jan '99 – 31 Dec '00		1 Jan '01 – 31 Dec '05		1 Jan '06 – 31 Dec '10		1 Jan '11 – 31 Dec '15	
	Weight (%)	Currency Amount	Weight (%)	Currency Amount	Weight (%)	Currency Amount	Weight (%)	Currency Amount	Weight (%)	Currency Amount	Weight (%)	Currency Amount	Weight (%)	Currency Amount	Weight (%)	Currency Amount	Weight (%)	Currency Amount	Weight (%)	Currency Amount
US dollar	33.0	0.4000	33.0	0.400	42.0	0.540	42.0	0.4520	40.0	0.572	39.0	0.582	39.0	0.5820	45.0	0.5770	40.0	0.6320	41.9	0.6600
Deutschmark (to 12/98)	12.5	0.3800	12.5	0.320	19.0	0.460	19.0	0.5270	21.0	0.453	21.0	0.446								
Pound sterling	9.0	0.0450	7.5	0.050	13.0	0.071	12.0	0.0893	11.0	0.081	11.0	0.105	11.0	0.1050	11.0	0.0984	11.0	0.0903	11.3	0.1110
French franc (to 12/98)	7.5	0.4400	7.5	0.420	13.0	0.740	12.0	1.0200	11.0	0.800	11.0	0.813								
Japanese yen	7.5	26.0000	7.5	21.000	13.0	34.000	15.0	33.4000	17.0	31.800	18.0	27.200	18.0	27.2000	15.0	21.0000	17.0	18.4000	9.4	12.1000
Euro (from 1/99)													32.0	0.3519	29.0	0.4260	34.0	0.4100	37.4	0.4230
Canadian dollar	6.0	0.7100	5.0	0.070																
Italian lira	6.0	47.0000	5.0	52.000																
Dutch guilder	4.5	0.1400	5.0	0.140																
Belgian franc	3.5	1.6000	4.0	1.600																
Swedish krona	2.5	0.1300	2.0	0.110																
Australian dollar	1.5	0.0120	1.5	0.017																
Spanish peseta	1.5	1.1000	1.5	1.500																
Norwegian krone	1.5	0.0990	1.5	0.100																
Danish krone	1.5	0.1100	-	-																
Austrian schilling	1.0	0.2200	1.5	0.280																
South African rand	1.0	0.0082	-	-																
Saudi Arabian riyal	-	-	3.0	0.130																
Iranian rial	-	-	2.0	1.700																

Notes: 1. Recall that, when instituted in 1969, the exchange rate of the SDR was said to be equal to US$1 (Rule O-3 of the IMF Rules and Regulations accompanying the First Amendment). However, following the first US dollar devaluation in terms of gold in May 1972, the SDR became effectively revalued at $1.08571, and after the second dollar devaluation in February 1973 became equal to $1.20635. This instability eventually prompted the Executive Board to adopt the standard basket above in 1974, after some prompting from both the Committee of Twenty and Fund staff. (See Chapter 2, pp. 52, 65; also M. de Vries, The IMF 1972–8, vol. 1 (Washington: 1985), pp. 284–6; 290–1.) 2. A sample valuation of a given currency in terms of the SDR may be calculated using published exchange rates. For the value of the US dollar in terms of the SDR on 6 August 1990, start with the SDR currency amounts as found in the correct column above, and as reproduced below. Then take the published exchange rates for the US dollar for that day, and find the value of each currency amount in terms of the US dollar. Then add these amounts:

Table 5.1 (*Continued*)

	SDR Valuation on 6 August 1990				SDR Valuation on 30 December 2010		
	Currency Amount	Exchange Rate per $, 6/8/90	US $ Equiv.		Currency Amount	Exchange Rate per $, 30/12/10	US $ Equiv.
US dollar	0.4520	1.00000	0.452000	US dollar	0.6600	1.00000	0.660000
Deutschmark	0.5270	1.57620	0.334348				
Pound sterling	0.0893	1.8722*	0.167187	Pound sterling	0.1110	1.54350	0.171329
French franc	1.0200	5.28800	0.192890				
Japanese yen	33.4000	149.82	0.222934	Japanese yen	12.1000	81.630000	0.148230
				Euro	0.4230	1.32500	0.560475
		SDR 1 = $1.369359				**SDR 1 = $1.54003**	

* = standard cross rate for sterling exchange rates

Source: Rates to 1985 from Finance and Development, Sept. 1982, p. 32; otherwise from various IMF Survey and Press Releases at http://www.imf.org
Table for SDR valuation on 6 August 1990 from IMF Survey, Special Supplement, August 1990, and for 30 December 2010 from http://www.imf.org/external/np/tre/sdr/sdrbasket.htm (accessed 6 June 2011).

Above all, the decision to provide SDRs with the possibility of becoming the principal reserve asset occurred because of a desire on the part of most Directors to say something positive after the Fund had decided to negate the role of gold. The Legal Department had prepared three alternative versions of Article VIII, Section 7 by the end of May 1975. Immediately prior to its discussion of these versions, the Executive Board referred to the communiqué of the Interim Committee that advocated that the role of gold be reduced as a precursor to the SDR taking the 'central place in the international monetary system'.[135] While it could be argued that the effective demonetization of gold as far as the Fund was concerned was understandable given that the US could not reestablish convertibility, it was less obvious that its formal replacement should be the SDR. What had become apparent, however, was a general desire to affirm a definitive role for SDRs in Article VIII, Section 7, which would not only reduce the role of gold as a reserve asset, but effectively nominate a prospective replacement. While many seemed willing to reduce the role of gold, at the time not all seemed willing to jump confidently into the abyss of an international monetary system with no stable core reserve asset, which this implied. The US executive director had expressed a worry that many shared, namely how well the new system would work, and this no doubt contributed to the avowed role of the SDR in the new system, as well as the incorporation of other features in the new amendment which we will address in the next section.

It should also be acknowledged that the G10 and bilateral diplomacy had some bearing on the inclusion of this phrase in the Second Amendment. Echoing the controversy over the SDR in the First Amendment, it was again a US–French compromise, ironed out both bilaterally and within the G10, which gave further impetus to the final version of Section 7, Article VIII to be included in the Second Amendment of the Articles of Agreement. In a press communiqué of the G10 in December 1975, they advised that they had resolved their differences and would include the pertinent phrase concerning the role of SDRs in a new system at the upcoming Jamaica meeting which approved the new Articles of Agreement.[136]

American–French differences were also concentrated on the more fundamental question of the nature of the exchange rate system under Article IV. Jacques de Larosière, who became managing director of the IMF in 1978, headed the French delegation in intensive bilateral discussions between the US and France from August to November 1975.[137] Initially, the French strongly favoured a renewed commitment for fixed exchange rates. However, the compromise struck over Article IV between the US and France ended in legalized flexible exchange rates (Section 2(b)), with the Fund overseeing the 'efficient operation' of the system as a whole (Section 3). In addition provisions were made for an eventual return to a par value system, should 85% of the membership approve (Section 4 and Schedule C).[138]

As during the First Amendment, some of the groundwork for the US–French compromise was outside the Fund and even G10. The first public economic summit amongst the five largest western economies (the G5, eventually the G7 with the inclusion of Italy and Canada) took place in November of 1975, at Rambouillet, outside Paris.[139] While Rambouillet has been heralded as the meeting which ironed out American–French differences, in effect it was the culmination of negotiations which had taken place throughout the previous six months, not only between Edwin Yeo and Jacques de Larosière, but also at the Interim Committee meeting in Washington in early September that included meetings by the US and French finance ministers, Simon and Fourcade.[140] As one critic pointed out, the agreement reached at Rambouillet was:

> . . . the fruit of negotiations that had already been going on for several months between delegations of the two countries, headed . . . by Edwin Yeo and Jacques de Larosière. The issue had also been discussed at the IMF Interim Committee and Assembly [*sic*] meetings (Washington, 31 August – 1 September 1975) by the US and French finance ministers, Simon and Fourcade . . . [141]

Thus, the Rambouillet summit and other bilateral and multilateral diplomatic initiatives outside the Fund did play their part in the successful conclusion of the Second Amendment. This time, however, and unlike during the First Amendment discussions, policy disagreements had been largely institutionalized at the Fund. Furthermore, judging by the results, the leverage enjoyed by the French or their European partners was now even lower than it had been during the First Amendment negotiations.

There were thus at least three other conceptual differences in the way in which the Second Amendment was negotiated vis-à-vis the first. First of all, unlike First Amendment discussions, one reason for the success of the Jamaica Agreement lay in the intense discussion *within* the Fund between 1974 and 1976. Second, French and other European reticence concerning a flexible exchange rate system could be—and indeed was—focused in the European arena with respect to European exchange rates. In addition, the intensive discussions surrounding the Second Amendment had demonstrated that international monetary agreement on a public system of liquidity provision was proving more and more elusive. With the new arrangements consolidating themselves over the course of the negotiations, it must be admitted that the credence given to the SDR in the Second Amendment had less to do with the real functioning of the international monetary system and more to do with the legacy of the First Amendment and the C-20 only a few years before. Embodied within the Second Amendment, however, were important elements of flexibility that would have a bearing on future changes to international monetary arrangements. These elements bear further attention.

5.9 Less Obvious Accomplishments of the Second Amendment: Enabling Powers and Automaticity

The evolution of the Second Amendment as a whole is indicative of many changes that took place—reflecting changing attitudes within the Fund and among its most important members as well as conditions in the international monetary system itself. Many of the debates reflected disquiet at the implications of the Amendments; certainly the debates on the Council reflect this. On the other hand, the Second Amendment did succeed in introducing elements of flexibility into the functioning of the Fund and its constitutional abilities to adapt to changing international monetary conditions. Given the upheaval since the negotiation of the First Amendment establishing SDRs—the suspension of dollar convertibility, the first oil-price shock, explosion in Eurobank lending, and the short-lived Smithsonian Agreement—the fact that this flexibility was built in to the Second Amendment must be considered a considerable achievement.

While it was true that fundamental reform did not take place, it has been argued here that the flexibility embodied in the Second Amendment has been overlooked. There has been some recognition of this flexibility, but little acknowledgement of its importance. Very early on, for example, John Williamson in his examination of Jamaica soon after the agreement was concluded argued that the significance of the Jamaica Agreement was the legalization of prevailing international monetary relations.[142] He went on to observe, however, that while Bretton Woods generally defined the rights and obligations in the system, what followed was rather a 'set of conventions and practices that have evolved out of a mixture of custom and crisis'.[143] This was characterized as an international monetary 'non-system', although Williamson did acknowledge that the new agreement was to embody a degree of flexibility that was not prevalent under the previous regime. Joseph Gold, responsible for the drafting of most of the proposed and adopted Articles, went further than this and argued that the enabling powers embodied in the Second Amendment made room for the Fund's involvement in the evolution of the international monetary system—without the necessity for further amendment of the Articles, a point echoed more recently by the Fund's Independent Evaluation Office.[144]

Indeed the protracted negotiations over the amended articles during the two-year period before ratification, plus the raising of the voting power required for further amendments from 80 to 85 per cent, all suggest that future amendments will be even more difficult to achieve.[145] This is not as great a problem as it could have been, however. While the Second Amendment did not make it easier for the Fund itself to amend the Articles (this had been true since Bretton Woods), the flexibility embodied in the enabling powers of the Fund to adapt to changing international monetary conditions were made *more* explicit in the Second Amendment.

The Council is an example of this in that provisions have been made for its creation within the Articles. Also, concerning exchange arrangements, under Article IV Section 4 the Fund may reinstitute par values,[146] and a schedule (Schedule C) also exists for their reestablishment. Furthermore, the phrase that a (future) *objective* of the IMF and its membership is to make the SDR the principal reserve asset in the international monetary system is included in the Articles. While all these accomplishments may be viewed as merely a convenient means of obtaining agreement to allow a floating rate regime, the documents and minutes of the negotiation of the Second Amendment do not solely support this interpretation. While it is true that opportunities were missed to endorse further reform proposals, embodied within the Second Amendment was the means to allow reform without amendment. These enabling powers are important and have tended to be overlooked by most commentators. As noted, despite the impasse over the Fourth Amendment allocations from 1997 until 2009, the IMF was able to respond to the calls for additional liquidity easily, and the SDR allocations were a core element in this response.

In some respects, this flexibility was also legacy of the C-20.[147] While the C-20 did not succeed in uniting behind a cohesive plan of reform, it did succeed in at least laying some of the groundwork for the 'evolutionary path to reform', as Joseph Gold has characterized it.[148] The character of the Articles of Agreement after the Second Amendment changed from that of a constitution in which member states duties and responsibilities were clearly outlined to one in which many initiatives for reform, such as SDRs becoming the principal international reserve asset (Article VIII, Sec. 7, Art. XXII) and providing for a return to par values (Article IV, Sec. 4; Schedule C), were included in the Articles and which in fact could be operative under different international monetary arrangements.[149] This is a crucially important feature, and one which even harks back to the mechanism surrounding Keynes's plans for an ICU as noted in Chapter 1.

5.10 Summary

The negotiations concerning the Second Amendment within the IMF were protracted and represented a real attempt to salvage prospects along the lines of those set out in the First Amendment. US policy after the failure of the Smithsonian Agreement had changed, first haltingly but then firmly, to strong support for a flexible exchange rate system.

In the Second Amendment negotiations, US opposition to proposals such as the link prevailed; its support for proposals such as the Council did not succeed as completely, however. US power in this context was not 'absolute', and an analogy may be drawn between the 'negative capability' of the US at the Fund with the similar capacity of the Federal Reserve in the formulation of US international monetary policy—that is that opposition to initiatives could succeed; proposition of initiatives, however, and seeing them through to fruition, was a different issue.

Without US support then the failure of comprehensive international monetary reform and SDR-related proposals was almost inevitable. Despite this, however, the IMF did enjoy limited success in providing the framework for a future reformed system under the Second Amendment. Understandably, most previous analyses of the Jamaica Agreement have pointed to the fact that it completely disestablished the role of gold, or legalized a flexible exchange rate system. What has been emphasized in this chapter, however, is that the Second Amendment provided a framework for future reform in the Jamaica Agreement, and that this is a positive accomplishment that has been largely overlooked. The flexibility embodied in the articles of the Second Amendment can easily encompass real political change in international monetary arrangements in the future, something that could not be said of the IMF's Articles of Agreement in their previous two incarnations.

In addition, with important supporters of the Bretton Woods system from the Fund's earliest days still at the Fund (e.g. Jacques Polak and Joseph Gold), and even though Fund staff were of course beholden to the executive directors, much evidence exists in the documents relating to the Second Amendment that suggests that Fund staff—indeed the Fund as an entity in itself—was successful in putting forward its own interests, and in exerting reformist pressure. We have witnessed this from the earliest days of the Second Amendment: in the influence of the C-20 and then Fund staff themselves in setting much of the initial agenda for the discussions. It would be wrong to suggest that these influences succeeded in causing the US to change its priorities, or to maintain that the Council or par value schedules were greater accomplishments than they were. Rather the main point here is to point out that previous analyses which have pointed to the failure of reform under the Second Amendment have tended to overlook these achievements—especially given the circumstances. Also, the Second Amendment established the groundwork for a continued role for the Fund under the new arrangements. Paradoxically, in the next few years this was to pave the way at the Fund for a declining identification of its own interests under these new arrangements with a role for the SDR.

Thus the negotiations leading to the Second Amendment of the Fund's Articles of Agreement cannot be judged a failure. Perhaps given the reform initiatives of the C-20 they seemed to be so to contemporary critics, but in the light of subsequent international monetary developments the Fund succeeded in salvaging important elements of flexibility in the amendments—amendments that also encompassed an SDR, including a greater role for it in the future.[150] Of course, international monetary arrangements and changes in US policy meant that in practice the SDR would have little in the way of a real role for the next 30 years. Nonetheless, under difficult circumstances, the Fund sought to preserve a role for the SDR in the Second Amendment. What remains to be examined is what this would mean for the SDR—and the IMF's relationship to it—during the international monetary arrangements of the de jure post-Bretton Woods monetary era.

Notes

1. The efforts of the Fund's chief archivist, Ms Gertrude Long, as well as the secretary of the Fund, Mr Leo Van Houtven, were successful in making these documents available to this author. The documents and minutes have been compiled in six hardback volumes entitled *Documents Relating to the Second Amendment of the Articles of Agreement of the International Monetary Fund.* Three volumes of these are documents of the Fund, three volumes are minutes of the Executive Board, prepared for limited distribution in 1980. (An index followed in 1986.) The Documents are abbreviated DAA (Draft Amendment of the Articles), SM (Staff Memorandum), EBD (Executive Board Document), or Press Release. The minutes are abbreviated EBM (Executive Board Minutes.) The titles of documents and minutes are provided in Appendix 1 of this book, below. Like other contemporary Fund Staff Memoranda and Departmental Memoranda examined by this author, these texts were embossed with the proviso that they are 'Documents of the International Monetary Fund and not for public use'; at the time this was in order to establish confidentiality before official Fund policy is agreed upon, and thus to aid in the establishment of consensus. In 1996, the IMF began to increase public access to archives; see http://www.imf.org/external/np/arc/eng/archive.htm#access (accessed 6 June 2011).
2. Prior to being made more widely available through the IMF's new archive policies as of the mid-1990s, availability of Fund Staff Memoranda (SMs) and Departmental Memoranda (DMs) was facilitated through interview visits to Washington and the welcome assistance of a number of ex-Fund staff as noted in n. 1, together with information provided by Jacques Polak, Sir Joseph Gold, and William Coats Jr.
3. *International Herald Tribune*, 13 January 1976, p. 9. As quoted in Benjamin Cohen, *Organizing the World's Money*, Basic Books (New York: 1977), p. 115.
4. Although Tom de Vries quotes Simon paraphrasing Shakespeare less enthusiastically by saying 'all's well that ends', in 'Jamaica, or the Non-Reform of the International Monetary System', *Foreign Affairs*, no. 54, April 1976.

5. See Robert Triffin, 'Jamaica: 'Major Revision or Fiasco?', in E. M. Bernstein *et. al. Reflections on Jamaica*, Princeton, International Finance Section, April 1976, p. 45.
6. 'The Quest for Stability', an address to the European-Atlantic Group, London, by Otmar Emminger, 19 February 1976, as quoted in Brian Tew, *The Evolution of the International Monetary System 1945–77*, Hutchinson (London: 1977), p. 203.
7. See E. M. Bernstein, *Reflections on Jamaica, op. cit.*
8. John Williamson, *The Failure of World Monetary Reform, op. cit.*, p. xi.
9. Tom de Vries, 'Jamaica, or the Non-Reform of the International Monetary System', *Foreign Affairs*, no. 54, April 1976.
10. Fritz Machlup, 'Between Outline and Outcome the Reform was Lost', in E. M. Bernstein *et. al. Reflections on Jamaica, op. cit.*, p. 30.
11. Andrew Crockett, *International Money—Issues and Analysis*, Nelson (Walton-on-Thames: 1982), p. 214; Herbert G. Grubel, *The International Monetary System*, Penguin (Harmondsworth, Middx: 1984), p. 112; Maurice Levi, *International Finance*, McGraw-Hill (Tokyo: 1983), pp. 143–4.
12. The Executive Directors came to be known as the Executive Board following the Second Amendment (Article XII, Section 3(a)).
13. IMF Document No. SM/74/72, p. 1 (p. 2, vol. 1 of Documents).
14. Despite the C-20's realization that agreement was not forthcoming on international monetary reform, in its last communiqué (13 June 1974), it recommended that the Executive Board prepare draft amendments to the Articles of Agreement. Furthermore the communiqué went on to say that it envisaged that the draft amendments 'would be presented for the approval of the Board of Governors *at latest* by the date fixed for completion of the current general review of Fund quotas, ie. by February 1975' (emphasis added). Document of the C-20, sixth and final press communiqué, p. 226.
15. Ratification required endorsement from three-fifths of the Fund's membership, representing four-fifths of the voting power at the IMF.
16. De Vries, *The IMF in a Changing World 1945–85, op. cit.*, p. 117.
17. Joseph Gold, 'The Second Amendment of the Fund's Articles of Agreement', IMF Pamphlet Series, No. 25, 1978.
18. C-20 *International Monetary Reform*, Documents of the C-20, IMF, 1974. Pt 1, section 31, p. 18.
19. Articles of Agreement(3), 1978. Schedule D (pp. 87–90), and Article XII, Section 1, which stipulates that the Council will come to fruition 'if the Board of Governors decides, by an eighty-five percent majority of the total voting power, that the provisions of Schedule D shall be applied' (p. 37)
20. IMF Document No. SM/74/72, pp. 1, 2, vol. 1 of Documents). (See also n. 14, above.)
21. Ibid.
22. Press Release no. 74/52 'Communiqué of the Committee of the Board of Governors on International Monetary Reform and Related Issues' (including detailed statement). Documents, vol. 1, no. 1.
23. See J. J. Polak, 'Thoughts on an International Monetary System Based Fully on the SDR', *op. cit.*; also Alexandre Kafka, 'Some IMF Problems After the Committee of

Twenty' paper prepared for the conference in honour of Jacques J. Polak, 4 April 1991 (mimeo).

24. Documents: SM/74/72, 3 April 1974. Possible Changes in the General Account, vol. I, part 1, pp. 1–5.

    Minutes: EBM/74/35, and EBM/74/36, both 19 April 1974. Possible Changes in the General Account, vol. II, part 1, pp. 1–9 and 10–30, respectively.
25. Press Release (Committee of Twenty). Document 74/32, 13 June 1974, vol. I, part 1, pp. 12–13.
26. 'By-Laws, Rules and Regulations of the IMF', 43rd issue, 1 August 1986, IMF. By-Law section 14, Terms of Service, para. (d), p. 8; see also rule C, pp. 22–4.
27. 'By-Laws, Rules and Regulations of the Fund', section 6, para (a), pp. 3–4.
28. Garritsen de Vries, *The International Monetary Fund 1972–78,* vol. II, p. 1029.
29. Ibid. pp. 1051, 1056.
30. While deputy managing directors have traditionally been from the US, since the Fund's inception the managing directors have been European. The *quid pro quo* for this arrangement is that World Bank presidents have been American—an unwritten understanding that appears unlikely to survive G20-sponsored IFI governance reform affecting these two Bretton Woods institutions as the following sentence appeared in paragraph 21 of the Pittsburgh G20 Summit Declaration in September, 2009: 'As part of a comprehensive reform package, we agree that the heads and senior leadership of all international institutions should be appointed through an open, transparent and merit-based process', as at: http://www.g20.utoronto.ca/2009/2009communique0925.html (accessed 15 June 2011). Following his resignation, the disgraced Dominique Strauss-Kahn was replaced by French Finance Minister Christine Lagarde. This was accomplished under extraordinary circumstances; despite another European heading the IMF, consistent with the wording of the G20 leaders' statement at Pittsburgh an 'open, transparent and merit-based process' was noted by both candidates and IMF member countries throughout the selection process.
31. Executive Directors, IMF Annual Reports (1974–6).
32. Margaret Garritsen de Vries, *The IMF 1972–78*, vol II, *op. cit.*, (Washington, DC: 1985), p. 984.
33. Ibid. The remaining hours were spent as follows: Trust Fund and related topics—40 hours; oil facility—29 hours; Sixth General Review of Quotas—20 hours; buffer stock and compensatory financing facilities—15 hours; world economic outlook—14 hours; regular consultations and consideration of requests for the use of the Fund's resources—100 hours.
34. See also Appendix 2, below.
35. 'By-Laws, Rules and Regulations—International Monetary Fund', 43rd issue, 1 August 1986. Rule C-10, p. 43.
36. Margaret Garritsen de Vries, *The IMF 1972–78*, vol. II, *op. cit.*, p. 988.
37. DAA/74/1, 9 July 1974. Draft Amendments of Establishment of a Council, vol. I, part 1, pp. 15–31.
38. EBM/74/92, 24 July 1974. Draft Amendments—Establishment of a Council, vol. II, part 1, pp. 31–55.

39. DAA/74/1 Supplement 1, 6 August 1974. Draft Amendments on Establishment of a Council—Restructured Version, vol. I, part 1, pp. 32–9;
    DAA/74/1 Supplement 2 (explanatory notes), 7 August 1974, vol. I, part 1, pp. 40–50;
    DAA/74/1 Supplement 3 (further explanatory notes), 14 August 1974, vol. I, part 1, pp. 51–66.
    DAA/74/1 Supplement 4, 18 November 1974, vol. I, part 1, pp. 67–92.
    DAA/74/1 Supplement 5, 13 December 1974, vol. I, part 1, pp. 93–105.
    DAA/74/1 Supplement 6, 13 December 1974, vol. I, part 1, pp. 106–14.
40. 25 October: EBM/74/133 and EBM/74/134, vol. II, part 1, pp. 281–6 and 287–303, respectively.
    1 November: EBM/74/136 and EBM/74/137, vol. II, part 1, pp. 304–21 and 322–37, respectively.
    8 November: EBM/74/141, vol. II, part 1, pp. 338–48.
    3 March 1975: EBM/75/26 and EBM/75/27, vol. II, part 1, pp. 650–72 and 673–93, respectively.
    3 May 1975: EBM/75/28, vol. II, part 1, pp. 694–716.
    5 August 1975: EBM/75/76, vol. II, part 2, pp. 1265–86.
41. Four Comprehensive Articles of Agreement drafts were published, often with subsequent corrections and supplements. See: DAA/75/2, 14 March 1975, vol. I, part 1, pp. 457–837; DAA/75/9, 27 May 1975, vol. I, part 2, pp. 1101–261; DAA/76/1, 14 January 1976, vol. I, part 2, pp. 1676–767; DAA/76/6, 9 February 1976, vol. I, part 3, pp. 2243–336.
42. DAA/74/1.
43. EBM/75/26, Draft Amendments—Establishment of a Council, 3 March 1975, vol. II, part 1, pp. 653–5.
44. EBM/74/141, Draft Amendments—Establishment of a Council, 8 November 1974, vol. II, part 1, pp. 340–1.
45. *Proposed Second Amendment to the Articles of Agreement of the International Monetary Fund: A Report by the Executive Directors to the Board of Governors* (IMF, March 1976), Part II, Ch P, section 5; reproduced in Garritsen de Vries, *The IMF 1972–78*, vol. III (documents). The Directors pointed out that this procedure would make the Council most resemble the Board of Governors in the way it conducted its voting. Developing country reticence was thus understandable.
46. Alexandre Kafka, 'Some IMF Problems After the Committee of XX'—paper prepared for a conference in honour of Jacques J. Polak (mimeo), 4 April 1991, p. 5 (note 8).
47. Joseph Gold, 'Voting Majorities in the Fund—Effects of the Second Amendment of the Articles', IMF Pamphlet No. 20 (Washington, DC: 1977), p. 12.
48. EBM/74/134, Draft Amendments—Establishment of a Council, 25 October 1974, vol. II, part 1, pp. 301–2.
49. Article XII, Section 1, *Articles of Agreement*, IMF 1982, p. 37.
50. The provision whereby an 85 per cent majority was required for amendment of the Articles enjoyed both developed and developing country support. See EBM/

75/87, Comprehensive Draft Amendment—Elimination of Brackets, 20 May 1975, vol. II, part 2, p. 1392.

51. On the link, for example, see DAA/74/9, 'Draft Amendment on the "Link" and on Other Holders of Special Drawing Rights'. On the substitution account, see SM/75/87, 'Substitution of SDRs for Currencies in Fund Drawings—Alternative Proposals for Article V, Section 3(f)'.
52. Committee of Twenty, *Outline of Reform, op. cit.*, para. 2(e), p. 8, and para. 24, p. 15.
53. Margaret Garritsen de Vries, *The IMF 1972–1978, op. cit.*, vol. I, p. 205.
54. Ibid. p. 17.
55. Ibid. pp. 17–18. Emphasis added. The two forms of the proposed link were either to allocate SDRs directly to developing country members, or alternatively to development finance organizations (DFOs).
56. Committee of Twenty, 'Report of the Technical Group on the SDR/Aid Link and Related Proposals', 9 July 1973, in C-20, *Outline of Reform, op. cit.*, pp. 95–111.
57. DAA/74/9, Draft Amendment on the 'Link' and on Other Holders of Special Drawing Rights, 31 July 1974, pp. 242–9.
    DAA/74/9, Supplement 1, Revised Draft Amendment on the 'Link' etc., 8 January 1975, pp. 250–61.
58. EBM/74/130, Draft Amendments—The 'Link' and Other Holders of SDRs, 18 October 1974, vol. II, part 1, pp. 262–80.
59. Ibid. p. 274.
60. Ibid. p. 274.
61. EBM/74/145, Draft Amendments—Program of Work, 15 November 1974, vol. II, part 1, p. 366, para. 1.
62. Ibid. p. 375.
63. Ibid. p. 375.
64. Ibid. p. 377.
65. Ibid. p. 380.
66. Ibid. p. 380.
67. EBM/74/160, Amendment of Articles of Agreement—Draft Report to Interim Committee, 19 December 1974, vol. II, part 1, p. 417. (Zulu later became head of the Fund's Africa Department.)
68. The following documents all referred to the C-20's directions on the link, and included the two alternative draft proposals on an SDR/aid link directly to developing countries or the DFOs. See DAA/74/16, Draft Report to the Interim Committee on Amendment of the Articles of Agreement, 10 December 1974, vol. I, part 1. pp. 359, 372–3; DAA/74/16 Revision 1, 22 December 1974, vol. I, part 1, pp. 392, 405–6; DAA/74/16 Revision 2, 24 December 1974, vol. 1, part 1, pp. 423, 437–8.
69. Press Release 75/2 (Interim Committee), 16 January 1975, vol. I, part 1, p. 456.
70. Peter Kenen, 'Financing, Adjustment, and the International Monetary Fund', Brookings Studies in International Economics (Washington, DC: 1986), pp. 59–60.
71. Committee of Twenty, *Outline of Reform*, Annex 7, pp. 41–2; also Technical Group Report on Intervention and Settlement, pp. 112–40, and Technical Group Report on Global Liquidity and Consolidation, pp. 162–82. Even in this case, however, Fund staff had begun toying with the idea in its consideration of allowing

transfers of SDRs from the General Account of the Fund to Fund members. See SM/71/171, 1 July 1971, 'Transfer of Special Drawing Rights Held in the General Account of Participants Making Purchases from the Fund', *passim* in SM/75/87, vol. I, part 1, p. 938.

72. C-20, *Outline of Reform*, Part 1, para. 28, p. 17
73. Interim Committee, 10-11/6/75, Sections 6, 7. Communiqué reprinted in de Vries, *The IMF 1972–78, op. cit.*, vol. 3, p. 222. (The Interim Committee met three times in 1975 instead of its normal twice.)
74. SM/75/94, A Substitution Account for Gold, 24 April 1975, vol. I, part 1, p. 942.
75. SM/75/205, 29 July 1975, Possible Provisions of a Gold Substitution Account, vol. I, part 2, pp. 1413, 1415.
76. EBM/75/156, Annex I, 26 September 1975, Observations by J. de Groote on an Alternative Approach to the Gold Substitution Account, vol. II, part 2, pp. 1671–7. EBM/75/156, Annex II, 26 September 1975, Statement by Mr Kafka on the Gold Problem and the Need for a Gold Substitution Account, vol. II, part 2, pp. 1678–84.

    The Research Department schemes (SM/75/94 and SM/75/205), and Mr de Groote's paper initially appeared in Garritsen de Vries' 1972–8 Fund history volumes (vol. 3, documents); Mr Kafka's did not.
77. EBM/75/156, Annex I, 26 September 1975, vol. II, part 2, p. 1671.
78. Ibid. p. 1672.
79. Interim Committee, 10-11/6/75, Sections 6, 7. Communiqué reprinted in de Vries, *The IMF 1972–78, op. cit.*, vol. 3, p. 313.
80. EBM/75/156, Annex II, 26 September 1975, vol. II, part 2, p. 1680.
81. EBM/75/156, 26 September 1975, vol. II, part 2, p. 1662
82. Ibid. p. 1670.
83. Ibid. p. 1652.
84. Correspondence with the author.
85. EBM/75/156, 26 September 1975, vol. II, part 2, p. 1661.
86. Margaret Garritsen de Vries, *The IMF 1972–78, op. cit.*, vol. II, pp. 678–82.
87. Recall that under the First Amendment the reconstitution provision stipulated that holders of SDRs had to hold an average of 30 per cent of their total allocation over a five-year period.
88. *Articles of Agreement of the International Monetary Fund—As Modified by the Proposed Amendment* (with typewritten palimpsests), IMF (Washington, DC: 1968), Article XXV, Section 6(b), p. 48.
89. DAA/75/12, Reconstitution, 21 July 1975, vol. I, part II, p. 1397.
90. Ibid. p. 1399.
91. Ibid.
92. EBM/75/135, Reconstitution, 30 July 1975, vol. II, part 2, pp. 1513–19.
93. Ibid. p. 1515.
94. Ibid.
95. EBM/75/163, Draft Amendment—Changes and Outstanding Issues, 6 October 1975, vol. II, part 2, Reconstitution, pp. 1750–3.
96. EBM/75/187, Draft Amendment—Changes and Outstanding Issues, 4 December 1975, vol. II, part 3, p. 1930.

97. Ibid. p. 1930.
98. Ibid. p. 1931.
99. SM/75/292 and Correction 1, Draft Amendment of the Executive Directors to the Interim Committee, 11, 12 December 1975, vol. 1, part 2, Attachment VI, p. 1571.
100. EBM/75/197, Draft Report to Interim Committee, 15 December 1975, vol. II, part 3, p. 2026.
101. SM/75/292, Revision 1, 19 December 1975, vol. I, part 2, pp. 1575–99; SM/75/292, Revision 2, 23 December 1975, vol. I, part 2, pp. 1600–16; and SM/75/292, Revision 3, 24 December 1975, vol. I, part 2, pp. 1617–35, respectively.
102. EBM/75/204, Draft Report to Interim Committee, 22 December 1975, vol. II, part 3, Reconstitution, pp. 2081–2.
103. EBM/75/206, Draft Report to Interim Committee, 23 December 1975, vol. II, part 3, Reconstitution, pp. 2108–9.
104. Press Communique of the Interim Committee, 7–8 January 1976, para. 7(g), reproduced in Garritsen de Vries, *The IMF 1972–1978, op. cit.*, vol. III (documents), p. 228.
105. DAA/76/1, Comprehensive Draft Amendment, 14 January 1976, vol. I, part 2. Article XIX, section 6(b), p. 1731.
106. DAA/76/11, Proposed Second Amendment to the Articles of Agreement of the IMF, March 1976, vol. 1, part 3. Text pp. 2751–839.
107. Executive Board Decision No. 5936-(78/168)S, 25 October 1978, reproduced in Garritsen de Vries, *The IMF 1972–1978*, vol. III (documents), p. 557.
108. G24, 21st Meeting of Ministers Communiqué, 27 September 1980, as at: http://www.g24.org/PDF/09-80ENG.pdf (accessed 15 June 2011).
109. John Williamson, 'A New SDR Allocation?', *op. cit.*, pp. 38–41.
110. EBM/75/135 Reconstitution, 30 July 1975, vol. II, part 2, p. 1517.
111. Ibid. p. 1515.
112. DAA/74/14 Objectives of Draft Amendments Already Issued, 28 September 1974, vol. I, part 1, pp. 340–4.
113. Ibid. p. 341.
114. C-20, *Outline of Reform, op. cit.*, part I, The Reformed System, p. 8.
115. *Articles of Agreement of the IMF—as modified by the Proposed [First] Amendment* (with typewritten palimpsests), IMF (Washington: 1968). Art. XXI, section 1, p. 40.
116. *Articles of Agreement*, IMF, 1986, Article XV, Section 1, p. 50.
117. *Articles of Agreement of the IMF—as modified by the Proposed [First] Amendment* (with typewritten palimpsests), Article XXIV, section 1(a), p. 42.
118. Ibid. Article XXIV, section 1(b), p. 42.
119. For a later Robert Triffin analysis of this explosion, see 'How to End the World 'Infession': Crisis Management of Fundamental Reforms?', in Masera and Triffin, (eds), *Europe's Money—Problems of European Monetary Co-ordination and Integration*, Clarendon Press (Oxford: 1984); see also Geldolph Kessler, 'The Need to Control International Bank Lending', *BNL Quarterly Review*, March 1980.
120. Article VIII (General Obligations of Members), Section 7: 'each member undertakes to collaborate with the Fund and with other members in order to ensure

that the policies of the member with respect to reserve assets shall be consistent with the objectives of promoting better international surveillance of international liquidity and making the special drawing right the principal reserve asset in the international monetary system'; and Article XXII, General Obligations of Participants, which expresses the same declaration. IMF Articles of Agreement (1986), ibid. pp. 33 and 65.

121. DAA/75/2, Comprehensive Draft Amendment of the Articles of Agreement, 14 March 1975, vol. I, part 1, p. 549.
122. DAA/75/2, Supplement 5, 13 May 1975, vol. 1, part 1, p. 732.
123. SM/75/120, Supplement 1, Supplementary Notes on the Comprehensive Draft Amendment, 23 May 1975, vol. I, part II, Para. 20, p. 1016.
124. The additional two years it took to achieve ratification of the Second Amendment by sufficient member governments tends to confirm this supposition.
125. EBM/75/15, Draft Amendments—Use of Fund Resources, 12 February 1975, vol. II, part 1, p. 579.
126. EBM/75/68 Comprehensive Draft Amendment—Provisions on Special Drawing Account, 30 April 1975, vol. II, part 2. Managing Director's statement, p. 1143.
127. EBM/75/192, Draft Amendment—Changes and Outstanding Issues—Provisions Relating to Gold, 10 December 1975, p. 1958.
128. Ibid. p. 1958.
129. see n. 124, above.
130. Alexander Mountford, 'The Historical Development of IMF Governance', IMF Independent Evaluation Office *Background Paper* no. BP/08/02, May 2008, as at: http://www.ieo-imf.org/eval/complete/pdf/05212008/BP08_02.pdf (accessed 6 June 2011).
131. EBM/75/163:2, 6 October 1975, pp. 1738–53 (1–2, 7–20), vol. II, part 2.
132. EBM/75/160, 1 October 1975, pp. 1709–17 (1–9), vol II, part 2.
133. DAA/75/9 Draft Amendment of the Articles of Agreement (inc. supplement), 27 May 1975, pp. 1101–261 (arts: 1–97, supplements: various, not including Article VIII, section 7), vol. 1, part 2. The first comprehensive draft amendment was presented on 14 March 1975. The view to making SDRs the principal reserve asset was not mentioned in this draft—the proposed wording of Article VIII, section 7, at this stage simply read: 'Each member undertakes to collaborate with the Fund and with other members regarding the policies of the member with respect to gold' (DAA/75/2, 14 March 1975, p. 505 (41)). Also, the provisional Article XXII at this stage simply referred to future allocations of SDRs in an effort to either supplement reserves, achieve balance of payments equilibrium, or improve the adjustment process—again no mention of making the SDR the principal reserve asset (ibid. p. 533 (69)).
134. EBM/75/9, 27 May 1975, p. 1141 (35).
135. Press communiqué of the Interim Committee 16 January 1975 (Press Release No. 75/2, p. 456 (3)).
136. EBD/75/276, vol. 1, part 2, 19 December 1975, pp. 1655–6 (1–2).
137. Margaret Garritsen de Vries, *The IMF in a Changing World 1945–85, op. cit.*, p. 115. The US delegation was headed by Ed Yeo.

138. Articles of Agreement, Section 4 (pp. 6–9) and Schedule C (pp. 84–7).
139. Actually, these meetings had been taking place since the early 1970s; it was only in 1975 that they were made public and more formal. See F. Lisle Widman, *The Making of International Monetary Policy*, The International Law Institute (Washington, DC: 1982), p. 66.
140. Guido Garavoglia, 'From Rambouillet to Williamsburg: A Historical Assessment', in Cesare Merlini (ed.), *Economic Summits and Western Decision-Making*, Croom Helm/European Institute of Public Administration (Brussels: 1984), pp. 5–7.
141. Ibid. p. 7.
142. John Williamson, 'The Benefits and Costs of an International Monetary Nonsystem', in E. M. Bernstein *et al. Reflections on Jamaica*, Princeton International Essay in Finance no. 115, April 1976, p. 54.
143. Ibid.
144. Joseph Gold, Pamphlet 25, *op. cit.*, p. 16. On the IEO, see n. 130 above.
145. The Third Amendment, formally enacted in 1992, was limited to disciplining recalcitrant borrowers from the IMF. It had little bearing on the international monetary system, nor on the framework for possible reform that has existed since the Second Amendment. (See IMF *Articles of Agreement* following the Third Amendment (Washington, DC: 1992).)
146. Articles of Agreement (1986), *op. cit.*, Article IV, section 4, pp. 8–9.
147. De Vries, *The IMF in a Changing World 1945–85*, p. 117. In fact the increase in the voting proportion necessary for new amendments was increased from 80 to 85 percent during the sixth general review of quotas. This review reduced the US voting strength to below 20 per cent (currently 16.74 per cent after 2010 revisions), which still amounted to an effective veto of any fundamental changes to IMF quotas and Amendment to the Articles.
148. Joseph Gold, 'The Second Amendment of the Fund's Articles of Agreement', IMF Pamphlet Series, No. 25. 1978, p. 3.
149. IMF Articles of Agreement (Washington, DC: 1982), pp. 33, 65; 8–9, 84–7.
150. In his speculative pamphlet entitled 'Thoughts on an International Monetary Fund Based Fully on the SDR' (IMF Pamphlet no. 28), J. J. Polak noted that additional amendments to the Articles would be necessary for an international monetary system based *fully* on the SDR. Subsequent work, however, has also considered what could be accomplished without additional amendments. See Polak 'The Impasse Concerning the Role of the SDR', in Wietze Eizenga, E. Frans Limburg, and Jacques J. Polak (eds), *The Quest for National and Global Economic Stability*, Kluwer Academic Publishers (Dordrecht: 1988); Kenen 'Use of the SDR to Supplement or Substitute for Other Means of Finance', in George M. von Furstenberg (ed.), *International Money and Credit: The Policy Roles*, IMF (Washington, DC: 1983), p. 357; and 'Changing Views About the Role of the SDR and Implications for Its Attributes', in S. Dell (ed.), *The International Monetary System and its Reform*, vol. II, North-Holland for the UN (Amsterdam: 1987); most recently 'Enhancing International Monetary Stability: A Role for the SDR?', IMF Strategy, Policy, and Review Department, 7 January 2011.

6

SDRs after the Second Amendment

6.1 Introduction

As we have seen in the previous few chapters, there was a growing divergence between an avowed role for the Special Drawing Right (SDR) epitomized by the Second Amendment and the evolution of a system in which its role was increasingly marginalized. The Fund's deep involvement with the Second Amendment negotiations was the apogee of its close association with the SDR until the 2008 financial crisis. Although it remained a champion of a role for the asset, as the 1980s dawned the International Monetary Fund (IMF) came to realize that its future role was no longer inexorably tied to progress with respect to the SDR. This reflected the ability of the Fund to adapt to the new international monetary arrangements without having to hark back to a world of fixed rates, public responsibility for liquidity provision—and an SDR.

Indeed within a few short years of the Second Amendment the Fund sponsored a conference in the IMF's Executive Board Room at which the need for the SDR was questioned by the Fund managing director, despite general support from the participants.[1] Furthermore this attitude of de Larosière was not unique at the Fund: the IMF research director at the time, William Hood, himself also began to wonder about the purpose and role of SDRs.[2] Ironically, further away from the Fund, the SDR continued to attract steady attention, but in general only a paucity of interest in the SDR could be identified as the flexible exchange rate system took hold.

This chapter will examine these changes, again focusing upon evolving Fund and US influences, which has proven useful in our investigation thus far. The continued evolution of the Fund under new arrangements also merits closer attention. As we shall see, the Fund did continue to marginally improve the mechanisms surrounding the SDR. However despite these efforts, as time progressed the SDR appeared less relevant to the needs of the international monetary system and to the evolving role of the Fund within it. The efforts, too, were piecemeal—when the difficulties associated with the negotiation of the Second Amendment were recalled, the Fund naturally shied away from attempting to mobilize support for any initiative which threatened to open up the Articles of Agreement to large scale revision. This was understandable—when raisons d'être for the asset were being questioned, it was prudent to scale back ambition.

Indeed the lack of a strong push for a third SDR allocation after the 1980s debt crisis may be said to have severely retarded prospects for the SDR until the late 1990s; after all, it was then that a liquidity shortage was experienced most acutely, even if it was primarily by less developed countries. Whereas in the 1970s some efforts were successful in accommodating the SDR to the new international monetary order, this process virtually halted in the 1980s. The IMF increasingly turned attention to enhanced lending packages, partly in response to the debt crisis. But conditionality was attached to the provision of these resources (which would not necessarily have been the case with SDR allocations). In this regard, as new IMF funding facilities proliferated for members in financial crisis, it is notable that the minor third amendment to the Fund articles—facilitating suspended member voting rights of those not fulfilling financial obligations—was recommended by the Interim Committee in May 1990 and accepted only a month later by the Executive Board. It was not until the late 1990s and early 2000s, with the reemergence of more systemic international monetary instability, that interest in the SDR was rekindled.

Thus, one of the most obvious reasons for the marginalization of the SDR at the end of the twentieth century lies in the continued evolution of the international monetary system away from that for which the SDR was designed. The SDR in this new system will be the focus of this chapter and, to this end, let us first turn to an examination of the second SDR allocation—an allocation which took place for very different reasons than the first, but was to be the last major successful initiative involving the SDR for a generation.

6.2 Accomplishment through Compromise: The Second SDR Allocation

As already explained, under flexible rates the character and use of owned reserve assets, including SDRs, changed greatly. During the first allocation SDRs were a supplement to existing reserve assets. However, as the First Basic Period drew to a close, and time came to consider an allocation for the Second Basic Period (1973–7, extended to 1978), it quickly became apparent that with global reserves having increased by approximately SDR 68 billion

Table 6.1. Transfers of SDRs, 1970–2010

	Millions of SDRs									
	Annual averages									
	1/1/1970 – 4/30/1978	1/5/1978 – 4/30/1981	1/5/1981 – 4/30/1983	1/5/1983 – 4/30/1987	1/5/1987 – 4/30/1996	1/1/70– 4/30/1999	2000	2004	2008	2010
Transfers among participants and prescribed holders										
Transactions with designation										
From own holdings	222	271	743	165	–	**5,016**	–	–	–	–
From purchase of SDRs from Fund	41	1,174	1,553	1,744	110	**14,727**	–	–	–	–
Transactions by agreement	439	771	1,262	3,121	6,353	**10,7949**	6,639	1,140	1,051	4,010
Prescribed operations	–	–	277	520	1,245	**18,586**	293	228	1,132	1
Fund-related operations	–	–	–	43	295	**5,092**	684	925	1,366	874
Net interest on SDRs	42	161	259	285	342	**6,405**	214	117	211	20
Total	**743**	**2,377**	**4,092**	**5,878**	**8,345**	**157,775**	**7,831**	**2,410**	**3,760**	**4,905**
Transfers from participants to General Resources Account										
Repurchases	306	809	702	991	2,126	**41,517**	3,826	2,981	542	17
Charges	259	620	1,233	2,574	1,791	**39,192**	2,600	2,456	694	896
Quota payments	24	1,704	175	1,591	1,452	**33,741**	528	16	47	–
Interest received on General Resources Accounts holdings	16	135	551	307	127	**4,137**	138	1	101	8
Assessments/reimbursements	1	2	2	4	4	**79**	3	18	4	5
Total	**606**	**3,269**	**2,663**	**5,466**	**5,499**	**118,666**	**7,094**	**5,472**	**1,388**	**926**
Transfers from General Resources Account to participants and prescribed holders										

Continued

Table 6.1. *Continued*

	Millions of SDRs									
	Annual averages									
	1/1/1970 – 4/30/1978	1/5/1978 – 4/30/1981	1/5/1981 – 4/30/1983	1/5/1983 – 4/30/1987	1/5/1987 – 4/30/1996	1/1/70– 4/30/1999	2000	2004	2008	2010
Purchases	172	1,474	2,227	2,554	3,056	**66,151**	3,592	3,500	719	36
Repayments of Fund borrowings	–	88	86	614	970	**13,050**	–	–	–	–
Interest on Fund borrowings	4	27	184	443	226	**4,332**	18	–	–	–
In exchange for other members' currencies										
Acquisitions to pay charges	–	3	95	896	293	**7,211**	1,577	1,398	359	252
Acquisitions to make quota payments	–	114	–	–	–	**341**	–	–	–	–
Reconstitution	210	33	–	–	–	**1,555**	–	–	–	–
Remuneration	26	165	605	1,536	999	**21,158**	1,747	947	303	88
Other (refunds, adjustments, etc.)	29	7	22	17	82	**1,299**	1,008	84	753	49
Total	**442**	**1,911**	**3,218**	**6,059**	**5,626**	**115,097**	**7,942**	**5,929**	**2,134**	**425**
Total Transfers	**1,792**	**7,556**	**9,971**	**17,404**	**19,469**	**391,538**	**22,867**	**13,811**	**7,282**	**6,256**
General Resources Account Holdings at end of period	**1,371**	**5,445**	**4,335**	**1,960**	**825**	**3,572**	**2,724**			
SDR allocations	*9,300*	*12,000*	–	–	–	*21,300*	–	–	–	*18,2550*

Note: 1st column: period from creation of SDR until Second Amendment; 2nd column: period of second SDR allocation; 4th column: period before transactions with designation abandoned
Source: *IMF Annual Report*, 1999, and various subsequent issues

between 1970–2—over ten times the amount in the previous three year period—there was little support for another allocation.[3]

Different circumstances prevailed, however, as the Second Basic Period drew to a close in 1978. John Williamson refers to two rather defeatist reasons which help to explain support for the second SDR allocation in 1979–81 of SDR 12 billion. He points out that proponents of its enhanced usefulness used the argument that since the relationship between reserves and international monetary order had been somewhat weakened, and since Euromarkets could be relied upon for some liquidity provision, allocating further SDRs could not *hurt* the system. The allocation was also a pact between those who supported this negativistic argument and those who believed in a Keynesian stimulus: 'an alliance between the promoters of long-run change to a more SDR-centred system and the advocates of short-run stimulus'.[4] Thus underlying the second SDR allocation was the belief, even among SDR proponents, that flexible exchange rates, borrowed reserves, and increased capital mobility made this further increase in official liquidity almost superfluous. As Williamson himself points out, the emphasis was now on demand- rather than supply-oriented theories of reserve supply and the provision of official reserves would not alter the fact that borrowed reserves were in many cases more easily acquired from Euromarkets, at least for the creditworthy.

There was another reason why a second allocation of SDRs occurred. This was the continued quiet influence of the Fund. The Fund managing director, Johannes Witteveen, strongly supported an allocation, and canvassed financial officials in 1976, a year before a report to the Board was required.[5] Throughout this book we have witnessed a gradually increasing role and profile for the Fund itself, both for its staff and especially its managing director, in initiating and furthering its own international monetary objectives. Until the late 1970s, this included promotion of the SDR. The chances for success were naturally strongest for initiatives supported by its most important members, but even after the breakdown of Bretton Woods, the Fund continued to press for changes in which its role could be fostered. At times, this included SDR initiatives. We witnessed this during the negotiation of the first and particularly second amendment; it was still true later, both during the time of the second SDR allocation and also during the discussions surrounding a substitution account, particularly during the tenure of Witteveen, and became true again in response to the international financial crisis in 2008–9. While the Fund had formally distanced itself from the SDR due to prevailing ideas about international liquidity provision, it nonetheless was willing to reflect intermittent interest in the asset at its nadir in the late 1980s and early 1990s.

At this time, although managing director Witteveen strongly supported an SDR allocation, he realized that support among the membership was

Table 6.2. SDR holdings as a percentage of total SDR allocations and of non-gold reserves, 1970–2010

			Non-industrial Countries	
	All Participants	Industrial Countries	Developing Countries	Net Debtor countries*
Holdings of SDRs as Per Cent of Cumulative Allocations				
1970	93.8	101.4	73.5	72.9
1971	92.3	103.3	63.2	64.7
1972	90.2	100.0	64.4	65.2
1973	93.4	105.7	60.8	60.9
1974	94.6	106.2	64.3	64.4
1975	94.5	106.5	63.1	62.8
1976	95.1	108.4	59.8	58.8
1977	91.7	105.7	54.9	53.6
1978	85.3	95.6	58.1	56.6
1979	90.3	97.0	74.5	71.5
1980	91.9	96.8	81.0	75.6
1981	74.5	81.0	60.8	53.5
1982	74.6	81.9	59.1	51.5
1983	79.8	95.1	47.4	32.4
1984	69.8	80.4	47.3	34.6
1985	78.4	95.2	42.8	29.8
1986	87.3	105.3	49.0	35.6
1987	90.8	110.0	49.9	36.4
1988	96.2	115.9	54.4	40.6
1989	93.1	116.3	43.5	30.7
1990	97.2	121.9	44.4	29.4
1991	96.8	120.7	45.9	34.6
1992	96.8	121.2	44.6	36.5
1993	63.0	73.1	41.6	35.1
1994	71.0	77.9	56.3	47.7
1995	90.9	105.1	60.4	49.8
1996	91.4	102.4	67.9	56.6
1997	87.2	99.8	60.5	47.8
1998	95.0	107.0	69.4	56.1
1999	81.1	94.6	52.5	46.3
2000	84.6	95.0	62.5	56.6
2001	86.6	101.6	54.6	46.5
2002	91.5	107.7	56.9	44.7
2003	93.0	102.4	72.0	57.7
2004	96.3	105.6	76.3	23.5
2005	96.2	96.3	96.0	33.0
2006	81.8	85.3	74.3	20.2
2007	86.0	92.3	72.4	11.4
2008	86.7	92.5	74.2	13.8
2009	87.5	95.2	70.2	10.0
2010	98.3	101.7	91.6	79.8
Holdings of SDRs as Per Cent of Non-gold Reserves				
1970	7.5	9.0	4.3	5.0
1971	9.2	9.9	6.1	7.7
1972	8.9	9.3	7.2	9.6
1973	7.8	8.7	5.0	6.4
1974	7.2	9.2	3.6	4.6

1975	6.0	8.9	2.4	3.9
1976	5.4	8.3	2.0	3.3
1977	4.4	7.4	1.4	2.3
1978	3.5	5.3	1.4	2.1
1979	4.6	5.8	2.9	3.6
1980	5.6	7.1	3.5	4.4
1981	4.8	6.2	2.9	3.5
1982	5.3	6.9	3.0	3.7
1983	5.3	7.2	2.3	2.3
1984	4.2	5.6	2.0	2.1
1985	4.4	6.3	1.6	1.6
1986	5.0	6.7	2.0	2.2
1987	4.7	5.7	2.0	2.4
1988	4.4	5.1	2.0	2.5
1989	3.9	4.7	1.5	1.7
1990	3.8	4.6	1.5	1.4
1991	3.3	4.3	1.3	1.3
1992	3.1	4.4	1.0	0.8
1993	2.1	2.8	0.9	0.7
1994	2.0	2.7	1.0	0.8
1995	2.5	3.5	1.0	0.8
1996	2.0	2.9	0.9	0.7
1997	1.7	2.6	0.7	0.5
1998	1.7	2.7	0.7	0.5
1999	1.5	2.8	0.5	0.4
2000	1.2	2.2	0.5	0.5
2001	1.1	2.3	0.4	–
2002	1.1	2.1	0.3	–
2003	0.9	1.9	0.4	–
2004	0.8	1.7	0.3	–
2005	0.7	1.3	0.4	–
2006	0.5	0.9	0.2	–
2007	0.4	0.9	0.2	–
2008	0.4	0.9	0.1	–
2009	3.7	6.7	2.0	–
Mar. 2010	3.5	6.4	1.9	–

* Net debtor countries' holdings of SDRs are less than their cumulative allocations of SDRs.

Source: *IMF Annual Report*, appendices I, II; various issues

lukewarm: in 1977, Witteveen had again written to the Board of Governors and Executive Board noting that:

> I now wish to report that at the present time I am not in a position to make a proposal [on SDR allocations] with respect to the next (third) basic period, which starts on January 1, 1978.[6]

However, just over a year later, in acknowledging the Interim Committee's recommendations at its meeting in September 1978, Witteveen was able to reverse his decision and was able to recommend a new allocation of SDR 4 billion for each of the next three years, a proposal which was accepted. Importantly, Witteveen had also persuaded the Executive Board to prepare a report on the substitution account for the Interim Committee, which bore fruit when the Interim Committee reported back the following year. Revealingly, J. J. Polak admitted in 1980 in a speech at Georgetown University Bankers' Forum that this support for the substitution account was a tactical move by Witteveen in an effort to break the deadlock over SDR allocations.[7] However, when the deadlock was broken and SDR allocations were agreed upon for only the second time in 1978, the substitution account was also again on the international agenda.

These developments were revealing of the continued importance of the role of the managing director, especially concerning SDR initiatives. This echoes our findings with respect to the important role of individuals and their ideas in the formulation of evolving US policy attitudes towards the SDR in Chapters 3 and 4. Following Witteveen's actions, the new IMF managing director Jacques de Larosière continued to strongly support an allocation in meetings with Fund Executive members individually and in small groups.[8] He succeeded in keeping the issue of an allocation alive after an apparent stalemate in early 1978 at the Interim Committee meeting in Mexico City. In late 1978 in Washington, at the third of four Interim Committee meetings chaired by Denis Healey, the Committee was able to recommend that to the Executive Board that an SDR allocation take place.[9] This support was echoed during the lengthy tenure of Michel Camdessus, who persevered in supporting the fourth amendment discussions over allocations to new Fund members, which were agreed to in 1997 (although not ratified until 2009). As Fund historian James Boughton succinctly summarized:

> ... Camdessus fought a lengthy political battle to persuade industrial and developing countries to authorize a unique round of SDR allocations targeted primarily at the new members, who had never received any allocations.[10]

Jumping forward, financial market innovations during the first years of the new millennium made SDRs look even less relevant to international monetary arrangements than they had the previous decade under Camdessus. Thus, little substantive progress on SDRs was in evidence when either Horst Köhler or Rodrigo de Rato were IMF Managing Directors. However, the international financial crisis in 2008–9 meant that new Managing Director Dominique Strauss-Kahn could continue the work of Michel Camdessus, first in generating support for the long-delayed ratification of the Fourth Amendment to the Fund Articles, and then by maintaining that the SDR could play a further constructive role in enhancing international monetary arrangements as the world haltingly emerged from crisis.[11]

All these were undeniable accomplishments; after all, the previous allocation had been 30 years earlier, when the US and Germany, both of which had come to oppose SDR allocations, agreed to support a second allocation at the end of 1978 as part of a 'package' of measures. These included an increase in Fund quotas under the Seventh General Review as part of a coordinated plan for economic growth.[12] Crudely, this locomotive theory of growth involved surplus countries such as Japan and Germany reflating and increasing domestic demand, which in turn would stimulate sluggish demand in the US. It was an unabashedly macro-economic plan, involving agreement at a succession of economic summits, with proposals aimed at increasing demand for goods and services in surplus countries acting as a locomotive to pull the world economy out of recession.[13] Importantly, the US also favoured the idea as a means of reducing downward pressure on the dollar. Also, as we saw in Chapter 3, the Carter administration Treasury was more sensitive to international macro-economic management than its predecessor, and after 'talking down the dollar', worked hard to improve the dollar's prospects internationally.[14]

The fact that this package also implicitly helped the dollar meant that the stalemate over an SDR allocation could be overcome. This was particularly true if, as Williamson points out, one could please both advocates of a short-term stimulus, as well as those Fund members such as Canada and the UK who at the time still favoured both that SDRs comprise a stable component of international reserves and that improvements take place in the characteristics of the asset. And these points also remained valid to those who advocated a role for the SDR in the international monetary system, as the newly agreed to Second Amendment stipulated. Buttressing these arguments, as Table 6.2 indicates, by 1978, SDRs as a percentage of total non-gold reserves had declined dramatically to its lowest level thus far: 3.6 per cent.

In addition, at this time the Interim Committee also recommended that further changes take place in the characteristics and use of the SDR, which included a closer identification of SDR interest rates with those of the market and a halving of the reconstitution requirement to 15 per cent. At this stage, in terms of the functioning of the SDR during the second allocation, we can see that with the allocation accompanied by changes to the reconstitution provision, and an interest rate beginning to approximate a market rate, SDRs were used slightly differently. Table 6.1 illustrates this, particularly when contrasted with the tables in Chapter 2, which best capture the way SDRs were used during the first allocation.

We observed in Chapter 2 that the SDR department worked relatively smoothly during the first allocation; by and large this continued during the second allocation under different circumstances. Table 6.1 points to continued SDR use following the first allocation; indeed when charges and interest payments are included in total SDR transfers, we may also note a steady absolute increase in SDR use. (See also Table 3.1.) We may note a shift among SDR transactions, however. During the second allocation, and then through the 1980s, the proportion of transfers to the General Resources Account fell, while transactions by agreement among Fund members increased dramatically (and, as countries were encouraged to sort out SDR transactions among themselves, transactions with designation became superfluous and then dropped to nil). Indeed the transfers between the General Resources Account and members rising in the mid-1970s and then falling in the late 1980s mirrors the prospects for SDR use during this same period. Until the early 1980s, SDR use increased at the Fund, helped by transfers from the General Resources Account, where charges and quota payments could also be made and received in SDRs. By the late 1980s, with designation, reconstitution, and transfers from the General Resources Account no longer big factors in SDR use, use of the SDR stagnated and then fell (see Table 6.1). By the early 1990s, momentum behind SDR use even at the Fund had dissipated.

In that time, however, the essence of SDRs under flexible rates had changed, as had the institution which had responsibility for SDRs. As the international monetary framework within which SDRs functioned changed so did the role (and the apparent prospective role) of SDRs. As we saw at the end of Chapter 1, and as we shall see later, the private sector did show interest in the SDR—this has been downplayed by many observers. This would wither, however, without further official support, which the IMF could not generate in the 1980s.

Functioning under different international monetary arrangements, SDRs were also used slightly differently than during the first allocation that we examined in Chapter 2. But it is notable that, despite the lack of any real support in the 1980s, total SDR transfers increased until the early 1990s. In addition, despite little sustained support, there were additional changes in the character of SDR use: a reduction in transactions by designation and an increase in transactions by agreement, for example. These did not point to any practical difficulties in SDR use; on the contrary Fund members had simply become more accustomed to dealing with each other in SDRs, a process that continued after the abolition of reconstitution in 1981. During the 1980s, then, although a small minority of members viewed SDR holdings as a nuisance,[15] the SDR Department continued to function smoothly.

Finally, the benefits of Special Drawing Account membership also became sufficiently clear to those few members who had elected not to join the SDR department at its inception; by 1978 all but one had done so, and in 1980 Kuwait made SDR participation universal.[16] As Fund membership continued to increase, this led to another problem: without a mechanism to allocate SDRs to new members, a growing gap prevailed between those members who joined the Fund prior to the Second Amendment and those who did not. This was resolved in the late 1990s through the negotiation of the Fourth Amendment to the Fund's articles. Ultimately, and like the Third Amendment negotiations, this was essentially a technical exercise that had no significant systemic implications other than equitability (a slightly more ambitious plan collapsed in rancour at the IMF annual meetings in Madrid in 1994). But it did concern the SDR. Even so, even though a protracted four-year discussion had culminated in an Executive Board approval of the amendment—which also implied a special allocation of 21.5 billion SDRs to new members on an agreed upon formula contained therein—it was not until the global financial crisis of 2008–9 that US ratification paved the way for its formal approval and disbursement in September 2009. And at that time it was dwarfed by the SDR 161.2 billion ($250 billion) that had been allocated a month earlier as part of the global package to respond to the crisis that had been agreed to in London. Nonetheless, it was very apparent that the Second Amendment and smooth second allocation had paved the way for an accommodation of SDRs under post-Bretton Woods arrangements.

6.3 The Substitution Account and the Continued Institutional Evolution of the IMF

In Chapter 3 we noted the substitution account in the context of US policy attitudes towards the idea, and in Chapter 5 we examined a version of it in the form of the gold substitution account discussions during the Second Amendment negotiations. We noted that the C-20 had investigated the idea as well. We now turn to look at the idea in the context of the evolution of the IMF's attitudes towards it—and the SDR in general.

Long before the SDR was even invented, the notion existed of a substitute for existing reserve currencies. We noted antecedents in Keynes' Bancor and, as early as 1962, UK Chancellor of the Exchequer Reginald Maudling proposed a Mutual Currency Account (MCA) at the IMF Annual Meeting:

> ...under which countries could continue to acquire the currency of another country which was temporarily surplus in the markets and use it to establish claims on a mutual currency account which they could themselves use when their situations were reversed. Such claims...would attract the guarantee that attaches to holdings in the Fund.[17]

The idea of an MCA also received attention in the Ossola Report: countries could deposit any currency with the Fund and receive a 'gold value guarantee'.[18] When the proposal was revived in the late 1970s it was a different Fund, encompassing the evolution we have noted throughout this book, which considered it. The managing director was increasingly important, an Interim Committee was now in place, the Fund in general had a higher profile, and SDRs were operating in a very different international monetary environment.

As noted in Chapter 2, when the SDR was instituted towards the end of the 1960s, the Fund's managing director, reflecting prevailing sentiment among most of the G10, was at pains to point out that the SDR was not designed, nor should it be construed, as a substitute for reserve currencies. Ironically, although the Fund was at pains to make this case, we saw how the Volcker Group had considered a substitution account precisely because of this as early as 1969—at this time, and later when it was discussed, it was at a period of dollar weakness. The IMF that considered the idea in the late 1970s, however, was an institution that had changed, both in its ability to adapt to the changing international monetary environment, and in a waning willingness to identify itself with an entity that was for a time increasingly marginalized.

Institutionally, there was change that did *not* transpire at the Fund, and which affected prospects for the SDR and the substitution account proposals. As we noted in the last chapter, the Council of Governors did not succeed the C-20. Rather, the Interim Committee was established. The Interim Committee remained one of the most important committees in the IMF that could lay some claim to speak for all the Fund's members. While its role was consultative, it became evident that the Interim Committee had become a focus for reform amongst the Fund's membership, despite being constituted organizationally along the same lines as the Executive Board.[19] The evolution of this committee—including its ultimate institutionalization as a permanent body as the reconstituted International Monetary and Financial Committee (IMFC) in 1999—and its relationship to the SDR, is important.

The Interim Committee was not a policy-making body nor even an organization with its own staff. Nonetheless, during the post-Bretton Woods era it became the committee through which many of the proposals affecting the SDR were honed. As its name suggested, the Interim Committee was a compromise. As the C-20 hurriedly published its report in the wake of the breakdown of the Smithsonian Agreement, it agreed that a reformed system was impossible to institute. It was also agreed that a 'Council of Governors' would evolve; this, too, however, could not be agreed upon either in 1972 or during the Second Amendment negotiations, and instead the then managing director of the Fund, Johannes Witteveen, suggested that another compromise be instituted: an 'interim' committee, known officially with some long-windedness as the 'Interim Committee of the Board of Governors on the International Monetary System' until the Second Amendment. It was initially believed that the Interim Committee would be interim for two years as the Council of Governors eventually transpired.[20] The Fund's former historian, Margaret Garritsen de Vries, compared the Interim Committee to Keynes's plans in 1944, supported by many countries, for a 'body of senior financial officials to meet several times to consider Fund business'.[21] In 1944 Keynes's plans were blocked by the US, who feared inactive executive directors. In 1974, however, the Interim Committee was seen as a compromise that the Americans could support, which was echoed in 1999 as it became permanent (although its powers did not change).

We saw that developing countries were wary of a Council to succeed the Interim Committee during the Second Amendment negotiations. Despite this wariness, however, the Interim Committee strongly supported the idea of a substitution account, although, since its influence was circumscribed, it was unable to do more than recommend to the Executive Board from time to time that work continue on the proposal. Unlike the C-20, whose brief was to consider the reform of the international monetary system, the Interim Committee's role was merely to 'supervise' the system. Secondly, the Committee 'recognized' the role of executive directors, in that its role was consultative, and hence subordinate to the executive directors. Thirdly, the Interim Committee was not allowed deputies, but had to rely on Fund staff. These latter two conditions were carefully inserted 'to avoid undermining the authority of the Executive Board'.[22] In addition, Interim Committee meetings were managed carefully by the Fund before they took place: the agenda was prepared by the managing director and discussed by the Executive Board, then agreed with the Committee's chairman, and finally dispatched to its members.[23] Despite this, it did not turn out to be as toothless as some had feared. Indeed Alexandre Kafka who, as we have seen, was thankful that the Council never came to pass, mused that the Interim Committee had become a:

> ... powerful new decision-making entity at ministerial level. Its recommendations can address all matters subject to the Articles of Agreement, including those delegated by the Board of Governors to the Executive Board.[24]

The Interim Committee contributed to the success of the second allocation, the gradual increase in the interest rate on SDRs, and the abolition of the reconstitution provision for SDR users. However, its lack of success or interest in some other SDR proposals, including the substitution account, served as an important indication to the Fund about the relative strength and support for international monetary initiatives. In this way the Committee was in effect an early warning system to the Fund of the relative chances of success of varying initiatives amongst its membership.

This process is furthered by the strong links between the Fund and the Committee. Although the Committee has its own chairman, the Fund managing director could strongly influence the Interim Committee. With nominal control over the agenda of Interim Committee meetings, this proved to be an important ingredient in how the Fund addressed—or did not address—SDRs in the new system. As noted, the managing director of the Fund between 1973 and 1978, Johannes Witteveen, was a strong supporter of the SDR and of the Fund maintaining a role in the provision of international liquidity despite the moves to private liquidity provision. Indeed the period of his tenure as managing director was crucially important in keeping the SDR on the agenda and, in a wider context, forging a role for the Fund in a post-Bretton Woods era. He was instrumental in gaining approval for an oil facility in 1974 and 1975 in the wake of the first oil price rise, which also instituted the new practice of the Fund borrowing from members. Similarly, in 1974 the extended facility was instituted to facilitate medium term balance of payments support for developing countries. In 1975, the compensatory financing facility, first instituted in 1963 to relieve balance of payments shortfalls arising from a decline in export receipts, was liberalized to make entitlements larger and payment to receiving countries quicker.

Also under Witteveen's auspices following the Second Amendment to the Articles of Agreement, the Fund decided to sell one-sixth of its gold for the benefit of the Fund's poorest members through a series of low-interest loans repayable over a ten-year period. During the first 18 months of the Trust Fund's operations, from January 1976 to June 1978, 43 countries received loans totalling SDR 841 million (US$1.023 billion) which, according to Margaret Garritsen de Vries, 'was considerably larger than had been expected when it was inaugurated'.[25]

The Fund's auctions of gold continued through the 1980s, and while the decision to use the surplus from the sale of gold in this manner also had a bearing upon the lack of success of the substitution account, it was an important step in the demonetization of gold, which developing countries also supported. Quota increases were also a feature of the Witteveen period, as was a new temporary supplementary facility that became known as the Witteveen facility. The impasse over SDRs continually reflected in successive Interim Committee communiqués, however, could not but strongly indicate to the managing director responsible for the Committees agenda, and the Fund as a whole, that further SDR initiatives were at a stalemate at best. However, during this time, the Fund steadily increased quotas—by 50.9 per cent in 1978 (with special increases for 11 members), 47.5 per cent in 1983, 50 per cent in 1990, 45 per cent in 1997, as well as supplementing the General Arrangements to Borrow (GAB) with the New Arrangements to Borrow in 1997 for G-10 members to SDR 34 billion, and then increased borrowing considerably to finance additional resources for members—first the oil facility, then the supplementary financing facility, Compensatory and Contingency Financing Facility (CCFF) in 1987, the Buffer Stock Financing Facility (BSFF)—essentially to stabilize commodity prices (which had essentially become moribund)—and then successively the Extended Fund Facility, the Structural Adjustment Facility in 1986 (replaced by the Enhanced Structural Adjustment Facility in 1987), the Poverty Reduction and Growth Facility (1999—since also replaced) all of which, unlike SDRs, had varying degrees of conditionality and costs attached to their use.[26]

This contrasted considerably with ongoing plans for a substitution account. The C-20's proposal was sketched out in a brief annex (and was also addressed in two of the technical reports),[27] and was ambitiously expected to initially accept $50 billion in deposits.[28] The Committee admitted that much remained to be resolved, and included many suggestions including the establishment of an 'SDR intervention system' (possibly mandatory), whereby 'commercial banks would intermediate in SDR transactions between central banks without themselves holding SDRs'.[29]

Although the issue of the dollar substitution account was kept alive following the C-20 Report, for a while it lay relatively dormant. The developed economies were preoccupied with a new agreement on exchange rates, and the developing countries, apart from the continued preoccupation with the link and petrodollar recycling, were not fully convinced of the potential benefits of the proposal, aside from its apparent ability to deal with gold as well (see Chapter 5 on the gold substitution account). This was true at the Interim Committee, for instance, which did not mention SDRs or the account in some of its announcements—in the relatively terse communiqué of October 1974 for instance, which hid deep disagreements over the future of the international monetary system, and at the second meeting of 1976. After all, for developing countries the priority was not substitution but securing any kind of reserves at all—particularly dollars which would enhance prospects for additional private liquidity provision.

By the time the Second Amendment was agreed upon, however, the substitution account had returned to the Interim Committee agenda. A substitution account was not the only SDR-related issue which periodically rose to the surface in Interim Committee communiqués—in 1975 it had recommended a review of link proposals, along with a return to the par value system outlined by the C-20,[30] and in 1977 pressed the Executive Board to 'review characteristics and uses of SDRs' to aid its becoming the principal reserve asset.[31] And although prospects for a substitution account were relatively muted following the moves to generalized floating, they were more firmly resurrected in 1978, when managing director Witteveen again proposed that a substitution account be reconsidered. Part of the reason for this was an effort to break the deadlock over SDR allocations, as we have seen.[32] In any case, this move by Witteveen served its avowed purpose but also served to indicate that a substitution account was back on the international monetary agenda. Another indication that this was so is that the Interim Committee promoted it as well.

Understandably the Interim Committee saw fit to support the substitution account following the rekindling of interest in the US. This coincided with the end of Witteveen's, and the beginning of de Larosière's, terms as IMF managing director—and as noted in Chapter 3, with the Carter administration and a relatively activist State Department (including Richard Cooper as Under-Secretary of State for Economic Affairs). During the first of the IMF's biannual meetings in 1979, the notion of a voluntary substitution account was endorsed. Again, this was a time of US dollar weakness, when worries were being expressed over the instability that could occur in a world of multi-currency reserves. While this made a substitution account attractive to some dollar reserve holders at the time, the Interim Committee also stressed that a substitution account would be a positive development simply by enhancing the role of the SDR. The US was keenly aware of the potential to help the dollar, as well as its potential threat. Denis Healey, the Chairman of the Interim Committee at the time underlined the latter by pointing out that the substitution account should be seen '... primarily as a possible reinforcement for the SDR [not]... as a buttress for reserve currencies'.[33] Jacques de Larosière, speaking to the Administrative Committee on Coordination of ECOSOC, also said that he supported the substitution account, and stated that he was 'pleased to be able to announce' that the Interim Committee had 'decided in favour of having the IMF's Executive Board consider the idea of a Substitution Account'.[34]

Activity by the Fund then intensified. The Interim Committee persevered with increasing tenacity in 1979, and at its second 1979 meeting in Belgrade called for the Executive Board to give 'priority' to the idea.[35] Of course it cannot be denied that US consideration of the proposal was important for this progress, but nonetheless Interim Committee support contributed to the momentum. The new chairman of the Committee, Italy's Treasury Secretary F. M. Pandolfi expressed optimism regarding prospects for the recommendation.[36]

After Belgrade, the next Interim Committee meeting was scheduled for Hamburg in April of 1980. As the Hamburg meeting approached, the Fund itself became confident of some sort of agreement. Normally reticent in its public pronouncements, press interest in the substitution account led the Fund to somewhat uncharacteristically publicize its support for a plan before it had been officially sanctified by its membership. In February, the Treasurer of the Fund even went so far as to suggest that the prospective substitution account would involve approximately US$20 billion in its initial phase.[37] Thus the Fund, through both the Interim Committee and its own staff, threw its weight behind the new proposals, even to the point of presenting it as a fait accompli before formal agreement. This was not typical of cautious Fund behaviour, and indicated that agreement in early 1980 had almost been realized. Endorsement seemed tantalizingly close. The US was discussing it seriously, as we saw in Chapter 3. Academic, policy, and business journals turned to the mechanics of how a substitution would work in practice.[38] With a foreword from former managing director Witteveen, the influential G30 endorsed a substitution account in 1980, arguing that it offered

> ... an alternative to the further diversification of currency reserves ... would therefore contribute to exchange rate stability ... [and] in the long term would also facilitate an orderly reduction in the reserve currency role of the dollar.[39]

This report did not advocate *mandatory* asset settlement (a compulsory move to an SDR-based system), but did say that the substitution account should be permanent.[40] *The Economist*, too, expected the endorsement of a substitution account at Hamburg, and noted that the G30 had emphatically endorsed it.[41]

Needless to say, this general optimism and excitement was premature. In truth there were clues before the Hamburg meeting took place that no agreement would be forthcoming, as noted in Chapter 3. The IMF was aware of the difficulties, as was revealed in the *IMF Survey* just before to the IMF Hamburg meetings. In the issue just before to the meeting, the *Survey* focused on the *agenda* of the Hamburg meeting on the front page of the fortnight's issue preceding the meeting, intimating that little progress had been made in the final few weeks.[42] Outside the Fund, support for the account was still prevalent: indeed sensing an impasse in mid-April, *The Economist*, often sceptical of SDR schemes, published a leading article lauding the substitution account, encouraging the Interim Committee to 'be bold', and also somewhat puzzlingly reasoned that it would be accepted because '... the lawyers and diplomats who have fettered it are in retreat'.[43] Three weeks later, however, the paper had to admit that it had never even made it to the discussion table at Hamburg.[44] Even more percipiently, *The New York Times* observed that the anticipated agreement had been shelved 'for at least a year, and perhaps indefinitely'.[45]

As observed in Chapter 3, it was the US policy that ultimately baulked at the proposal. We have seen how seriously the proposal was taken by US policy makers despite the exchange risk problem, and we can infer from this that reserve diversification (from the dollar to other currencies), or at least dollar weakness, was assumed to be a long-term problem. As Peter Kenen observed, once pressure on the dollar had waned, support for substitution rapidly dissipated.[46] Compounding this, the second oil price hike occurred, and, domestically, the political climate in the US was changing as well. President Carter appointed Paul Volcker as head of the Federal Reserve, and it was plain that Volcker's role was to restore confidence in the US economy as well as the health of the dollar on the foreign exchange markets. As noted, there were other important factors in the US policy process at this time, particularly Congressional involvement, which made US policy makers increasingly cautious despite a flurry of interest.

In addition, compounding the exchange risk problem from the US perspective was a dollar 'overhang'. Whereas under the Bretton Woods system it was official balances that were problematic, under post-Bretton Woods arrangements concern was increasingly noted with respect to a *private* dollar overhang. Official reserve holders might be cajoled into supporting the dollar, but once the substitution account had been agreed to the Treasury was worried again about private confidence in the dollar.[47] Who would stop portfolio shifts into other currencies, and, above all, how could the exchange risk then be addressed in a manner which would satisfy the US *and* SDR holders? This remains a key issue that continues to receive quiet attention at the Fund and elsewhere, and would have to be resolved in the event of a greater role for the SDR in the international monetary system.

The substitution account was not a panacea for all existing international monetary ills under post-Bretton Woods arrangements. It was true that some advocated that it aided the ultimate cause of the amended IMF articles (especially the principal reserve asset Articles VIII (7) and XXII), although more cautious critics at the time suggested that in the first instance it was simply more of a means of minimizing the instability caused by apparent moves to a multi-currency reserve system. This was not a universal sentiment, however. Without support from all its sponsors, a substitution account was not *inherently* stabilizing, and some large dollar holders would have preferred their recently devalued store of value (i.e. dollars) to simply appreciate. This was true of developing countries as well as other large dollar holders such as Germany, as a critic there pointed out:

> It is impossible to achieve monetary stability by institutional exchange of one asset for another. It can only be achieved by an economic policy which engenders trust and convinces the market that the world's major currency is once again capable of exercising its function as a store of value.[48]

Thus, while a substitution account would have enhanced the role of the SDR, it did not follow that it would have aided stability or other systemic goals. This experience is salutary given current discussion over a greater role for SDRs today: unless all major dollar reserve holders agree (and this would only be the case if dollar weakness was viewed to be both chronic and endemic), portfolio managers would be reticent to diversify further into SDRs. And if they did, and then wanted to move back into dollars at a different exchange rate, who would be responsible for prospective exchange losses? Without a more fully developed private market in the asset, SDRs would be both less liquid and more risky—and hence less attractive substitutes for the dollar or indeed other reserve assets.

Aside from the nature of the SDR and US policy change, there were other reasons for the substitution account's demise in its latest guise. J.J. Polak characterized the reason for this lack of success, and indeed other initiatives for progress with the SDR, succinctly: 'As always, although support for the SDR is broad, it is not deep'.[49] As the second oil shocks occurred America's experiments with 'convoy' or 'locomotive' theories of growth in conjunction with Japan and Germany dissipated, as did any willingness to experiment with the substitution account. Reflecting primary US concern under the new Federal Reserve Chairman, Paul Volcker, proposals that risked contributing to increased inflation were firmly quashed. Rather than an endorsement of a substitution account, which had been predicted by the financial press, by the time the Interim Committee had convened the US had already indicated to its G5 partners that the idea was not going to be supported by the US. As Polak wrote: 'At the meeting of the Interim Committee in Hamburg in April 1980 the idea [of the substitution account] was unceremoniously buried.'[50]

Indeed SDR proponents had to admit that the US had legitimate reasons for shying away from a substitution account. As Peter Kenen noted later:

> At a meeting I attended on the eve of the Hamburg Summit, the then Secretary of the Treasury dismissed the whole notion abruptly, and I went back to my office at the Treasury somewhat disappointed. But if I were in his shoes today, I too might be worried about the size of the contingent obligation that the United States might have to assume and the difficulty of persuading the US Congress to approve the necessary legislation.[51]

Despite intellectual interest in the idea, the failure of the substitution account proposals halted any real progress on the SDR, which, Williamson reminds us, was reinforced by the Fund's decision to suspend allocations in 1981.[52]

To recapitulate, then, 1979–80 was really a last hurrah for the SDR for a generation: a new allocation was agreed upon, and academic and policy interest was relatively high. In the US, senior officials at the Treasury and the State Department had been seriously considering new ideas associated with the substitution account, and the press was taking an interest in the idea as well. The Fund and other policy makers encouraged this interest as well, including associated ideas such as an SDR clearinghouse.

Nonetheless, the substitution account did fail. Paradoxically, however, it may be said that this points both to the continued influence of the Fund on the international monetary agenda, and to the evolution of the IMF under the new international monetary arrangements. The Fund had influence: the substitution account *was* seriously discussed, and the Fund had promoted an idea only half-heartedly supported by many of its member states. Indeed as Alexandre Kafka, the long-standing Brazilian executive director later observed, in his estimation the Fund retained important functions with respect to international oversight as well as being a source of liquidity (even if it was conditional), and had become flexible under the new system:

> Significant effective regulatory powers have been retained by the Fund, despite the loss of its jurisdiction over the choice of the worldwide exchange rate system.... At the same time the Fund has remained—*or perhaps become even more than in the past*—a flexible instrument through its financial functions to meet the international financial repercussions of all sorts of shocks.[53]

At the same time the IMF was developing a stronger conception of its own interests as an institution. The failure of the substitution account, however, also indicated to the Fund that there were limits to its influence, and that henceforth its role in post-Bretton Woods arrangements would not necessarily be an intertwined with that of the SDR until international monetary conditions were more conducive to a role for it.

The ultimate unacceptability of the substitution account reflected the importance of the US to the success of any reform proposal. However, given the US disquiet in the early 1970s over the potential of the SDR to act as an alternative reserve asset, the seriousness with which the US took the substitution account proposals in the late 1970s was important. Its failure, however, indicated to the Fund that continued promotion of the SDR could threaten its legitimacy under the new arrangements. The Fund continued its evolution into an institution *für sich*. Until 1980, this meant advocating the SDR; this was not to characterize how the IMF chose to exhibit its influence in the succeeding decade however.

More broadly, despite the apparent marginalization of prospects for the SDR, its primary 'internal' sponsor, the C-20, was reconstituted first as the Interim Committee in 1974, and then as the International Monetary and Financial Committee in 1999. Gradually losing its interim status, a committee whose initial and primary raison d'etre was to consider international monetary reform became a permanent body among whose explicit purposes was to supervise the management and adaptation of the international monetary and financial system, '...and in this connection' review 'developments in global liquidity and the transfer of real resources to developing countries', consider proposals by the Board to amend the Articles, and deal with sudden disturbances that might threaten the system.[54] Quietly, whether it be through the Second Amendment results or institutional developments following its adoption, international monetary arrangements were evolving that were consistent with a greater role for SDRs at a more propitious time. This is not to say that such developments were inevitable; simply that prudent steps continued to be taken to facilitate a greater role for SDRs when and if the Fund's membership so desired.

6.4 Developing Countries and SDRs Under Post-Bretton Woods Arrangements

Although their influence on the international monetary system is not large, the changing role and perceptions of developing countries are important for an understanding of the marginalization of the SDR. At the outset, it is worth recalling that one of the main reasons for this lack of influence at the Fund is the apportioning of national voting interests roughly in accordance with each country's importance in world trade. Apart from the oil producers, declining real commodity prices meant that, aside from a few cases, developing country influence did not increase in the post-Bretton Woods era until the nascent emergence of the BRIC countries (Brazil, Russia, India, and China) as key players in the first decade of the twenty-first century.

As a reflection of a proportionately stronger voice in other fora, developing countries have expressed support for the SDR outside the Fund—at the Group of 77 within the UN General Assembly and in other UN specialized agencies such as the UNDP and UNCTAD.[55] These organizations have very little practical influence on the Fund, although the Fund's relationship with the UN has been subject to agreement since 1947.[56] But it is such organizations (especially the G24 and UNCTAD) that are more likely to question the fundamentals of international monetary arrangements. This harks back to the interest the UN had with respect to international monetary needs in the 1950s, when it reminded the Fund of its responsibilities with respect to liquidity.[57] And with respect to developing country needs specifically, this has been a concern of other international institutions since the arguments of Raul Prebisch, Argentinian Secretary of ECLA, asked whether the structure of the international monetary system itself was detrimental to developing country interest.[58] As the system evolved, the Fund regularly sent delegations to ECOSOC and UNCTAD. While shared work was relatively rare, there was limited joint work in the 1980s (noted below), and the UN's Stiglitz Report in 2009 was particularly well-timed for influence given its release on the heels of the international financial crisis. It, too, called for more consideration of a greater role for SDRs.[59]

There are two other developing country committees whose activities are more closely linked to those of the Fund. While they are more explicitly concerned with Fund business, neither of them are official Fund organizations. The first of these is the Development Committee which, like the Interim Committee, was formed in October 1974 upon the recommendation of the C-20. Its full name, the 'Joint Ministerial Committee of the Boards of Governors of the Bank and the Fund on the Transfer of Real Resources to the Developing Countries' reveals that its representatives come from both the World Bank and IMF and that their brief is limited to the transfer of resources (rather than any structural or institutional questions, for instance). The second is the Group of 24 (G24), which was formed at the Group of 77 meeting in Lima in 1972 'to represent the interests of the developing countries in negotiations on international monetary matters'.[60] The G77 continues to rely on the G24 for expertise in international monetary issues.[61]

Calls for reform within the Fund, particularly on the link, came from the G24 and the Development Committee. Influence, however, was naturally limited. Occasionally, when developing country frustrations came to light, as they did at the G24 meeting in Mexico City in April of 1978 and the Annual Meeting of the IMF in Madrid in 1994, the Fund cautioned against too much impatience. In Mexico City, for instance, the G24 complained of an inability to produce concrete results regarding transfer of resources and expressed frustration that stumbling blocks to reform tended to be of a technical nature and lacked focus.[62] In its report on the Development Committee, however, the Executive Board made it clear that the committee had no real power and that it and, by extension, the G24, were just talking shops—simply 'forum[s] for finance ministers'—a candid admission.[63] Madrid collapsed with managing director Camdessus and developing countries rejecting a compromise allocation similar to that which ultimately transpired in the Fourth Amendment discussions.

With respect to the SDR, it would be misleading to suggest that the G24 and the Development Committee were automatically in favour of all SDR proposals, or reform proposals generally. For instance, when discussions on the Interim Committee and the proposed Council of Governors were taking place, developing countries feared that a Council would downgrade the voice of their Governors on the Board.[64] Alexandre Kafka was one of the strongest opponents of a Council, as we have noted. Second, while perennially supporting SDR allocations, it is interesting to note that in general developing countries were only lukewarm about the idea of a substitution account. Of course, they were individually far from the largest reserve holders, but immediate financial considerations caused some hesitation as well.[65] Developing countries were well aware that a healthy dollar reserve balance, which outside the franc zone was by far their most important reserve asset, was the best means of continued access to Euromarket finance.[66] Both developing country committees regularly reminded the Fund of the necessity to keep open the flows of capital to their countries; failing this they concentrated upon recommendations concerning special IMF facilities for balance of payments problems, on concessionary terms if possible. On less immediate questions, developing countries preferred to expend their diplomatic energy in an attempt to improve the link between the SDR and development finance. Their lack of success in this matter, however, was reflected in resorting to forums outside the Fund to call for an SDR link. From the UNCTAD V conference in Manila in May and June of 1979 to G24-sponsored work, to the UN General Assembly's Stiglitz report in 2009, calls to revive the SDR, including through the link, were ignored. Only George Soros's call for an allocation linked to development finance, which appeared suddenly in 2002, received much attention—and even then was viewed as quixotic by most observers.[67]

G24 work included three research volumes published in 1987 and two more 1990—these and other related documents, some of which have been noted, were published by UNCTAD.[68] Some of the papers have been published elsewhere; many authors were also developing country policy-makers, such as V. B. Kadam of the Indian Reserve Bank, Salvador Arriola of the Ministry of

Finance and Public Credit in Mexico City, and G. O. Nwankwo, Executive Director of the Central Bank of Nigeria. Much of this work concerned balance of payments adjustment and development finance, and individual country experience with these problems (including, in the latter two volumes, the debt crisis), but others examined systemic problems, including those relating to the SDR. Many of the issues with respect to the SDR are familiar, such as the substitution account and improvements to the mechanisms surrounding SDR use. Others were intertwined with broader and more nebulous issues of reform. Although comprehensive however, this work had little impact. For developing country views to have an effect it was necessary to appeal at the Fund.

The G24 and Development Committee have taken little initiative in promoting the idea of the Fund acting as a clearinghouse for the private market in the SDR. While it is true that the lack of a large private market in SDRs remains an impediment to further countries pegging to the SDR, there have been suggestions that an SDR would be an optimal peg for a majority of developing countries, *and* that a larger market in SDRs would serve to enhance its role in the international monetary system.[69] John Williamson has noted this lukewarm support:

> It has always puzzled me as to why the Group of 24 has never taken up the cause of creating an SDR clearinghouse. This is not a topic where the industrial countries would have a strong interest in resisting developing country demands: it is one where the developing countries have never taken an initiative. Yet such a step could be of significant value to most developing countries in resolving the dilemma they face in choosing whether to peg to a basket or a single currency.[70]

Furthermore, Williamson goes on to argue that such a move could aid the cause of South–South trade. However, the two development committees tended to press for assistance for immediate balance of payments need. Still, the idea of an SDR clearinghouse, or lender of last resort in the case of private market transactions, has resurfaced. Although arguably precluded by the limited list of official holders at the IMF, John Williamson has periodically been joined by Peter Kenen, and more recently Barry Eichengreen and DeAnne Julius, in calling for a greater role for SDRs in private markets. Julius notes that complementing an increase in SDR supply through allocations should be commensurate moves to expand SDR demand by the IMF allowing SDR accounts by private actors, and through the creation of a settlement system (or clearing house).[71] Although Julius suggests that it would be possible to design a system that could minimize US exchange risk exposure in the event of holders converting SDRs back into dollars, neither Eichengreen nor Kenen, despite being attracted by the idea, are as sanguine.

At the Fund developing countries have had limited influence on the success of additions to Fund resources, a subsidy account for the oil facility, and the Heavily Indebted Poor Countries (HIPC) initiative being just two examples. And as we noted in the previous chapter, individual executive directors had influence on Second Amendment discussions. But support for the substitution account, and indeed SDR allocations, were subsidiary to their quest for the link and other forms of Fund liquidity to aid immediate balance of payments problems. By the late 1970s, developing country influence in the international system was weakening, and was dealt a death-blow by the financial repercussions of the second oil shock in 1979–80. In this context it could be argued that the more immediate problems of developing countries were furthered by seeking to open credit lines with the West rather than supporting an SDR whose attributes with respect to immediate problems were less and less apparent.

Indeed the two development committees' proposals, as revealed in their communiqués, often reflected concerns already expressed in the Interim Committee and in the Fund itself. Initially, they were disappointed that no link between SDR allocations and development finance was forthcoming in the First Amendment to the Fund's Articles that established SDRs.[72] When trying to reach a consensus on the proposed amendments to the Fund's Articles, developing countries, while continuing to press for a link, had the immediate problems of petrodollar recycling and reserve growth to concern themselves with. It was only in retrospect that the G24 began to note and regret the decline in the role of SDRs.[73] It was also at this time that the G24 expressed strong support for a gold substitution account, which had been mooted by the Fund's Research Department in 1975.[74] Again, it is interesting to note that developing countries, who tend to hold much less of a proportion of their reserves in gold than developed economies, supported a gold substitution account, whereas support for a dollar substitution account was more muted. There were important reasons for developing countries and their representative committees devoting their energy to more pressing problems than the sometimes esoteric and arcane discussions surrounding the SDR. However their reticence to become more involved in these discussions remains a factor in the lack of success of the substitution account and other initiatives. A lack of influence coupled with a lack of political support did not translate into unbridled enthusiasm for SDR initiatives—and again we cannot ignore the shorter term gains of the creditworthy among the developing countries when dollar reserves were relatively accessible on the market.

Williamson writes of steps necessary for the SDR to become a vehicle currency 'to perform the functions of "international money" at the private level'.[75] Several alternatives are considered, ranging from the SDR becoming the sole currency peg and intervention currency, to unilateral developing country moves to an SDR peg. Although conjectural, Williamson argues that *if* the necessary changes of (political) attitude took place, the technical obstacles would 'not really be all that great'.[76] This again echoes a persistent theme that we noted at the outset of this book: technical problems associated with a greater role for the SDR are not insurmountable. In considering other parameters, such as the exchange rate system and coordination of economic policy, Williamson notes that reformist initiatives in all spheres could be initiated by developing countries acting in unison, although it would be necessary for any participants to an alternative system to 'accept the fact that more structured arrangements will necessarily imply some limitation of national sovereignty'.[77] This is an important insight, and is as true for developed as it is for developing countries. It has an important precedent in the belated establishment of the third Bretton Woods institution when the WTO replaced the GATT in 1994. In this case, an implicit acceptance of 'pooled sovereignty' was evident. This understanding is not as evident in the international monetary domain. How governments and the IMF consider this issue will have a bearing on future international reform, as well as the SDR.

There were other limited calls for the SDR from developing country representatives. In his discussion of international monetary reform, Ariel Buira, Deputy Governor of the Bank of Mexico, advocated additional allocations of SDRs.[78] He also calls for an allocation skewed to favour developing countries. A core problem with SDR development finance proposals, however, is that advocacy of a 'link' tends to impede prospects for an allocation in the developed countries for broader system purposes.[79] Thus, even amongst academic and other proponents of the SDR, there was a notable lack of cohesive support for any specific SDR initiatives as the 1980s dawned. Whether the substitution account, an SDR clearinghouse, or a 'link', it could not be shown convincingly—or in any case agreed upon—that any of these initiatives was important to the functioning of the international monetary system. Furthermore, even within link-related discussions, proposals proliferated—in addition to 'asymmetric', or 'selective', allocations in favour of developing countries, the UN Stiglitz Commission revisited a proposal for the IMF to buy bonds from multilateral development banks, and George Soros suggested that developed countries agree among themselves to donate their new holdings to developing countries through a new international body.[80]

Importantly, even during periodic and increasingly frequent debt crises, when an SDR allocation was advocated, Dornbusch and Fischer pointed out that an allocation would not resolve some of the issues inherent in the debtors predicament:

> A new SDR allocation is clearly a desirable measure. But it must also be clear that it is not a solution to the debt problem, neither for large nor for small debtors. If the

> SDRs are used to pay off debts, the reserve inadequacy problem remains. If they are not used, the debt problem remains. This is none the less an opportune time to present a case that clearly stands on its own merits.[81]

The case for an allocation could be made on its own merits, independent of debt ratios or reserve inadequacy. And the case for additional SDRs to buttress reserves can be made even more strongly if reserves ratios versus trade in goods and services (versus world merchandize trade) are used:

> The case [for an SDR allocation] is reinforced when reserves are measured not, as is customary, relative to world merchandise trade but rather relative to world trade in goods and services.... The case is strengthened by taking into account the effect of increased variability of the value of trade in goods and services.[82]

But, ultimately, developing countries did not make the SDR a policy priority. It was an esoteric subject; systemic needs that may have favoured them—and may have indeed favoured developing countries a priori with additional liquidity in the system—seemed an abstraction at a time when conventional reserves were more and more important to access capital markets. While isolated calls continued, by the early 1980s SDR advocacy at the IMF and even G24 essentially ceased for another 15 years. When references appeared at all, successive pronouncements by the Fund acknowledged that little progress on the SDR was forthcoming.

Such promotion of the asset that did take place was not sustained—nor did it have much influence. In addition, developing country support for a link undermined more neutral support for an SDR allocation, and support for more market-based initiatives, such as an SDR clearinghouse, were lukewarm. Under these arrangements enhancements to the mechanisms associated with the asset also slowed. And even when developing countries were united—on the link for example—they were unable to prevail. As the Fund slowly decoupled its future from that of the SDR, so did developing countries.

6.5 Towards the Fourth Amendment and the Response to the International Financial Crisis

As the twentieth century drew to a close, with a flexible exchange rate system firmly entrenched, the role of the SDR, and indeed the Fund, was questioned. By the early 1980s the Fund made net withdrawals from the world economy (after including repayments of earlier loans), and *The Economist* observed that '...cockier bankers questioned the need for the IMF at all'.[83] And it was not only bankers who felt this way: George Shultz, Secretary of State under President Reagan, joined William Simon (who had served under Presidents Nixon and Ford) and former Citibank chairman Walt Wriston in similarly questioning the need for the IMF.[84] In the 1980s and 1990s, then, much of the remaining impetus behind Fund SDR initiatives rested within the relatively small degree of latitude of the managing director, the Interim Committee (and then IMFC), Fund staff, as well as limited academic and policy maker interest. Until the global financial crisis in late 2008, this was most clearly in evidence in support for the Fourth Amendment discussions in the late 1990s and early 2000s.

Relatively muted official voices in support of SDRs were evident on the IMF Board of Governors, which continued to reflect the prevailing attitudes of their governments and sought to ensure that these were represented on the Executive Board. As high representatives of their respective governments, usually ministers of finance, at a time when the 'Washington Consensus' on free markets and financial liberalization was effectively advocated, this was only to be expected.[85] During this 1980s and 1990s Board of Governors' resolutions concerning SDRs were few, reflecting the Fund's structure which delegates full authority to the managing director and Executive Board. Even in the 1970s, apart from the provision to increase allocations and abolish the reconstitution provision, and the Jamaica Agreement of course, only three resolutions concerning SDRs were passed: in March 1972, SDRs were made the Fund's unit of account, in January 1974 the Bank for International Settlements was made the first prescribed holder of SDRs outside the Fund, and in March 1974 the Fund extended the suspension of the 'equal value provision' (in Article XXV), enabling European countries to use their holdings of SDRs in payments amongst themselves.[86] Later, statements on SDRs dried up (with the occasional half-hearted nod towards making the SDR the principal international reserve asset as per the revised articles); after 1997 statements repeatedly referred to the fact that a new allocation endorsed by the Fourth Amendment would take place in accordance with the special 85 per cent majority formula necessary to formally approve it. In other words, without US ratification, no Fourth Amendment allocation could take place.

In the early 1990s, however, IMF members first agreed to a Third Amendment to the Articles of Agreement. This was a relatively minor technical amendment that reflected the Fund's concentration on the provision of conditional liquidity programmes, largely for developing countries. As noted, in the wake of the second oil shock and growing debt problems in the developing world, the Fund had expanded its activity in this area with a number of loan programmes and facilities. Repayments, however, were not always timely.

The Third Amendment facilitated suspension of voting and related rights of members consistently in arrears, and could only be applied to members already ineligible to use the General Resources Account. As the US Treasury recently stated, at the time of approval there was little support from developed countries for the provision of unconditional financial resources through the SDR:

> ... many IMF member governments felt that countries seeking to use SDRs often needed conditional support through an IMF program rather than through an unconditional reserve asset such as the SDR.[87]

It is noteworthy that as conditional financing rather than SDRs was increasingly relied upon for the liquidity needs of its poorer members, the threat of voting right suspension was viewed as an incentive for these members to meet financial obligations. Developing countries understandably emphasized their immediate liquidity needs, particularly as debt increased. While at least one critic has argued that this was an ineffective means of encouraging adherence to loan obligations, it is noteworthy that arrears fell following the ratification of this amendment.[88] The Third Amendment represented an acknowledgement of the primary importance attached to conditional liquidity provision, backed up by domestic adjustment as necessary, which was increasingly challenging as crises became more frequent.

In this context, it became apparent that if the SDR was to have a role to play then, in addition to being more manageable, it was important to make the SDR more acceptable to the private market, which had plainly not occurred.[89] Although the first Eurobonds denominated in SDRs had been issued in 1975, further progress has not been forthcoming.[90] David Lomax postulated now familiar reasons for this in an article for a Fund conference based upon a survey of private banks, noting that official support was necessary for a market in the asset to develop.[91]

The apparent willingness of private intermediaries to establish a market in SDRs should not be underestimated. We have seen earlier how, once instituted, a private SDR market quickly established itself in the early 1970s—so much so that the US regulatory authorities became alarmed.[92] Over a decade later, *Euromoney* published a survey that examined the bond, syndicated loan, floating rate note, certificate of deposit, and other markets in SDRs and other composite instruments. It gave high marks to the idea of a basket as a hedging instrument, and many authors, most of whom were bankers, wrote of the practicalities of SDR-denominated assets. (An example of an SDR Certificate of Deposit is Figure 6.1 given below.) Repeatedly, however, these bankers noted the lack of official support for these nascent markets. We have witnessed developing country indifference to them, but this was just as true of developed countries.

This contrasted greatly with first the ECU and then the Euro, which enjoyed fundamentally important political support in the EU, particularly France and Germany.[93] The comments of the editor of the volume are representative of other authors (most of them bankers with practical experience

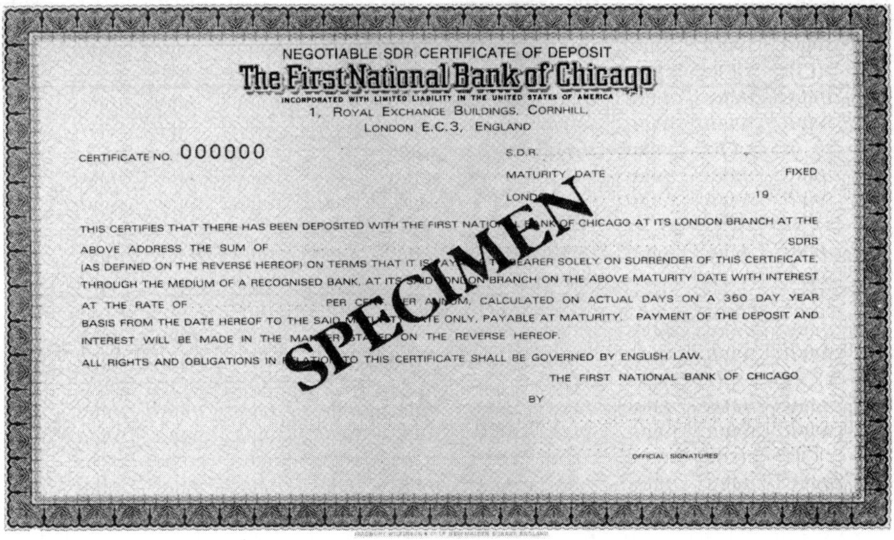

NEGOTIABLE SDR CERTIFICATE OF DEPOSIT

The First National Bank of Chicago

INCORPORATED WITH LIMITED LIABILITY IN THE UNITED STATES OF AMERICA

1, Royal Exchange Buildings, Cornhill,
London E.C.3, England

CERTIFICATE NO. 000000

S.D.R.

MATURITY DATE FIXED

LONDON 19

THIS CERTIFIES THAT THERE HAS BEEN DEPOSITED WITH THE FIRST NATIONAL BANK OF CHICAGO AT ITS LONDON BRANCH AT THE ABOVE ADDRESS THE SUM OF SDRS (AS DEFINED ON THE REVERSE HEREOF) ON TERMS THAT IT IS PAYABLE TO BEARER SOLELY ON SURRENDER OF THIS CERTIFICATE, THROUGH THE MEDIUM OF A RECOGNISED BANK, AT ITS SAID LONDON BRANCH ON THE ABOVE MATURITY DATE WITH INTEREST AT THE RATE OF PER CENT PER ANNUM, CALCULATED ON ACTUAL DAYS ON A 360 DAY YEAR BASIS FROM THE DATE HEREOF TO THE SAID MATURITY DATE ONLY, PAYABLE AT MATURITY. PAYMENT OF THE DEPOSIT AND INTEREST WILL BE MADE IN THE MANNER STATED ON THE REVERSE HEREOF.

ALL RIGHTS AND OBLIGATIONS IN RELATION TO THIS CERTIFICATE SHALL BE GOVERNED BY ENGLISH LAW.

THE FIRST NATIONAL BANK OF CHICAGO

BY

OFFICIAL SIGNATURES

SPECIMEN

For the purposes of this Certificate an SDR is the aggregate of the following amounts of the following currencies (being, at the date hereof, the components of one Special Drawing Right of the International Monetary Fund):—

Currency	Amount
U.S. Dollar	0.5400
Deutsche Mark	0.4600
Japanese Yen	34.0000
French Franc	0.7400
Pound Sterling	0.0710

Payment of the deposit and interest will, save as provided below, only be made in U.S. dollars. For the purpose of calculating the amount of these payments the U.S. dollar value of an SDR shall be that fixed by the International Monetary Fund for a Special Drawing Right comprising the currencies and amounts listed above as at two business days (which shall be days upon which banks are open for business in both London and New York City) prior to the Maturity Date stated on the face hereof. If the International Monetary Fund shall not fix the U.S. dollar value of such a Special Drawing Right on such day, payment of each SDR deposited as stated on the face hereof will be made in the currencies and amounts listed above and payment of interest on each such amount will be made in such respective currencies.

All payments will be made by draft or telegraphic transfer on New York City or, in the case of a payment in any currency other than U.S. dollars, on the principal financial centre applicable to such other currency.

Figure 6.1. SDR certificate of deposit

Source: A. Papa, 'SDR Certificates of Deposit', in L. de V. Wragg (ed.), *Composite Currencies SDRs, ECUs and Other Instruments*, Euromoney Publications, London, 1984. (Used with permission)

of SDR-denominated assets). They also point to the lack of support for the SDR by its sponsors:

> ... the intellectual case in favour of the SDR as both a borrowing and investing vehicle is a sound one, [although] the actual demand for such services has depended on cost (or yield) differentials between the SDR and the major international currencies, most particularly the US dollar ...
>
> [The lack of an SDR clearing house] may also explain why the corporate sector generally has been slow to exploit SDR services.... Corporate interest has centred on the ECU, where trading and settlement of the unit in its own right has developed, possibly as a result of extensive political support.[94]

Similar comparisons today between the Euro and SDR would also lead to the same conclusions (although it is noteworthy that *'arrière-pensées'* on the long-term desirability of the Euro and its predecessor the ECU have a long history, and include long-standing private German doubts).[95]

The 'private' ECU received early and sustained official backing from the then EC and its member governments—and it already had a clearinghouse, for instance, through the BIS. Indeed as early as 1984 outstanding ECU bond issues were larger than every currency apart from the US dollar, Deutschmark, pound sterling, and Canadian dollar.[96] While we have noted that there remained some reticence about long-term prospects for the ECU, this dissipated as the political commitment to what was to be its successor, the Euro, strengthened in the late 1990s. There is little doubt that marketplace success is dependent upon official support. And the Euro, although on a smaller scale, was a much more ambitious experiment in that it supplanted most European currencies. As many observers have noted, most famously Robert Mundell, the case for SDRs was rarely made on this basis, but rather it become the 'principal' (rather than sole) international reserve asset.[97]

Although the ECU and Euro are not entirely analogous to the role of SDRs, the European assets have always enjoyed considerable *political* support by the EU and its member states, particularly France and Germany. In the case of SDRs, with the role of the Fund to provide important clearinghouse functions restricted, the willingness of private intermediaries to involve themselves—albeit in a limited way—with transactions denominated in SDRs has been downplayed. It was the lack of sufficient official backing—if not opposition—that caused this market to dry up, not private reluctance to engage in and experiment with SDRs in the first place.

While many critics (Williamson, Kenen, Chrystal, Lomax, Julius, Eichengreen) continue to advocate an SDR clearinghouse to further these markets, an important stumbling block in the revised Articles of Agreement has complicated matters.[98] To a large degree commercial acceptability for the SDR is prohibited by Article XVII, section 3, which prescribes holders of SDRs outside those official institutions specified by the IMF. Until now, SDR transactions that have taken place in the private market have been developed on their own, creating a parallel market in SDRs. The protracted negotiations over the Fund's articles has meant extreme reluctance to tamper with them again; this has led to a number of proposals for an independent SDR clearinghouse, including, as we have seen, Williamson urging developing country support for the idea.[99]

It should be recalled that initial plans for a substitution account foundered partly because of fears of US Congressional rejection. In turn, this was due to the understandable difficulties of ascribing US responsibility for exchange risk—that is for maintaining the dollar value of SDRs purchased by dollar holders substituting SDRs for dollar reserves. In the 1980s, as now, the question remains: if IMF member countries exchanged reserve currencies—particularly the dollar—for SDRs, was this to be a 'one way' substitution (in which case would it seem less attractive to portfolio managers)? If not, who would absorb exchange risk in the event of SDR appreciation? Most recently, DeAnne Julius suggests a 'controlled two-way substitution account', tying the size of the account to SDR allocations. While she acknowledges that this could limit the SDR's attractiveness to surplus country portfolio managers, eligibility for private sector SDR holdings would enhance its appeal, particularly for international trade and investment purposes. Peter Kenen has reexamined his earlier work in support of a substitution account, observing that reserve currency diversification had resumed, and that SDRs could preclude 'potentially disruptive diversification and [achieve] more orderly growth in the stock of reserves'. He set out a number of simulations dealing with the costs of setting up such an account, most of which involved significant costs to the US. But he also notes that these costs:

> ...must be weighed against another cost that cannot be readily quantified: the effect of reserve currency diversification by central banks that now hold far larger reserves than they are apt to need to cope with balance-of-payments problems.[100]

As noted, Kenen also cautioned that after the US refused to take sole responsibility in 1980 for maintaining the dollar value of SDR denominated claims on the account, 'the subject lay dormant for nearly three decades.' The Fund also had become less and less willing to risk scarce political capital in support of such a major change to international monetary arrangements.

However the Fund and its membership continued to support minor but important steps taken in the 1980s and 1990s to enhance the attractiveness and marketability of the SDR. Reducing the basket of currencies upon which the SDR was based from an unwieldy sixteen to the five then major currencies of the industrialized world, with the Euro replacing the Deutschmark and French franc in 1999, was key (see Table 5.1),[101] as was the interest rate gradually approaching the average of that obtained on short term money market instruments of the component currencies. It could be argued that the latter represented an impetus to bolster a parallel private market in SDRs, but this was short lived. Nonetheless, since the early 1980s the rate of interest on the SDR has been 100 per cent of the combined market rate of the five constituent currencies of the SDR,[102] and the interest rate on the SDR began to be determined weekly:

> ... by reference to a combined market interest rate, which is the weighted average of interest rates on specified short-term domestic obligations in the money markets of the same five countries whose currencies are included in the SDR valuation basket.[103]

With very minor technical changes, this means of interest rate determination remains in effect today, although of course based on four currencies rather than five.

The marginalization of the SDR under post-Bretton Woods arrangements was due to a lack of success in three main areas: lack of agreement on the need for additional Fund sponsored liquidity in the system, either universally or skewed towards developing countries; the failure of any kind of substitution account to be accepted; and the failure of a parallel private market in SDRs to develop. Changing and increasingly complex US policy determination was a common factor in all these fields. In addition, the Fund could not be said to be responsible for the moves to a largely demand-determined system for liquidity provision. While it could work on technical enhancements consistent with its mandate, its capacity to address the rise in importance of Eurocurrency markets, especially in the wake of the oil price rise, was extremely limited.

Despite its marginalization, the SDR continued to capture the imagination of many academically oriented critics, both within and outside the Fund. Another allocation, which virtually all IMF members favoured as the Fourth Amendment to the Fund articles was agreed to, was periodically supplemented by a few calls for an international monetary system based fully on the SDR. In particular, J. J. Polak's IMF pamphlet called for a 'major amendment of the Articles of Agreement' which would result in a Fund 'in which transactions could be conducted entirely in SDRs'—although he does acknowledge that given the experience of drawn-out ratification of the Jamaica Agreement his proposals would probably be of long- rather than near-term interest.[104] John Williamson and Peter Kenen have more recently added to this literature, the former noting that China and the US may find an enhanced role for SDRs in their interests; Peter Kenen focusing on its desirability in the event of further reserve-currency diversification.[105] In both cases this work builds on their previous contributions to debate over international monetary reform 20 to 30 years earlier.

In the meantime, new proposals involving SDRs were sporadic. The IMF had followed up on its 1983 sponsorship of a conference that dealt with SDRs by focusing almost exclusively on its role in a 1996 conference.[106] Notably, although a variety of views were expressed at the latter conference, most acknowledged at most an attenuated role. Ten years later, at a 2006 conference hosted by the IIE on *Reforming the IMF for the 21st Century*, SDRs were almost absent. Editor Edward Truman noted that the IMF managing director, Rodrigo de Rato, had been silent on the issue of SDRs and one paper dealt with the issue. In a nutshell, an ostensibly demand-driven liquidity system made the SDR superfluous. Notwithstanding the fact that the demand for liquidity was a complicated issue, reconciling prevailing attitudes with long term systemic needs and any role for the SDR was difficult. J. J. Polak (and Peter B. Clark) acknowledged this dynamic in their relatively calm call for an SDR allocation in 2004. They noted that even if a modest allocation without amending the articles could be accommodated, 'one can only be sceptical about both the rationale and the feasibility of such proposals', due in part to recent increases facilitated through the New Arrangements to Borrow (NAB).[107]

Without further encouragement and political support from the Fund's membership—particularly the US—and unless increased exchange rate volatility produced a stronger desire for stability, prospects for the SDR remained limited. Politically there was little support, despite how well mechanisms surrounding the SDR worked. In 1992, Paul Volcker wrote that an SDR based system was impracticable 'however intellectually attractive the idea may seem' because it would involve the delegation of sovereign authority to a 'supranational world central bank'.[108] Although Volcker has more recently slightly softened this criticism,[109] his observation does indeed capture the dilemma of continuing intellectual interest for the idea as the SDR retreated to the margins of real debate. And understandable IMF reticence to promote the SDR in the face of continued disinterest from some of its membership, coupled with difficulties in the Articles of Agreement vis-à-vis Fund sponsorship of privately-traded SDRs, simply reflected political reality.

In response, some advocates argued that enhancements to the SDR could be accommodated without further amendments to the Articles. Sir Joseph Gold determined that should the establishment of a substitution account ever be reconsidered, it could go ahead without an amendment to the Fund's articles, under the broad Article V, Section 2(b), which stipulates that the Fund perform financial and legal services consistent with its purposes.[110] Peter Kenen has also noted that vast improvements could take place with a view to making the SDR the principal reserve asset 'without amending the Articles of Agreement',[111] and many have spoken of the possibility of the SDR clearinghouse not operated by the IMF that could take place without further amendment. The Fund was reluctant to explore these more fundamental ideas further, however. It was prudent to disengage a discussion of its future role with that of a close identification with the SDR.[112] In his inquiry into explanations for the SDR's lack of support, J. J. Polak noted the following:

> . . . a natural aversion of conservatively inclined governments against the concept of a banking function for the Fund. In the present international monetary system, commercial bank credit is the main source of reserves, just as it is the main source of cash balance in the domestic economy. To the extent that reserves are supplied by the SDR mechanism, the reserve-creating role of the commercial banks is reduced. Given the recent deflation in the enthusiasm of the commercial banks for extending credit abroad . . . some sharing of the privilege of creating credit . . . might not be a bad idea. But while this might be helpful to the system . . . it is not hard to understand that those governments for which privatization is an article of faith would not be keen to activate the provisions for official reserve creation unless there were an overwhelming case for doing so.[113]

Thus with the failure of a substitution account, the lack of an SDR clearing-house for private transactions, and the continuing evolution of the post-Bretton Woods system, the Fund looked to slowly divorce itself from the SDR. The life support system to which it had been attached in the Second Amendment had prompted only a few signs of recovery in the 1980s and early 1990s, among them the second allocation and the idea of a substitution account. And concerning the latter, its institutionalization did not occur. It had once seemed close, but then evaporated, mirage-like, as the strength of the dollar improved and the US regained the initiative over monetary arrangements. Prospects throughout this time indeed appeared dim: two critics took heart in 1985 that the G10 Dini report had not completely closed the door on the SDR, despite, the musings of a US official that it had done just that.[114] Throughout this period, the Interim Committee recognized the impasse that had transpired surrounding a further allocation. Successive communiqués continued to report that no consensus had emerged on the need for further allocations, although by the first 1986 meeting the Committee was admitting that most members favoured an allocation, even though 'broad support' was lacking.[115]

There were, however, intermittent revivals of interest in the asset: in 1988 *The Economist* published a cover story and further study on a prospective universal currency that it appropriately called the 'phoenix'.[116] But the SDR continued to generate limited traction on the official plane. For instance, also in 1988, the Institute of International Finance (IIF) in Washington, speaking on behalf of its international commercial bank membership, recommended a 'sizable allocation' (SDR 21.4 billion—very close to Fourth Amendment proposals ten years later) of SDRs to maintain orderly exchange markets and to ease financing problems of both deficit and surplus countries. In April 1991, in a policy reversal, Japan recommended that the Interim Committee discuss a new SDR allocation.[117] In late 1993, in a speech to the Parliamentary Assembly of the Council of Europe, the OECD Secretary-General called for another SDR allocation.[118] And in 1994, it was evident that the US was once again considering a limited SDR allocation in its preparation for the G7 summit in Naples and at the IMF Annual Meeting in Madrid.[119] Thus, having weathered difficult economic circumstances through the late 1980s and early 1990s, prospects for the SDR altered slightly. Nonetheless, in 1995 it would have been rash to assert that the world would soon be willing to reconsider an international monetary system with an important role for publicly sponsored liquidity provision.

Despite a stalemate concerning further allocation,[120] and muted enthusiasm for further improvements such as the establishment of an SDR clearing-house—even one that might not require amendments to the Articles of Agreement—a proposed Fourth Amendment was endorsed by the Board of Governors. This Amendment set the stage for a greater role for the SDR, since it redressed the anomaly of new Fund members—many of whom were developing countries—who had not been allocated SDRs. It also implicitly meant that an asymmetrical allocation—even to redress one that emerged because of constraints inherent in the articles—was possible. Ratification, however, of course depended on the approval of three-fifths of IMF membership and 85 per cent of voting power (i.e. US support).

Once endorsed, stalemate ensued for 11 years. The cause was not aided by Michel Camdessus's successor, Rodrigo de Rato, who was relatively silent on the issue of SDRs.[121] In addition, as part of their response to increasing balance of payments crises in the developing world, the Fund had considered an allocation, including to new members. But this was rejected by Michel Camdessus and developing countries in an embarrassing outcome of the IMF Annual Meeting in Madrid in 1994. As former US executive director Karin Lissakers has noted:

> The Executive Board has not seriously considered a general allocation since the bloody fight over the resumption of SDR allocations at the annual meetings in Madrid [in 1994]. The Fourth Amendment notwithstanding, I believe it is fair to say that if, by the time I left the Executive Board [in 2001] the SDR provisions had simply been erased from the Articles, few of my colleagues would have shed a tear.[122]

This is a candid observation. Between 1994 and 2006, then, at a time when the Fourth Amendment was agreed to (but not ratified), few IMF Board members were concerned about SDRs at all. Nonetheless, Lissakers makes the case for SDRs for classic reasons: a sudden need for international liquidity. And this is indeed what happened in response to the international financial crisis.

The financial crisis in 2008 heralded a significant reexamination of SDR attributes. It was remarkable how quickly the international community reacted as global credit lines dried up dramatically in late 2008. Recognizing the gravity of the situation, central bankers and G7 and G20 finance ministers responded immediately and sought to inject additional liquidity into the global economy. The SDR was a fundamentally important component of the response. In the run up to its London meeting in April 2009, the G20 recommended injecting a gargantuan $1.1 trillion into the world economy (supplemented by the Federal Reserve increasing its own balance sheet by a further trillion dollars).[123] As part of this package, a special SDR allocation of $250 billion was endorsed, as was ratifying the Fourth Amendment to the Fund's Articles of Agreement and considering other reforms to the governance of the Fund.[124]

By August, the IMF Board of Governors approved the Fourth Amendment, 12 years after the initial proposal. After 12 years of reluctance by the US Administration to present the proposal to Congress, it was approved as part of a much bigger package of measures and funds to respond to the international financial crisis. Even more importantly, a special SDR allocation of $250 billion (SDR 161.2 billion) was agreed to, with $100 billion of this committed to emerging markets and developing countries, $18 billion of which was allocated to low-income countries. These allocations had the result of increasing the proportion of SDRs among total non-gold reserves to levels not seen since the mid-1980s, and as a proportion of world trade to unprecedented levels (see Illustration 6.1).

The significance of these moves for the SDR cannot be understated—not only because they placed the SDR at the heart of international monetary relations but because the SDR was associated with such a successful response to a crisis. The *zeitgeist* had changed. In an IMF account of the breaking of this 12-year old stalemate, attention to Congressional approval of what had been a US Administration proposal looms large, reflecting the growing importance of US Congress to international monetary policy that was investigated in Chapters 3 and 4 above.[125] And the SDR was acclaimed in the international spotlight for the first time in almost 40 years. In reporting on the April G20 London meeting, *Time* magazine published an article strongly supportive of the role of the SDR titled 'Why Supplanting the Dollar Would Be Good for America'.[126] And in March, as the G20 London conference loomed, China issued a carefully timed call for 'special consideration' of the SDR 'to act as a super-sovereign reserve currency', which has loomed large in subsequent consideration of SDRs due to China's large surpluses and newfound influence on international monetary matters.[127]

Although the special allocation of SDR 161.1 billion was considerably more significant than the SDR 21.4 billion that was allocated as a result of the

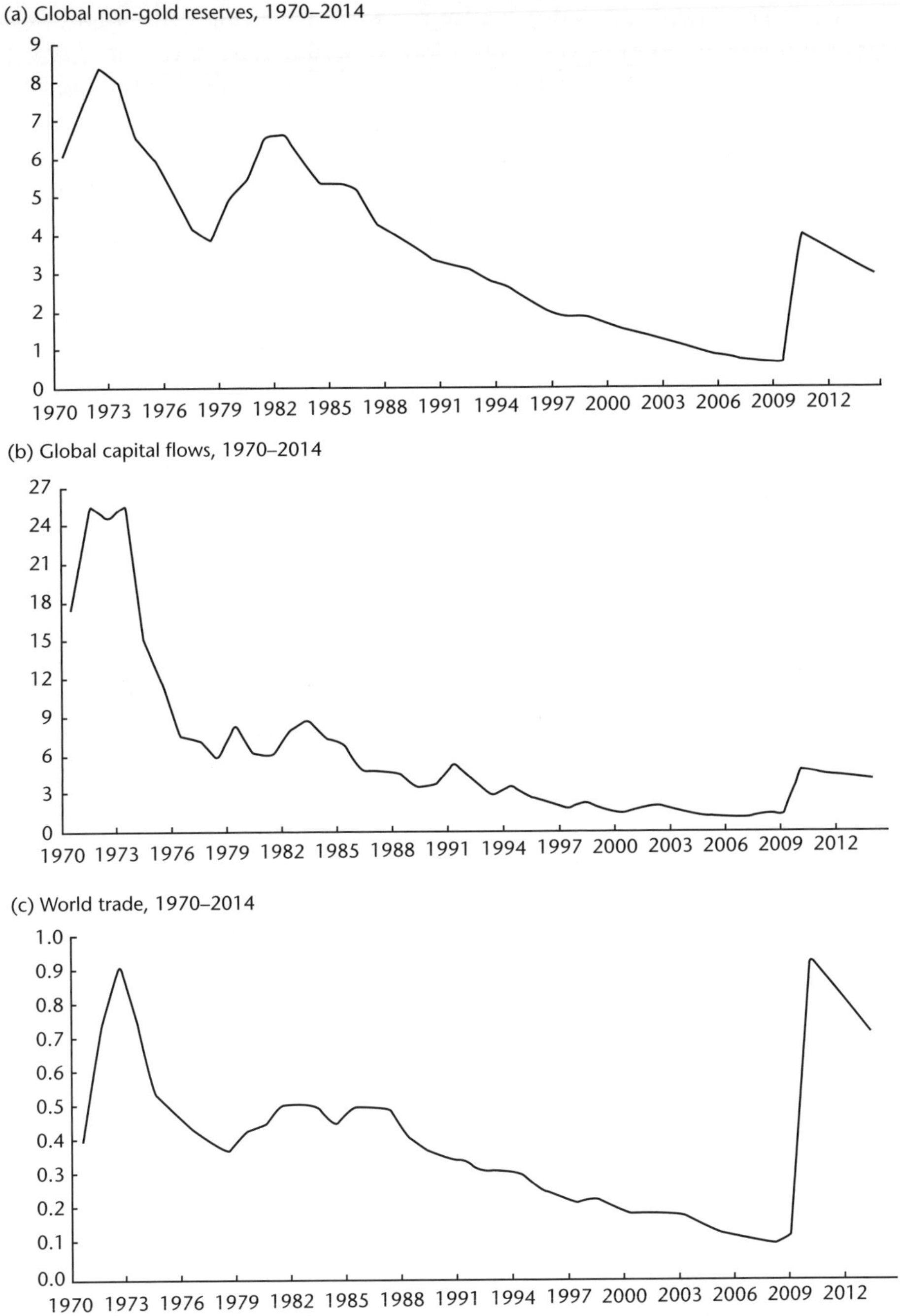

Source: 'Proposal for a General Allocation of SDRs', prepared by Finance, Legal, and Strategy, Policy and Review Departments, IMF, 9 June 2009, as at: http://www.imf.org/external/np/pp/eng/2009/060909.pdf

Illustration 6.1. SDRs as a share of (a) global non-gold reserves; (b) global capital flows; and (c) world trade, 1970–2014

Fourth Amendment, the latter is important in that it implicitly implies the desirability of an asymmetrical allocation, skewed in part in favour of developing countries, for the first time. While this served to address the growing anomaly of countries that joined the IMF after 1981 having never received an allocation, it also broke new ground in justifying SDR allocations. And, above all, the international financial package showed that at the height of the financial crisis the Fund and its most important members—including the US and now China—were willing to consider comprehensive changes to the international monetary system. Even more importantly, it was evident that any new international monetary arrangements once again encompassed a key role for the SDR.

It is also remarkable how international monetary debate has rejuvenated interest in SDRs since the crisis. As we have seen, apart from a few proponents on the margins of international monetary debates, SDRs were ignored or tolerated as an anachronism, even when international monetary reform was discussed.[128] Indeed, even when development issues were discussed—such as during the run-up to the Millenium Development Goals agreed to at the UN in 2000, neither SDRs nor international monetary reform figured prominently in the discussion of how to enhance poverty alleviation efforts in developing countries to meet these goals.[129]

We have already witnessed the return to earlier debates in the discussion of the substitution account and SDR clearinghouse. Williamson and others have also returned to note the desirability of regular SDR allocations in response to a greater global demand for liquidity that simply cannot be responded to by the US necessity to increase a deficit.[130] José Ocampo, in a paper for the G24, implicitly defers to the international financial crisis, but the Stiglitz Commission, which called for deep reforms of the global system, notes the desirability of regular allocations in part due to the asymmetric burden on adjustment on deficit countries (because of their net liability positions and deflationary bias), noting further the return of the Triffin dilemma, that is that 'an *international* reserve system based on a *national* currency is inherently unstable'.[131]

These observations will be familiar. In many respects they echo unresolved debates over international monetary reform in the 1970s. The financial crisis has given sudden and new impetus to the prospective contribution to SDRs to international liquidity, international monetary reform, and increasingly international monetary stability. In a nutshell, current difficulties associated with the US providing sufficient liquidity for global economic growth—and difficulties in the short to medium term for the EU, China, or others to do so—suggests that a pooling of currency risk embodied in SDR reserves could be a stabilizing influence in an increasingly multi-currency reserve system with growing liquidity needs.

A prospective link of SDR allocations to climate change is one of a few new proposals that have few antecedents. Under a George Soros suggestion, developed countries would lend $100 billion worth of SDRs already allocated to a special green fund for the developing world, jump-starting forestry, land-use, and agricultural projects; in addition IMF gold reserves would be used to guarantee interest payments and repayment of the principal. Soros optimistically maintains that public pressure could generate momentum to support this in the US: 'The mere fact that tapping SDRs requires Congressional approval in the US ensures that nothing will happen without public pressure'.[132] Supported by then managing director Dominique Strauss-Kahn, IMF staff have also produced a position note on the subject.[133] Notably, however, since the Climate Conference in Copenhagen in 2009 there has been little other interest expressed in the proposal.

Nonetheless policy makers have a full agenda. China's call for 'special consideration' of the SDR 'to act as a super-sovereign reserve currency' continues to be taken seriously.[134] In his recent call for an SDR substitution account, C. Fred Bergsten has appealed to the US to support an 'expanded role' for the international currency in *Foreign Affairs*.[135] And France called the reform of international monetary arrangements a priority for 2011 in its capacity as G8 and G20 host. Regular allocations, a substitution account, and an SDR clearinghouse are paramount among these revisited issues; still others involve a modified link, such as those encompassed by George Soros's plea for pooled developed country SDR donations for developing countries), and the Stiglitz Report's endorsement of additional SDR allocations (through a 'link' or otherwise) and an evolutionary approach to a reform through a 'Reserve Currency Association', whereby a number of countries would pool reserves.[136] And in this context, with limited issues thus far, the significance of the IMF decision in 2009 to issue SDR-denominated bonds is yet to be determined.

As the twenty-first century unfolds, an international monetary system underpinned by private liquidity provision in US dollars no longer seems as inevitable as it did only ten years ago. But workable alternatives are not as clear either. Three new and rapid developments: the Euro, the rise of BRIC countries—particularly China—and the persistent liquidity needs of the poorest countries, all, for different reasons, suggest that a greater role for an SDR in international monetary arrangements may once again appeal to the US and other members as a potential source of stability, a prospective buttress to the dollar, a source of development finance, and even an element in modified international monetary arrangements. This essentially echoes the dynamics in the late 1960s and early 1970s when the international monetary system was previously in a state of transition.

In particular, in the event of a sustained period of dollar weakness, the attributes of an SDR as a source of international monetary stability—as well as a source of liquidity—will return.[137] (Not incidentally, concerns about SDRs being inflationary or profligate will have to be addressed in this regard.[138]) As noted in Chapter 3, at times of dollar weakness, reserves tend to diversify and the possibility of exchange rate volatility increases.[139] A component money such as the SDR will tend to be more stable during these periods. In the wake of the international financial crisis new interest has in part been facilitated by the quiet accomplishments embodied in the SDR that were approved during, and as a result of, the accomplishments inherent in the Second Amendment to the Fund's Articles of Agreement.

6.6 Summary

At times it appeared that, for all practical purposes, the SDR was unlikely to survive as anything more than a *numéraire*—much like 'gold francs' at the Bank for International Settlements until replaced by the SDR in 2003. After all, the SDR was created to augment liquidity under a fixed exchange rate system with largely public responsibility for liquidity provision. By the 1980s and 1990s, with the world seemingly awash with liquidity provided largely by private financial intermediaries (at least for those deemed creditworthy), the SDR could arguably have been abandoned as an irrelevant anachronism.[140] One reason why this did not transpire is because it became a symbol for reform. When even this failed, however, for a limited time the Fund sought to adapt it to the new system. And when support for even this role waned, the Fund effectively—but not completely—divorced its role from that of progress associated with the SDR until the late 1990s.

Without official support, it was asking a lot for SDRs to be taken seriously by a private market that was emerging from the constraints of Bretton Woods. The fact that this market had shown some willingness to include SDRs as a component in portfolio strategies in the early 1970s and 1980s was significant. Without official backing, however, particularly for an SDR clearing-house, the market evaporated. Consequently, the role of SDRs as the new international monetary arrangements consolidated themselves became more difficult to envisage. Calls for international monetary reform and SDRs following the adoption of flexible exchange rates became further removed from the policy-making process (witness the lack of response to UNCTAD/G24 calls for further SDR allocations), and were relegated to the fringes of official debate until recently.

Quietly, however, limited interest in the SDR was always in evidence. In his study of the impasse surrounding the SDR during the 1980s, J. J. Polak noted continued interest in the SDR exemplified by a new link-related proposal (though the word 'link' is not used) to make 'post-allocation adjustments to the distribution of SDRs'.[141] Later, the Fund tweaked mechanisms associated with it, including with respect to its valuation and interest rate. The IMF's 1983 and 1996 volumes on international monetary reform—and the SDR—served to keep SDRs at least intermittently on the international agenda, and sporadic academic and policy-making interest in honing the mechanism continued to exist. In addition, in an effort to enhance its appeal to detractors of a role for the SDR, calls were also made for reinstatement of the reconstitution provision and, as noted, George Soros made an important call for an SDR allocation in 2002.[142]

All these developments appear insignificant in light of the response to the global financial crisis in 2008–9, with the ratification of the Fourth Amendment of the Articles of Agreement (and the allocation of SDR 21.4 billion), together with the injection of SDR 161.2 billion ($250 billion) through a special SDR allocation.[143] Future developments are of course conjectural. However, the important but relatively neglected legacy of the Jamaica Agreement, followed by complementary work of a limited number of policy-makers, academics, and institutions, suggests a reversal of the marginalization of SDRs that transpired through much of the post-Bretton Woods monetary era.

It cannot be denied that international monetary developments made this is an unlikely scenario until recently. But in much the same way as its numerous proponents heralded over 40 years ago, the contribution of the SDR to a stable international monetary system is once again a subject for serious debate. Few underlying issues are new, but new actors and increasingly complex policy making suggests that new approaches will be necessary to enhance or reform international monetary arrangements. In this context, subjects such as an SDR allocation, the substitution account, a link to development finance, and an SDR clearinghouse for private market transactions in the asset have re-emerged as core issues on the international monetary agenda.

Notes

1. George M. von Furstenberg (ed.) *International Money and Credit: The Policy Roles*, IMF (Washington, DC: 1983). In the introduction to the 1983 volume Jacques de Larosière asked rhetorically '. . . how should we see the role of the SDR? Is it needed?' (p. 2). Despite limited academic and policy making interest, at the official level this trend continued—for example, in a summary of an IMF study published in the early 1990s entitled 'Issues in the Evolving International Monetary System', SDRs were not mentioned. See IMF *Survey*, 26 October 1992, pp. 321, 329–32.

2. Interview with William C. Hood, Vienna, Virginia.
3. Margaret Garritsen de Vries, *The International Monetary Fund 1972–1978—Cooperation on Trial*, vol. II, IMF (Washington, DC: 1985), p. 872.
4. J. Williamson, 'A New SDR Allocation?', *op. cit.*, p. 12.
5. Margaret Garritsen de Vries, *The International Monetary Fund 1972–1978, op. cit.*, vol II, p. 873.
6. Witteveen report 29/6/77, reproduced in de Vries, *The IMF, 1972–78*, vol. 3, no. 3, p. 274.
7. IMF *Survey*, 27/10/80, vol. 9, no. 20, p. 337.
8. Margaret Garritsen de Vries, *The International Monetary Fund 1972–1978, op. cit.*, vol. II, p. 880.
9. Interim Committee Communiqué, 24 September 1978, para. 4, as reproduced in M. Garritsen de Vries, *op. cit.*, vol III (documents), p. 240.
10. James Boughton, 'Michel Camdessus at the IMF: A Retrospective', *Finance and Development*, March 2000, vol. 37, no. 1, as at: http://www.imf.org/external/pubs/ft/fandd/2000/03/boughton.htm (accessed 8 June 2011).
11. As the Fund released a paper on enhancing international monetary stability at a Washington conference in early 2011, then managing director Strauss-Kahn noted the potential contribution of the SDR in this regard, noting the prospective role for SDR-denominated bonds. See 'Toward a More Stable International Monetary System', address by Dominique Strauss-Kahn, 10 February 2011, as at: http://www.imf.org/external/np/speeches/2011/021011.htm (accessed 16 June 2011). In response to the Fund paper and the managing director's speech, the Executive Board recommended further work: http://www.imf.org/external/np/sec/pn/2011/pn1122.htm (accessed 16 June 2011).
12. Margaret Garritsen de Vries, *The International Monetary Fund 1972–1978, op. cit.*, vol II, pp. 881–2.
13. Jacques Pelkmans, 'Collective Management and Economic Cooperation', in Cesare Merlini (ed.), *Economic Summits and Western Decision-Making*, European Institute of Public Administration/Croom Helm (Beckenham: 1984). Despite the controversy surrounding the notion, Pelkmans writes that 'The coordination of economic expansion has played a role right from the start at Rambouillet', p. 119.
14. As we saw in Chapter 3 these measures included sales of SDRs, the issuing of 'Carter bonds' (securities denominated in foreign currencies), and an increase in swap lines with the major surplus countries (West Germany, Switzerland, and Japan).
15. Australia was one example mentioned to this author.
16. Since then, however, with several new IMF members, including those created by the break-up of the Soviet Union in the early 1990s, an anomaly had been created in that 40 states became members of the IMF but had not been allocated SDRs. It was exactly this anomaly that led to the Fourth Amendment of the Fund Articles of Agreement being agreed to in 1997, but not ratified until the US formally agreed to it in the wake of the financial crisis in 2009.
17. As quoted in 'The Proposed Substitution Account in the IMF', *Midland Bank Review*, Winter 1979, p. 21. Like the Maudling Plan referred to in Chapter 1, this would

have particularly lent itself to supporting the role of sterling under Bretton Woods arrangements.

18. Ibid. p. 22.
19. With the expansion of the Executive Board to include Saudi Arabia and China, the Interim Committee then consisted of 22 members rather than the initial 20, with 11 members from the developed countries, 11 from developing countries. In addition, each committee member was entitled to appoint up to seven associates from its geographical grouping. Executive Board members also attended Committee meetings, in addition to the Fund's managing director, deputy managing director, and senior Fund staff. Altogether up to 200 people could be present at the twice annual meetings; about half of the meetings are held in Washington, DC. (See Margaret Garritsen de Vries, *The IMF in a Changing World 1945–85, op. cit.*, pp. 158–61, 168.) Although the Interim Committee never became a 'Council' with additional powers, it was formally succeeded by the permanent International Monetary and Financial Committee in 1999. Since 1992, reflecting the expansion in the Executive Board membership, membership has increased to 24. See Alexander Shakow, 'The Role of the International Monetary and Financial Committee in IMF Governance', in Ruben Lamdany and Leonardo Martinez-Diaz (eds), Studies of IMF Governance: A Compendium, International Evaluation Office of the International Monetary Fund, 2009 as at: http://www.ieo-imf.org/pub/pdf/16956_IEO_Gov_Compend_WEB.pdf (accessed 8 June 2011).
20. Margaret Garritsen de Vries, *The IMF in a Changing World 1945–85, op. cit.*, pp. 158–9.
21. De Vries, *The IMF, 1972–1978, op. cit.*, vol. 2, no. 3, p. 967.
22. Ibid. p. 968.
23. Ibid. p. 970.
24. Alexandre Kafka, 'Some IMF Problems After the Committee of XX'—paper prepared for a conference in honour of Jacques J. Polak (mimeo), 4 April 1991, p. 5.
25. De Vries, *The IMF in a Changing World 1945–85, op. cit.*, p. 119.
26. By the time of the global financial crisis in 2009, IMF lending facilities funded through the General Resources Account (as opposed to the SDR Account) comprised long running Stand-By Arrangements (terms for which were made more flexible at that time), a new Precautionary Credit Line (PCL) as well as a Flexible Credit Line (FCL) for loans based on balance of payments need, with the FCL replacing four other programmes: the never used Contingent Credit Line and Short-Term Liquidity Facility, as well as the Supplementary Reserve Facility and Compensatory Financing Facility. For developing countries in particular, in the wake of the financial crisis the 1975 Extended Fund Facility (EFF) was supplemented by a succession of Concessional Rate Facilities: the 1999 Poverty Reduction and Growth Facility (PRGF—which was sometimes administered in consultation with the World Bank), now superseded by an Extended Credit Facility (ECF) and a new Rapid Credit Facility (RCF); and the 2008 Exogenous Shocks Facility (ECF), the latter now superseded by a Standby Credit Facility. See relevant IMF 'Factsheets' at: http://www.imf.org/external/np/exr/facts/sba.htm, http://www.imf.org/external/np/exr/facts/poor.htm (accessed 8 June 2011); also Jonathan E. Sanford and Martin

A. Weiss, 'The Global Financial Crisis: Increasing IMF Resources and the Role of Congress', Congressional Research Service, 14 May 2009, as at: http://www.fas.org/sgp/crs/misc/R40578.pdf (accessed 8 June 2011).

27. Just prior to the C-20, J. J. Polak submitted a substitution account proposal to the Executive Board, which also incorporated aspects of the link. See Chapter 2, p. 61.
28. See also Joanne Gowa, 'Hegemons, IOs, and Markets: The Case of the Substitution Account', in *International Organization*, vol. 38, no. 4, Autumn 1984, p. 664.
29. This was one of many suggestions that could not be agreed upon within the wider framework of a substitution account. See C-20 Report, 'Report of Technical Group on Intervention and Settlement', pp. 112–38 (p. 137 re.: quotation).
30. Communiqué, Interim Committee, 15-16/1/75, sections 6.I.(d), and 6.II., reprinted in de Vries, *The IMF 1972–1978, op. cit.*, vol. III, p. 219.
31. Interim Committee Communiqué 29/4/77, Section 5, reprinted in ibid. p. 232. This language, however, was simply a way of conveying reluctance to endorse SDR-related initiatives.
32. IMF *Survey*, 27/10/80, vol. 9, no. 20, p. 337.
33. IMF *Survey*, 19/3/79, vol. 8, no. 6, p. 90.
34. IMF *Survey*, 23/4/79, vol. 8, no. 8, p. 126.
35. IMF *Survey*, 15/10/79, vol. 8, no. 19, p. 315.
36. Ibid. p. 315.
37. 'Monetary Swap Plan Outlined', *The New York Times*, Monday, 4/2/80, p. D1.
38. In the financial community, Dorothy Sobol, whose earlier work examined European policy towards the SDR, published an article for the Federal Reserve Bank in New York, reviewing the antecedents and existing issues behind a substitution account; the FRB Dallas also published an article in a similar vein, as did Midland Bank in the UK.
39. 'Towards a Less Unstable International Monetary System—Reserve Assets and a Substitution Account', a Report by the Reserve Assets Study Group of the Group of Thirty (London: 1980), pp. 6–7.
40. Ibid. p. 9
41. *The Economist*, 9/2/80, p. 84, and 23/2/80, p. 20.
42. IMF *Survey*, 7/4/80.
43. 'Funny Money Turning Serious', *The Economist* leading article, 19/4/80, p. 16.
44. *The Economist*, 3/5/80, p. 82.
45. 'Dollar Plan for IMF is Shelved', *The New York Times*, Friday, 25/4/80, p. D1.
46. See also Chapter 3, p. 102.
47. 'Dollar Plan for IMF is Shelved', *The New York Times*, Friday, 25/4/80, p. D1.
48. Dieter Gehrmann, 'Substitution Account: No Solution for International Monetary Problems', *Intereconomics* (Hamburg), May–June 1980, as quoted in Joanne Gowa, 'Hegemons, IOs, and Markets: The Case of the Substitution Account', *op. cit.*, p. 665. In addition, it could also be argued that the existence of a substitution account, if it was voluntary, could be destabilizing, unless it clearly supplanted the dollar as the reserve and intervention currency. If not, the problem of instability could manifest itself even more strongly than under the nascent multi-currency system which appeared likely in the late 1970s, and again looks possible in 2011.

49. Interview remarks with the author, Washington. As noted, Kenen's corollary to this statement is on p. 102.
50. J. J. Polak, 'The Impasse Concerning the Role of the SDR', *The Quest for National and Global Economic Stability* (Dordrecht: 1988).
51. Peter Kenen, 'Renovation of the Global Reserve Regime: Concepts and Proposals', CEPS Working Paper no. 208, June 2010, p. 7 as at: http://www.princeton.edu/ceps/workingpapers/208kenen.pdf (accessed 8 June 2011).
52. John Williamson, 'A New SDR Allocation?', *op. cit.*, p. 1.
53. Alexandre Kafka, 'Some IMF Problems After the Committee of XX'—paper prepared for a conference in honour of Jacques J. Polak (mimeo), 4 April 1991, pp. 28, 29 (emphasis added).
54. 'IMF Board of Governors Approves Transformation of Interim Committee', IMF Press Release no. 99/47, http://www.imf.org/external/np/sec/pr/1999/PR9947.htm (accessed 8 June 2011).
55. 'Measures to Strengthen the SDR'—A Report to the Group of 24, UNDP/UNCTAD Project INT/75/015, Studies on International Monetary and Financial Issues for the Developing Countries, UNCTAD Document No. UNCTAD/MFD/TA/11 GE.81-51666. This paper, under the auspices of project director Sidney Dell, recommended, among other things, an increase in SDR allocations of SDR 16 billion, which would be allocated disproportionately in favour of non-oil developing countries (p. 14). See also UNCTAD Discussion Paper No. 1, M.M. Sakbani, 'The Enduring Financial and Monetary Consequences of the US Freeze: An SDR Recycling Proposal', which proposed that the recycling process of OPEC surpluses by linked to SDR substitution (p. 11).
56. Under Article II of the 'Agreement between the United Nations and International Monetary Fund' which came into force on 15 November 1947, representatives of the UN are entitled to attend meetings of the Fund's Board of Governors, and representatives of the Fund may attend meetings of the UN's General Assembly. Under Article XI, the Fund is required to notify the Economic and Social Council (ECOSOC) of any agreements with other specialized agencies. See *Selected Decisions of the International Monetary Fund and Selected Documents*, 13th Issue, IMF (Washington, DC: 1987), pp. 457–8, 462.
57. See Chapter 1, pp. 13, 15, 19 above.
58. Raul Prebisch, *Theoretical and Practical Problems of Economic Growth*, ECLA (Mexico City: May, 1951), UN Document No. E/CN-12/221. While Prebisch's arguments influenced leftist theorists as diverse as André Gunder Frank and the dependencia theorists, Samir Amin and even Immanuel Wallerstein, they also influenced a number of more reformist critics, such as Lester Pearson (former UN diplomat and Canadian Prime Minister) in *Partners in Development* and the Brandt Commission in *North-South: a Programme for Survival?*, Pan Books (London: 1980).
59. Joseph Stiglitz (Chair) 'Report of the Commission of Experts of the President of the United Nations General Assembly on Reforms of the International Monetary and Financial System', United Nations General Assembly (New York: 21 September

2009), at: http://www.un.org/ga/econcrisissummit/docs/FinalReport_CoE.pdf (accessed 8 June 2011).

60. IMF *Survey*, vol. 16, no. 8, 20/4/87, p. 116.
61. Margaret Garritsen de Vries, *The International Monetary Fund, 1972–78, op. cit.*, vol. II, pp. 979–80.
62. Communiqué, G24, in de Vries, *The International Monetary Fund, 1972–78, op. cit.*, vol. III, p. 623–6.
63. Report by the Executive Board on the Development Committee, ibid. p. 624.
64. Margaret Garritsen de Vries, *The International Monetary Fund, 1972–78, op. cit.*, vol. 2, no. 3, pp. 971–2.
65. For instance, a link between the institution of a substitution account and its possible negative impact on developing country access to private financial markets was judged to be relatively small, although the gains from participation in an account, especially if reserves were relatively well diversified, would not necessarily be great either. See P. M. Oppenheimer, 'Impact of a Substitution Account on Euro-Currency and Related Lending to Developing Countries', in S. Dell (ed.), *The International Monetary System and its Reform*, part I, North-Holland for the UN (Amsterdam: 1987), pp. 221, 226.
66. Reserve holdings are one indicator used in measuring a country's financial health. See also ch. 2, pp. 46—50, above.
67. IMF *Survey*, 18/6/79, vol. 8, no. 12, pp. 186–7. And see *George Soros on Globalization*, Public Affairs—Perseus Books (Cambridge, MA: 2002)
68. See preface to S. Dell (ed.), *The International Monetary System and Its Reform* —Papers prepared for the Group of Twenty-Four by a United Nations project directed by Sidney Dell 1979–86; five volumes, published by North-Holland in cooperation with the United Nations (Amsterdam: 1987 (vols. 1–3) and 1990 (vols. 4–5)), vol. I, p. vii; also the foreword to same by Gamani Corea, Secretary-General of UNCTAD, pp. vii–ix.
69. On the former, see David A. Brodsky and Gary P. Sampson, 'The Sources of Exchange Rate Instability in Developing Countries: Dollar, French Franc and SDR Pegging Countries', *Weltwirtschaftliches Archiv*, No. 1 (1984); Gerald Helleiner, *The Impact of the Exchange Rate System on the Developing Countries: A Report to the Group of Twenty-Four* (UNDP/UNCTAD Project, INT/75/015, 1980)—later incorporated in S. Dell (ed.) *The International Monetary System and its Reform* (*op. cit.*); and John Williamson, 'A Survey of the Literature on the Optimal Peg', *Journal of Development Economics* (August 1982). On the latter, see Peter B. Kenen, 'Use of the SDR to Supplement of Substitute for Other Means of Finance', in George M. von Furstenberg (ed.), *International Money and Credit: The Policy Roles* (*op. cit.*).
70. John Williamson, 'Exchange Rate Policy for Developing Countries—A Case for Collective Action', *Journal of Foreign Exchange and International Finance* (India), vol. 1, no. 1. (1987), p. 42.
71. John Williamson and Michael Gavin, Chapter IV, International Liquidity, *International Monetary Issues in 1985*, A Report to the Group of Twenty-Four, Institute for International Economics (mimeo), 7/1/85. See also Peter Kenen, 'Use of the SDR to Supplement of Substitute for Other Means of Finance', in George M. von

Furstenberg, *International Money and Credit: The Policy Roles*, IMF, Washington, 1983 and 'Renovation of the Global Reserve Regime: Concepts and Proposals'", CEPS Working Paper no. 208, June 2010. See also Barry Eichengreen, 'Commercialize the SDR', as at www.project-syndicate.org/commentary/eichengreen4/English (accessed 8 June 2011), and 'Out-of-the-box thoughts about the international financial architecture', *Journal of International Commerce, Economics and Policy*, vol. 1, no. 1, 2010. DeAnne Julius's paper 'A Roadmap for SDR Evolution' appeared in a 2010 Chatham House Report *Beyond the Dollar: Rethinking the International Monetary System*, Paola Subacchi and John Driffill (eds).

72. Margaret Garritsen de Vries, *The International Monetary Fund, 1966–71: System Under Stress*, IMF (Washington, DC: 1978), pp. 84–5, 110–11, 219–20, 245–6.
73. G24 Communiqué, 6/1/76, as at: http://www.g24.org/PDF/01-76ENG.pdf (accessed 16 June 2011).
74. Ibid. para. 8.
75. John Williamson, 'International Monetary Reform: A Survey of the Options', in S. Dell, *op. cit.*, vol. 1, p. 234.
76. Ibid. p. 237.
77. Ibid. p. 273.
78. Ariel Buira, 'The nature and direction of international monetary reform', in S. Dell (ed.), *op. cit.*, vol. III, p. 778–80.
79. Peter Kenen, *Financing, Adjustment and the IMF*, Brookings Studies in International Finance (Washington, DC: 1986), pp. 59–60; see also 'The Substitution Account as a First Step Toward Reform of the International Monetary System', Peterson Institute for International Economics Policy Brief no. PB10-6, March 2010, as at: http://www.piie.com/publications/pb/pb10-06.pdf (accessed 16 June 2011).
80. Ernest Aryeetey, 'A Development-focused Allocation of the Special Drawing Rights', United Nations University (UNU) World Institute for Development Economics Research (WIDER) Discussion Paper no. 2003/3, January 2004, as at: http://www.wider.unu.edu/publications/working-papers/discussion-papers/2004/en_GB/dp2004-003/(accessed 16 June 2011).
81. Rudiger Dornbusch and Stanley Fischer, 'The world debt problem', in S. Dell (ed.), *op. cit.*, vol. III, p. 950.
82. Ibid.
83. *The Economist*, supplement on the Fund, 26/9/81, p. 8. Needless to say, this hubris was reversed within a year; following the Mexican debt moratorium and other sovereign debt difficulties, bankers were grateful for the Fund's presence.
84. George P. Shultz, William E. Simon, and Walter Wriston, 'Who needs the IMF?', *Wall Street Journal*, 3 February 1998.
85. A survey of governors' statements at annual meetings is illustrative of the different positions that are reconciled or laid out at the Fund by the Executive Board and Fund staff. The Board of Governors is only directly involved in the management of the Fund at the annual meeting; resolutions that are passed concerning the bylaws of the Fund may be passed by postal vote.
86. Board of Governors—Resolution no. 27-3, 20/3/72; no. 29-1, 21/1/74; no. 29-2, 4/3/74, respectively, in de Vries, *The IMF, 1972–78*, *op. cit.*, vol III, p. 281.

87. 'Report to Congress on the Use of Special Drawing Rights by IMF Member Countries', US Treasury, August 2010, as at: http://www.treasury.gov/about/organizational-structure/offices/International-Affairs/Documents/Report%20to%20Congress%20on%20SDR%20Use%20–%20August%202010.pdf (accessed 8 June 2011).
88. John W. Head, 'Suspension of Debtor Countries' Voting Rights in the IMF: An Assessment of the Third Amendment to the IMF Charter', *Virginia Journal of International Law*, vol. 33, 1993.
89. K. Alec Chrystal, 'International Money and the Future of the SDR', *Princeton Essays in International Finance* no. 128.
90. U. Sacchetti, 'The SDR: Ten Years of Experience', *BNL Quarterly Review*, December 1979, p. 393.
91. David Lomax, 'International Moneys and Monetary Arrangements in Private Markets', in G. M. von Furstenberg, *op. cit.* Like Chrystal and Sacchetti, Lomax notes that the SDR must receive further institutional support from the IMF, and perhaps even other international agencies such as the BIS to provide a market clearing role (as it did for the ECU).
92. See Chapter 2, pp. 66–7, above.
93. See, e.g. Peter Modeen, 'Operating in SDRs', in L. de V. Wragg (ed.), *Composite Currencies—SDRs, ECUs, and other Instruments*, Euromoney Publications (London: 1984).
94. L. de V. Wragg, 'The development of commercial uses of the SDR', in L. de V. Wragg (ed.), *op. cit.*, pp. 51, 52.
95. In the wake of the EMS crisis in late 1992, for example, the issue market in ECUs dried up completely. The 1992 crisis was by no means the first, however, and as we have seen since the birth of the Euro, crises have not been banished. A prescient discussion of current pressures on the Euro affecting some of its members is reflected in earlier German reticence for the asset in the absence of greater economic integration—see Wilhelm Nolling (President of the State Central Bank, Hamburg and member of the Central Monetary Policy Council of the Bundesbank), 'Why Real Integration Should Come First', in which he cautions against 'extensive private use of the Ecu and a premature further institutional development of the EMS', *Financial Times*, Wednesday, 27/3/85, p. 17. Although the Euro was flawlessly introduced in 2001, following the global financial crisis in 2009, strains in the Euro system have re-emerged. Since the German-backed bailouts of Greece in 2010 and 2011 and Ireland in 2011 these calls have proliferated, including in Germany. See, for example, 'EU Cacophony Reveals Market Doubts on Euro Zone', as at: http://uk.reuters.com/article/2011/02/14/uk-eurozone-doubts-idUKLNE71D02Y20110214 (accessed 8 June 2011).
96. 'The Role of the SDR in the International Monetary System', IMF *Occasional Paper no. 51*, (Washington: March, 1987), pp. 50, 51.
97. The apogee of post-Bretton Woods hopes for the SDR rested with J. J. Polak, 'Thoughts on an International Monetary Fund Based Fully on the SDR', IMF Pamphlet no. 28, 1979. Robert Mundell's more recent thoughts on a world currency that does not supplant others is in 'The International Monetary System and

the Case for a World Currency', Leon Koźmiński Academy of Entrepreneurship and Management (WSPiZ) and TIGER, Distinguished Lectures Series n. 12, Warsaw, 23 October 2003, as at: http://www.tiger.edu.pl/publikacje/dist/mundell2.pdf (accessed 8 June 2011).

98. Peter B. Kenen, 'Use of the SDR to supplement or substitute for other means of Finance', in George M. von Furstenberg, *op. cit.*, p. 257.
99. Denominating commodities such as oil in SDRs, first suggested in the late 1970s as the dollar fell and the prospects of a multicurrency reserve system increased—needless to say echoed in the wake of the 2008 financial crisis when the same set of circumstances prevailed—are hampered because of the lack of liquid markets in SDRs.
100. Peter Kenen, 'The Substitution Account as a First Step Toward Reform of the International Monetary System', Peterson Institute for International Economic Policy Brief no. PB10-6, March 2010, p. 7.
101. Decision No. 6631-(80/145) G/S, 17 September 1980, in *Selected Decisions, op. cit.*, 13th issue, p. 324.
102. Ibid. pp. 7–8.
103. IMF *Survey*, vol. 16, September 1987, Supplement on the Fund, p. 7.
104. J. J. Polak, 'Thoughts on an International Monetary Fund Based Fully on the SDR', IMF Pamphlet Series, No. 28. (Washington, DC: 1979), p. 3. Although noting that he was writing in a personal capacity, Polak was the IMF's research director at the time. Polak addresses the reasons for the lack of progress with the SDR during the 1980s in 'The Impasse Concerning the Role of the SDR' (*op. cit.*).
105. John Williamson, 'Why SDRs Could Rival the Dollar', Peterson Institute Policy Brief no. PB09-20, September 2009; Peter Kenen, 'An SDR Based Reserve System', *Journal of Globalization and Development*, vol. 1, no. 2, 2010, as at: http://www.bepress.com/jgd/vol1/iss2/art13 (accessed 8 June 2011).
106. George M. von Furstenberg (ed.), *International Money and Credit: The Policy Roles* (Washington, DC: 1983); Michael Mussa, James M. Broughton, and Peter Isard (eds), *The Future of the SDR in Light of Changes in the International Financial System—Proceedings of a Seminar held in Washington, D.C. 18–19 March 1996*, IMF (Washington, DC: 1996).
107. Peter B. Clark and Jacques J. Polak, 'International Liquidity and the role of the SDR in the International Monetary System', *IMF Staff Papers*, vol. 51, no.1, 2004.
108. Paul Volcker and Toyoo Gyohten, *Changing Fortunes, op. cit.*, p. 295.
109. See Chapter 4, pp. 122–3; also Mr. Volckere's involvement in the Palais-Royal initiative, as at n. 35, Chapter 4, above.
110. De Vries, *The IMF 1972–78, op. cit.*, vol. II, p. 771, n. 11.
111. P. Kenen, 'Changing views about the role of the SDR and implications for its attributes', in S. Dell (ed.), *The International Monetary System and its Reform*, vol. II, North-Holland for the UN (Amsterdam: 1987), p. 379.
112. As managing director Michel Camdessus's second term progressed, however, he, in common with most of his predecessors and successors, expressed his support for a universal SDR allocation. See IMF *Survey*, 2 May 1994; 'IMF Split Over Plan to Boost World Reserves', *Financial Times*, 3 October 1994, p. 1.

113. J. J. Polak, 'The Impasse Concerning the Role of the SDR', *op. cit.*, p. 183
114. See John Williamson and Michael Gavin, 'International Monetary Issues in 1985—A Report to the Group of Twenty-Four', Institute for International Economics (mimeo), 7/1/85, p. 38.
115. IMF *Survey*, vol. 15, no. 8. 21/4/86, p. 116.
116. 'Get Ready for a World Currency' (cover story), *The Economist*, 9/1/88, pp. 9–10, 74–5. This was all the more notable since less than three years earlier in a survey on international monetary reform, *The Economist* had written 'The cranks who think that there should be a world currency or that money should be based on something solid (granite was one suggestion in your correspondent's postbag) may all be talking nonsense . . . ', *The Economist*, special survey on International Monetary Reform, 5/10/85, p. 5.

    This particular form of hedging is not untypical. Many of the observers who have at times referred to the idealism and impracticality inherent in an SDR-based system have hedged their bets by writing that in preparing for the long term (ie. the twenty-first century), work on an international currency, and the SDR, must continue. See, for example, R. N. Cooper, 'A Monetary System for the Future', *Foreign Affairs,* Fall 1984, pp. 166–84, and more recently Paul Volcker, 'Toward a Single World Currency to Level the Playing Field', *International Herald Tribune*, as at: http://www.iht.com/articles/2000/01/31/edpaul.2.t_0.php (accessed 8 June 2011).
117. *Financial Times*, 26/4/91, p. 8.
118. OECD Press Release: 'Address by Mr Jean-Claude Paye, Secretary General of the OECD, to the Parliamentary Assembly of the Council of the Council of Europe', Strasbourg, Thursday, 30 September 1993, p. 8.
119. See 'US and Britain Propose Boost to Reserves of Poorer IMF Members', *Financial Times*, 19 September 1994, p. 18.
120. See 'IMF Split Over Plan to Boost World Reserves', *Financial Times*, 3 October 1994, p. 1; also 'Spanner in the Rolls-Royce Engine', *Financial Times*, 4 October 1994, p. 17.
121. Edwin Truman (ed.), *Reforming the IMF for the 21st Century*, Peterson Institute for International Economics (Washington, DC: April 2006).
122. Karin Lissakers, 'Is the SDR a Monetary Dodo? This Bird May Still Fly', in Edwin Truman (ed.), *Reforming the IMF for the 21st Century, op. cit.*, p. 484.
123. See 'Federal Reserve's Exit Strategy'—Federal Reserve Board Chairman Bernanke's statement to the House Committee on Financial Services, 10 February 2010, as at: http://www.federalreserve.gov/newsevents/testimony/bernanke20100210a.htm (accessed 8 June 2011).
124. Para 5 of the Leader's statement read as follows: 'The agreements we have reached today, to treble resources available to the IMF to $750 billion, to support a new SDR allocation of $250 billion, to support at least $100 billion of additional lending by the MDBs, to ensure $250 billion of support for trade finance, and to use the additional resources from agreed IMF gold sales for concessional finance for the poorest countries, constitute an additional $1.1 trillion programme of support to restore credit, growth and jobs in the world economy. Together with

the measures we have each taken nationally, this constitutes a global plan for recovery on an unprecedented scale.' See London Summit—Leaders' Statement, 2 April 2009—see: http://www.g20.org/Documents/g20_communique_020409.pdf (accessed 8 June 2011).

125. 'US Congress Vote Marks Big Step for IMF Reform, Funding', *IMF Survey online*, 18 June 2009; available at: http://www.imf.org/external/pubs/ft/survey/so/2009/NEW061809A.htm (accessed 16 June 2011).
126. 'Why Supplanting the Dollar Would Be Good for America', *Time*, 9 April 2009.
127. Soros's call for an SDR allocation focused on development appeared in his 2002 work *George Soros on Globalization*, Public Affairs—Perseus Books (Cambridge, MA: 2002); the Bank of China's Governor Zhou Xiaochuan's call for a greater role for SDRs appeared in a short paper prior to the G20 meetings in London entitled 'Reform the International Monetary System'—see: http://www.pbc.gov.cn/publish/english/956/2009/20091229104425550619706/20091229104425550619706_.html (accessed 16 June 2011).
128. See, for example, Michael Bordo and Barry Eichengreen (eds), *A Restrospective on the Bretton Woods System: Lessons for International Monetary Reform,* University of Chicago Press/NBER (Chicago: 1993); also Edwin Truman, *Reforming the IMF for the 21st Century*, Peterson Institute for International Economics (Washington, DC: April 2006).
129. UN Millenium Project at: http://www.unmillenniumproject.org/reports/index_overview.htm (accessed 8 June 2011); see also the follow-up report in 2005 at: http://www.unmillenniumproject.org/documents/overviewEng36-55LowRes.pdf (accessed 8 June 2011).
130. John Williamson, 'Why SDRs Could Rival the Dollar', Peterson Institute Policy Brief no. PB09-20, September 2009.
131. José Antonio Ocampo, 'Special Drawing Rights and the Reform of the Global Reserve System', Group of 24, September 2009, p. 4, http://www.g24.org/PDF/jao0909.pdf (accessed 16 June 2011).
132. George Soros 'Financing the Fight Against Climate Change', http://www.project-syndicate.org/commentary/soros55/English (accessed 8 June 2011), December 2009.
133. 'IMF Proposes 'Green Fund' for Climate Change Financing', World Economic Forum, IMF Survey Press Release, 30 January 2010; see also 'Financing the Response to Climate Change', Hugh Bredenkamp and Catherine Pattillo, IMF Staff Position Note SPN10/06, 25 March 2010.
134. Re Bank of China's Governor Zhou call for a greater role for SDRs, see n. 127, above. This was followed by a G20 meeting in Nanjing in March 2011 (suggested by French President and G20 host Nicolas Sarkozy) at which the relationship between the Chinese Yuan and SDR was discussed.
135. Bergsten, C. Fred. 'The Dollar and the Deficits: How Washington Can Prevent the Next Crisis', Foreign Affairs, vol. 88, no. 6, November/December 2009. See also John Williamson, 'Why SDRs Could Rival the Dollar', Peterson Institute *Policy Brief* no. PB09-200, September, 2009.

136. 'Report of the Commission of Experts of the President of the United Nations General Assembly on Reforms of the International Monetary and Financial System' (the 'Stiglitz Report'), 21 September 2009, pp. 115–20. See http://www.un.org/ga/econcrisissummit/docs/FinalReport_CoE.pdf (accessed 16 June 2011) .
137. 'Reserve Shifts Can Be Destabilizing'—see H. Johannes Witteveen, 'Developing a New International Monetary System: A Long-Term View', the1983 Per Jacobsson Lecture (Washington, DC: 1983), p. 6, as at: http://www.perjacobsson.org/lectures/1983.pdf (accessed 8 June 2011); echoed in Peter Kenen's observation that reserve shifts by central banks have in general been destabilizing. Peter Kenen, 'Use of the SDR to Supplement or Substitute for Other Means of Finance', *op. cit.*, 1983; also his 'The Substitution Account as a First Step Toward Reform of the International Monetary System', Peterson Institute Policy Brief no. PB10-6, March, 2010, *op. cit.*
138. Richard Cooper, 'Is SDR Creation Inflationary?', special annex to 'Enhancing International Monetary Stability—A Role for the SDR?', IMF Strategy, Policy, and Review Department, 7 January 2011, as at: http://www.imf.org/external/np/pp/eng/2011/010711.pdf (accessed 8 June 2011).
139. In September 2010, Malaysia's central bank bought renminbi-denominated bonds for its reserves, facilitated in part to China having opened its domestic interbank bond market to foreign central banks. See 'Malaysian bond boost for Renminbi', in http://www.ft.com/cms/s/0/fecc16fc-c417-11df-b827-00144feab49a.html (accessed 8 June 2011). And in November 2010, Russia admitted that the Canadian dollar was an increasing part of Russian reserves—see 'Russia Adds Canadian Dollar to Reserves, Australian Currency May Be Next', http://www.bloomberg.com/news/2010-11-24/russia-adds-canadian-dollar-to-reserves-eyes-other-currencies.html (accessed 8 June 2011).
140. An idea entertained by the Fund (see nn. 1 and 2, Chapter 6, above), and forewarned by Richard Cooper (see Conclusion, p. 241, below).
141. J. J. Polak 'The Impasse Concerning the Role of the SDR', *op. cit.,* p. 186. This in fact continued to be echoed even during the nadir for SDR prospects—the US and UK, for exampled, proposed a limited SDR allocation that was to evolve into the Fourth Amendment proposals. See 'US and Britain Propose Boost to Reserves of Poorer IMF Members', *Financial Times*, 18 September 1994, p. 18.
142. During the 1980s by J. J. Polak in ibid. pp. 185–6, and more forcefully by John Williamson in 'A New SDR Allocation?', *op. cit.,* pp. 38–40. Regarding George Soros's call, see n. 127, above.
143. London Summit—Leaders' Statement, 2 April 2009—see: http://www.g20.org/Documents/g20_communique_020409.pdf (accessed 8 June 2011).

7

Conclusion

There are a number of themes concerning the Special Drawing Right (SDR) that emerged from our examination of the genesis of the Rio Agreement in Chapter 1. These set the stage for our investigation in the rest of the book. First of all, the Rio Agreement and the institution of SDRs was a compromise that had many important antecedents dating back to the Bretton Woods negotiations at the end of the World War II. The essence of the Rio Agreement lay simply in the institution of the SDR, which was to be administered by an International Monetary Fund (IMF) rejuvenated by the First Amendment to its Articles of Agreement. Notably, despite the reform encompassed in the revised Articles, SDRs were a buttress to prevailing international monetary arrangements, particularly the role of the dollar. The entity that came to fruition was a new form of liquidity, created by fiat, with the intention of supplementing existing reserve assets as needed. Despite this understatement, the birth of SDRs heralded widespread enthusiasm for its future role, including one in the private market. Without further political support, however, this optimism was misplaced. And the character of SDRs as a prospective substitute rather than simply a supplement for existing reserve assets under Bretton Woods arrangements also complicated matters: this potential 'substitutability' of SDRs for other reserve assets, particularly the dollar, was a characteristic which was to periodically reemerge during the next 40 years, and which coloured its future development in the eyes of both its supporters and detractors.

In Chapter 2 we examined the mechanisms surrounding SDRs during the First Allocation in 1970–2. The SDR Department functioned smoothly at this time, a very difficult period of transition from Bretton Woods arrangements. The SDR's primary purpose, however, was to shore up prevailing arrangements, and it was at precisely the time of the first allocation that Bretton Woods arrangements broke down. In its current guise, SDRs could not respond to an explosion in global liquidity. Partly in response to this, the SDR was seized upon by many observers, including those at the Fund and the Committee of Twenty, as a key element in prospective reform plans for the post-Bretton Woods system—although it must be recalled that the institution of the C-20 was in fact an attempt to address increasingly irreconcilable views on the international monetary system. For a time, the Fund was to link the future of its role in international monetary system with that of a role for SDRs. In a pattern that was to be repeated, the nascent acceptance of the SDR in private markets was not encouraged.

Plainly, a role for the SDR was circumscribed in the new system, and some of the reasons for this were ascertained in the changing role of the US in international monetary arrangements, which was the focus of Chapters 3 and 4. The growing divergence between the reform plans and prospects for the SDR, echoed later in optimistic prognoses for the SDR as their marginalization continued, necessitated an injection of political realism, indeed a neo-realist approach to an examination of US policy determination. In Chapter3, we noted increasing complexities in the formulation of US policy reflected in the continuation of a form of 'ad hoccery' and the growing complexities in international monetary policy determination within the US administration. With respect to the SDR, by the early 1980s, apart from brief periods of interest inevitably at a time of dollar weakness, the US had abandoned a greater role for it for and would continue to do so for the next 30 years.

Disparate strains in policy formulation in the US administration also prompted a closer look at the SDR and the US international monetary policy process in Chapter 4. This confirmed a number of findings: first, the notions of 'ad hoccery' in US policy making, in the tradition of Robert Roosa, then, with a different emphasis, Nixon's 'benign neglect' (simply called 'muddling through' by Gowa[1]) is also discernable in the US approach to international monetary relations in the post-Bretton Woods era, notwithstanding the fact that the US undeniably turned away from the SDR. Second, the importance of both individual policy makers and their ideas, as well as the institutional structure of the state apparatus in which they operate, should not be discounted in any account of the evolution of US international monetary policy towards the SDR. This is certainly true at the Treasury and Federal Reserve, but also the State Department and in the growing role of Congress. These themes do not lend themselves easily to a comprehensive *theory* of US policy making, although as an explanation it does point to a confirmation of the strains we noted in Chapter 3.

One of the most important phenomena in this context is that the increasing role of Congress is fundamental to an understanding of the growing complexity of US international monetary policy formulation in the post-Bretton Woods era, as well as US policy approaches to the SDR. While we noted the long term cyclical nature of Congressional power in US policy determination, we also noted the strong involvement of Congress in US international monetary policy in the 1970s, including an unequivocal 'no' to the substitution account well before the administration came to this same conclusion. This increased role of Congress had negative consequences for the SDR, with the 12-year hiatus between implicit US administration approval of the Fourth Amendment in 1997 and Congress's concurrence in 2009 only the most recent example of this. Finally, changing structural influences in US international monetary policy determination all tended to reinforce the moves away from the SDR as post-Bretton Woods arrangements consolidated themselves. Until the financial crisis in 2008, a greater role for SDRs under these new arrangements was increasingly perceived as antithetical to US interests.

As this dynamic first became evident, however, the Second Amendment negotiations began, and this necessitated a return to an examination of the IMF and its relationship to the SDR. One theme that emerged throughout this book is that the Fund has evolved into an entity with its own perspective and views concerning the functioning of the international monetary system. An appreciation of the changing role of the IMF as an international institution is extremely important in any account of the evolution of recent international monetary arrangements. Related to the growth of other international institutions, such as the EU and the UN, this is not a surprising development in postwar international relations, as noted by Robert Keohane and others, but it has not been given commensurate attention with respect to the IMF.[2] In part, this niche for the IMF has been due to a succession of strong managing directors and Fund staff that worked on utility and future of SDRs despite the evolution of monetary arrangements away from public international monetary management.

Chapter 5 and the negotiation of the Second Amendment consolidated two of our most important themes—the fundamental importance of the US to the success or more particularly failure of SDR initiatives, and yet also the continued evolution of the IMF as an independent institution with its own agenda and interests, which were linked to the fortunes of the SDR through the Second Amendment negotiations and beyond. Noting the importance of the US regarding the *failure* of initiatives is to note a 'negative capability' of the US—first, regarding the Fed's position in US policy determination, and second with respect to the US stance at the Fund as a whole. Domestically, in much the same way that the Federal Reserve has a stronger capacity to block US international monetary policy initiatives rather than to garner support for them, the US at the Fund has a stronger capacity to block initiatives it opposes rather than guarantee support for proposals that it supports.

Indeed the Fund had a strong influence on the agenda of the negotiations of the Second Amendment to its Articles of Agreement. This resulted in important achievements vis-à-vis the flexibility embodied in the Jamaica Agreement,[3] which also included the incorporation of a role for the SDR in international monetary arrangements should its membership ever decide that to be necessary. And a case has been made for a reappraisal of the relative achievements of the First and Second Amendments of the Fund's Articles of Agreement: over time the accomplishments of the First Amendment have arguably been over-emphasized whereas the opposite is true of the Second Amendment. In turn, however, this was to have longer-term implications for the SDR: following the Second Amendment the continuation of an admittedly circumscribed role for the Fund under the new international monetary arrangements was established. As the Fund adjusted itself to the new system, however, seeds were sown for a decreasing identification of its role with that of its prime *casus belli* in the years before the Second Amendment, namely the SDR.

In the final chapter, as post-Bretton Woods arrangements consolidated themselves, it became apparent that earlier aspirations engendered by the IMF for the SDR were not to be realized. Again this had much to do with continuing power asymmetries among the key players in the post-Bretton Woods system, particularly, of course, the continued influence of the US and the widespread acceptance of these arrangements. Developing country influence on these arrangements, and on the SDR, proved to be even less than had appeared to be the case in the 1970s. Recognizing this, the Fund gradually disengaged from a more important role for the SDR in the international monetary system, while quietly accommodating changes that could accommodate a greater role for it in the future. Despite official pronouncements, approval in principle of the Fourth Amendment to the Articles of Agreement in 1997 (not ratified until 2009) was just one of several developments affecting the SDR that turned out to be more significant than they appeared at the time.

In many respects, the evolution of the international monetary system since 1971 seemed irrelevant to the mechanisms surrounding the SDR as it evolved. Nonetheless, variable but continued interest in the SDR was evident. Initially, Eurobanks took the SDR seriously, and began denominating various financial derivatives in SDRs in the 1970s and early 1980s. Without further official support, however, these markets never really developed and instead, the SDR was not abandoned but rather awkwardly grafted on to the new system. As a result, it did not grow into a strong supporting branch of the new international monetary arrangements. Indeed the marginalization of the SDR at times appeared so far advanced that, in Richard Cooper's words, at times it appeared 'in danger of atrophying into irrelevance'.[4] In this book, however, a case has been made for a reexamination of influences on the development of the SDR to better understand its recent history and future prospects. This reexamination is also valuable in the context of the evolution of US and IMF post-Bretton Woods international monetary policies, and the politics of international monetary relations in general.

The transition to post-Bretton Woods arrangements for SDRs may therefore be viewed as painful and disappointing only when measured against the very grand hopes for them that we witnessed at their birth. As post-Bretton Woods monetary arrangements consolidated themselves, the US increasingly perceived SDRs as irrelevant to their national interests. The IMF, after closely identifying its own future prospects with the SDR, eventually came to a similar conclusion with respect to both its own and wider systemic interests. Notably, however, both the US and IMF turned to SDRs to assist in responding to the international financial crisis in 2009. With the ratification of the Fourth Amendment to the Articles of Agreement and resultant allocation of SDR 21.4 billion, as well as the special allocation of SDR 161.2 billion, SDRs again became a significant component of international reserves. Significantly, this transpired under a very different system of liquidity provision and indeed very different international monetary circumstances than initially envisioned for the asset.

Thus, for the first time in over 30 years, SDRs are an important item on the international monetary agenda. Notably, many underlying issues remain similar to those unresolved 30 years ago. Old files are being revisited on the desirability of a clearinghouse for SDRs in the private market, regular allocations of SDRs—perhaps biased towards development finance—and the advantages of an SDR substitution account. The Fund, including successive managing directors interested in these same underlying issues, as well as an international monetary community taking into account newly important actors such as the BRICs—particularly China—have begun to reexamine the prospective role of the SDR, emphasizing its potential role in enhancing international monetary stability.[5]

In many respects, SDRs have returned to where they were when awkwardly introduced to the world in the late 1960s: full of promise and potential to buttress existing and reformed international monetary arrangements. In sum, the short but chequered history of the SDR is more relevant than ever to debates about the future of a stable international monetary system and a healthy international economy that depends on it.

Notes

1. Joanne Gowa, *Closing the Gold Window* (*op. cit.*)
2. The UN and *some* of its related agencies' contribution to the changing nature of international society had enjoyed its heyday in the 1960s and 1970s. See J. Martin Rochester, 'The Rise and Fall or International Organization as a Field of Study', *International Organization*, Autumn 1986.

3. As noted in Chapter 6, Peter Kenen, DeAnne Julius and the late Jacques Polak have all suggested that in limited aspects the role of SDRs could be further enhanced without additional amendments.
4. R. N. Cooper—comment on P. B. Kenen's 'Use of the SDR to supplement or substitute for other means of finance' in G. M. von Furstenberg (ed.), *International Money and Credit: The Policy Roles*, *op. cit.*, p. 361.
5. One of the implicit concerns addressed in this context is the instability that can result in a multiple reserve currency system, particularly at a time of dollar weakness. See 'Enhancing International Monetary Stability – A Role for the SDR?', IMF paper prepared by the Strategy, Policy, and Review Department, 7 January 2011, as at: http://www.imf.org/external/np/pp/eng/2011/010711.pdf (accessed 8 June 2011).

APPENDIX 1

IMF documents and executive board minutes relating to the Second Amendment to the IMF's Articles of Agreement

The following is a table of contents for the three volumes of documents and three volumes of minutes relating to the negotiation of the Second Amendment of the IMF's Articles of Agreement in 1974–6. (In the volumes themselves, the contents pages list the documents by document number only.) The volumes were released to a limited audience in 1980 and an index followed in 1986. In 1996, the IMF began to increase public access to documentation. See also notes at the end of this Appendix.

Appendix 1

Documents

Volume I, Part 1—Documents Issued 3 April 1974–13 May 1975

Document No.	Title	Page Refs.
SM/74/72	Possible Changes in the General Account	1–5
Press Release 74/32	Communiqué of the Committee of the Board of Governors on International Monetary Reform and Related Issues (inc. detailed statement)	6–14
DAA/74/1	Draft Amendments on Establishment of a Council (inc six supplements)	15–14
DAA/74/2	Draft Amendment of Provisions on Repurchase (inc. supplements)*	115–46
DAA/74/3	Payments on Changes in Quotas, Charges, Interest, Remuneration, Distribution of Net Income (inc. supplement)*	147–71
DAA/74/4	Draft Amendments on Use of the Fund's Resources (inc. supplement)*	172–86
DAA/74/5	Draft Amendments on Legalization of Floating (inc. supplements)	187–214
DAA/74/6	Commentary on Draft Amendments DAA/74/2, 3 and 4*	215–19
DAA/74/7	Draft Amendment of Provisions on Reconstitution*	220–5
DAA/74/8	Draft Amendment on Avoidance of Trade Measures for Balance of Payments Reasons (inc. supplement)	226–41
DAA/74/9	Draft Amendment on the 'Link' and on Other Holders of Special Drawing Rights*	242–61
DAA/74/10	Draft Amendment on Investment	262–81
DAA/74/11	Draft Provisions of Article XXV on Operations and Transactions in SDRs (inc. supplement)*	282–324
DAA/74/12	Draft Amendments on SDRs: Opting Out*	325–30
DAA/74/13	A General View of Proposed Amendments to the Articles*	331–9
DAA/74/14	Objectives of Draft Amendments Already Issued*	340–3
DAA/74/15	Special Majorities and Participations for the Adoption of Decisions	344–55
DAA/74/16	Draft Report to the Interim Committee on Amendment of the Articles of Agreement (inc. revisions)*	356–449
DAA/75/1	Annotated List of DAA Memoranda on Revised Draft Amendments of the Articles of Agreement*	450–3
Press Release 75/2	Press Communiqué of the Interim Committee of the Board of Governors on the International Monetary System	454–6
DAA/75/2	Comprehensive Draft Amendment of the Articles of Agreement (and corrections) and Supplements*	457–837
DAA/75/3	Commentary on Comprehensive Draft Amendment of the Articles of Agreement*	838–74
SM/75/68	Direct Fund Financing of Buffer Stocks	875–82
DAA/75/4	Special Majorities and Participations for the Adoption of Decisions under the Comprehensive Draft Amendment of the Articles of Agreement	883–95
DAA/75/5	Comprehensive Draft Amendment—Distribution and Delegation of Powers	896–932
DAA/75/6	Majority Required for Decisions to Admit Governments to Membership and Prescribe Terms for Membership	933–6
SM/75/87	Substitution of SDRs for Currencies in Fund Drawings—Alternative Proposals for Article V, Section 3(f)*	937–40
SM/75/94	A Substitution Account for Gold	941–4
EBD/75/113	Comprehensive Draft Amendment of the Articles of Agreement—Commentary by Mr Cross on Alternative Approach to Article IV on Exchange Rate Arrangements	945–50
EBD/75/111	Remarks by Mr Smit—Draft Amendment of the Articles of Agreement—Revised Provisions on Gold	951–4
DAA/75/7	Draft Provisions on Gold: Variant C	955–9
DAA/75/8	Termination of Par Values	960–9
SM/75/112	Buffer Stocks and Compensatory Financing (and revisions)	970–82
SM/75/114	The Majority for Decisions on the Method of Valuation of the SDR (Article XIX, Section 2)*	983–5

Volume I, Part 2—Documents Issued 16 May 1975–28 January 1976

Document No.	Title	Page Refs.
SM/75/120	Draft Report of the Executive Directors to the Interim Committee on Amendment (inc. revisions and supplements)*	987–1100
DAA/75/9	Draft Amendment of the Articles of Agreement (inc. supplement)*	1101–261
DAA/75/10	Draft Amendment of the Articles of Agreement: Changes	1262–382
EBD/75/143	Aide-Mémoire of the Chairman of the Interim Committee	1383–90
DAA/75/11	Draft Amendment of the Articles of Agreement—Effect of Purchases Under the Buffer Stock Facility on a Member's Reserve Position in the Fund	1391–4
DAA/75/12	Reconstitution (inc. supplement)*	1395–402
DAA/75/13	Decisions on Valuation of SDR—Majority of Voting Power*	1403–9
SM/75/205	Possible Provisions of a Gold Substitution Account	1410–15
SM/75/211	Reconsideration of the Norm of 75% in Relation to Draft Amendments, Quota Payments, and the Possibility of Establishing 100% as the Norm	1416–27
SM/75/217	Report on the Work of the Executive Directors Since the Third Meeting of the Interim Committee (inc. revisions)*	1428–43
Press Release 75/40	Press Communiqué of the Interim Committee of the Board of Governors on the International Monetary System	1444–7
SM/75/237	Changes in the Norm of 75% Quota—Legal Implications	1448–51
DAA/75/14	Draft Amendment of the Articles of Agreement—Provisions Relating to the 'Norm' (inc. supplement)	1452–67
DAA/75/15	Draft Amendment of the Articles of Agreement—Provisions	1468–77
DAA/75/16	Draft Article V, Section 3(e) and Draft Article V, Section 7(j)*	1478–80
DAA/75/17	Draft Amendments of the Articles of Agreement—Revised Provisions Relating to Investment (inc. supplements)	1481–92
DAA/75/18	Revised Draft Provision on the Method of Valuation of the SDR: Article XIX, Section 2*	1493–4
DAA/75/19	Draft Amendment of the Articles of Agreement—Gold Substitution Account*	1495–502
EBD/75/261	Conference on the Law of the World	1503–4
DAA/75/20	Draft Amendments—Revised Provisions on Gold (inc. supplements)	1505–34
DAA/75/21	Majorities Under the Comprehensive Draft Amendment	1535–45
DAA/75/22	Draft Amendment of the Articles of Agreement—Provisions Relating to the 'Norm' (inc. supplements)	1546–56
SM/75/292	Amendment of the Articles of Agreement—Draft Report of the Executive Directors to the Interim Committee (inc. correction, revisions, and supplements)*	1557–635
DAA/75/23	Draft Amendment of the Articles of Agreement—Gold Substitution Account*	1636–43
DAA/75/24	Drafts on Exchange Arrangements (inc. supplement)	1644–54
EBD/75/276	Communiqué of the Ministerial Meeting of the Group of Ten*	1655–6
DAA/75/25	Latest Versions of Provisions of Comprehensive Draft Amendment (inc. correction and supplement)	1657–73
DAA/76/1	Comprehensive Draft Amendment	1676–767
DAA/76/2	Amendment—Majorities	1768–73
DAA/76/3	Amendment—Residual Issues*	1774–82
DAA/76/4	Comprehensive Draft Amendment (inc. supplement)*	1783–994

Appendix 1

Volume I, Part 3—Documents Issued 2 February 1976–25 June 1976

Document No.	Title	Page Refs.
DAA/76/5	Draft Report to the Board of Governors on Amendment (inc. revision and supplements)	1995–2242
DAA/76/6	Comprehensive Draft Amendment: Latest Version (inc. corrections)*	2243–336
DAA/76/7	Comprehensive Draft Amendment: Appointment of Executive Directors Under Article XII, Section 3(c)	2337–40
DAA/76/8	Comprehensive Draft Amendment: Election of Executive Directors Under Article XII, Section 3(b)	2341–54
DAA/76/9	Comprehensive Draft Amendment (inc. supplement)*	2355–451
DAA/76/10	Draft Decision of the Executive Directors on Amendment (inc. supplements)	2452–8
DAA/76/11	Proposed Second Amendment to the Articles of Agreement—Report by the Executive Directors to the board of Governors	2459–839
EBS/75/199	Disposition of Gold Under Schedule B, Paragraph 7(a) of Proposed Second Amendment	2840–2
SM/76/145	Second Amendment of the Articles—A First Syllabus of Changes in and Additions to Policies and Decisions of the Fund	2843–8

Minutes

Volume II, Part 1—Minutes of Executive Board Meetings from 19 April 1974 to 4 April 1975

Minute No.	Title	Date	Page Refs.
EBM/74/35	Possible Changes in the General Account	19/4/74	1–9
EBM/74/36	Possible Changes in the General Account	19/4/74	10–30
EBM/74/92	Draft Amendments—Establishment of a Council	24/7/74	31–55
EBM/74/101	Draft Amendments—Provisions on Repurchase	9/8/74	56–68
EBM/74/104	Draft Amendments—Payments on Changes in Quotas, Charges, Interest, Remuneration, and Distribution of Net income	15/8/74	69–83
EBM/74/107	Draft Amendments—Payments on Changes in Quotas, Charges, Interest, Remuneration, and Distribution of Net Income*	4/9/74	84–107
	Draft Amendments—Use of Fund Resources		
EBM/74/108	Draft Amendments—Use of Fund Resources	4/9/74	108–22
EBM/74/109	Draft Amendments—Legalization of Floating	6/9/74	123–48
EBM/74/110	Draft Amendments—Legalization of Floating Draft Amendments—Investment	6/9/74	149–64
EBM/74/111	Draft Amendments—Provisions on Reconstitution*	9/9/74	165–75
EBM/74/113	Draft Composite Resolution—Committees of Board of Governors and Immediate Steps*	11/9/74	176–82
EBD/74/177	7. Special Interests of Developing Countries*	6/9/74	183–4
	9. Amendments to the Articles of Agreement*		

EBM/74/116	Draft Amendments—Provisions of Article XXV on Operations and Transactions in SDRs*	16/9/74	185–98
EBM/74/117	Draft Amendments: a. Provisions of Article XXV on Operations and Transactions in SDRs*	16/9/74	199–215
	b. SDRs: Opting Out*		
EBM/74/118	Draft Composite Resolution—Committees of Board of Governors and Immediate Steps	18/9/74	216–21
EBM/74/119	Draft Composite Resolution—Committees of Board of Governors and Immediate Steps	18/9/74	222–34
EBD/74/177 (rev. 1)	7. Special Interests of Developing Countries*	12/9/74	235–6
	9. Amendments to the Articles of Agreement*		
EBM/74/122	Draft Composite Resolution—Committees of Board of Governors and Immediate Steps*	20/9/74	237–46
EBM/74/128	Draft Amendments—Avoidance of Trade Measures	16/10/74	247–61
EBM/74/130	Draft Amendments—The 'Link' and Other Holders of SDRs*	18/10/74	262–80
EBM/74/133	Draft Amendments—Establishment of a Council	25/10/74	281–6
EBM/74/134	Draft Amendments—Establishment of a Council	25/10/74	287–303
EBM/74/136	Draft Amendments—Establishment of a Council	1/11/74	304–21
EBM/74/137	Draft Amendments—Establishment of a Council	1/11/74	322–37
EBM/74/141	Draft Amendments—Establishment of a Council	8/11/74	338–48
EBM/74/144	Draft Amendments—A General View of Proposed Amendments to Articles	13/11/74	349–63
EBM/74/145	Draft Amendments—Program of Work	15/11/74	364–86
EBM/74/159	Amendment of Articles of Agreement—Draft Report to Interim Committee	19/12/74	387–411
EBM/74/160	Amendment of Articles of Agreement—Draft Report to Interim Committee	19/12/74	412–31
EBM/74/161	Amendment of Articles of Agreement—Draft Report to Interim Committee	20/12/74	432–47
EBM/74/164	Amendment of Articles of Agreement—Draft Report to Interim Committee*	23/12/74	448–70
EBM/74/165	Amendment of the Articles of Agreement—Report to Interim Committee	23/12/74	471–5
EBM/75/9	Draft Amendments—Payments on Changes in Quotas, Charges, Interest, Remuneration, and Distribution of Net Income	3/2/75	476–99
EBM/75/10	Draft Amendments—Payments on Changes in Quotas, Charges, Interest, Remuneration, and Distribution of Net Income*	3/2/75	500–17
EBM/75/13	Draft Amendments—Payments on Changes in Quotas, Charges, Interest, Remuneration, and Distribution of Net Income	10/2/75	518–37
	Draft Amendments—Provisions on Repurchase and Transitional Provisions on Payment of Additional Subscriptions		
EBM/75/14	Draft Amendments—Provisions on Repurchase and Transitional Provisions on Payment of Additional Subscriptions*	10/2/75	538–57
EBM/75/15	Draft Amendments—Provisions on Repurchase and Transitional Provisions on Payment of Additional Subscriptions	12/2/75	558–80
	Draft Amendments—Use of Fund Resources		
EBM/75/18	Draft Amendments—Use of Fund Resources	19/2/75	581–99
EBM/75/19	Draft Amendments—Provisions on Operations and Transactions in SDRs and on Opting Out*	19/2/75	600–13
EBM/75/21		24/2/75	614–33

Continued

Minute No.	Title	Date	Page Refs.
	Draft Amendments—Provisions on Operations and Transactions in SDRs and on Opting Out		
EBM/75/22	Draft Amendments—Provisions on Operations and Transactions in SDRs and on Opting Out	24/2/75	634–49
	Draft Amendments—Participants and Other Holders of SDRs*		
	Draft Amendments—Reserve Distribution of Net Income and Investment		
EBM/75/26	Draft Amendments—Establishment of a Council	3/3/75	650–72
EBM/75/27	Draft Amendments—Establishment of a Council	3/3/75	673–93
EBM/75/28	Draft Amendments—Establishment of a Council	5/3/75	694–716
EBM/75/33	Comprehensive Draft Amendment—Article III	21/3/75	717–40
EBM/75/34	Comprehensive Draft Amendment—Article V	21/3/75	741–60
EBM/75/35	Comprehensive Draft Amendment—Article V	24/3/75	761–81
EBM/75/36	Comprehensive Draft Amendment—Article V	24/3/75	782–99
EBM/75/41	Comprehensive Draft Amendment—Provisions on Gold	31/3/75	800–18
EBM/75/42	Comprehensive Draft Amendment—Article V	31/3/75	819–33
EBM/75/47	Comprehensive Draft Amendment—Article V	4/4/75	834–50

Volume II, Part 2—Minutes of Executive Board Meetings from 19 April 1974 to 4 April 1975

Minute No.	Title	Date	Page Refs.
EBM/75/48	Comprehensive Draft Amendment—Article V	7/4/75	851–9
EBM/75/49	Comprehensive Draft Amendment—Article V	7/4/75	860–81
EBM/75/50	Comprehensive Draft Amendment—Provisions on Gold	9/4/75	882–98
EBM/75/51	Comprehensive Draft Amendment—Provisions on Gold	9/4/75	899–919
	Comprehensive Draft Amendment—Article IV		
EBM/75/53	Comprehensive Draft Amendment—Article IV	11/4/75	920–33
EBM/75/54	Buffer Stocks—Direct Fund Financing	14/4/75	934–61
EBM/75/55	Comprehensive Draft Amendment—Article IV*	14/4/75	962–78
EBM/75/58	Comprehensive Draft Amendment—Article IV	18/4/75	979–91
EBM/75/59	Comprehensive Draft Amendment—Article IV	18/4/75	992–1006
EBM/75/60	Comprehensive Draft Amendment—Article IV	21/4/75	1007–25
EBM/75/61	Comprehensive Draft Amendment—Article IV and V*	21/4/75	1026–47
EBM/75/62	Comprehensive Draft Amendment—Article V*	23/4/75	1048–63
EBM/75/63	Comprehensive Draft Amendment—Article V*	23/4/75	1064–71
EBM/75/64	Comprehensive Draft Amendment—Article V*	25/4/75	1072–82
EBM/75/65	Comprehensive Draft Amendment—Article V and XII	25/4/75	1083–98
EBM/75/66	Comprehensive Draft Amendment—Article XII*	28/4/75	1099–115
EBM/75/67	Comprehensive Draft Amendment—Article XXI and XXX*	28/4/75	1116–34
EBM/75/68	Comprehensive Draft Amendment—Provisions on General Account—Article XXX and Schedule B	30/4/75	1135–49
	Comprehensive Draft Amendment—Provisions on Special Drawing Account—Articles XIX–XXI*		
EBM/75/69	Comprehensive Draft Amendment—Articles XX–XXIII*	30/4/75	1150–65

EBM/75/70	Comprehensive Draft Amendment—Provisions on Gold*	2/5/75	1166–92
EBM/75/71	Comprehensive Draft Amendment—Article V and VIII*	2/5/75	1193–209
EBM/75/72	Comprehensive Draft Amendment—Article XXIII*	5/5/75	1210–30
EBM/75/73	Comprehensive Draft Amendment—Article XXIII and XXIX*	5/5/75	1231–44
EBM/75/75	Comprehensive Draft Amendment—Provisions on Gold - Article V	7/5/75	1245–64
EBM/75/76	Comprehensive Draft Amendment—Provisions on Gold Comprehensive Draft Amendment—Establishment of a Council—Article XII and Schedule J	8/5/75	1265–86
EBM/75/78	Comprehensive Draft Amendment—Article IV	12/5/75	1287–310
EBM/75/79	Comprehensive Draft Amendment—Article IV	12/5/75	1311–20
EBM/75/82	Buffer Stocks and Compensatory Financing—Report to Interim Committee	16/5/75	1321–31
EBM/75/84	Comprehensive Draft Amendment—Elimination of Brackets*	19/5/75	1332–44
EBM/75/85	Comprehensive Draft Amendment—Elimination of Brackets*	19/5/75	1345–62
EBM/75/86	Comprehensive Draft Amendment—Elimination of Brackets*	20/5/75	1363–83
EBM/75/87	Comprehensive Draft Amendment—Elimination of Brackets*	20/5/75	1384–411
EBM/75/88	Comprehensive Draft Amendment—Article IV, V, and XXX	22/5/75	1412–32
EBM/75/89	Comprehensive Draft Amendment—Article V, Section 12(c) Comprehensive Draft Amendment—Redrafts of Miscellaneous Amendments	23/5/75	1433–43
EBM/75/90	Comprehensive Draft Amendment—Redrafts of Miscellaneous Provisions Comprehensive Draft Amendment—Report to Interim Committee*	23/5/75	1444–78
EBM/75/91	Comprehensive Draft Amendment—Supplementary Notes* Comprehensive Draft Amendment—Report to Interim Committee	27/5/75	1479–506
EBM/75/127	Draft Amendment—Buffer Stock Facility—Effect of Purchases on a Members Position in the Fund	21/7/75	1507–11
EBM/75/135	Reconstitution*	30/7/75	1512–19
EBM/75/137	SDR—Decisions on Valuation—Majority of Voting Power*	18/8/75	1520–28
EBM/75/140	Reconsideration of 75 Per Cent Norm	20/8/75	1529–51
EBM/75/141	Reconsideration of 75 Per Cent Norm	21/8/75	1552–60
EBM/75/147	Program of Work	15/9/75	1561–77
EBM/75/151	Draft Amendment—Changes and Outstanding Issues—The Norm	22/9/75	1578–83
EBM/75/152	Draft Amendment—Changes and Outstanding Issues—The Norm	22/9/75	1584–92
EBM/75/153	Draft Amendment—Changes and Outstanding Issues—Fund Transaction in Gold	24/9/75	1593–604
EBM/75/154	Draft Amendment—Changes and Outstanding Issues—Fund Transactions in Gold	24/9/75	1605–25
EBM/75/155*	Gold Substitution Account*	26/9/75	1626–41
EBM/75/156	Gold Substitution Account	26/9/75	1642–84
EBM/75/159	Draft Amendment—Changes and Outstanding Issues—Other Operations and Transactions	1/10/75	1685–708
EBM/75/160	Draft Amendment—Changes and Outstanding Issues	1/10/75	1709–17

Continued

Minute No.	Title	Date	Page Refs.
EBM/75/161	Draft amendment—Changes and Outstanding Issues—Repurchase, and Provision of Freely Usable Currencies	3/10/75	1718–29
EBM/75/162	Draft Amendment—Changes and Outstanding Issues—Provision of Freely Usable Currencies	3/10/75	1730–7
EBM/75/163	Draft Amendment—Changes and Outstanding Issues—Method of Valuation of the SDR, Obligation to Collaborate on Policies Regarding Gold,Obligation of Reconstitution*	6/10/75	1738–53
EBM/75/164	Draft Amendment—Changes and Outstanding Issues—Investment*	8/10/75	1754–68
EBM/75/165	Draft Amendment—Changes and Outstanding Issues—Investment	8/10/75	1769–74

Volume II, Part 3—Minutes of Executive Board Meetings from 10 November 1975 to 14 July 1976

Minute No.	Title	Date	Page Refs.
EBM/75/175	Draft Amendment—Changes and Outstanding Issues—The Norm	10/11/75	1775–90
EBM/75/178	Draft Amendment—Changes and Outstanding Issues—Provisions Relating to Gold*	19/11/75	1791–813
EBM/75/179	Draft Amendment—Changes and Outstanding Issues—Provisions Relating to Gold	19/11/75	1814–30
EBM/75/180	Draft Amendment—Changes and Outstanding Issues—Provisions Relating to Gold	24/11/75	1831–47
EBM/75/182	Draft Amendment—Changes and Outstanding Issues—Provisions of Freely Usable Currencies	26/11/75	1848–54
EBM/75/183	Draft Amendment—Changes and Outstanding Issues—Investment Draft Amendment—Changes and Outstanding Issues—The Norm	1/12/75	1855–78
EBM/75/185	Draft Amendment—Changes and Outstanding Issues—Provisions Relating to Gold	3/12/75	1879–97
EBM/75/186	Draft Amendment—Changes and Outstanding Issues—Provisions Relating to Gold	3/12/75	1898–916
EBM/75/187	Draft Amendment—Changes and Outstanding Issues – Investment Draft Amendment -- Changes and Outstanding Issues—The Norm Draft Amendment—Changes and Outstanding Issues—Reconstitution*	4/12/75	1917–34
EBM/75/189	Draft Amendment—Changes and Outstanding Issues—Gold Substitution Account	5/12/75	1935–43
EBM/75/191	Draft Amendment—Changes and Outstanding Issues—Valuation of the SDR*	8/12/75	1944–9
EBM/75/192	Draft Amendment—Changes and Outstanding Issues – The Norm Draft Amendment—Changes and Outstanding Issues—Provisions Relating to Gold*	10/12/75	1950–72

EBM/75/193	Draft Amendment—Changes and Outstanding Issues—Provisions Relating to Gold	10/12/75	1973–89
EBM/75/194	Draft Amendment—Changes and Outstanding Issues—Reconstitution*	10/12/75	1990–2003
	Draft Amendment—Changes and Outstanding Issues—Investment		
EBM/75/196	Report by Staff	15/12/75	2004–11
EBM/75/197	Draft Amendment—Draft Report to Interim Committee*	15/12/75	2012–28
EBM/75/199	Majorities	17/12/75	2029–40
EBM/75/201	Draft Amendment—Changes and Outstanding Issues—Gold Substitution Account	19/12/75	2041–7
EBM/75/202	Draft Amendment—Changes and Outstanding Issues—Gold Substitution Account	19/12/75	2048–54
EBM/75/203	Report by Staff	22/12/75	2055–71
	Draft Amendment—Changes and Outstanding Issues—Exchange Arrangements		
EBM/75/204	Draft Amendment—Draft Report to Interim Committee*	22/12/75	2072–82
EBM/75/205	Draft Amendment—Changes and Outstanding Issues—Exchange Arrangements	23/12/75	2083–102
EBM/75/206	Draft Amendment—Draft Report to Interim Committee*	23/12/75	2103–19
	Draft Amendment—Changes and Outstanding Issues—Exchange Arrangements		
EBM/75/207	Draft Amendment—Changes and Outstanding Issues—Exchange Arrangements	23/12/75	2120–52
	Draft Amendment—Report to Interim Committee		
EBM/76/7	Comprehensive Draft Amendment—Residual Issues*	26/1/76	2153–75
EBM/76/8	Comprehensive Draft Amendment—Residual Issues	26/1/76	2176–91
EBM/76/11	Comprehensive Draft Amendment—Majorities*	30/1/76	2192–216
EBM/76/12	Comprehensive Draft Amendment—Majorities*	2/2/76	2217–49
EBM/76/13	Comprehensive Draft Amendment*	2/2/76	2250–75
EBM/76/14	Comprehensive Draft Amendment	4/2/76	2276–98
EBM/76/17	Amendment—Draft Report to Board of Governors	13/2/76	2299–306
EBM/76/18	Amendment—Draft Report to Board of Governors	13/2/76	2307–20
EBM/76/20	Amendment—Draft Report to Board of Governors	18/2/76	2321–36
EBM/76/23	Amendment—Draft Report to Board of Governors*	23/2/76	2337–65
EBM/76/33	Comprehensive Draft Amendment—Residual Issues—Election and Appointment of Executive Directors	5/3/76	2366–76
EBM/76/34	Comprehensive Draft Amendment—Residual Issues—Election of Executive Directors	8/3/76	2377–98
EBM/76/35	Comprehensive Draft Amendment—Residual Issues—Election of Executive Directors	8/3/76	2399–420
EBM/76/36	Comprehensive Draft Amendment—Residual Issues—Appointment of Executive Directors	9/3/76	2421–39
	Amendment—Draft Report to Board of Governors*		
EBM/76/37	Amendment—Draft Report to Board of Governors	10/3/76	2440–53
	Comprehensive Draft Amendment—Residual Issues—Election and Appointment of Executive Directors		
EBM/76/38	Comprehensive Draft Amendment—Residual Issues—Election and Appointment of Executive Directors	10/3/76	2454–77
	Amendment—Draft Report to Board of Governors		
EBM/76/39	Comprehensive Draft Amendment—Residual Issues—Election and Appointment of Executive Directors	10/3/76	2478–91
	Amendment—Draft Report to Board of Governors		
EBM/76/41	Amendment—Draft Report to Board of Governors	12/3/76	2492–504
EBM/76/42	Amendment—Draft Report to Board of Governors, and Residual Issues—Freely Usable Currencies	15/3/76	2505–22

Continued

Minute No.	Title	Date	Page Refs.
EBM/76/43	Amendment—Draft Report to Board of Governors, and Residual Issues—Freely Usable Currencies	15/3/76	2523–38
EBM/76/44	Amendment—Draft Report to Board of Governors*	16/3/76	2539–61
EBM/76/45	Comprehensive Draft Amendment—Residual Issues—Election and Appointment of Executive Directors Amendment—Draft Report to Board of Governors* Comprehensive Draft Amendment—Schedule K	17/3/76	2562–88
EBM/76/46	Comprehensive Draft Amendment—Election and Appointment of Executive Directors	17/3/76	2589–602
EBM/76/51	Amendment - Report to Board of Governors, Draft Resolution, and Decision*	24/3/76	2603–13
EBM/76/52	Amendment—Final Review of Texts, and Closing Date for Governors Vote	n.d.	2614–27
EBM/76/53	Amendment—Press Conference	29/3/76	2628–30
EBM/76/71	Proposed Second Amendment of the Articles of Agreement—Governors Agreement	n.d.	2631–3
EBM/76/103	Amendment—First Syllabus of Changes and Additions	14/7/76	2634–40

N.B. An asterisk indicates that the document was identified in the Fund's 1986 index as directly related to issues surrounding the SDR. However other documents—on the gold substitution account, or the Council, for example—also affected prospects for the SDR, and are addressed/referred to above where relevant.

Staff memoranda (SMs), departmental memoranda (DMs), and other Fund documents dealing with the Second Amendment were stamped with the proviso that they were documents of the IMF and not for public use. The DMs were also prefaced with the remark 'Any views expressed in the Departmental Memoranda (DM) Series represent the opinions of the authors and, unless otherwise indicated, should not be interpreted as official Fund views'. Relevant research departments responsible for their preparation, rather than individual authors, are thus indicated.

This documentation comprises six hardback volumes, plus an index.

Abbreviations are as follows:

SM	Staff Memorandum
DAA	Draft Article(s) of Agreement
EBD	Executive Board Document
EBM	Executive Board Minute

APPENDIX 2

(a) IMF managing directors to date; (b) IMF executive directors during the negotiation of the Second Amendment to the IMF Articles of Agreement, 1974–6; and (c) Senior IMF Staff during the negotiation of the Second Amendment to the IMF Articles of Agreement, 1974–6

(a) Fund managing directors to date

May 1946 – August 1951	Camille Gutt (Belgium)
August 1951 – September 1956	Ivar Rooth (Sweden)
September 1956 – May 1964	Per Jacobsson (Sweden)
September 1964 – August 1973	Pierre-Paul Schweitzer (France)
September 1973 – June 1978	H. Johannes Witteveen (Netherlands)
June 1978 – January 1987	J. de Larosière (France)
January 1987 – May 2000	Michel Camdessus (France)
May 2000 – June 2004	Horst Köhler (Germany)
June 2004 – November 2007	Rodrigo de Rato (Spain)
November 2007 – May 2011	Dominique Strauss-Kahn (France)
July 2011 –	Christine Lagarde (France)

(b) Executive directors during the negotiation of the Second Amendment to the IMF Articles of Agreement (Jamaica Agreement), April 1974 – July 1976

Executive directors	
Appointed	
1. United States (21.87%)	
William B. Dale	1965–74
Sam Y. Cross	1974–81
2. United Kingdom (9.19%)	
Anthony K. Rawlinson	1972–5
William S. Ryrie	1975–80
3. Germany (5.29%)	
Günther Schleiminger	1968–74
Eckard Pieske	1974–9

Executive directors	
Appointed	
4. France (4.96%)	
Jacques Henri Wahl	1973–8
5. Japan (3.98%)	
Kaichi Kawaguchi	1972–6
Elected	
6. 4 member states (3 in SDR Dept in 1975) (4.83%)	
Francesco Palamenghi-Crispi (Italy)	1967–76
Lamberto Dini (Italy)	1976–80
7. 5 member states (4.66%)	
Robert Bryce (Canada)	1971–4
Bernard J. Drabble (Canada)	1974–81
8. 5 member states (4.48%)	
Pieter Lieftinck (Netherlands)	1955–76
9. 14 member states (8 in SDR Dept in 1975) (2.75%)	
Nazih Ahmed Deif (Egypt)	1970–6
10. 3 member states (4.03%)	
P. S. N. Prasad (India)	1971–5
S. Jagannathan (India)	1975–6
11. 4 member states (3.87%)	
Jacques de Groote (Belgium)	1973–94
12. 5 member states (3.78%)	
Per Åsbrink (Sweden)	1973–6
13. 11 member states (10 in SDR Dept in 1975) (3.56%)	
Byanti Kharmawan (Indonesia)	1968–82
14. 4 member states (3.66%)	
Lindsay B. Brand (Australia)	1970–5
R. J. Whitelaw (Australia)	1975–81
15. 17 member states (16 in SDR Dept in 1975) (3.29%)	
S. B. Nicol-Cole (Sierra-Leone)	1972–4
Horace R. Monday, Jr. (Gambia)	1974–6
16. 7 member states (3.35%)	
Guillermo Bueso (Honduras)	1972–4
Francisco Suárez (Mexico)	1974–6
17. 7 member states (3.29%)	
Alexandre Kafka (Brazil)	1966–98

18. 9 member states (3.27%)	
Jahangir Amuzegar (Iran)	1973–80
19. 6 member states (2.95%)	
Carlos Massad A. (Chile)	1970–4
Roberto Gavaldá (Argentina)	1974–6
20. 18 member states (2.93%)	
Antoine W. Yaméogo (Upper Volta)	1966–76

NB: i. Percentage of Special Drawing Account Votes (roughly analogous to General Account Votes) at 30 April 1975 are indicated for each group.

ii. For elected executive directors, the number of countries in each group is also indicated. Countries in each group usually share historical ties, economic similarities, or geographical proximity.

(c) Senior Fund staff during the negotiation of the Second Amendment to the IMF Articles of Agreement (Jamaica Agreement), April 1974–July 1976

The General Counsel	Joseph Gold
The Economic Counsellor	J. J. Polak
Administration Department	Phillip Thorson*
African Department	Mamoudou Touré*
Asian Department	Tun Thin*
Central Banking Service	J. V. Mládek*
European Department	L. A. Whittome*
Exchange & Trade Relations Department	Ernest Sturc*
Fiscal Affairs Department	Richard Goode*
IMF Institute	Gérard Teyssier*
Legal Department	Joseph Gold*
Middle Eastern Department	John W. Gunter*
Research Department	J. J. Polak*
Secretary's Department; Secretary:	W. Lawrence Hebbard
Treasurer's Department; Treasurer:	Walter Habermeier
Western Hemisphere Department	Jorge Del Canto*
Bureau of Language Services	J. S. Haszard*
Bureau of Statistics	Earl Hicks*
Office in Europe (Paris)	Jean-Paul Sallé* Leo Van Houtven*
Office in Geneva	Edgar Jones*
Chief Editor	Norman Humphreys

* Director or Acting Director

APPENDIX 3

Senior US treasury staff with international monetary responsibilities, 1965–90

Secretary	
1961–5	Douglas Dillon
1965–8	Henry H. Fowler
1968–9	Joseph Barr
1969–71	David Kennedy
1971–2	John Connally
1972–4	George Shultz
1974–7	William Simon
1977–9	W. Michael Blumenthal
1979–81	G. William Miller
1981–5	Donald Regan
1985–9	James Baker III
1989–90	Nicholas F. Brady

Under-Secretary for Monetary Affairs	
1961–4	Robert Roosa
1965–9	Fred Deming
1969–74	Paul Volcker
1974–5	Jack Bennett
1975–7	Edwin Yeo III
1977–80	Anthony M. Solomon
1980–1	Robert Carswell (acting)
1981–4	Beryl W. Sprinkel

Under-Secretary for International Affairs	
1989–90	David C. Mulford

Assistant Secretary (International Affairs)	
1961–2	John Leddy
1962–4	John Bullitt
1965–6	Merlyn Trued
1966–8	Winthrop Knowlton
1968–72	John R. Petty
1972–4	John Hennessey
1974–5	Charles Cooper
1975–7	Gerald Parsky
1977–81	C. Fred Bergsten
1981–2	Marc E. Leland
1984–9	David C. Mulford
1989–90	Charles H. Dallara

Senior Deputy Assistant Secretary (International Economic Policy)	
1985–9	Charles H. Dallara
1990	John M. Niehuss

Deputy Assistant Secretary (International Monetary Affairs)	
1970–3	Will Cates
1973–5	Sam Y. Cross
1975–80	F. Lisle Widman
1980–4	Thomas B.C. Leddy
1984–5	Charles H. Dallara
1985–6	James E. Ammerman (acting)
1986–90	Thomas J. Berger (acting to 1987)
1990	Robert M. Bestani

Deputy Assistant Secretary (Policy Coordination)	
1983–4	Jacob Dreyer (acting)

Deputy Assistant Secretary (International Affairs)	
1984–5	George R. Hoguet

Deputy to the Assistant Secretary and Secretary of the IMG (International Monetary Group)	
1964–81	George H. Willis

Special Assistant to the Assistant Secretary (International Affairs)	
1983–4	Lyn Withey
1985–6	John Donaldson
1986–7	Steven F. Tuardek

Director, Office of Industrial Nations	
1962–70	F. Lisle Widman

Director, Office of Industrial Nations and Global Analysis	
1987–9	Robert C. Fauver
1989–90	Donald C. Templeman

Director, Office of International Monetary Affairs	
1970–3	Sam Y. Cross
1973–5	F. Lisle Widman
1975–9	Donald E. Syvrud
1979–80	Thomas B.C. Liddy

Director, Office of International Monetary Policy	
1987–9	Barry S. Newman

Director, Office of Balance of Payments Analysis	
1987–9	Donald W. Curtis
1988–90	David J. Klock

Director, Office of Gold and Foreign Exchange Operations	
1964–74	T. Page Nelson
1974–	Fred Springborn

Director, Office of Bilateral Relations	
1970–1	Hal F. Reynolds
1971–2	James E. Ammerman
1972–3	Schubert J. Dyche

Director, Office of International Economic Analysis	
1973–4	Schubert J. Dyche

Director, Office of Foreign Investment	
1972–4	Ralph V. Korp
1974–6	James E. Griffin

Director, Office of International Banking and Portfolio Investment	
1977–80	Jerry M. Newman
1987–90	James E. Ammerman

Sources: F. Lisle Widman, *Making International Monetary Policy*, The International Law Institute, Georgetown University Law Center (Washington, DC: 1982); *The United States Government Manual*, Office of the Federal Register, National Archives and Records Administration, various issues.

Bibliography

A: Books and Articles

Akhtar, M. A. and Howard Howe. 'The Political and Institutional Independence of US Monetary Policy', Federal Reserve Bank of New York Research Paper no. 9110, May 1991.

Alessandrini, Pietro and Michele Fratianni. 'Resurrecting Keynes to Stabilize the International Monetary System', Social Science Research Network (SSRN) Working Paper, available at: http://papers.ssrn.com/sol3/papers.cfm?abstract_id=1031346 (accessed 8 June 2011) , December, 2008.

'A New International Reserve Asset', *The Bank of Nova Scotia Monthly Review*, Toronto, October 1967.

Aryeetey, Ernest. 'A Development-Focused Allocation of Special Drawing Rights', United Nations University, World Institute for Development Economics Research (WIDER), Helsinki. Discussion Paper No. 2003/3, as at: http://www.wider.unu.edu/publications/working-papers/discussion-papers/2004/en_GB/dp2004-003/_files/78091737731499054/default/dp2004-003.pdf (accessed 8 June 2011), January 2004.

Avramovic, D. 'Transfer of Resources to Developing Countries', in S. Dell (ed.), *The International Monetary System and its Reform (for the G-24) vol. 5*, North-Holland for the UN (Amsterdam: 1990).

Axelrod, Robert (ed.). *Structure of Decision*, Princeton University Press (Princeton: 1976).

Balogh, Thomas. 'Old Fallacies and New Remedies: The SDRs in Perspective', *Bulletin of the Oxford University Institute of Economics and Statistics*, vol. 32, no. 2, May 1970.

Bauer, Peter. 'Inflation, SDRs and Aid', *Lloyds Bank Review*, no. 109, July 1973.

Bauer, Peter. 'The SDR Link Scheme—A Comment', *Lloyds Bank Review*, no. 111, January 1974.

Bennett, Jack. 'A Free Dollar Makes Sense', *Foreign Policy*, no. 21, Winter 1975–6.

Bergsten, C. Fred. *The Dilemmas of the Dollar—The Economics and Politics of United States International Monetary Policy*, Council on Foreign Relations Book/New York University Press (New York: 1975).

Bergsten, C. Fred. *Toward a New International Economic Order: Selected Papers of C. Fred Bergsten 1972–1974*, Lexington Books/D.C. Heath and Co. (Lexington, MA: 1975).

Bergsten, C. Fred. *Managing International Economic Interdependence: Selected Papers of C. Fred Bergsten, 1975–1976*, Lexington Books/D.C. Heath and Co. (Lexington, MA: 1977).

Bergsten, C. Fred. *The International Economic Policy of the United States: Selected Papers of C. Fred Bergsten, 1977–1979*, Lexington Books/D.C. Heath and Co. (Lexington, MA: 1980).

Bergsten, C. Fred. 'The Dollar and the Deficits: How Washington Can Prevent the Next Crisis', *Foreign Affairs*, vol. 88, no. 6, November/December 2009.

Best, Jacqueline. *The Limits of Transparency: Ambiguity and the History of International Finance*, Ithaca, NY (Cornell University Press: 2005).

Bird, Graham. 'SDR Distribution, Interest Rates and Aid Flows', *World Economy*, vol. 4, no. 4, December 1981.

Bird, Graham. *International Financial Policy and Economic Development—A Disaggregated Approach*, St Martin's Press (New York: 1987).

Bird, Graham. 'The Political Economy of the SDR: The Rise and Fall of an International Reserve Asset', *Global Governance*, vol. 4, no. 3, 1998.

Bird, Graham. *The IMF and the Future: Issues and Options Facing the Fund*, Routledge (London: 2003).

Bird, Graham. 'The SDR Aid Link: It's Now or Never', *Development Policy Review*, vol. 28, no. 1, January 2010.

Black, Stanley W. 'International Money and International Monetary Arrangements', in R. W. Jones and P. B. Kenen (eds), *Handbook of International Economics*, North-Holland (Amsterdam: 1985).

Bordo, Michael D. 'The Bretton Woods International Monetary System', October 1991 NBER Conference Paper: Bordo and Eichengreen (eds), *A Restrospective on the Bretton Woods System: Lessons for International Monetary Reform*, University of Chicago Press\NBER (Chicago: 1993).

Boyer, Jan E. and Edwin M. Truman. 'The United States and the Large Emerging-Market Economies: Competitors or Partners?', in C. Fred Bergsten, *The United States and the World Economy—Foreign Economic Policy for the Next Decade*, Institute for International Economics (Washington, DC: 2005).

Buchan, Alastair. *Power and Equilibrium in the 1970s,* Chatto and Windus (London: 1973).

Buchanan, Michael and Jim O'Neill. 'Global Reserve Currencies and the SDR', Global Economics Paper no. 196—Goldman Sachs Global Economics Commodities and Strategy Research, available at: https://360.gs.com (accessed 8 June 2011).

Buira, Ariel (ed.). *The IMF and World Bank at Sixty*, Anthem Press (London: 2005).

Bull, Hedley. *The Anarchical Society*, Columbia University Press (New York: 1979).

Bristow, Richard L. 'SDR bonds and notes', in L. de V. Wragg (ed.), *Composite Currencies—SDRs, ECUs and Other Instruments*, Euromoney Publications (London: 1984).

Brown, Brendan. *The Dollar – Mark Axis on Currency Power*, Macmillan (London: 1979).

Broz, J. Lawrence and Michael Brewster Hawes, 'US Domestic Politics and International Monetary Fund Policy, paper prepared for 8th Annual International Society for New Institutional Economics Conference (ISNIE), Tucson, Arizona, 30 September – 3 October 2004 (later published as 'Congressional Politics of Financing the International Monetary Fund', in *International Organization*, vol. 60, no. 2, Spring 2006), as at: http://dss.ucsd.edu/~jlbroz/broz_hawes_isnie.pdf (accessed 16 June 2011).

Byrne, William J. 'Evolution of the SDR', *Finance and Development*, September 1982.

Camdessus, Michel et. al. 'How Should the IMF be Reshaped? Three Points of View on the IMF in the 21st Century', in *Finance and Development*, IMF vol. 41, no. 3, September 2004, at: http://www.imf.org/external/pubs/ft/fandd/2004/09/pdf/larosier.pdf (accessed 16 June 2011).

Camdessus, Michel, Alexandre Lamfalussy, Tommaso Padoa-Schioppa, et. al. 'Reform of the International Monetary System: A Cooperative Approach for the Twenty First Century', Palais-Royal Initiative, 18 January 2011, at: http://www.elysee.fr/president/root/bank_objects/2011-007.Palais-Royal_Initiative-Final_version_of_the_Report-Jan_ 18.pdf (accessed 8 June 2011).

Chrystal, K. Alec. 'International Money and the Future of the SDR', Princeton Essay in International Finance no. 128, International Finance Section, Princeton, NJ, June 1978.

Chrystal, K. Alec. 'The Role of the Special Drawing Right in the International Monetary System', in S. Dell (ed.), *The International Monetary System and its Reform (for the G-24) vol. 5*, North-Holland for the UN (Amsterdam: 1990).

Coats, Warren. *Special Drawing Rights—Operations and Role in Development Finance*, Allied Publishers Ltd. (New Delhi: 1990).

Coats, Warren. 'Time for a New Global Currency?', *New Global Studies*, vol. 3, no. 2, 2009, as at: http://www.bepress.com/ngs/vol3/iss1/art5/ (accessed 16 June 2011).

Cohen, Benjamin J. 'International Reserves and Liquidity' (including comments by Ronald McKinnon and Rudi Rhomberg), in P. B. Kenen (ed.) *International Trade and Finance—Frontiers for Research*, Cambridge University Press (Cambridge: 1975).

Cohen, Benjamin J. *Organizing the World's Money—The Political Economy of International Monetary Relations*, Macmillan (Basingstoke: 1979).

Cohen, Benjamin J., in collaboration with Fabio Basagni. *Banks and the Balance of Payments*, Rowman and Allanheld (Montclair, NJ: 1981).

Cohen, Benjamin J. *In Whose Interest?—International Banking and American Foreign Policy*, Yale University Press (New Haven: 1986).

Cohen, Benjamin J. *The Future of Money*, Princeton University Press (Princeton: 2006).

Cohen, Benjamin J. *Global Monetary Governance*, Routledge (New York: 2007).

Cohen, Benjamin J. 'The Transatlantic Divide: Why are American and British IPE So Different?', *Review of International Political Economy*, vol. 14, no. 2, May 2007.

Cohen, Benjamin J. 'The Multiple Traditions of American IPE', in Mark Blyth (ed.), *Routledge Handbook of International Political Economy (IPE)—IPE as a Global Conversation*, Routledge (Abingdon: 2009).

Cohen, Benjamin J. 'The Future of Reserve Currencies', Finance and Development, IMF, September 2009, available at: http://www.imf.org/external/pubs/ft/fandd/2009/09/cohen.htm (accessed 8 June 2011).

Cohen, Stephen D. *International Monetary Reform 1964–69: The Political Dimension*, Praeger (New York: 1970).

Cohen, Stephen D. *The Making of United States International Economic Policy—Principles, Problems, and Proposals for Reform*, Praeger Publishers (New York: 1988).

Coombs, Charles A. *The Arena of International Finance*, John Wiley & Sons (New York: 1976).

Coombs, Charles A. and Guillaume Guindey. *Reflections on the International Monetary System*, The 1980 Per Jacobsson Lecture (Basle: 1980).

Cooper, Richard N. 'Is There a Need for Reform?', in *The International Monetary System: Forty Years After Bretton Woods*, Conference Series No. 28, FRB Boston (Boston: 1984).

Cooper, Richard N. 'A Monetary System for the Future', *Foreign Affairs*, vol. 63, no. 1, Fall 1984.

Cooper, Richard N. *The International Monetary System—Essays in World Economics*, MIT Press (Cambridge, MA: 1987).

Cooper, Richard N. 'Proposal for a Common Currency Among Rich Democracies', *National Bank of Austria Working Paper* 127, available at: http://www.oenb.at/de/img/wp127_tcm14-42690.pdf (accessed 8 June 2011), June 2006.

Cooper, Richard N. 'The Future of the Dollar', Peterson Institute Policy Brief no. PB09-21, Peterson Institute for International Economics (Washington, DC: 2009), available at: http://www.petersoninstitute.org/publications/pb/pb09-21.pdf (accessed 8 June 2011).

Cooper, Richard N. 'Necessary Reform? The IMF and International Financial Architecture', *Harvard International Review*, vol. 30, no. 4, Winter 2009, available at: http://hir.harvard.edu/index.php?page=article&id=1845 (accessed 8 June 2011).

Corden, W. Max. *Inflation, Exchange Rates and the World Economy—Lectures on International Monetary Economics*, Oxford University Press (Oxford: 1981).

Corden, W. Max. 'Is There an Important Role for an International Reserve Asset Such as the SDR?', in George M. von Furstenberg (ed.), *International Money and Credit: The Policy Roles*, IMF (Washington, DC: 1983).

Corden, W. Max. 'The Logic of the International Monetary System', in F. Machlup et. al., *Reflections on a Troubled World Economy*, St Martin's Press (New York: 1983).

Crockett, Andrew. *International Money—Issues and Analysis*, Academic Press/Harcourt Brace Jovanovich (New York: 1977).

Crovitz, L. Gordon. 'Micromanaging Foreign Policy', in *The Public Interest*, special issue on the American Congress, no. 100, summer 1990.

Daane, J. Dewey. 'Much Ado About International Monetary Reform' (remarks by J. Dewey Daane, member, Board of Governors of the Federal Reserve System before the Cleveland Business Economists Club, Cleveland, Ohio, 17 February 1969), in *Economic Review*, Federal Reserve Bank of Cleveland, February 1969.

Dam, Kenneth W. *The Rules of the Game—Reform and Evolution in the International Monetary System*, University of Chicago Press (Chicago: 1982).

Davidson, Paul. *International Money and the Real World*, Macmillan (London: 1982).

Davidson, Roger H. 'Subcommittee Government: New Channels for Policy Making', in T. E. Mann and N. J. Ornstein (eds), *The New Congress*, American Enterprise Institute for Public Policy Research (Washington, DC: 1981).

Davidson, Roger H. and Walter J. Oleszek. *Congress Against Itself*, Indiana University Press (Bloomington, IN: 1977).

Dell, Sidney. 'Measures to Strengthen the SDR'—includes supporting papers by Alec Chrystal, Peter Kenen, Berito Legarda and John Williamson, in S. Dell (ed.), *The International Monetary System and its Reform* (for the G-24), vol. 2, North-Holland for the UN (Amsterdam: 1987).

Dell, Sidney (ed.). *The International Monetary System and Its Reform*—Papers prepared for the Group of Twenty-Four by a United Nations project directed by Sidney Dell 1979–86; five volumes, published by North-Holland in cooperation with the United Nations (Amsterdam: 1987 (vols. 1–3) and 1990 (vols. 4–5)).

Despres, Emile, Charles Kindleberger, and Walter S. Salant. 'The Dollar and World Liquidity—A Minority View', *The Economist*, London, 5 February 1966.

Destler, I. M. *Making Foreign Economic Policy*, Brookings Institution (Washington, DC: 1980).

Destler, I. M. 'Trade Consensus, SALT Stalemate: Congress and Foreign Policy in the 1970s', in T. E. Mann and N. J. Ornstein (eds), *The New Congress*, American Enterprise Institute for Public Policy Research (Washington, DC: 1981).

Destler, I. M. *American Trade Politics*, Institute for International Economics and The Twentieth Century Fund (Washington, DC: 1992).

Destler, I. M. and C. Randall Henning. *Dollar Politics: Exchange Rate Policymaking in the United States*, Institute for International Economics (Washington, DC: 1989).

De Kock, M. H. *Central Banking* (4th edn). Crosby Lockwood Staples (London: 1974).

De Vries, Tom. 'Jamaica, Or the Non-reform of the International Monetary System', *Foreign Affairs*, vol. 54, April 1976.

Dominguez, Kathryn M. 'The Role of International Organizations in the Bretton Woods System', in Bordo and Eichengreen (eds), *A Restrospective on the Bretton Woods System: Lessons for International Monetary Reform*, University of Chicago Press/NBER (Chicago: 1993).

Dreyer, Jacob S., Gottfried Haberler, and Thomas D. Willett (eds). *The International Monetary System—A Time of Turbulence* (Conference Proceedings). American Enterprise Institute for Public Policy Research (Washington, DC: 1980).

Dreyer, Jacob S. *Composite Reserve Assets in the International Monetary System*, JAI Press (Greenwich, CT: 1977).

Eichengreen, Barry. *Global Imbalances and the Lessons of Bretton Woods*, MIT Press (Cambridge, MA: 2006).

Eichengreen, Barry. 'Commercialize the SDR', 27 April 2009, as at: http://www.project-syndicate.org/commentary/eichengreen4/English (accessed 8 June 2011).

Eichengreen, Barry. 'The Dollar Dilemma: The World's Top Currency Faces Competition', *Foreign Affairs*, vol. 88, no. 5, September/October 2009.

Eichengreen, Barry. 'Out-of-the-Box Thoughts About the International Financial Architecture', *Journal of International Commerce, Economics and Policy*, vol. 1, no. 1, 2010.

Emminger, Otmar. 'The Dollar's Borrowed Strength', Group of Thirty Occasional Paper 19 (New York: 1985).

Feinberg, Richard E. 'The Changing Relationship Between the World Bank and the International Monetary Fund', in *International Organization*, vol. 42, no. 3, Summer 1988.

Fellner, William. 'Gold and the Uneasy Case for Responsibly Managed Fiat Money', in F. Machlup *et al.*, *Reflections on a Troubled World Economy*, St Martin's Press (New York: 1983).

Fleming, J. Marcus. 'The SDR: Some Problems and Possibilities', IMF *Staff Papers*, vol. XVIII, 1971

Flor, Elena. 'The Debate About the SDR as a Global Reserve Currency and SDR Denominated Securities', as at: http://www.uclouvain.be/cps/ucl/doc/triffin/documents/SDR_Flor_nov09.pdf (accessed 8 June 2011).

Fridriksson, Ingimundur. 'Aspects of the International Monetary System: International Reserves and International Exchange Rate Regimes', Norges Bank Staff Memo, no. 9, 2010, as at: http://www.norges-bank.no/upload/publikasjoner/staff%20memo/2010/staff_memo_0910.pdf (accessed 8 June 2011).

Garber, Peter M. 'The Collapse of the Bretton Woods Fixed Exchange Rate System', in Bordo and Eichengreen (eds), *A Restrospective on the Bretton Woods System: Lessons for International Monetary Reform*, University of Chicago Press/NBER (Chicago: 1993).

Gardner, Richard N. *Sterling—Dollar Diplomacy—Anglo-American Collaboration in the Reconstruction of Multilateral Trade*, Clarendon Press (Oxford: 1956).

Genberg, Hans and Alexander K. Swoboda. 'The Provision of Liquidity in the Bretton Woods System', in Bordo and Eichengreen (eds), *A Restrospective on the Bretton Woods System: Lessons for International Monetary Reform*, University of Chicago Press/NBER (Chicago: 1993).

Gilbert, Milton. *Quest for World Monetary Order—The Gold–Dollar System and Its Aftermath*, a Twentieth Century Fund Study, with posthumous editing by Peter Oppenheimer and Michael Dealtry, John Wiley & Sons (New York: 1980).

Gilpin, Robert. *US Power and the Multinational Corporation*, Basic Books (New York: 1975).

Glenon, Michael J., Thomas M. Franck, and Robert C. Cassidy, Jr. *United States Foreign Relations Law: Documents and Sources, vol. IV—International Economic Regulation*, Oceana Publications, Inc. (New York: 1984).

Gold, Joseph. 'Special Drawing Rights: Renaming the Infant Asset', IMF *Staff Papers*, vol. 23, July 1976.

Gourevitch, Peter. 'The Second Image Reversed: The International Sources of Domestic Politics', *International Organization*, vol. 32, Autumn 1978.

Gowa, Joanne. *Closing the Gold Window—Domestic Policy and the End of Bretton Woods*, Cornell University Press (Ithaca, NY: 1983).

Gowa, Joanne. 'Hegemons, IOs and Markets: The Case of the Substitution Account', in *International Organization*, vol. 38, no. 4, Autumn 1984.

Gowa, Joanne. 'Public Goods and Political Institutions: Trade and Monetary Policy Processes in the United States', in *International Organization*, vol. 42, no. 1, Winter 1988.

Greider, William. *Secrets of the Temple—How the Federal Reserve Runs the Country*, Simon and Schuster (New York: 1987).

Group of Twenty (G20). *The Group of 20—A History*; published at the meeting of G20 Finance Ministers and Central Bank Governors, Cape Town, South Africa, November 2007, as at: http://www.g20.org/Documents/history_report_dm1.pdf (accessed 8 June 2011).

Group of Twenty (G20). *Leaders Statement—The Global Plan for Recovery and Reform, London, 2 April 2009*, as at: http://www.g20.org/Documents/final-communique.pdf (accessed 8 June 2011).

Grubel, Herbert G. *The International Monetary System*, Penguin Books (Harmondworth: 1984).

Guindey, Guillaume and Charles A. Coombs. 'Reflections on the International Monetary System', The 1980 Per Jacobsson Lecture (Washington, DC: 1980).

Halm, George N. (ed.). *Approaches to Greater Flexibility of Exchange Rates—The Bürgenstock Papers*, Princeton University Press (Princeton: 1970).

Head, John W. 'Suspension of Debtor Countries' Voting Rights in the IMF: An Assessment of the Third Amendment to the IMF Charter', *Virginia Journal of International Law*, vol. 33, 1993.

Healey, Denis. *The Time of My Life*, Michael Joseph (London: 1989).

Helleiner, Gerald K. 'The Less Developed Countries and the International Monetary System', *Journal of Development Studies*, April/July 1974.

Helleiner, Eric. 'The IMF and the SDR: What to Make of China's Proposals?', in B. Momani and Eric Santor (eds), *The Future of IMF Reform: A Canadian Perspective* (Waterloo, Canada: 2009), available at: http://www.cigionline.org/sites/default/files/The%20Future%20of%20the%20IMF_0.pdf (accessed 8 June 2011).

Heller, H. Robert, and Mohsin S. Khan. 'The Demand for International Reserves Under Fixed and Floating Exchange Rates', IMF *Staff Papers*, vol. XXV (Washington, DC: 1978).

Hennessy, J. M. 'The Time for Monetary Muddling is Over', CSFB Research Presentation (expanded version of *Wall Street Journal* article 28 October 1987), Credit Suisse First Boston (London, 1987).

Henning, C. Randall. 'US Interests and the International Monetary Fund', Peterson Institute for International Economics Policy Brief no. PB09-12, June 2009, as at: http://www.piie.com/publications/pb/pb09-12.pdf (accessed 8 June 2011).

Hirsch, Fred. 'SDRs and the Working of the Gold Exchange Standard', IMF *Staff Papers*, vol. 18, July 1971.

Hirsch, Fred and Michael W. Doyle. 'Politicization in the World Economy: Necessary Conditions for an International Economic Order', in F. Hirsch, M. W. Doyle, and Edward Morse, *Alternatives to Monetary Disorder*, 1980s Project/Council on Foreign Relations—McGraw-Hill (New York: 1977).

Ikenberry, G. John, David A. Lake, and Michael Mastando, 'Introduction: Approaches to Explaining American Foreign Economic Policy', in *International Organization*, vol. 42, no. 1, Winter 1988.

Ikenberry, G. John. 'Conclusion: An Institutional Approach to American Foreign Economic Policy', in *International Organization*, vol. 42, no. 1, Winter 1988.

Ikenberry, G. John. 'The Political Origins of Bretton Woods', in Bordo and Eichengreen (eds), *A Restrospective on the Bretton Woods System: Lessons for International Monetary Reform*, University of Chicago Press/NBER (Chicago: 1993).

Intergovernmental Group of Twenty-Four on International Monetary Affairs and Development (Group of 24), Communiqué, 1 October 2004, at: http://www.g24.org/PDF/09-04ENG.pdf (accessed 16 June 2011).

Jacobsson, Erin E. *A Life for Sound Money—Per Jacobsson, His Biography*, Clarendon Press (Oxford: 1979).

Jelley, Colin. 'The SDR Clearing Mechanism', in L. de V. Wragg (ed.), *Composite Currencies—SDRs, ECUs and Other Instruments*, Euromoney Publications (London: 1984).

Jones, Ronald W. and Peter B. Kenen (eds). *Handbook of International Economics, vol. 2* (international monetary economics), North-Holland (Amsterdam: 1985).

Jovović, Dejan. 'Evolution of Special Drawing Rights', *Review of International Affairs* (Yugoslavia), no. 837, 20 February 1985.

Julius, DeAnne. 'A Roadmap for SDR Evolution', in Subacchi and Driffill (eds), *Beyond the Dollar: Rethinking the International Monetary System*, A Chatham House Report (London: 2010), as at: http://www.chathamhouse.org.uk/files/16146_r0310_ims.pdf (accessed 8 June 2011).

Kadan, V. B. 'Implications for Developing Countries of Current Proposals for a Substitution Account', in S. Dell (ed.), *The International Monetary System and its Reform,* (for the G24) vol. 1, North-Holland for the UN (Amsterdam: 1987).

Kafka, Alexandre. 'Some IMF Problems After the Committee of Twenty' (mimeo—prepared for a conference in honour of Jacques J. Polak), 4 April 1991.

Kahn, Professor Lord. 'SDRs and Aid', *Lloyds Bank Review*, no. 110, October 1973.

Katzenstein, Peter (ed.). *Between Power and Plenty—Foreign Economic Policies of Advanced Industrial States*, University of Wisconsin Press (Madison, WI: 1978).

Kazmi, S. Aqdas Ali Kazmi, 'Special Drawing Rights and International Liquidity', *Punjab University Economist* (Pakistan), vol. VIII, 1970.

Kelkar, Vijay L., Praveen K. Chaudhry, and Marta Vanduzer-Snow, 'Time for Change at the IMF', in *Finance and Development*, IMF, March 2005, vol. 42, no. 1. at: http://www.internationalmonetaryfund.org/external/pubs/ft/fandd/2005/03/pdf/kelkar.pdf (accessed 16 June 2011).

Kenen, Peter B. (ed.). *International Trade and Finance—Frontiers for Research,* Cambridge University Press (Cambridge: 1975).

Kenen, Peter B. 'The Analytics of a Substitution Account', *Banca Nazionale del Lavoro Quarterly Review*, no. 139, December 1981.

Kenen, Peter B. 'The Role of the Dollar as an International Currency', Group of Thirty Occasional Paper 13 (New York: 1983).

Kenen, Peter B. 'Use of the SDR to Supplement or Substitute for Other Means of Finance', in George M. von Furstenberg, *International Money and Credit: The Policy Roles,* IMF (Washington, DC: 1983).

Kenen, Peter B. 'Financing, Adjustment, and the International Monetary Fund', Brookings Discussion Paper in International Economics no. 26, Brookings Institution, Washington, DC: February 1985.

Kenen, Peter B. 'Macroeconomic Theory and Policy: How the Closed Economy was Opened', in R. W. Jones and P. B. Kenen (eds), *Handbook of International Economics,* North-Holland (Amsterdam: 1985).

Kenen, Peter B. 'Financing, Adjustment, and the International Monetary System', *Studies in International Economics*, The Brookings Institution (Washington, DC: 1986).

Kenen, Peter B. 'Changing Views About the Role of the SDR and Implications for its Attributes', in S. Dell (ed.), *The International Monetary System and its Reform*, vol. II, North-Holland for the UN (Amsterdam: 1987).

Kenen, Peter B. 'The Future of the SDR', in Michael Mussa, J. M. Boughton, and P. Isard (eds). *The Future of the SDR*, IMF (Washington, DC: 1996).

Kenen, Peter B. 'The Substitution Account as a First Step Toward Reform of the International Monetary System', Peterson Institute for International Economics Policy Brief no. PB10-6, March 2010, as at: http://www.piie.com/publications/pb/pb10-06.pdf (accessed 8 June 2011).

Kenen, Peter B. 'An SDR Based Reserve System', *Journal of Globalization and Development*, vol. 1, no. 2, 2010, as at: http://www.bepress.com/jgd/vol1/iss2/art13 (accessed 8 June 2011).

Kenen, Peter B. 'Renovation of the Global Reserve Regime: Concepts and Proposals', CEPS Working Paper no. 208, June 2010, as at: http://www.princeton.edu/ceps/workingpapers/208kenen.pdf (accessed 8 June 2011).

Kenen, Peter B. 'Beyond the Dollar', mimeo—paper prepared for the Allied Social Science Association Meetings, Denver, CO, January 2011.

Keohane, Robert O. *After Hegemony: Cooperation and Discord in the World Political System*, Princeton University Press (Princeton: 1984).

Keohane, Robert O. *International Institutions and State Power—Essays in International Relations Theory*, Westview Press (Boulder, Co: 1989).

Keohane, Robert O. and Joseph S. Nye, Jr. '*Power and Interdependence* revisited', in *International Organization,* vol. 41, no. 4, Autumn 1987.

Kessler, Geldolph A. 'The Need to Control International Bank Lending', *Banca Nazionale del Lavoro Quarterly Review,* no. 132, March 1980.

Keynes, J. M. *Activities 1944–1946: The Transition to Power,* collected works of J. M. Keynes, vol. XXIV (Donald Moggridge (ed.)), Macmillan and Cambridge University Press (Cambridge: 1979).

Keynes, J. M. *Activities 1940–1944: Shaping the Post-War World—The Clearing Union,* collected works of J. M. Keynes, vol. XXV (Donald Moggridge (ed.)), Macmillan and Cambridge University Press (Cambridge: 1980).

Keynes, J. M. *Activities 1941–1946: Shaping the Post-War World—Bretton Woods,* collected works of J. M. Keynes, vol. XXVI (Donald Moggridge (ed.)), Macmillan and Cambridge University Press (Cambridge: 1980).

Khambata, Dara M. *The Practice of Multinational Banking—Macro-Policy Issues and Key International Concepts*, Quorum Books (New York: 1986).

Kindleberger, Charles P. 'Key Currencies and Financial Centres', in F. Machlup *et al.*, *Reflections on a Troubled World Economy*, St Martin's Press (New York: 1983).

King, Kenneth. *US Monetary Policy and European Responses in the 1980s*, Chatham House Paper 16, Royal Institute of International Affairs/Routledge & Kegan Paul (London: 1982).

Klopstock, Fred H. 'Implications of a Substitution Account for the Eurocurrency Markets', in S. Dell (ed.), *The International Monetary System and its Reform* (for the G24) vol. 1, North-Holland for the UN (Amsterdam: 1987).

Krasner, Stephen. *Defending the National Interest*, Princeton University Press (Princeton: 1978).

Krupnick, Alan J. 'SDR: Super-Duper Reserve?', FRB Philadelphia *Business Review,* July 1971.

Laney, Leroy O. 'SDR Substitution, the Dollar, or Multiple Reserve Assets: Where are We Bound from Here?', in *Voice,* Federal Reserve Bank of Dallas, July 1980.

Levi, Maurice. *International Finance—Financial Management and the International Economy*, McGraw-Hill (Tokyo: 1983).

Lissakers, Karin. 'Is the SDR a Monetary Dodo? This Bird May Still Fly', in Edwin Truman (ed.), *Reforming the IMF for the 21st Century*, Peterson Institute for International Economics (Washington, DC: April 2006).

Lockhart, Tessa Eliott. 'A Re-evaluation of Special Drawing Rights During the Global Financial Crisis in 2009'—IPE Working Paper 3/2009, Istanbul Bilgi University, as at: http://web.me.com/eatonak/IPEWorkingPapers/page6/files/SDR%20Paper.pdf (accessed 8 June 2011).

Lomax, David F. 'International Moneys and Monetary Arrangements in Private Markets', in George M. von Furstenberg (ed.), *International Money and Credit: The Policy Roles,* IMF (Washington, DC: 1983).

Machlup, Fritz. 'Plans for Reform of the International Monetary System', Special Papers in International Economics, No. 3, International Finance Section, Princeton University (Princeton: May 1962).

Machlup, Fritz. *Remaking the International Monetary System: The Rio Agreement and Beyond,* Johns Hopkins Press (Baltimore: 1968).

Machlup, Fritz, Gerhard Fels and Hubertus Müller-Groeling (eds.). *Reflections on a Troubled World Economy—Essays in Honor of Herbert Giersch,* Trade Policy Research Centre (London) and St Martin's Press (New York: 1983).

Mann, Thomas E. and Norman J. Ornstein (eds.). *The New Congress,* American Enterprise Institute for Public Policy Research (Washington, DC: 1981).

Martin, William McChesney. 'Toward a World Central Bank?' (background paper for 7th Per Jacobsson Foundation lecture meeting, Basle; includes commentaries by Karl Blessing, Alfredo Machado and Harry Johnson), Washington, DC, 1970.

Mayer, Helmut and Hiro Taguchi. 'Official Intervention in the Exchange Markets: Stabilising or Destabilising?', BIS Economic Paper no. 6, (Basle: March 1983).

McKinnon, Ronald I. *Money in International Exchange—The Convertible Currency System,* Oxford University Press (Oxford: 1979).

McKinnon, Ronald I. 'The Case for Internationalizing American Monetary Policy', (draft of paper presented to Annual Symposium of Euro-American Relations and Global Economic Interdependence), College of Europe, Bruges, Belgium, September 1984.

Meltzer, Allan. 'US Policy in the Bretton Woods era', in *FRB St Louis Review*, vol. 73, no. 3, May/June 1991.

Merlini, Cesare. *Economic Summits and Western Decision-Making,* European Institute of Public Administration and Croom Helm (Beckenham: 1984).

Milward, Alan S. *War, Economy and Society 1939–1945* (vol. 5 of the History of the World Economy in the Twentieth Century (general editor: Wolfram Fischer), University of California Press (Berkeley and Los Angeles: 1977)).

'Ministry without Portfolio', *The Economist* special survey on the IMF, 26 September 1981.

Mountford, Alexander. 'The Historical Development of IMF Governance', IMF Independent Evaluation Office (IEO) *Background Paper* BP/08/02, May 2008, as at: http://www.ieo-imf.org/eval/complete/pdf/05212008/BP08_02.pdf (accessed 8 June 2011).

Mudd, Douglas R. 'International Reserves and the Role of Special Drawing Rights', in *FRB St Louis Review*, January 1978.

Mundell, Robert. 'The International Monetary System and the Case for a World Currency', Leon Koźmiński Academy of Entrepreneurship and Management (WSPiZ) and TIGER, Distinguished Lectures Series n. 12, Warsaw, 23 October 2003, as at: http://www.tiger.edu.pl/publikacje/dist/mundell2.pdf (accessed 8 June 2011).

Mundell, Robert and Milton Friedman, 'One world, One money?', *Policy Options/ Options Politiques*, Institute for Research in Public Policy (IRPP), Montreal, May 2001.

Mundell, Robert and Jacques J. Polak. *The New International Monetary System*, Columbia University Press (New York: 1977).

Myers, Robert J. (ed). *The Political Morality of the International Monetary Fund*, vol 3. of Ethics and Foreign Policy, Carnegie Council on Ethics and International Affairs/ Transaction Books (New Brunswick, NJ: 1987).

Nau, Henry R. *The Myth of America's Decline—Leading the World Economy into the 1990s*, Oxford University Press (New York: 1990).

Nedersjö, Anna-Karin. 'Special Drawing Rights—Oiling the Wheels', *Sveriges Riksbank Economic Review*, no. 2 (Stockholm: 2003).

Nye, Joseph S. Jr. *Bound to Lead—The Changing Nature of American Power*, Basic Books (New York: 1991).

Nye, Joseph S. Jr. and Robert Keohane. *Power and Interdependence*, Little, Brown & Co. (Boston: 1977).

Ocampo, José Antonio. 'Special Drawing Rights and the Reform of the Global Reserve System', Group of 24, September 2009, available at: http://www.g24.org/PDF/jao0909.pdf (accessed 16 June 2011).

Ocampo, José Antonio. 'Building an SDR-based Global Reserve System', *Journal of Globalization and Development*, vol. 1, no. 2, 2010, as at: http://www.bepress.com/jgd/vol1/iss2/art14 (accessed 8 June 2011).

Odell, John. *US International Monetary Policy: Markets, Power, and Ideas as Sources of Change*, Princeton University Press (Princeton, NJ: 1982).

Oppenheimer, Peter. 'Impact of a Substitution Account on Eurocurrency and Related Lending to Developing Countries', in S. Dell (ed.) *The International Monetary System and its Reform* (for the G24), vol. 1, North-Holland for the UN (Amsterdam: 1987).

Ornstein, Norman J. 'The House and The Senate in a New Congress', in T. E. Mann and N. J. Ornstein (eds), *The New Congress*, American Enterprise Institute for Public Policy Research (Washington, DC: 1981).

Padoan, Pier Carlo. *The Political Economy of International Financial Instability*, Croom Helm (Beckenham: 1986).

Papa, Angelo. 'SDR Certificates of Deposit', in L. de V. Wragg (ed.), *Composite Currencies—SDRs, ECUs and Other Instruments*, Euromoney Publications (London: 1984).

Pārsā, Parviz. 'Special Drawing Rights: Background and Analysis', *Tahqiqat-e eqtesadi (Quarterly Journal of Economic Research* (Tehran)), vol. 8, Spring 1971.

Pastor, Robert A. *Congress and the Politics of US Foreign Economic Policy 1929–1976*, University of California Press (Berkeley and Los Angeles: 1980).

Pauls, B. Dianne. 'US Exchange Rate Policy: Bretton Woods to Present', in *Federal Reserve Bulletin*, vol. 76, no. 11, November 1990.

Polak, Jacques J. 'The Role of the International Monetary Fund', in *The International Monetary System: Forty Years After Bretton Woods*, Conference Series No. 28, FRB Boston (Boston: 1984).

Polak, Jacques J. 'The Impasse Concerning the Role of the SDR', in Wietze Eizenga, E. Frans Limburg, and Jacques J. Polak (eds), *The Quest for National and Global Economic Stability*, Kluwer Academic Publishers (Dordrecht: 1988).

Polak, Jacques J. 'Should the SDR Become the Sole Financing Technique for the IMF?', in Michael Mussa, James M. Broughton, and Peter Isard (eds), *The Future of the SDR in Light of Changes in the International Financial System*—Proceedings of a Seminar held in Washington, DC 18–19 March 1996, IMF (Washington, DC: 1996).

Posner, Michael (ed.). *Problems of International Money*, IMF and Overseas Development Institute (Washington, DC: 1986).

Rabushka, Alvin. 'From Austerity to Growth: A New Role for the IMF', in R. J. Myers (ed.), *The Political Morality of the International Monetary Fund*, Transaction Books (New Brunswick, NJ: 1987).

Rawson, Tessa G. 'A Response to the Allocation of Special Drawing Rights in 2009, and Their Role in the Reform of the International Monetary System', as at: http://web.me.com/eatonak/IPE/page21/files/Tessa%20Rawson-.pdf (accessed 8 June 2011).

'Reserves and International Liquidity', BIS Economic Paper No. 22, Monetary and Economic Department (Basle: June 1988).

Rhomberg, Rudolf R. 'Balance of Payments Financing and Reserve Creation', IMF *Staff Papers,* vol. XXXII (Washington, DC: 1985).

Rieke, Wolfgang. 'The Development of the Deutschemark as a Reserve Currency', (including appendix: 'The Functioning of the ECU') in *Reserve Currencies in Transition,* Group of Thirty (New York: 1982).

Rohrlich, Paul Egon. 'Economic Culture and Foreign Policy: The Cognitive Analysis of Economic Policy Making', *International Organization,* vol. 41, no. 1, Winter 1987.

Roosa, Robert. *Reserve Currencies in Transition,* Group of Thirty (New York: 1982).

Roosa, Robert. 'The Multiple Reserve Currency System', in *Reserve Currencies in Transition,* Group of Thirty (New York: 1982).

Russett, Bruce. 'The Mysterious Case of Vanishing Hegemony; or is Mark Twain Really Dead?', *International Organization,* vol. 39, no. 2, Spring 1985.

Sacchetti, Ugo. 'The SDR: Ten Years of Experience', *Banca Nazionale del Lavoro Quarterly Review,* no. 131, Rome, December 1979.

Sakbani, M. M. 'A Critique of the Prevailing Monetary System: Principal Themes of a Reformed System', UNCTAD *Reprint Series,* no. 16, July 1981 (reprinted from *Third World Quarterly,* vol. 3, no. 3, July 1981).

Sakbani, M. M. 'The Enduring Financial and Monetary Consequences of the US Freeze: An SDR Recycling Proposal', UNCTAD Discussion Paper No. 1 (Geneva: 1982).

Samuels, Nathaniel. 'Dealing with the International Debt Issue', in A. K. Henrikson, *Negotiating World Order—The Artisanship and Architecture of Global Diplomacy,* Scholarly Resources Inc. (Wilmington, DE: 1987).

Sanders, Elaine J. M. 'SDR Syndicated Loans', in L. de V. Wragg (ed.), *Composite Currencies—SDRs, ECUs and Other Instruments,* Euromoney Publications (London: 1984).

Scammell, W. M. *The Stability of the International Monetary System*, Macmillan Education (Basingstoke: 1987).

Schwartz, Anna J. *Money in Historical Perspective—Part III, International Monetary Arrangements*, University of Chicago Press (Chicago: 1987)

'SDRs—A New Asset Supplementing Reserves for Growth in Free World Trade', in *Business Review* (FRB Dallas), December 1970.

Sil, Rudra, and Peter J. Katzenstein, 'Analytical Eclectism in the Study of World Politics: Reconfiguring Problems and Mechanisms Across Research Traditions', American Political Science Association's *Perspectives on Politics*, vol. 8, no. 2, June 2010.

Sinclair, Barbara, 'Coping with Uncertainty: Building Coalitions in the House and the Senate', in T. E. Mann and N. J. Ornstein (eds), *The New Congress*, American Enterprise Institute for Public Policy Research (Washington, DC: 1981).

Sniderman, Mark S. 'The Business Economist at Work: The Research Department of the Federal Reserve Bank of Cleveland', in *Business Economics* (FRB Cleveland), July 1991.

Sobol, Dorothy M. 'A Substitution Account: Precedents and Issues', *FRBNY Quarterly Review*, Summer 1979, at: http://www.newyorkfed.org/research/quarterly_review/1979v4/v4n2article8.pdf (accessed 8 June 2011).

Sobol, Dorothy M. 'The SDR in Private International Finance', *FRBNY Quarterly Review*, Winter 1981–2 at: http://www.newyorkfed.org/research/quarterly_review/1981v6/v6n4article5.pdf (accessed 8 June 2011).

Sobol, Dorothy M. *Europe Confronts the Dollar—The Creation of the SDR, 1963–69*, Garland Publishing Co. (New York: 1982).

Soros, George. 'Special Drawing Rights for the Provision of Public Goods on a Global Scale', remarks at the Roundtable on 'New Proposals for Financing for Development', Peterson Institute for International Economics, as at: http://www.iie.com/publications/papers/paper.cfm?ResearchID=447 (accessed 8 June 2011).

Soros, George. *George Soros on Globalization*, Public Affairs—Perseus Books (Cambridge, MA: 2002).

Soros, George. 'Financing the Fight Against Climate Change', 10 December 2010, as at: http://www.project-syndicate.org/commentary/soros55/English (accessed 8 June 2011).

Solomon, Robert. *The International Monetary System 1945–1981*, Harper & Row (New York: 1982).

Steele, D. B. 'The Case for Global Economic Management and UN System Reform', in *International Organization*, vol. 39, no. 3, Summer 1985.

Steil, Benn. *Financial Statecraft: The Role of Financial Markets in American Foreign Policy*, Yale University Press (New Haven: 2006).

Steil, Benn. 'The End of National Currency', *Foreign Affairs* (New York: May/June 2007), available at: http://www.foreignaffairs.com/print/62614 (accessed 8 June 2011).

Steil, Benn and Manuel Hinds. *Money, Markets, and Sovereignty*, Yale University Press (New Haven, CT: March 2009).

Stiglitz, Joseph E. (Chair) 'Report of the Commission of Experts of the President of the United Nations General Assembly on Reforms of the International Monetary and Financial System', United Nations General Assembly (New York: 21 September 2009), at: http://www.un.org/ga/econcrisissummit/docs/FinalReport_CoE.pdf (accessed

8 June 2011); preliminary report and other documentation at: http://www.un.org/ga/president/63/commission/financial_commission.shtml (accessed 8 June 2011).

Strange, Susan. 'The Politics of International Currencies', *World Politics,* vol. XXIII, no. 2, 1971.

Strange, Susan. *International Monetary Relations*, vol. 2 of International Economic Relations of the Western World 1959–71 (Andrew Shonfield (ed.)), RIIA and Oxford University Press (Oxford: 1976).

Strange, Susan. 'Politics, Trade and Money' (draft of paper presented to Annual Symposium of Euro-American Relations and Global Economic Interdependence), College of Europe, Bruges, Belgium, September 1984.

Strange, Susan. *Casino Capitalism,* Basil Blackwell (Oxford: 1986).

Strange, Susan. 'The Persistent Myth of Lost Hegemony', in *International Organization,* vol. 41, no. 4, Autumn 1987.

Subacchi, Paola and John Driffill (eds). 'Beyond the Dollar—Rethinking the International Monetary System, A Chatham House Report' (London: 2010), as at: http//www.chathamhouse.org.uk/files/16146_r0310_ims.pdf (accessed 8 June 2011).

Swoboda, Alexander K. 'Credit Creation in the Euromarket: Alternative Theories and Implications for Control', Group of Thirty Occasional Paper no. 2 (New York: 1980).

'The Proposed Substitution Account in the IMF', *Midland Bank Review,* Winter 1979.

The International Monetary System: Forty Years After Bretton Woods, Conference Series No. 28, FRB Boston (Boston: 1984)

The US Dollar—Recent Developments, Outlook, and Policy Options, A Symposium Sponsored by the Federal Reserve Bank of Kansas City, Jackson Hole, Wyoming, 21–23 August 1985, FRB Kansas City (Kansas City: 1985).

Tew, Brian. *The Evolution of the International Monetary System 1945–1977,* Hutchinson (London: 1979).

Teunissen, Jan Joost (ed.). *Fragile Finance—Rethinking the International Monetary System,* FONDAD (The Hague: 1992), available at: http://www.fondad.org/product_books/pdf_download/26/Fragile_Finance-BookComplete.pdf (accessed 16 June 2011).

Thirlwall, A. P. (ed.) *Keynes and International Monetary Relations,* Macmillan (London: 1976).

Toniolo, Gianni (ed.). *Central Banks' Independence in Historical Perspective,* Walter de Gruyter (Berlin: 1988).

'Towards a Less Unstable International Monetary System—Reserve Assets and a Substitution Account', Group of Thirty Reserve Assets Study Group, Group of Thirty (New York: 1980).

Triffin, Robert. *Gold and the Dollar Crisis—The Future of Convertibility,* Yale University Press (New Haven: 1960).

Triffin, Robert. '"Europe and the Money Muddle" Revisited', *Banca Nazionale del Lavoro Quarterly Review,* no. 124, Rome, March 1978.

Triffin, Robert. 'The Future of the International Monetary System', *Banca Nazionale del Lavoro Quarterly Review,* no. 132, Rome, March 1980.

Truman, Edwin M. *A Strategy for IMF Reform,* Institute for International Economics (Washington, DC: February 2006).

Truman, Edwin M. (ed.). *Reforming the IMF for the 21st Century*, Peterson Institute for International Economics (Washington, DC: April 2006).

Truman, Edwin M. 'How the Fund Can Help Save the World Economy', *Financial Times* op. ed., 5 March 2009, available at: http://www.iie.com/publications/opeds/oped.cfm?ResearchID=1140 (accessed 16 June 2011).

Ugeux, Georges. 'SDR Floating Rate Notes', in L. de V. Wragg (ed.), *Composite Currencies—SDRs, ECUs and Other Instruments*, Euromoney Publications (London: 1984).

UNCTAD. 'Development and Recovery: The Realities of the New Interdependence', Report by the Secretary of UNCTAD to the sixth session of the Conference, document no. TD/271/Rev. 1, New York, 1984.

UNDP/UNCTAD. 'Measures to Strengthen the SDR', Report to the Group of Twenty-Four, UNDP/UNCTAD Project INT/75/015. (Studies on International Monetary and Financial Issues for the Developing Countries, document no. UNCTAD/MFD/TA/11 GE.81-51666.) (Geneva: March 1981).

Van Ypersele, J. 'A Central Position for the Special Drawing Right in the Monetary System', *Banca Nazionale del Lavoro Quarterly Review,* vol. 30 (Rome: 1977).

Vernon, Ray. *Sovereignty at Bay: The Multinational Spread of US Enterprise*, Basic Books (New York: 1971).

Volcker, Paul A. 'The Political Economy of the Dollar'—The Fred Hirsch Memorial Lecture, Warwick University, Coventry, England, 9 November 1978, as reproduced in FRBNY *Quarterly Review,* vol. 3, no. 4, Winter 1978–9.

Volcker, Paul A. and Toyoo Gyohten. *Changing Fortunes: The World's Money and the Threat to American Leadership*, Times Books (New York: 1992).

Wallerstein, Immanuel. *The Politics of the World Economy—The States, The Movements and the Civilisations,* Cambridge University Press (Cambridge: 1988).

Walter, Andrew. *World Power and World Money*, St Martin's Press (New York: 1993).

Waltz, Kenneth. *Theory of International Politics*, Addison-Wesley (Reading, MA: 1979).

Weatherford, M. Stephen. 'The International Economy as a Constraint on US Macro-Economic Policymaking', in *International Organization,* vol. 42, no. 4, Autumn 1988.

Widman, F. Lisle. *Making International Monetary Policy*, International Law Institute, Georgetown University Law Center (Washington, DC: 1982).

Willett, Thomas D. 'US Monetary Policy and World Liquidity' (paper of the 95th annual meeting of the American Economic Association), *American Economic Association,* vol. 73, no. 2, May 1983.

Williamson, John. 'International Liquidity', fifth survey in applied economics for the Social Science Research Council and the Royal Economic Society, *The Economic Journal,* September 1973.

Williamson, John. *The Failure of World Monetary Reform*, Thomas Nelson and Sons Ltd (Sunbury-on-Thames: 1977).

Williamson, John. *The Open Economy and the World Economy*, Basic Books (New York: 1983).

Williamson, John. 'A New SDR Allocation?', Institute for International Economics Policy Analysis in International Economics Study No. 7, March 1984.

Williamson, John. 'International Liquidity: Are the Supply and Composition Appropriate?', in *The International Monetary System: Forty Years After Bretton Woods*, Conference Series No. 28, FRB Boston (Boston: 1984).

Williamson, John and Michael Gavin. 'International Monetary Issues in 1985'—A Report to the Group of Twenty Four, Institute for International Economics, 1985 (mimeo).

Williamson, John. 'Exchange Rate Policy for Developing Countries—A Case for Collective Action', *Journal of Foreign Exchange and International Finance* (India), vol. 1, no. 1, 1987.

Williamson, John. 'International Monetary Reform: A Survey of the Options', in S. Dell (ed.), *The International Monetary System and its Reform* (for the G24), vol. 1, North-Holland for the UN (Amsterdam: 1987).

Williamson, John. 'Reforming the IMF: Different or Better?' in R. J. Myers (ed.), *The Political Morality of the International Monetary Fund,* Transaction Books (New Brunswick, NJ: 1987).

Williamson, John. 'Understanding Special Drawing Rights', Peterson Insititute for Internaitonal Economics Policy Brief no. PB09-11, June 2009, available at: http://www.iie.com/publications/pb/pb09-11.pdf (accessed 8 June 2011).

Williamson, John. 'Why SDRs Could Rival the Dollar', Peterson Institute for International Economics Policy Brief no. PB09-20, September 2009, available at: http://www.iie.com/publications/pb/pb09-20.pdf (accessed 8 June 2011).

Wilson, P. R. D. *International Economics—Theory, Evidence and Practice,* Harvester Press (Brighton: 1986).

Witteveen, H. Johannes *et al.* 'Towards a Less Unstable International Monetary System—Reserve Assets and a Substitution Account', A Report by the Reserve Assets Study Group of the Group of Thirty (London: 1980).

Witteveen, H. Johannes. 'Developing a New International Monetary System: A Long-Term View', the1983 Per Jacobsson Lecture (Washington, DC: 1983), as at: http://www.perjacobsson.org/lectures/1983.pdf (accessed 8 June 0211).

Woolley, John T. *Monetary Politics—The Federal Reserve and the Politics of Monetary Policy,* Cambridge University Press (Cambridge: 1984).

Wragg, L. de V. (ed.). *Composite Currencies—SDRs, ECUs and Other Instruments,* Euromoney Publications Ltd. (London: 1984).

Zedillo, Ernesto *et al.* 'Report of the High-level Panel on Financing for Development' [Zedillo Report], United Nations, New York, 2001, at: http://www.un.org/esa/ffd/a55-1000.pdf (accessed 8 June 2011).

B: US Government Documents

(i) Annual Reports and Miscellaneous Documents

——Annual Report of the National Advisory Council on International Monetary and Financial Policies. Annual.

——Annual Report of the Secretary of the Treasury on the State of the Finances. Annual.

——Declassified US documents: papers of Dean Acheson, Harry S. Truman Library. 1962 US Treasury memoranda concerning the G10 stand-by arrangements. US declassified document nos. 86–1918 and 86–1919.

——Economic Report of the President—together with the Annual Report of the Council of Economic Advisers. Annual.

Ferguson, Roger W. Jr. Vice Chairman, Federal Reserve Board of Governors. 'The Future of the International Financial Architecture', remarks to the Banco de España and IMF Conference, Madrid Spain, 15 June 2004, as at: http://www.imf.org/external/np/res/seminars/2004/60/pdf/fergus.pdf (accessed 8 June 2011).

——FRB Staff Studies, FRBNY Annual Reports (individual FRB articles above).

——Maintaining the Strength of the United States Dollar in a Strong Free World Economy. US Treasury, January 1968 (and progress report, December 1968).

——'Report to Congress on the Use of Special Drawing Rights by IMF Member Countries', US.

Treasury, August 2010, as at: http://www.treasury.gov/about/organizational-structure/offices/International-Affairs/Documents/Report%20to%20Congress%20on%20SDR%20Use%20–%20August%202010.pdf (accessed 8 June 2011).

Sanford, Jonathan E. and Martin A. Weiss, 'The Global Financial Crisis: Increasing IMF Resources and the Role of Congress', Congressional Research Service Report no, R40578, as at: http://www.fas.org/sgp/crs/misc/R40578.pdf (accessed 8 June 2011).

(ii) Joint Economic Committee—Hearings, Reports, and Documents

——JEC Reports on the Economic Reports of the President (Annual, usually March).

——'International Payments Imbalances—and Need for Strengthening International Financial Arrangements', Report of the Subcommittee on International Exchange and Payments (Henry Reuss, chairman), 87th Congress, 1st session, 1961.

——'Next Steps in International Monetary Reform' Hearing before the Subcommittee on International Exchange and Payments. 9 September 1968.

——'The Euro-dollar Market and its Public Policy Implications', paper by Ira O. Scott, Jr., no. 12 of Economic Policies and Practices. Submitted 20 February 1970.

——Making Floating Part of a Reformed Monetary System Report of the Subcommittee on International Economics. 93rd Congress, 1st session, 9 January 1974.

——Exchange Rate Policy and International Monetary Reform Report of the Cubcommittee on International Trade, Investment and Monetary Policy of the House Committee on Banking, Currency and Housing, and the JEC Subcommittee on International Economics. 94th Congress, 1st session, August 1975.

——The Proposed IMF Agreement on Gold, Report of the Subcommittee on International Economics. 94th Congress, 1st session, 17 December 1975.

(iii) Senate Committees

——'The International Financial Crisis', Hearings before the Subcommittee on International Finance and Resources, Senate Finance Committee. 30 May – 5 June 1973.

——'Causes and Cures of World Inflation', Hearings before the Subcommittee on International Finance and Resources, Senate Finance Committee. 26 January, 17 February 1976.

——Amendment of the Bretton Woods Agreements Act, Report Senate Foreign Relations Committee, no. 94—1148, 10 August 1976 (printed).

——Amendment of the Bretton Woods Agreements Act and Other International Monetary Matters, Report of the Senate Banking, Housing, and Urban Affairs Committee no. 94–1295, 22 September 1976 (printed).
——Bretton Woods Agreements Amendments Act of 1977, Report of Senate Committee on Foreign Relations no. 95–603, 15 November 1977 (printed).
——Bretton Woods Agreements Act—Amendments of 1978, Report of the Senate Committee on Banking, Housing, and Urban Affairs no. 95–698, 13 March 1978 (printed).
——Multilateral Action on International Economic Issues, Report from Senate Foreign Relations Committee no. 95–977, 12 July 1978 (printed).
——Bretton Woods Agreements Amendments Act of 1980, Report of the Senate Foreign Relations Committee no. 96–693, 9 May 1980 (printed).

(iv) House of Representatives Committees
——'To Authorize the United States to Participate in Increases in the Resources of the Asian Development Bank, the International Monetary Fund, and the International Bank for Reconstruction and Development', Hearings before the House Committee on Banking and Currency, 91st Congress, 2nd session,16–17 April 1970.
——Increase US Participation in International Monetary Banks—Communication from the President to the House Banking and Currency Committee no. 91–383, 14 September 1970 (printed).
——US Participation in the Supplementary Financing Facility of the International Monetary Fund Communication form the Chairman, National Advisory Council on International Monetary and Financial Policies no 95–224, 20 September 1970 (printed).
——International Monetary Fund Appropriation, 1981, Report to the House Committee on Appropriations no. 96–1263.

C: IMF Documents

Access to IMF archival material has been gradually increased over the past twenty years, including by virtue of a 1996 Board Decision allowing the managing director to declassify documentary materials in the custody of the archives. Much Fund documentation now falls into the public domain 5/10/20 years after date of writing.

(i) Second Amendment Documents and Minutes

See Appendix 1 for a detailed list of contents of the following:

Documents Relating to the Second Amendment of the Articles of Agreement of the International Monetary Fund, 3 vols. documents (Staff Memoranda, Draft Articles of Agreement), 3 vols. minutes of the Executive Board (Washington, DC: 1980). Index, 1986.

(ii) Departmental Memoranda (DMs) and related documents
DM/70/2, 'International Monetary Problems and Special Drawing Rights', Research Department, 14 January 1970.

DM/77/18, 'Control over International Liquidity—A Summary of the Views Expressed by the Participants in the Fleming Memorial Conference', Financial Studies Division, Research Department, 28 February 1977.

DM/77/38, 'International Units of Account: A Comparison', Treasurer's Department, 20 April 1977.

DM/77/64, 'Differential Economic Treatment in Favor of Less Developed Countries', Exchange and Trade Relations Department, 15 July 1977.

DM/79/91, 'The European Monetary Fund: External Relationships', Research Department, 10 December 1979.

DM/80/40, 'Price Deflators for Special Drawing Rights (SDRs) Over the Past Decade', Research Department, 30 May 1980.

DM/82/4, 'Has the SDR Been Used as The First Line Reserve Asset? (A statistical examination of SDR uses)', Treasurer's Department, 27 January 1982.

DM/82/29, 'Some Aspects of Using the SDR to Invoice Private International Goods and Services Transactions', Treasurer's Department, 23 April 1982.

DM/82/41, 'Official and Private SDRs: Their Relationship and Its Future', Treasurer's Department, 24 June 1982.

DM/84/11, 'Demand for International Reserves and Effects Reserve Increases on the World Economy: An Annotated Bibliography', Financial Studies Division, Research Department, 22 February 1984.

DM/85/27, 'The Level and Structure of Interest Rates on SDR-Denominated Financial Assets', Treasurer's Department, 3 May 1985.

DM/85/81, 'Pegging to a Basket of Currencies: Conceptual and Operational Issues', Research Department, 26 December 1985.

DM/86/14, 'Currency Pegs for Developing Countries and Experiences with the SDR as a Standard Basket: A Review and Appraisal', Treasurer's Department, 14 February 1986.

DM/86/48, 'Holding and Use of SDRs by Fund Members', Treasurer's Department, 28 July 1986.

———'SDR Allocation in the Eighth Basic Period—Basic Considerations', prepared by the Research and Treasurer's Departments, 16 November 2001; available at: http://www.imf.org/external/np/tre/2001/111601.pdf (accessed 8 June 2011).

——— 'Proposal for a General Allocation of SDRs', Finance, Legal, and Strategy, Policy and Review Departments (in collaboration with the Research Department, 9 June 2009; available at: http://www.imf.org/external/np/pp/eng/2009/060909.pdf (accessed 8 June 2011).

——— 'Allocation of Special Drawing Rights for the Ninth Basic Period: Draft Executive Board Decision and Managing Director Report to the Board of Governors', Finance, Legal, and Strategy, Policy and Review Departments, 16 July 2009; available at: http://www.imf.org/external/np/pp/eng/2009/071609.pdf (accessed 8 June 2011).

(iii) IMF Occasional Papers, Pamphlets, etc.

Occasional Paper No. 6. Joseph Gold, 'The Multilateral System of Payments—Keynes, Convertibility, and the International Monetary Fund's Articles of Agreement', August 1981.

Occasional Paper No. 28. Research Department, 'Exchange Rate Volatility and World Trade', July 1984.

Occasional Paper No. 43. Maxwell Watson *et al.*, 'International Capital Markets—Developments and Prospects', February 1986.

Occasional Paper No. 51. Research and Treasurer's Departments, 'The Role of the SDR in the International Monetary System', March 1987.

Occasional Paper No. 270. Altish R. Ghosh, Jonathan D. Ostry, and Charalambos Tsangarides, 'Exchange Rate Regimes and the Stability of the International Monetary System', 2010.

Pamphlet No. 12. Joseph Gold, 'The Reform of the Fund', 1969.

Pamphlet No. 13. Joseph Gold, 'Special Drawing Rights—Character and Use', 1970.

Pamphlet No. 14. Joseph Gold, 'Special Drawing Rights—The Role of Language', 1971.

Pamphlet No. 17. Walter Habermeier, 'Operations and Transactions in SDRs—The First Basic Period', 1973.

Pamphlet No. 18. J. J. Polak, 'Valuation and Rate of Interest of the SDR', 1974.

Pamphlet No. 19. Joseph Gold, 'Floating Currencies, Gold, and SDRs—Some Recent Legal Developments', 1976.

Pamphlet No. 20. Joseph Gold, 'Voting Majorities in the Fund—Effects of Second Amendment of the Articles', 1977.

Pamphlet No. 21. Joseph Gold, 'International Capital Movements Under the Law of the International Monetary Fund', 1977.

Pamphlet No. 22. Joseph Gold, 'Floating Currencies, SDRs and Gold—Further Legal Developments', 1977.

Pamphlet No. 25. Joseph Gold, 'The Second Amendment of the Fund's Articles of Agreement', 1978.

Pamphlet No. 26. Joseph Gold, 'SDRs, Gold, and Currencies—Third Survey of New Legal Developments', 1979.

Pamphlet No. 28. J. J. Polak, 'Thoughts on an International Monetary Fund Based Fully on the SDR', 1979.

Pamphlet No. 33. Joseph Gold, 'SDRs, Currencies, and Gold—Fourth Survey of New Legal Developments', 1980.

Pamphlet No. 36. Joseph Gold, 'SDRs, Currencies, and Gold—Fifth Survey of New Legal Developments', 1981.

Pamphlet No. 37. 'The International Monetary Fund—Its Evolution, Organization, and Activities', 1984.

Pamphlet No. 40. Joseph Gold, 'SDRs, Currencies, and Gold—Sixth Survey of New Legal Developments', 1983.

Pamphlet No. 41. Michael Ainley, 'The General Arrangements to Borrow', 1984.

Pamphlet No. 44. Joseph Gold, 'SDRs, Currencies, and Gold—Seventh Survey of New Legal Developments', 1987.

Pamphlet No. 45. 'Financial Organization and Operations of the IMF', Treasurer's Department, 2001, available at: http://www.imf.org/external/pubs/ft/pam/pam45/pdf/pam45.pdf (accessed 8 June 2011).

Pamphlet No. 53. Leo Van Houtven, 'Governance of the IMF—Decision Making, Institutional Oversight, Transparency, and Accountability', 2002, available at: http://www.imf.org/external/pubs/ft/pam/pam53/pam53.pdf (accessed 8 June 2011).

Staff Position Note SPN/09/26. Isabelle Mateos y Lago, Rupa Duttagupta and Rishi Goyall, 'The Debate on the International Monetary System', 11 November 2009, available at: http://www.imf.org/external/pubs/ft/spn/2009/spn0926.pdf (accessed 8 June 2011).

Staff Position Note SPN 10/06. Hugh Bredenkamp and Catherine Pattillo, 'Financing the Response to Climate Change', 25 March 2010, available at: http://www.imf.org/external/pubs/ft/spn/2010/spn1006.pdf (accessed 8 June 2011).

Working Paper WP/09/116. Barry Eichengreen, 'Out of the Box Thoughts about the International Financial Architecture', May 2009, at: http://www.imf.org/external/pubs/ft/wp/2009/wp09118.pdf (accessed 8 June 2011).

(iv) Other IMF Publications and Documents

Annual Report, International Monetary Fund.

Articles of Agreement of the International Monetary Fund as Modified by the Proposed [First] Amendment (includes typewritten palimpsests), n.d. (1968).

Articles of Agreement of the International Monetary Fund [after Second Amendment], reprinted May, 1982.

Articles of Agreement of the International Monetary Fund [after Fourth Amendment], available at: http://www.imf.org/external/pubs/ft/aa/ (accessed 8 June 2011).

Boughton, James. B. *Silent Revolution—The International Monetary Fund 1979–1989*. (Washington, DC: 2001); complete text available at: http://www.imf.org/external/pubs/ft/history/2001/ (accessed 8 June 2011).

Boughton, James B. 'Evolution of the SDR: Paper Gold or Paper Tiger?'—chapter 18 of James Boughton, Silent Revolution—The International Monetary Fund, 1979–89. 1 October, 2001, available at: http://www.imf.org/external/pubs/ft/history/2001/ch18.pdf (accessed 8 June 2011).

'By-Laws, Rules and Regulations—International Monetary Fund', 43rd Issue, 1 August 1986.

Clark, Peter B. and Jacques J. Polak. 'International Liquidity and the Role of the SDR in the International Monetary System', IMF Staff Papers, vol. 51, no. 1, 2004; available in Staff Papers Archive at: http://www.imf.org/external/pubs/ft/staffp/2004/01/pdf/clark.pdf (accessed 8 June 2011).

Coats, Warren L. R., Reinhard W. Furstenberg, and Peter Isard, 'Does the SDR System Generate Permanent Resource Transfers?', IMF Working Paper WP/88/33, Washington, DC, 1988.

Coats, Warren Jr. 'In Search of a Monetary Anchor: A "New" Monetary Standard', IMF Treasurer's Department document (not numbered), 13 April 1990.

De Vries, Margaret Garritsen. *The International Monetary Fund 1966–1971—The System Under Stress. vol. 1, Narrative; vol. 2. Documents* (Washington, DC: 1976).

De Vries, Margaret Garritsen. *The International Monetary Fund 1972–1978—Cooperation on Trial. vols. 1 and 2, Narrative and Analysis; vol. 3, Documents.* (Washington, DC: 1985).

De Vries, Margaret Garritsen. *The IMF in a Changing World 1945–85* (Washington, DC: 1986).

'Enhancing International Monetary Stability—A Role for the SDR?', IMF Strategy, Policy, and Review Department, 7 January 2011, at: http://www.imf.org/external/np/pp/eng/2011/010711.pdf (accessed 8 June 2011).

'Evolution of the SDR Outside the Fund', in George M. von Furstenberg (ed.), *International Money and Credit: The Policy Roles,* IMF (Washington, DC: 1983)

Horsefield, J. Keith. *The International Monetary Fund 1945–65. vol. 1, Chronicle; vol. 2,* (with M.G. de Vries *et al.*) *Analysis; vol. 3, Documents* (Washington, DC: 1969).

International Financial Statistics (annual yearbooks); also annual supplements: no. 6 'Supplement on International Reserves', 1983; no. 14 'Supplement on International Liquidity', 1987; no. 15 'Supplement on Trade Statistics', 1988.

IMF Staff Papers, quarterly (DMs, SMs, mentioned above in Appendix 1, often became staff papers).

IMF Survey, 23 times p.a., plus supplements and index.

'International Monetary Reform—Documents of the Committee of Twenty', Committee on Reform of the International Monetary System and Related Issues (Committee of Twenty), 1974.

'Is SDR Creation Inflationary?', Report by Richard Cooper, Harvard University, as Independent External Consultant, IMF, January 2011, at: http://www.imf.org/external/np/pp/eng/2011/010711a.pdf (accessed 8 June 2011).

Madeiros, Carlos, and Simon Nocera. 'The Potential Role of the SDR in Diversified Currency Portfolios of Central Banks', IMF Working Paper WP/88/81, Washington, DC 1988.

Mussa, Michael. 'The Rationale for SDR Allocation Under the Present Articles of Agreement of the International Monetary Fund', in Michael Mussa, James M. Broughton, and Peter Isard (eds), *The Future of the SDR in Light of Changes in the International Financial System—Proceedings of a Seminar held in Washington, DC, 18–19 March 1996, IMF (Washington, DC: 1996).*

Mussa, Michael, James M. Broughton, and Peter Isard (eds). *The Future of the SDR in Light of Changes in the International Financial System* – Proceedings of a Seminar held in Washington, DC, 18–19 March 1996, IMF (Washington, DC: 1996).

'Possible Further Improvements in the Existing SDR', in George M. von Furstenberg (ed.), *International Money and Credit: The Policy Roles,* IMF (Washington, DC: 1983).

'Proposal for a General Allocation of SDRs', IMF Finance, Legal and Strategy, Policy, and Review Departments, June 9 2009; available at: http://www.imf.org/extend/np/pp/eng/2009/060909.pdf (accessed 8 June 2011).

'Proposed Amendment of Articles of Agreement—New Facility Based on Special Drawing Rights, Changes in Fund Rules and Practices', Executive Directors, Report to the Board of Governors, April 1968.

'Reserve Accumulation and International Monetary Stability', Prepared by the Strategy, Policy and Review Department, 13 April 2010, as at: http://www.imf.org/external/np/pp/eng/2010/041310a.pdf (accessed 8 June 2011).

'SDR Allocation in the Eighth Basic Period—Basic Considerations', IMF Research and Treasurer's Departments, available at: http://www.imf.org/external/np/tre/2001/111601.htm (accessed 16 June 2011).

Selected Decisions of the International Monetary Fund—and Selected Documents. various.

Summary Proceedings, Annual Meetings of IMF Board of Governors. Annual.

'The Evolving Role of the SDR in the International Monetary System', in George M. von Furstenberg (ed.), *International Money and Credit: The Policy Roles* (Washington, DC: 1983).

'The Fund's Mandate—An Overview', IMF Strategy, Policy, and Review Department, 22 January 2010, available at: http://www.imf.org/external/np/pp/eng/2010/012210a.pdf (accessed 8 June 2011).

'Towards a More Stable International Monetary System', Opening Remarks by Dominique Strauss-Kahn, IMF Managing Director, 10 February 2011, as at: http://www.imf.org/external/np/speeches/2011/021011.htm (accessed 21 June 2011).

von Furstenberg, George M. (ed.) *International Money and Credit: The Policy Roles*, (Washington, DC: 1983).

D: Selected Interviews on the SDR or US International Monetary Policy were Conducted with the Following Individuals in London, Washington, DC, New York, Princeton, NJ, and Cambridge, MA, Concerning IMF Second Amendment and Subsequent Discussions

Peter Bakstansky, Vice-President, Federal Reserve Bank of New York (1975–2005), New York.

Jack Bennett, Under Secretary for Monetary Affairs, US Treasury 1974–5 (dec'd) (Deputy Under Secretary, Monetary Affairs, 1971–5, Deputy Assistant Secretary, International Affairs).

C. Fred Bergsten, Director, Peterson Institute for International Economics, 1981– (Other chief appointments include Assistant Secretary for International Affairs, US Treasury 1977–81, and Assistant for International Economic Affairs, National Security Council, Washington, DC).

Warren Coats, Jr., Advisor, Treasurer's Department, IMF (former Visiting Economist at the Board of Governors of the Federal Reserve System, and Chief of the Operations Division for SDRs and Administered Accounts, Treasurer's Department, IMF, Washington, DC).

Edwin Cohen, Under Secretary, US Treasury, 1972–3 (dec'd).

Richard Cooper, Maurits C. Boas Professor of International Economics, Harvard University, 1981—(Chairman, Federal Reserve Bank of Boston, 1990–2; Under Secretary for Economic Affairs, US State Department 1977–81; Deputy Assistant Secretary of State for International Monetary Affairs, US State Department 1965–6; Sr. Staff Economist, Council of Economic Advisers, 1961–3).

Sam Cross, Executive Vice-president, Federal Reserve Bank of New York, New York. (Also US Executive Director at the IMF 1975–80.)

Sir Joseph Gold, Senior Consultant, IMF, 1979–99 (dec'd) (with the Fund from 1946–99 and formerly General Counsel and Head of Legal Department 1960–79) (twice).

John Hennessy, Chairman and CEO, Credit Suisse First Boston Ltd. (Assistant Secretary, International Monetary Affairs, US Treasury 1972–4; Deputy Assistant Secretary, International Affairs, 1967–70).

William Hood, former Director of the Research Department, IMF (1979–86) and Canadian Deputy to the Committee of Twenty.

Peter Kenen, former Director of the International Finance Section, Princeton (consultant to US Treasury 1978–80; also to Federal Reserve Board and Council of Economic Advisers).

Jacques Polak, former President, Per Jacobsson Foundation, IMF (dec'd) (with the Dutch delegation to Bretton Woods, 1944; subsequently with the Fund from 1947, Director of the Research Department 1958–79, Economic Counsellor 1966–79, and advisor to the Managing Director of the Fund 1979–81. Executive Director of the Fund for the constituency comprising Cyprus, Israel, Netherlands, Romania, and Yugoslavia 1981–6) (twice).

Barry Newman, US Deputy Assistant Secretary; former Director, Office of International Monetary Policy, US Treasury.

Nathaniel Samuels, Deputy Under Secretary of State for Economic Affairs, 1969–72 US State Department (telephone interview).

Paul Volcker, while Frederick H. Schultz Professor of International Economic Policy, Princeton University, (Chairman, President Obama's Economic Recovery Advisory Board 2009–11; Group of Thirty Chairman of Board of Trustees 2006–; Chairman of the Board of Governors of the Federal Reserve System 1979–87, President of the New York Federal Reserve Bank 1975–9, Deputy Under Secretary for Monetary Affairs, US Treasury 1963–5, and Under Secretary for Monetary Affairs, US Treasury 1969–74).

Charls Walker, Deputy Secretary, US Treasury 1972–3, (Under Secretary, 1969–72).

Helen C. Walsh, former Assistant US Treasury Representative, US Embassy, London.

John Williamson, Peterson Institute for International Economics (IMF official 1972–4).

Index

NB. Italicized page numbers refer to references in footnotes